SOLVING PUBLIC PROBLEMS

SOLVING
PUBLIC PROBLEMS

A Practical Guide to
Fix Our Government and
Change Our World

BETH SIMONE NOVECK

Yale
UNIVERSITY
PRESS

New Haven and London

2021

Yale University Press books may be purchased in quantity for educational, business, or promotional use. For information, please e-mail sales.press@yale.edu (U.S. office) or sales@yaleup.co.uk (U.K. office).

Set in Scala type by Integrated Publishing Solutions.
Printed in the United States of America.

Library of Congress Control Number: 2020951416
ISBN: 978-0-300-23015-4 (hardcover : alk. paper)

A catalogue record for this book is available from the British Library.

This paper meets the requirements of ANSI/NISO Z39.48–1992 (Permanence of Paper).

10 9 8 7 6 5 4 3 2 1

For Amedeo Max

CONTENTS

AUTHOR'S NOTE

On January 6, 2021, a systematic, relentless campaign of grievance and falsehood, led by former President Donald Trump and stoked by members of the Republican Party in Congress and right-wing media, culminated in a violent attack on the Capitol. The incompetently planned but nonetheless deadly coup attempt counted among its leaders White supremacists, neo-Nazis, and devotees of the paranoid conspiracy theory QAnon. Yet support among Americans for the insurrection went way beyond the far-right fringe. According to YouGov about 45 percent of Republicans said they backed the attack on the Capitol, while 74 million Americans voted for Trump in 2020, despite his undisguised contempt for democratic institutions and decision-making both during the campaign and over the four years of his presidency. Watching these events, one could be forgiven for thinking that American democracy was reaching its final hours. I have written this book in the firm belief that this is not so.

The tools to solve the deepest problems of our democracy are in our own hands. Even during the past long year of COVID, when it seemed the whole world had come apart, I have seen countless examples of activists, community leaders, public servants, and changemakers—many of them young people from several countries—working with their governments to solve real problems, and overcoming strong political disagreement as they did so. I am not alone in my optimism: in the United States, 57 percent of adults believe that Americans can find a way to solve their problems, according to Pew Research. A majority also remains staunch in its belief that government and public institutions have a major role to play in addressing our big public challenges.

The way to deal with these challenges is, first and foremost, to involve citizens in the way we solve them. That means turning more power over to ordinary people. It means transforming the way we govern ourselves.

That task is now urgent, even existential. Within a generation, trust in government has declined to historic lows. With an uptick during the pandemic, until recently only 3 percent of Americans said they can trust the government in Washington to do what is right "just about always." Widening levels of inequality, stagnant wages, lack of social mobility, and a decline in life expectancy and quality have led many to feel that government is neither listening to nor working for them. The effect, says comedian Bill Maher, is that "America is full of fed-up, unhappy people, who just want to break shit."

Blaming the public sector for all the ills of America would be grossly unfair. Nevertheless, too often our government is indeed sclerotic and ineffective. We suffer from what Larry Lessig, a law professor at Harvard and an activist on electoral and campaign finance reform, calls "institutional corruption." Relentless media focus on demagogic personalities and the horse race between political parties—on political rather than governance outcomes—obscure the fact that there are far better ways to govern, and as this book shows, in hard times they are beginning to emerge.

At the height of the COVID-19 pandemic, some public institutions in this country and overseas did things differently. They collaborated across government and with external organizations. They responded to difficult problems by consulting the citizens directly affected by them and through the use of rapidly increasing quantities of data and predictive analytics. They took advantage of ordinary people's insight, passion, and power. They showed how successful government *could be* at improving people's lives if such novel ways of working were the norm.

For example, the urgency of the pandemic motivated the cities of Accra, Bahir Dar, Kampala, Kano, and Mutare, with the support of the United Nations Development Programme and The Governance Lab, to turn in 2021 to their citizens for help in tackling three big challenges: improving waste generation and management, building urban resilience in slums and informal settlements, and growing and supporting their informal economies. Asked to participate in this multi-city challenge, citizens contributed almost 300 detailed and practical proposals for solving these problems with a handful currently being chosen for implementation. Also in 2020, five cities in northern Mexico collaborated with residents in a separate multi-city challenge. These cities are now implementing citizen-designed projects to address urban mobility, post-pandemic economic relief, and the digital divide. They include a novel initiative to introduce new plantings into communal areas in Monterrey to absorb pollutants and a design for eco-friendly bike stations to reduce traffic in Hermosillo.

Examples of responsive institutions—those working *with* people to solve problems— exist around the world. In Taiwan, more than 200,000 people have collaborated in crafting 26 pieces of national legislation in an initiative known as vTaiwan. They have drafted laws on telemedicine and the digital economy. VTaiwan is just one example of the burgeoning "crowdlaw" movement, in which legislatures are turning to the use of new technology to engage their publics in lawmaking.

Innovation in government can also be found in the United States. In the past decade, even the U.S. Federal Government has been running a little-known program to source solutions to public problems from people across and outside government. Over a hundred federal agencies have used the website Challenge.gov to tap the intelligence and expertise of ordinary citizens. Right now, the Health Resources and Services Administration is asking for help on how to increase pediatric preventive care. The Department of Energy is running a competition for college students to design and build innovative buildings powered by renewable energy.

Where institutions are using more data and tapping the experience, know-how, and wisdom of ordinary people, they are able to do extraordinary things, create effective solutions to problems, and strengthen participatory democracy. Focusing only on people's opinions, which are often corrupted by misinformation and prejudice, can merely inflame divisions. Discovering and focusing on what people know and can do helps to overcome partisanship and produce powerful outcomes. These changes, in turn, increase people's faith that government can be made to work for them.

Such a transformation to new ways of working will not happen by itself. The African and Mexican city leaders who ran the multi-city challenges all went through eight training sessions. In Taiwan, Audrey Tang, the nation's digital minister, and a leading proponent of civil society-government collaboration, has set up a training program to educate government officials and turn them into "participation officers." U.S. federal agency officials have a community of practice in which they teach one another how to design and run a challenge on Challenge.gov.

The Biden-Harris Administration must complement its policy initiatives by training public servants in new ways of working. The White House must invest in upskilling, using new technology to ensure that political leaders and public servants learn better ways of solving public problems, and make that education available for free to state and local governments. To reverse the erosion of trust, the Biden Administration needs all public servants, not just small pockets of technologists or data scientists, to possess the innovation skills that foster more effective, agile, and responsive governing. As we learned during COVID-19—especially from our failures — the Administration can do better by working with citizens and with data to implement innovative solutions.

But it is not enough to train people inside institutions. If we want to tackle the acute challenges of our time—the immense strains on our system of government produced by the pandemic, economic recession, climate change, and systemic racism, among other problems—we need to democratize access to experiential and lifelong learning in public problem solving. We need to give tools and methods that will enable all people, but especially the young, to turn their passions into practical outcomes.

We must invest in teaching people how to design and lead social change, how to collaborate with communities, including marginalized and vulnerable groups. For if we create institutions that know how to listen, we still have to raise a next generation of leaders who know how to speak up. For example, instead of training students only in *business* entrepreneurship, universities and schools need to respond to students' demands to learn *public* entrepreneurship. We can support what the late congressman and civil rights activist John Lewis called "committed and determined people" who want to make a difference in their communities by helping them to acquire the skills needed to take projects from idea to implementation.

Too often, the gap between idea and implementation is a chasm. With all the tools and skills we now have at our disposal, it no longer needs to be. We can break intractable issues into manageable problems. We can use data and collaboration to understand those problems. We can partner with others to implement a shared solution.

This book provides a practical, how-to guide that uses these skills to achieve social change. It is written in the belief that with the widest possible deployment of these skills, we can, in the words of youth poet laureate Amanda Gorman, "raise this wounded world into a wondrous one" and move beyond the current woes of our politics to build a new confidence in the power of government and civil society to dramatically improve the lives of ordinary citizens. We may even, in our lifetimes, get a chance to play our part in honoring the "I Have a Dream" words of Dr. Martin Luther King, Jr. and "hew out of the mountain of despair a stone of hope . . . to transform the jangling discords of our nation into a beautiful symphony."

Beth Simone Noveck
March 2021
New York, NY

Introduction

Not having heard of it is not as good as having heard of it. Having heard of it is not as good as having seen it. Having seen it is not as good as knowing it. Knowing it is not as good as putting it into practice.

Xunzi, The Complete Text (3rd century BCE)

These are dark days in the United States. Crisis builds upon crisis. As I write, in early 2021, American deaths from COVID-19 far exceed four hundred thousand and continue to rise, making up over 20 percent of all global coronavirus fatalities. Many countries are locking down again in response to the ongoing outbreak. Demonstrations erupted in every state in the country and around the world in protest against the brutal murder in Minneapolis, Minnesota, of yet another unarmed Black man by four White police officers. Cops in full riot gear have arrested journalists, tear-gassed protestors, and clubbed pedestrians. In the United States, the integrity of our democratic elections and a peaceful transition of presidential power were in doubt due to widespread voter suppression and hyperpartisanship.

In response to the pandemic, President Donald Trump was incompetent at best, indifferent to science, and callous to the victims. In response to the death of George Floyd, the latest in a long list of police killings that expose the depth of White supremacy and racial injustice in the United States, the president's use of military force against Americans demonstrated a greater desire to incite violence than to end it. In response to rising and systemic inequality, an opioid blight that kills 128 Americans every day, and the persistent and existential threat of climate change, Trump had no response at all.

The United States may never have had a worse president than Trump. Yet the problems we face run so much deeper than one man. These are complex societal challenges that have no easy answer, no one-size-fits-all solution, no quick fix at the ballot box. There is a persistent sense that our institutions, especially government, are failing us. The origin of the loss of faith in our governments and institutions, a collective despair that helped to elect Trump, dates back years, even decades, exacerbated by the slow rate of change following countless disasters, from mass shootings to wildfires. Ronald Reagan famously said in his first Inaugural Address, "Government is not the solution to the problem; government is the problem."

I wrote this book because I believe that Reagan was wrong. Sometimes government can indeed be the problem. But I am certain that government can be the solution. In fact, without such governments, it is hard to see how our greatest problems can be solved at all.

Margaret Mead said, "Never doubt that a small group of thoughtful, committed citizens can change the world; indeed, it's the only thing that ever has." This is a book about Mead's thoughtful, committed citizens—whose numbers, I believe, are not small—and who seek to practice service. Many work inside government (regardless of who occupies the White House). Others work in the nonprofit and private sectors. Others are ordinary individuals who want to take action and improve their own communities. They are public problem solvers who want to live lives of purpose, and in an era of unprecedented interconnectedness and access to information driven by digital technology, their time has come.

I have the privilege to lead a team of engineers, designers, and policy professionals in the Office of Innovation in the state of New Jersey. When the COVID-19 pandemic hit in March 2020, we were able to use technology and data, and unprecedented levels of collaboration, to show how government can be nimble and effective, not a lumbering, unresponsive bureaucracy.

Working with the nonprofit Federation of American Scientists, we built a website and an Alexa skill to enable the public to pose questions about the virus to over six hundred scientists and to receive rapid, well-researched responses. A private-sector company lent us the tech and the talent to create a website—covid19.nj.gov—in three days. In eight months, the site has served well over twenty million individual users in a state of fewer than nine million people.

Even more challenging than the technology was the need to overcome the silos of government and persuade all agencies to put their COVID-19 information in one place. We had to edit legalese into plain English and scour different sources for content when government agencies did not provide it to us. We collaborated with Princeton, Rutgers, Montclair, and Rowan Universities to create a student editorial team to answer questions citizens submitted to the website.

A renowned professor of data science at New York University volunteered and assembled a crack team to produce the predictive analytics about the spread of the virus that enabled the governor of New Jersey to make daily decisions about the virus. Insights from the data were also used by the Department of Health, the Office of Homeland Security and Preparedness, State Police, and the Attorney General's Office and shared with the public at press briefings.

When we could not determine the number of deaths on the basis of race, because the testing labs were not providing that information, the Department of Human Services and the Department of Health shared key data with each other that enabled us to answer this question. What would have normally been accomplished in a year, or never, was done in a day.

In three days, we produced the nation's first state jobs site to list available positions in essential businesses and mitigate the crisis of unemployment. We posted over fifty thousand jobs in a wide range of businesses and salary levels. With a clear view of what we wanted to accomplish, we launched this site that was far from perfect and improved it as we went, knowing it was more important to risk failure than not to act quickly.

My team also worked with the federal government's Digital Service, a unit within the Executive Office of the President, to fix the state's process of certifying for unemployment. Recipients must attest weekly to being unemployed in order to receive benefits. With unemployment in New Jersey rising past 16 percent, the existing website was straining under the load. We also worked with the NGO Code for America to digitize the application process for food benefits, whose paper-based rules previously required going into a government office to demonstrate income level. Both problems were addressed in a week.

While we are proud of this work in New Jersey, it was insignificant compared with the outpouring of community volunteer efforts in response to the pandemic. A group called Invisible Hands, one of countless such mutual-aid organizations, coordinated ten thousand volunteers to deliver groceries to the elderly. Another volunteer group, United States Digital Response—"non-partisan, fast and free," according to its website[1]—organized and deployed over a thousand experienced technologists and designers to work pro bono alongside sixty state and local governments and NGOs struggling to cope with the crisis.

The unique conditions created by the pandemic made fusty organizations willing to bust through normal barriers to get things done and done quickly. But public problem solvers are not only born in extremis.

In my work as director of the Governance Lab, a nonprofit action research "do tank" based at New York University, I see such public problem solving—what I also like to call public entrepreneurship—in governments around the world. I have met pioneers like the public servants in Mexico City who crowdsourced a new constitution using the voice and power of ordinary people to bring more legitimacy to the lawmaking process or those at the US Departments of Education and Labor who, under President Obama, transformed their agencies' multibillion-dollar grantmaking programs. Any training programs developed with that money would have to be openly shared so that a community college course on welding or soil science would be freely shared for the benefit of workers.

In Helsinki, the Mayor's Office created the Climate Watch process and a website to enable citizens and city leaders to cocreate their community's climate-change plan. Civic technologists built these tools to make it possible for citizens to hold public officials accountable to meet the Climate Watch plan's 147 target goals.

In California, a fire chief built a national program and an app to enable anyone in participating communities trained in cardiopulmonary resuscitation to come to the aid of victims of sudden cardiac arrest, the third leading cause of death in the United States, killing nine out of ten of its victims. Using 911 and location data, the Pulsepoint app matches a victim experiencing cardiac arrest to a trained bystander. Now more than thirty-eight hundred communities across the United States and Canada are collaborating with a network of two million volunteer CPR-trained users, who have saved over one hundred thousand lives.

In Chile, city officials are working with researchers to use data from the public and private sector, such as satellite and telecom data, to look at the impact of gender on commuting patterns and help the city of Santiago design gender-responsive transportation options.

In New Jersey, education leaders have created the nation's first mandatory climate-education curriculum for K–12 to forge a new generation of informed climate activists. In Virginia, officials are taking down hurtful Confederate monuments that have dominated the landscape for a century, and in Barcelona, the city is opening up all of the data it collects for public benefit.

Public-sector entrepreneurs are solving a vast range of problems, from "using sensors to detect potholes; word pedometers to help students learn; harnessing behavioral economics to encourage organ donation; crowdsourcing patent review; and transforming Medellin, Colombia with cable cars," writes Mitchell Weiss, professor of public entrepreneurship at Harvard Business School, in the *Harvard Business Review*.[2] Echoing the Nobel Laureate Elinor Ostrom, the economist who coined the term "public entrepreneurship" in 1964, Weiss has written dozens of case studies, profiling the deep entrepreneurship of public leaders as part of his first-of-its-kind course on public entrepreneurship (http://www.inventadifference.co).[3] Perhaps more than anyone, Ostrom helped to popularize the idea that governments and the people who work for them can be innovative.

Public problem solvers, however, are not only in government or in wealthy countries. Ali Clare and Marcello Bonatto dove headlong into addressing the humanitarian crisis in Syria. Far from being overwhelmed by the magnitude of the suffering, they started Re:Coded, the largest coding program for conflict-affected young people in the Middle East. The couple teaches tech skills to Syrian refugees, especially women, in Iraq and Turkey using a network of mentors.

Given the right tools, ordinary citizens are doing more than voting. They are shaping world events. Ushahidi (Swahili for "witness") is a website created to crowdsource and map eyewitness reports of incidents of violence following the contested 2007 election in Kenya. Founders Juliana Rotich and Ory Orkolloh gave away these crisis-mapping tools, and today more than 150,000 activists have used Ushahidi to rescue victims from the Haitian earthquake in 2010, prevent forest fires in Italy and Russia, and crowdsource incidents of sexual harassment in Egypt, among other campaigns.

Similarly, the entrepreneur, designer, and academic Sean Bonner and his friends in Japan started Safecast after the Fukushima nuclear disaster in 2011. Today Safecast's global network of volunteers has collected more than 150 million measurements of radiation and air quality, making it the world's largest distributed data-collection project. Now the Japanese government, for example, uses Safecast's data, which are better than its own, to improve environmental policymaking.

Drawing on the lessons learned from these public problem solvers and public entrepreneurs, this book provides a practical guide for change agents —public servants, community leaders, students, activists, anyone who seeks to tackle public problems in the twenty-first century. It is not a theoretical book about social movements of the past but a hands-on set of methods for problem solvers of today.

I endeavor to show how leading change makers are defining problems that are urgent and matter to real people. The book teaches ways to use data to understand the breadth and nature of a problem and how to deepen understanding of the problem by using technology to work with the individuals and communities most affected by it. It offers techniques to tackle hard problems with rather than for communities. The book demonstrates how to scan sources rapidly for reliable evidence of what else has worked and how to build teams and partnerships that cross disciplines and sectors to launch a project in practice, crossing the chasm between idea and implementation. Law, policy, and institutions play a central role in these methods, but first and foremost, I aim to equip individuals with the combination of qualitative and quantitative skills needed to become powerful change makers and, by working differently, to improve the effectiveness, equity, and legitimacy of our institutions.

These skills are not intuitive, and can and must be learned. Just recently, I was asked to review the work of a civic leader who has devoted his career to improving sustainability but whose plastic recycling project, while it might build awareness of the problem, will never achieve impact because it is not connected to any institutional response to the blight of single-use plastics.

In a competition I judged last year, a passionate technologist proposed to use natural language processing to overcome a thorny problem in government, oblivious to the fact that the solution had been developed a decade ago. If she had known how to synthesize evidence and learn what else is out there, she could have used her talents to solve a genuine problem.

Students I coached last year have engineered a new form of beehive to combat the decline of the European honeybee yet, when we started, had little clue how to get cities to adopt their innovation. Similarly, the newly minted public servants I work with in a program to send recent college graduates to work in state government are very keen to help others but have little idea when they start out how to engage with citizens and build coalitions that can get things done.

For every person I meet who has made effective change, I meet ten with the desire but not the capacity to make a difference. It is perhaps no wonder that over 100 students enrolled in "Solving Public Problems" at New York University for the fall 2020 semester alone. Our democracies urgently need to produce citizens who can move from demanding change to making it. If we are to do more than vote occasionally or shout into the wind on Twitter, more people have to be able to take an initiative from idea to reality. We can all do good, but we must all do better.

Power, wrote Bertrand Russell, is the ability to produce intended effects.[4] This book seeks to make more people more powerful by creating public problem solvers inside and outside government. I believe we have never had better opportunities to do so. Power is shifting away from established organizations, institutions, and professions, a consequence both of democracy and of declining trust, writes the journalist and former politician Moises Naïm in his book *The End of Power*.[5] But whereas power is easier to obtain today, he argues, its diffuse nature in the contemporary world makes it harder to use and easier to lose. Naïm's analysis challenges us to wield power more thoughtfully and ethically, by staffing our institutions with people who understand twenty-first-century problem-solving skills and new forms of citizen-led democracy.

Around the world, it is a time of anxiety, a sense that humans are challenged, that we all need to do more. The political scientist Yuval Levin writes that we are suffering from "a distinct kind of institutional dereliction," in which we have allowed our institutions to become inefficient and ineffectual.[6] More bluntly, the activist Greta Thunberg asks, What we will tell our children, and their children, about our failure to act against the climate chaos unfolding around us? And at a protest in Atlanta after the killing of George Floyd, the activist and rapper Michael Santiago Render, better known as Killer Mike, delivered an anguished, powerful address:

> I watched a White officer assassinate a Black man, and I know
> that tore your heart out. I know it's crippling, and I have nothing
> positive to say in this moment. I'm mad as hell. . . . It is the

responsibility of us to make this better right now. . . . I want you
to go home. I want you to talk to ten of your friends. I want you
guys to come up with real solutions. . . . I don't have the answers,
but I do know we must plot. We must plan. We must strategize,
organize, and mobilize.[7]

This is a book about how to organize, mobilize, plot, and plan. It is a
book about what Representative John Lewis described as getting into good
trouble, necessary trouble. It is a book about how to devise but also implement real solutions. It is about the vast gap between our failing public institutions and the huge number of public entrepreneurs doing extraordinary
things—and how to close that gap and reform government through training and skill building. That training is not limited to the public sector but
designed for schools and universities as well as governments to empower
more capable, talented, determined, and compassionate problem solvers
working in the public interest. I do not argue for bigger or smaller government but for better, more equitable, and effective government—one that
offers not a knee to the neck but a hand to pull us to our feet, that knows
how to tackle challenges with the collective intelligence and wisdom of our
communities.

We cannot expect to tackle tomorrow's problems with yesterday's toolkit. In the twenty-first century, we must urgently equip ourselves with the
skills to solve public problems. The task of doing so falls to us all.

CHAPTER ONE

Public Problem Solving and the
New Public Entrepreneur

As an organizer, I start from where the world is, as it is, not as I would
like it to be. That we accept the world as it is does not in any sense
weaken our desire to change it into what we believe it should be. It is
necessary to begin where the world is if we are going to change it to
what we think it should be. That means working within the system.

Saul Alinsky, Rules for Radicals

THE PUBLIC PROBLEM SOLVER

In India, thousands of people, most of them poor, die every day from tuberculosis. Globally, over one billion people are affected by such tropical diseases. Yet despite US$150 billion in global pharmaceutical research and
development spending, a tiny 0.23 percent of that spending is focused on
tuberculosis. As a result, only two new drugs have been approved for tuberculosis in the past thirty years, and resistance to existing treatments is increasing. In 2008, Samir Brahmachari, former director general of the
Council of Scientific and Industrial Research of the Government of India,
set up the Open Source Drug Discovery project. His goal was to create a
website on which the best minds could collaborate and try to discover ther-
apies for neglected tropical diseases such as tuberculosis and malaria.[1]

Using this open-source platform, Brahmachari recruited college students, academics, and scientists from around the world and across India.
Since most of the locals came from remote villages, not elite universities,
they were an inexpensive team. Brahmachari organized them to undertake
the mammoth task of collecting, annotating, and extracting information
from the scientific literature on the tuberculosis pathogen. When the articles were not freely available online, students wrote to thousands of authors
to request free copies. With a mere $12 million grant from the council, Brah-
machari coordinated the incremental contributions of seventy-five hundred

participants from 130 countries in order to test a multitude of hypotheses.[2] This collaborative citizen science initiative identified six drugs approved by the US Food and Drug Administration as promising metabolic targets, including one in widespread use for type 2 diabetes.[3]

On the other side of the world from India, Latin America's cities are growing so rapidly that people are struggling to move around them. The residents of San Pedro, an affluent community of about 125,000 people outside Monterrey in Mexico, drive more than 122,000 cars and make well over half their trips in them rather than on public transport.[4] As a result, they spend ever more time in traffic. Before 2016, 85 percent of schoolchildren traveled to school in single-family cars, hurting their health and their capacity to study, as well as the environment.

That year, Graciela Reyes, a city councilor, launched the Desafíos, or Challenges, program to enable fifty members of the public to work with the municipality to create better policies and services. One big question these citizens were asked was: How can we reduce the time kids spend driving to school?

Using open data provided by the city about the location of schools and routes, a volunteer team of citizens, comprising two lawyers, a civil engineer, an architect, and a political scientist, worked with civil servants to develop a plan for getting kids to school. The truly unprecedented development came when the residents did more than simply suggest an alternative. Instead, they joined with the city's urban planners and officials to be coached over ten weeks by mentors around the country and the world in how to turn ideas into practical policies and services. Together these public officials and members of the public were able to craft a solution that worked. One year after the launch of a transportation plan that includes public transportation, busing, and walking, the city reports that fewer than a quarter of parents are driving their children to school.[5]

About twelve hundred miles north of San Pedro in Lakewood, Colorado, a midsized suburb of Denver, the urban planner Jonathan Wachtel has created a thirty-thousand-person-strong sustainability "workforce."[6] Previously, the city worked with residents in the usual way. Residents could go to a planning meeting to complain about plans that had already been made, but this left them frustrated and Wachtel—the town's single urban planner—overwhelmed.

In 2012, Wachtel launched the Sustainable Neighborhoods Program (after an initial pilot in 2010). The program encourages residents with the passion, ideas, and know-how to propose projects that they will develop and implement with their neighbors. As Wachtel explains, he wanted to change how he worked: "All the inquiries around green kept getting directed my way. . . . I was getting tired of not being able to say anything except thank you."[7]

The city supports neighborhood projects with technical advice, leadership coaching, and help to secure grants and navigate city bureaucracy. The approach enables the city to invest in feasible and impactful proposals by working with enthusiastic residents on projects capable of contributing to the city's sustainability goals. For example, when Morse Park neighborhood residents planted one hundred trees in 2018, it contributed to the city's goal of achieving 30 percent tree-canopy coverage by 2025.

Now eight neighborhoods covering a fifth of the city's population have joined the Sustainable Neighborhoods Program. More than five hundred resident-led events, workshops, and projects have reduced waste, conserved water, and improved energy efficiency. Participating neighborhoods are recognized through celebratory receptions with the mayor, in the city's newsletter, and in speaking opportunities for neighborhood leaders at schools, colleges, and professional conferences.

DEFINING PUBLIC PROBLEM SOLVING

Although Brahmachari, Reyes, and Wachtel did remarkable things, they are not activists or hackers or revolutionaries manning the barricades but public officials passionate about doing good in the world. They have not given up their professional "day jobs," nor did they simply look for the old solutions to their problems. Instead, they used the convening power of their positions to work differently and develop creative and effective approaches. In a world beset by profound and deepening problems that the global coronavirus pandemic of 2020 has only made worse, they recognized the need to work differently to accomplish their goals and change the world. I call these leaders "public problem solvers."

There is no preexisting single definition of public problem solving. It is not yet a defined field. Some people use the term "social innovator." Others prefer "change agent." Universities do not normally offer public-problem-solving courses or provide consistent career advice focusing on public-interest work in different sectors. Although some offer capstone projects and internships, there is generally no accepted "methods course" to teach people to take a project from idea to implementation. Nor is there a centralized and consistent set of data, crossing engineering, public policy, law, business, and other disciplines, about how many students want to do mission-driven work during or after university. Training programs for those who work in nonprofits or for government do not offer a problem-solving curriculum.

By contrast, "public-interest law" is a term of art in legal circles. Loosely speaking, it means performing legal work to serve the underdog and promote civil rights (as opposed to work to serve corporate economic interests). It does not refer to a body of law or a type of organization but, instead, covers using legal techniques such as litigation, law reform, and legal advocacy to advance the public good. Most law schools have a public-interest law program and provide career counseling for those who wish to do public-interest law. Resources such as the Public Service Jobs Directory (PSJD) comprise a network of more than two hundred member law schools and thirteen thousand law-related public-interest organizations.[8] Public-interest law has come to be understood as a broad but coherent field with a defined skill set.

Similarly, with the growth of entrepreneurship programs in universities, first in the 1970s and then their explosion in the past twenty-five years as a result of the dot-com boom, entrepreneurship is also well understood today. We all know what it means to start and grow a business. Thanks to the significant growth of business entrepreneurship programs in universities and community colleges over the past forty years, entrepreneurship has become a staple of university education, cutting across disciplines. In the early 1980s, about three hundred schools had entrepreneurship and small business programs. By the early 2000s, eager to help students become the next Mark Zuckerberg, more than sixteen hundred schools had created entrepreneurship programs offering over twenty-two hundred courses.[9] There is a robust scholarship on business formation as well as a pedagogical discipline focusing on teaching people to start their own businesses.

In *Public Problem Solving*, I seek to articulate a learnable set of tools that, when combined with subject-matter expertise, make it possible to design interventions that improve people's lives. In so doing, I hope to define what it means to take a public-interest project from idea to implementation. Public problem solvers possess a replicable skill set that can be applied to any public problem for making measurable change. These skills include the following:

1. *Problem definition.* Public problem solvers know how to define a problem that is urgent, that matters to real people, and that can be resolved.
2. *Data-analytical thinking.* They know how to use data and the analysis of data in order to understand the breadth and nature of the problem.
3. *Human-centered design.* They shun the closed-door practices of the past and design interventions in partnership with those whom they are trying to help, deepening their understanding of the problem by consulting people directly affected by it.
4. *Collective intelligence.* They adopt more participatory and democratic ways of working that build on the collective intelligence of communities.
5. *Rapid evidence review.* They take advantage of new technology to scan for the best available ideas and the best people who know what has worked.
6. *Powerful partnerships.* They know how to build teams and partnerships that cross many disciplines to become more effective at implementing change that others will adopt and accept.
7. *Measuring what works.* Finally, they use experimental techniques and collaboration to evaluate what has worked and what has not and either pivot or stay on course as a result. They know how to expand work that has a beneficial and measurable impact on people's lives.

The rest of this book explains these core skills for solving public problems in an effort to spur more of the same kind of data-driven and participatory problem solving exemplified in the work of Reyes, Brahmachari, and Wachtel.

Many of the skills and methods I lay out in this book are made possible by the development of new digital technologies in the past decade. Taken together, they offer a process for more agile and rapid means of action, implementation, and validation. They elevate evidence over politics and egos. They reject closed-door workings by professionals in favor of ways of identifying problems and interventions in collaboration with those who are most affected and most knowledgeable. They emphasize tapping the good ideas of communities and leveraging law and policy as well as technology to produce more just and effective results. They eschew rigid and rules-based ways of organizing work in favor of more flexible, experimental, and innovative approaches.

Yet public problem solvers are not reckless. Despite their willingness to innovate, they hold fast to the values of the public interest. They are ethically conscious of obligations to due process and equity. Rather than merely complying with rules, they act with alacrity, ingenuity, integrity, and a relentless focus on solving some of the most urgent and difficult challenges of our time.

Finally, public problem solvers are not content with slow and incremental approaches. They are impatient to deliver results in a short time, and they experiment with new processes and ways of working, despite the risks of doing so within a bureaucracy. Perhaps most importantly, they do not want simply to solve the problem in front of them but to institutionalize a process that others can learn from, copy, and scale up.

A NOTE ON SOLVING

Of course, complex or wicked societal problems of the kind discussed in this book can never be truly "solved." As Horst Rittel and Melvin Webber have written, "Social problems are never solved. At best they are only resolved—over and over again."[10] No matter how successful an intervention, there is always more to do. Even if a need is satisfied, it does not stay that way for long. A problem once solved rarely stays solved in the real world. We have to beware the political expediency that favors solving problems over the vastly more complex idea that problems can only be tackled.

Since our goal is to engage in activist and agile approaches—and to prescribe methods and tools for getting from idea to implementation—we always select those interventions that we can actually accomplish and that will improve conditions on the ground even if they are incremental answers to bigger problems. This is not to say that we cannot be ambitious or strive to help as many people as possible, but there are no magic bullets or single "solutions" to wicked, messy, complex problems.

Also, we are laser focused on going beyond good ideas that may in theory ameliorate a condition to address real-world *implementation* of interventions in actual communities with real stakeholders. Thus, by necessity, there will always be a degree of "satisficing" required, whether because of the politics, bureaucracy, inaction, or malevolence that get in the way of more aggressive change, but we must always try to make the lives of some people better. Change makers sometimes refer to the "Overton Window," meaning the range of acceptable interventions that are politically palatable or acceptable to the public at a given time. For example, Bernie Sanders's presidential campaigns helped to expand the Overton Window in health care and to make "Medicare for All" a mainstream idea. Sometimes the most we can hope for is to expand that Overton Window and open up debate to previously unpopular or unthinkable ideas.

Furthermore, problems have interdependent root causes, and while we may tackle one, we will never tackle them all. Hence, I use the terms "problem solving" and "solutions" with some skepticism, fully aware that whatever we do will never be enough. Our results will always be partial, not perfect. We must continue to protest, speak out, demand more. But we seek to do more than merely object. We seek to continuously develop and implement impactful interventions without letting the perfect be the enemy of action or engagement.

Engaging in public problem solving together is essential to strengthening democratic life. In earlier work, I have called this kind of robust cooperation "collaborative democracy" to distinguish it from deliberative democracy.[11] Collaborative democracy goes beyond the processes of deliberation, which would measure success by the diversity and quality of voices participating in a dialogue, such as a discussion between neighbors about a contentious policy issue. Collaborative democratic processes go beyond dialogue, taking advantage of new technologies to enable people to do more than talk and, instead, to make decisions and act together from a distance. Collaborative democratic processes like those in Lakewood or Monterrey are not limited to conversations in which people express opinions. On the contrary, they measure democracy in terms of the ultimate effectiveness of the problem-solving process—by the outcomes—rather than in terms of inputs to the dialogue.

WHY WE NEED MORE PUBLIC ENTREPRENEURS IN GOVERNMENT

While public problem solvers need not work for the public sector, there is real urgency to ensuring that those who do are trained to become public entrepreneurs. Public entrepreneurs (I will use that term and "public problem solvers" interchangeably throughout for simplicity) like Brahmachari, Reyes, and Wachtel use the power of data and of the crowd to disrupt and accelerate and the power of their institutions to convene, fund, and drive change.

These agile problem-solving skills are extraordinarily useful for anyone working to tackle a problem in the public interest, whether inside or outside government (and this book is designed for public problem solvers generally). But the declining trust in government and, as will be discussed in chapter 2 at greater length, the systematic degradation of capacity inside the public sector make it especially urgent to focus on ensuring that everyone who works for government (and the many more who work outside government) learns how to become a public entrepreneur, who knows how to use data and collective intelligence to solve public problems.[12] Right now, when a serious issue arises, like the coronavirus pandemic in 2020, leaders are too often turning to private-sector consultancies like McKinsey to manage response, fearful that government managers do not have what it takes. Despite a withering federal-government report about ethical improprieties, wild overcharging, a history of complicity with firing of workers and aiding and abetting Trump's policy of putting immigrant kids in cages, and, above all, no particular skills in or motivation to engage communities or promote participation, McKinsey and similar management consultants keep getting called on because they offer some assurance of getting things done.[13] Leaders are afraid to count on public servants. Yet management consultants are not accountable to the public, are not motivated by the values of equity or legitimacy, and are focused on short-term wins to guarantee them a contract renewal rather than motivated by public benefit.

If we want to create more capable, agile, and responsive leaders *inside* government, who put the public interest first, then this calls for strengthening capacity in the public sector by radically reshaping the curriculum with which we train public leaders and problem solvers and making that training more widely accessible and attractive.

There is a profound need to reimagine how we govern—how public entrepreneurs make policy decisions, design public services, and solve public problems. In particular, as other sectors of society have exploited new technologies to better achieve their goals and missions, people who work in and with government need to consider how governance can be more innovative, legitimate, and effective in the digital era.

The change is not political—not about selecting from among particular ideologies or policies. We need to innovate our policy toolkit across the ideological spectrum, with new techniques that center on the better use of big data and collective intelligence to solve problems. But knowing how to do so—instead of merely buying whatever the next vendor is selling to government—requires honing a set of skills and methods for creative problem solving.

PROBLEM SOLVING AND THE FUTURE OF WORK

In a world in which technology will transform every job, retraining, reskilling, and lifelong learning are crucial for thriving in the digital age. The World Economic Forum estimates that with retraining, 96 percent of the most immediately at-risk US workers would find decent jobs that offer higher wages.[14] In business, it has become routine to talk about nurturing talent by providing digital, data, and innovation training to help people work and think differently. In *The Innovator's DNA*, business school professors Jeff Dyer, Hal Greggersen, and Clayton Christensen explain that the ability to innovate is not innate but a learned set of practices that can and must be taught if businesses are to thrive. Christensen believes that innovative people possess five core skills: associating, questioning, observing, experimenting, and networking.[15] These are the skills that successful businessmen (most of the innovators whom the authors profile are men) use to discover and deliver what sells.

Yet, for all the talk about investing in private-sector training, we are not doing so nearly enough for the public sector or for public change makers. By failing to pay attention to the productivity of such training, we are failing to build the skill set of the twenty-first-century public servant.[16]

Whereas *The Innovator's DNA* is concerned with innovation to maximize profit, public entrepreneurs seek not to make money but to solve public problems. To equip public entrepreneurs to solve these problems, to create government that is not smaller or bigger but better, the public sector needs to nurture talent and to invest in training and the development of a new set of skills. The British Conservative politician and minister for the Cabinet Office Michael Gove declared in a much-publicized speech in June 2020, "The manner in which Government has rewarded its workers for many years now has, understandably, prized cognitive skills—the analytical, evaluative and, perhaps, above all, presentational. I believe that should change. Delivery on the ground; making a difference in the community; practicable, measurable improvements in the lives of others should matter more."[17]

Unfortunately, these data and collaborative skills that are needed to make practicable, measurable improvements in the lives of others—defining problems, data-analytical thinking, applying human-centered design, using collective intelligence, rapid evidence review, creating powerful partnerships, and measuring what works—are not in widespread and consistent use in public services.

A 2019 survey I designed and conducted to assess the use of innovative problem-solving skills of over four hundred local public officials in the United States shows that only half are using new data-analytical or collaborative skills in their work.[18] Only 28 percent of these public officials use agile techniques, developed in the technology industry, for working faster with greater testing and experimentation. While 60 percent say they use problem definition, not much more than half of the same group, when probed, say they know how to define a hypothesis, the most basic feature of problem definition.

The results were similar in Australia, where I worked with colleagues at Monash University to run a similar survey of almost four hundred mid- to senior-level public servants. Only a third of these Australian bureaucrats, on average, used innovative problem-solving skills.[19] In Paraguay in 2020, almost five hundred senior civil servants responded to the same survey. Again, fewer than half had defined a problem, only a third knew how to conduct an evidence review, and less than that had used collective-intelligence approaches to solve problems.[20]

Tellingly, however, the US, Australian, and Paraguayan surveys all revealed that once people knew and used an innovative skill, they applied it much of the time in their work. But the application is scattershot, and the skills are not combined into a process for taking a project from idea to implementation. For example, the people we surveyed may use human-centered design but not as part of a process that also includes problem definition; they are familiar with using data but not open innovation.

The public sector's failure to use creative problem-solving methods that take advantage of collective intelligence and data is widespread.[21] And it is no wonder, when public servants are not getting trained to work differently. The surveys showed that most people had been trained in each of six innovative problem-solving skills only between 8 and 30 percent of the time.[22]

In another example revealing the absence of adequate skills training, in June 2019, the government of Singapore adopted the mantra of "Singapore Together"—a commitment to making policies and delivering services *with* rather than *for* the public. But, despite this pronouncement, by late 2019, agencies had undertaken only a handful of one-off citizen juries and were no closer to engaging with citizens systematically or leveraging the public's collective intelligence.[23] This was not because of a lack of will but a lack of know-how and experience with citizen engagement.[24]

Lone innovators have always spontaneously sprung up in government, even within hierarchical bureaucracies and without training. But today's tools are making it easier and cheaper for *everyone* to adopt better methods for problem solving. There is no need to silo innovation in special digital or innovation agencies.

Of course, certain institutional and organizational conditions make it easier for innovators to thrive. But, ultimately, it is individuals who decide how money is spent and determine which issues become policy priorities and which topics become the subject of media attention, convenings, speeches, and politicians' campaign promises.

The futurist and architect Buckminster Fuller likened the power of the individual change agent to the trim tab, the small rudder that moves a big ship.[25] Public problem solvers know which tools to employ in order to design, develop, and implement solutions that work within the culture of their own organization. Such attention to innovation skills puts the focus squarely on the abilities of managers and leaders.[26] There has never been a more urgent need to train new leaders, passionate and innovative people who are determined to go beyond mere compliance with the rules and actually solve problems, especially in government.

Introducing new problem-solving approaches is also vitally important for reducing alienation and disengagement. Research on the meaning and nature of work shows that employees who enjoy autonomy and challenge are far more engaged and creative than those who do not. As the psychology professor Barry Schwartz wrote in the *New York Times* in 2015, all of us "want work that is challenging and engaging, that enables us to exercise some discretion and control over what we do, and that provides us opportunities to learn and grow. We want to work with colleagues we respect and with supervisors who respect us. Most of all, we want work that is meaningful— that makes a difference to other people and thus ennobles us in at least some small way."[27] A whole body of research shows that we are most motivated when we are helping others.[28] The most productive organizations are those whose employees work autonomously and creatively to solve problems faced by other people.[29] This is also true among public servants.[30]

Reframing the role of public servant as public entrepreneur requires abandoning the traditional view of public servants as technocratic brokers and decision-makers and thinking of them as compassionate conveners of conversations and coalitions between sectors in order to solve practical problems to the end of improving people's lives.

To be clear, public entrepreneurship does not in any way prescribe privatization or replacing public with market-based solutions. Nor does it call for government to work more like a business or to solve every problem using an app. On the contrary, the tools and techniques it explores aim to give voice to the needs of those who were previously excluded from public decision-making—which is all of us but especially the most vulnerable.

As such, public entrepreneurship is very tightly connected to and builds on my earlier books about democracy: *Wiki Government: How Technology Can Make Government Better, Democracy Stronger, and Citizens More Powerful*, which articulated a political theory of collaborative democracy, and *Smart Citizens, Smarter State: The Technologies of Expertise and the Future of Government*, which endeavored to make the case for institutions making better use of citizens' know-how and expertise.

This new book moves beyond theory, however, to focus on the day-to-day skills and practices of solving problems more democratically. It offers a manual for a broader audience beyond public administration and addresses all those who are working in or studying public problem solving and social innovation, whether on the job or in professional schools like business, law, engineering, or computer science, or those who simply want to take action in their communities. I endeavor to define public problem solving through a new set of organizational mind-sets and individual skill sets for public, as distinct from private, problem solving. In so doing, I also differentiate this work from the few earlier studies of public entrepreneurship that focus on case studies of innovative institutions but fail to look at individual capacity building.

Instead, this book uses examples from around the world, along with empirical survey data and in-depth interviews, to draw conclusions about the skills and abilities that public entrepreneurs need. If you see yourself as a potential public problem solver or public entrepreneur, I hope to offer more robust prescriptions for advancing your own projects, whether you are inside government or working from outside on mission-driven initiatives.[31]

The book should appeal to the academic as well as to the practitioner, whether a politician, public servant, or social entrepreneur. After explaining the historical and political context for public problem solving in chapter 2, subsequent chapters lay out a set of innovative heuristics for solving complex problems using a broader toolkit—one that includes big data and new technologies—than the traditional stuff of policy analysis and in much deeper dialogue and collaboration with data and communities.

Each chapter presents a different skill and explains its value and how it works in practice. Each chapter concludes with a "To Do" section that contains exercises for applying the skill to your own work. I have used these exercises over many years of training and coaching officials from governments around the world, from Singapore and New Zealand to Mexico and Ghana, as well as social innovators and students at universities like NYU, Yale, and Stanford. I taught my first version of a public-problem-solving course almost twenty years ago, in 2003. The exercises in this book are intended to help you apply innovative problem-solving practices to your own projects. They are a subset of the exercises I have collected from smart people and organizations pioneering some of these methods around the world. Interactive versions of these exercises and an accompanying online course are also available at https://solvingpublicproblems.org.

CONCLUSION

Open Source Drug Discovery is "no longer a project but a movement," Samir Brahmachari writes.[32] The Open Source Pharma Foundation, launched in 2018 to translate this crowdsourcing effort into clinical trials, took the generic diabetes drug Metformin and moved it into phase 2B clinical trials as a tuberculosis treatment. The process took less than a year and cost under $50,000.[33] By contrast, researchers at Tufts University estimate that the average drug costs $2.6 billion to develop.[34]

Similarly, Graciela Reyes not only ran the Desafíos program but oversaw a process whereby the municipality legislated to make the Desafíos model of coached collaboration with the public the new paradigm for government operations in San Pedro.[35]

Jonathan Wachtel is no longer the city's planner but is its sustainability manager, and Sustainable Neighborhoods has become a growing network of four cities with thousands of successful projects under the umbrella of a new nonprofit.

Given the complex, interdependent challenges facing our world—which have only grown since it succumbed to a pandemic and recession in 2020 —we must tackle our abundance of societal problems with ever-greater urgency. We can do so by adopting the techniques that these public entrepreneurs use. In addition, if more of the people who work in government adopt these techniques, we may also make government more effective and legitimate because it gets things that matter to real people done.

If the experiments and examples described in this volume are any indication, we can train people inside and outside government to work more openly and collaboratively, taking advantage of both data and human intelligence to improve and accelerate equitable problem solving and finding deep professional fulfillment along the way. How to do so is the subject of this book.

CHAPTER TWO

The Government That Governs
Least Governs Best

THE POLITICS OF PROBLEM SOLVING AND THE CRISIS OF TRUST

There is no more delicate matter to take in hand, nor more dangerous to conduct, nor more doubtful in its success, than to set up as a leader of changes. For he who innovates will have for his enemies all those who are well off under the existing order of things, and only lukewarm supporters in those who might be better off under the new.

Machiavelli, The Prince

THE CRISIS OF TRUST IN PUBLIC INSTITUTIONS

Louisville has some of the worst air quality in the United States. The air is particularly bad on the city's poor, predominantly African American, west side. Nitrogen dioxide and sulfur dioxide emitted by rubber and coal-fired power plants near residential neighborhoods force people to use emergency inhalers more than anywhere else in the city. In 2015, Louisville's chief innovation officer Ted Smith established AIR Louisville, a collaboration between the city government, the local university, and a spin-off social enterprise called Propellor. The result was the largest public-health study of respiratory disease ever conducted by a public-private collaboration.

The project enrolled more than one thousand city residents to track where, when, and why they suffered symptoms of asthma or chronic obstructive pulmonary disease (COPD). GPS-enabled medication sensors were distributed, and sufferers were notified on days that were likely to worsen their conditions. Propeller sensors collected 1.2 million data points from inhalers, including over 251,000 medication puffs, to help Louisville learn what causes asthma and COPD symptoms for its residents. The result of this innovative use of data and the collective action of citizens was an 82 percent decrease in the use of asthmatic rescue inhalers and twice as many symptom-free days for asthma sufferers. Now the city is doing more to fight the prevalence of these conditions by increasing tree coverage in high-risk asthma areas, working to route diesel-emitting trucks away from high-risk neighborhoods, and providing an Asthma Forecast Card to all citizens via the Smart Louisville automated alert system.[1]

Although not all governments undertake projects that are as innovative as Ted Smith's vision for AIR Louisville, many in the United States and other countries run their operations efficiently and ethically. They land planes on time, make sure that food and drugs are safe, educate and feed children without direct cost, and protect communities from crime and fraud. In the era of COVID-19, they have played an outsize role in helping our communities and tackling the global pandemic.[2] The economist Mariana Mazzucato's book *Entrepreneurial State* is devoted to debunking the myth that the private sector innovates whereas the public sector does not.[3] Her book shines a light on the policies and grants that helped to create the Internet, GPS, and biotech industries, for example. A government agency even lent Apple $500,000 before it went public, investing in and enabling one of the great technological innovation stories of today.

Despite government's many successes, however, public institutions are increasingly seen as unable to do their job and respond to the challenges of our time. From the Flint, Michigan, water crisis to unconscionable wait times for veterans to receive their medical care to the crisis in the United States postal system, government too often underperforms or fails to respond. Even where the administrative state functions well and without corruption, the public lacks confidence in its effectiveness. Although during the height of the coronavirus pandemic of 2020, trust in government globally saw a temporary uptick consistent with reactions to other crises like World War II or 9/11, Americans have said that the government in Washington was not rising to meet the challenge of the virus, and they are angry at its performance.[4] The number demanding "very major reform" is at an all-time-high.[5] Around the world, people are disenchanted with a political system they feel has failed them.

That belief is growing because public institutions are frequently inefficient, inflexible, and dysfunctional. In too many instances, such as the federal government's handling of the pandemic response in 2020, people do not trust government because government does not deserve our trust.[6] In the first four months of the pandemic, public leaders spent over $100 million on the management consulting firm McKinsey to increase the likelihood— or at least the perception—that government was getting things done.[7]

While people have complained about government and politics in every era, survey data confirm that trust in government in the United States is at an all-time low.[8] When Americans were asked, "How much time can you trust the government to do what is right?" in 1958, 73 percent surveyed responded, "just about always." By 2013, that number had dropped to 28 percent. In another survey, conducted in 2010, the proportion of Americans who had a "lot of confidence" that the federal government could solve the problems on its desk was a paltry 4 percent.[9]

Instead, voters typically see their government as a "chronically clumsy, ineffectual, bloated giant."[10] The United States has dropped in the *Economist*'s Democracy Index to twenty-fifth because of its poor rankings in the "functioning of government" category.[11] Both Republicans and Democrats hold this view, writes the Yale law professor Peter Schuck in *Why Government Fails So Often*. Schuck concludes that voters rate government so poorly because it does perform poorly. After conducting a meta-analysis of 270 assessments of US federal government programs conducted by both left- and right-wing think tanks as well as the Office of Management and Budget (OMB) and the Government Accountability Office (GAO), Schuck found that "only a small number of these assessments could be considered positive. The vast majority were either clearly negative or showed mixed results."[12]

Of course, any report that purports to scrutinize government failures may have an element of selection bias. Nonetheless, in reaching the "inescapable conclusion" that public dissatisfaction is justified by a genuine lack of effectiveness, Schuck cites the joint, bipartisan finding of Barack Obama's OMB director, Peter Orszag, and George Bush's OMB director, John Bridgeland. These two analysts wrote that "based on our rough calculations, less than $1 out of every $100 of government spending is backed by even the most basic evidence that the money is being spent wisely."[13]

Such conclusions lead the political scientist Paul Light to assert that "federal failures have become so common that they are less of a shock to the public than an expectation. The question is no longer if government will fail every few months, but where. And the answer is 'anywhere at all.'"[14]

This implosion of trust is compounded by a widening legitimacy gap —the sense that those who govern do not speak for us. While the American public actually agrees on many policy issues, Congress is increasingly partisan and polarizing, a divergence that has been growing since the 1980s. Every day is Election Day in Congress.[15]

Moreover, the preferences of the average American appear to have only a minuscule, near-zero, statistically insignificant impact on public policy. Arguably, voting matters little. The conservative theorists Bryan Caplan and Ilya Somin, both law professors at George Mason University, following in the tradition of Anthony Downs in his 1957 classic *Economic Theory of Democracy*, see voting, that basic form of democratic participation, as irrational and irrelevant.[16] They lay the blame at what they perceive to be the feet of incompetent citizens rather than with the design of our current institutions and how they work.[17] The political scientists Chris Achen and Larry Bartels (in work that has been extensively criticized) go so far as to say that voting is so irrational and voters so incompetent that everything from weather to shark attacks condition how people vote presumably more than an informed decision.[18]

The concern that rule of the people by the people is a myth also comes from the Left. As Jacob Hacker and Paul Pierson conclude in *Winner-Takes-All Politics*, the multibillion-dollar lobbying machine of organized business that emerged in the 1970s to fight the costs that Great Society social programs and protections demanded of business has continuously pushed through a legislative agenda designed to favor the rich over the middle class. Their book chronicles a systematic exclusion of the "everyman" from politics as a result of the marriage of big business and political power. Big corporations wield outsize influence.[19] As inequality has risen, they argue, people no longer feel that things are going well or that government is representing them. Perhaps one indicator of undue corporate influence is the growth in the number of lobbyists, which has risen from 175 in 1971 to over 11,000 today, either reflecting or causing Congress's tendency to favor wealthy business interests.[20] "The complexity and incoherence of our government," argues Stephen Teles, further adds to the challenge of participation. Legalisms, jargon, and complex rules often "make it difficult for us to understand just what that government is doing, and among the practices it most frequently hides from view is the growing tendency of public policy to redistribute resources upward to the wealthy and the organized at the expense of the poorer and less organized."[21] With legislation largely developed by professional staff and elected officials working behind closed doors, it is no wonder that rates of trust in Congress are at historic lows.

Lobbyists and advocacy groups vie for face time with legislators, while constituent emails and letters pile up in congressional offices. The hypothesis that Congress does not represent the American public and that public preferences do not guide Washington is borne out in practice. Politicians preen in front of cameras while passing the blame and the buck to future generations for ineffective lawmaking. Without tools or processes to foster a meaningful two-way conversation with elected or appointed officials, legitimacy suffers.

The crisis of trust in public institutions feeds a long-standing and highly partisan debate about the role of government, with the two poles of the debate having been defined as being between bigger or smaller government. "Big government" conjures negative images of sclerotic bureaucracy and intrusive overreach into private life. So-called small government conservatives see government as a primary impediment to solving problems, especially when regulations interfere with doing business. They call for limits on the size of government in order to prevent excessive intervention in the economy or private life.

However, couching the discussion about lack of trust in government in terms of the size of government creates a false dichotomy between big and small. While conservatives have a point about excessive bureaucracy, they also miss the point. Government has a vital role to play as independent and neutral arbiter for the public interest. We need strong government to safeguard the rule of law and the rights of minorities and to justly administer programs and services that work for all rather than just for some. As we have seen with COVID-19, we need government to play a coordinating role to ensure adequate availability and distribution of testing, vaccines, and personal protective equipment (PPE).

But being a proponent for the role of government does not have to equate with being satisfied with how government performs. Far from it. There is an increasing public outcry for the wealthy and corporations to pay their fair share in taxes. That is absolutely correct, but public institutions also have to do a better job at spending money and administering services. We also need to transform how government works to become more effective and efficient at problem solving with agility. Rather than bigger or smaller government, above all, we urgently need *stronger* but *better* government. We have ambitious challenges, and we need institutions that can keep up to fix the problems and respond to crises like the health-care needs of residents during a pandemic, exploding unemployment, rampant levels of hunger, widening inequality, worsening geopolitical relations, and the runaway ravages of climate change.

In order to make the case that better—more effective, efficient, and legitimate—government will result from changing working practices and learning a new set of skills in the twenty-first century, we first have to understand the urgency of the challenge. Thus, we dive in to understand the *origins* of the crisis of trust and lack of confidence in government in the United States and around the world.

ORIGINS OF THE CRISIS OF TRUST IN GOVERNMENT: AN AMERICAN VIEW

Increasingly dysfunctional public institutions have begotten and resulted from broader socioeconomic challenges that government has failed to address, further reinforcing the view that public institutions are not performing.

These challenges can be summed up in one phrase: for many Americans, their quality of life is either stagnant or declining. Anxiety about the future is rampant. While I have long been skeptical about complaints (rampant even before COVID) that life is worse today than it was in some bygone age, like most Americans I have the nagging sense, backed up by empirical evidence, that the world is going in the wrong direction.

In the United States, whereas life expectancy increased for most of the past sixty years, the rate of increase slowed over time, and life expectancy has been decreasing since 2014.[22] For the poor, life expectancy is dramatically lower.[23] For White women in the United States without a high school diploma, it has fallen by five years since 1990.[24] Rich American men now live fifteen years longer than their poorer fellow citizens do.[25] Life expectancy for Black men is far below that for every other demographic.[26]

The United Nations special rapporteur on extreme poverty has declared that almost a fifth of American children are in poverty and that children account for more than a fifth of homeless people.[27] A child in the United States is 57 percent more likely to die before the age of nineteen than a child in a peer country is.[28] In my home state of New Jersey, a Black mother is five times more likely to die from a pregnancy complication than an American White mother is, the worst such disparity in the nation.[29] The coronavirus only further highlighted the outcome disparity between Whites and minorities.[30] For example, in Los Angeles County, a UCLA study found Black and Latino residents were twice as likely to die of COVID-19 as non-Latino Whites. A University of California–San Francisco study found that 95 percent of people testing positive for COVID-19 in San Francisco's Mission District in April 2020 were Latino.[31]

"For ordinary Americans," writes the journalist Bob Herbert, "the story of the past several years has too often been about job cuts, falling wages, vanishing pensions and diminished expectations." While the income of the United States' bottom half remains stagnant—taking a significant toll on public health by many measures—the average pretax income of the top tenth of Americans has doubled since 1980, and that of the top 0.001 percent has risen sevenfold.[32] Inequality is at historically high levels and getting worse by the day.

This unnecessary income inequality is exacerbated by rising levels of unemployment. During the coronavirus epidemic, unemployment soared from 3.5 percent in February 2020 to almost 15 percent in April 2020, a figure that did not count the millions of workers who left the labor force entirely or those who were forcibly shifted to part-time work, not to mention those who had difficulty applying for unemployment insurance due to overburdened government websites. Low-wage workers faced the disproportionate brunt of the impact of unemployment.[33]

Uncertainty about the impact of technology on work further exacerbated the problem. From the axe to the calculator, new technologies have always transformed work. In 1900, 41 percent of Americans worked in agriculture; by 2000, it was only 2 percent. Likewise, the proportion of Americans employed in manufacturing has dropped from 30 percent in the post–World War II years to around 10 percent today. In both cases, new jobs emerged to replace the old ones.

Will that happen again? Or will it take years to recover? As technological innovation accelerates, no commonly accepted vision of the future of work or of its key drivers has emerged. "Certain activities are more likely to be automated, requiring entire business processes to be transformed, and jobs performed by people to be redefined, much like the bank teller's job was redefined with the advent of ATMs," writes the economist James Bessen in the *Atlantic*.[34]

Today, some people argue that new technologies of automation and artificial intelligence will actually create jobs—including entirely new categories of jobs.[35] Some people even imagine a world of superabundance where work will be about pursuing your passion, on your own terms. Others predict with equal and opposite conviction that machines and humans will wage a Darwinian struggle—and that machines will win. AI systems will take on tasks at the heart of middle- and high-skill jobs, while robots will perform menial work that once required low-skill human labor. The result will be massive unemployment, falling wages, and wrenching economic dislocation.[36] Whatever the future holds, present trends in the workplace are sharply exacerbating the unequal division of income and wealth between the high and low skilled, dislocating workers, depressing wages, and wreaking havoc with people's lives.

These bleak trends all contribute to levels of violence in the United States that are among the highest in wealthy countries. About 40 percent of Americans say they own a gun or live in a household with one, according to a 2017 survey. The rate of murder and manslaughter by firearm is the highest in the developed world.[37] In 2019, there were more mass shootings than there were days of the year. Notably, nearly two-thirds of gun deaths in the United States are suicides. The gun suicide rate is eight times that of other high-income countries.[38] The fear of violence is very real for Black and Hispanic Americans. Although half of the people shot and killed by police are White, Black Americans are shot at a disproportionate rate. In data measured from 2015, Black Americans account for less than 13 percent of the US population but are killed by police at more than twice the rate of White Americans. Hispanic Americans are also killed by police at a disproportionate rate.[39]

Pervasive racism besets too many of our social institutions and perpetuates catastrophic inequalities of income, incarceration, educational outcomes, and even life expectancy. The coronavirus pandemic, as with so many other problems, has disproportionately impacted communities of color. As of this writing, according to APM Research, the overall COVID-19 mortality rate for Black Americans is 2.4 times as high as the rate for Whites and 2.2 times as high as the rate for Asians and Latinos.[40]

Adding insult to injury, points out the Harvard philosopher Michael Sandel, is that this decreasing quality of life is coupled with a meritocratic "rhetoric of rising" from both political parties: if everyone has an equal chance to succeed in the American dream, then the failure to succeed is one's own fault. Inequality of outcomes is excused by supposed equality of opportunity. Yet it is not so easy to rise in the United States today. In reality, social mobility is more difficult in the United States today than in Canada or Europe. Thus, as inequality widens the smug pull-yourself-up-by-your-bootstraps refrain, coupled with a market-oriented technocratic approach to governing that excludes ordinary people, fuels populist discontent, societal frustration, anger, and disappointment at the tyranny of merit.[41]

ORIGINS OF THE CRISIS OF TRUST IN GOVERNMENT: A GLOBAL VIEW

Globally, exponential progress of science and technology in recent decades has made it possible for humans to live longer, healthier, more creative lives. We are more educated and more literate than ever before. Around the world, albeit to different degrees, levels of trade, prosperity, and mobility have all risen, spurred by the explosion of Internet and mobile phone technologies that accelerate the spread of ideas, culture, and people. Pre-COVID, global poverty had been decreasing, and life expectancies had been increasing (now over a hundred million people have been pushed into extreme poverty with over a million deaths, as of this writing, with both numbers expected to rise). Over the past forty years, however, the number of annual deaths among children less than five years of age has halved.[42]

These remarkable changes have also fueled the expectation that even our hardest global challenges can be tackled. Yet they also generate frustration. The more we undergo what the political commentator Moises Naím calls the "massive cognitive and emotional transformation" created by technological innovation, the more the public clamors for institutions that will help it to cope—and the more disappointed it feels when they fail to do so.[43]

High expectations coupled with growing inequality is a combustible mix. Across the Organisation for Economic Co-operation and Development (OECD), the average income of the richest 10 percent of the population is about nine times that of the poorest 10 percent.[44] Amazon's Jeff Bezos is anticipated to become the planet's first trillionaire by 2026. Around the globe, the richest 1 percent of people control 82 percent of the total wealth, and just forty-two people own the same amount of wealth as the poorest 50 percent of the global population, according to Oxfam.[45]

Equally, if not more, serious even than the problem of inequality, the impact of climate change threatens to reverse the gains that much of the global population has made in recent decades. At a historic UN Summit in September 2015, the leaders of 193 countries ratified seventeen Sustainable Development Goals. These include tackling poverty and inequality and promoting gender equality, good health, quality education, clean water, and sustainable cities.

But the need to reduce greenhouse-gas emissions is paramount. A string of UN and climate scientist reports, couched in ever more urgent language, are warning that pledges to limit warming to two degrees Celsius made at the Paris climate summit in 2015 will not be enough to stave off the life-threatening consequences of climate change for all species, including human beings.[46] If we do not halt the warming progression, the planet will soon hit a point of irreversible damage. The melting Antarctic ice cap, rising temperatures, and rising sea levels have already led to more and more intense hurricanes (so many to necessitate using the Greek alphabet in addition to the English one for naming all the Atlantic storms), more extreme and frequent wildfires, more droughts and heatwaves, and less predictable precipitation patterns, with the devastating human and economic consequences we are globally learning about first-hand.[47] Those catastrophes are expected to escalate. Over a million species are expected to go extinct as a result.[48] When the five warmest years in the global record have all come in the 2010s and the ten warmest years on record have all come since 1998, it is no wonder that climate change—and political inaction—top the list of anxiety-inducing problems.[49]

For many people, however, rising levels of violence provoke more immediate anxiety than do rising temperatures. Although levels of war-related violence and terrorism are declining overall, violence still plagues many societies. The number of deaths from terrorism has fallen off in recent years with the decline of Islamic State in Syria and Iraq. Yet far-right terrorism is on the rise in Western countries, and nineteen countries recorded more than one hundred deaths from terrorism of any kind in 2017, bringing the specter of random violence home for many people.[50] Moreover, people worry about terrorism a great deal.

Violence, climate change, and insecure economic conditions all generate migration flows, which have increased by almost 25 percent since 2011. There were an estimated 258 million international migrants in 2017,[51] and the number of people living in internal displacement is the highest in history. "Unresolved conflicts, new waves of violence, and extreme weather events were responsible for most of the new displacement we saw in 2018," writes Alexandra Bilak, director of the Internal Displacement Monitoring Centre.[52] As the number of international migrants reaches new highs, people around the world show "little appetite for more migration"—whether into or out of their countries, reports Pew Research.[53] In all of the twenty-seven countries Pew surveyed, less than a third say their nation should allow more immigrants to enter.

In many high-income countries, immigration is generating intense political division, especially in Europe. Dalia Research finds that antiestablishment parties are on the rise because Europeans are fed up with their political class. The nationalist Alternative for Germany (AfD), for example, has grown rapidly since its founding in 2013 and is now the biggest opposition party in the German Bundestag. Barely a third of people in Europe trust politicians to do the right thing. The distrust extends beyond the public sector to include business, government, NGOs, and media, and it is self-reinforcing. A sense that the system is broken only "increases a person's vulnerability to fear, ultimately causing deeper distrust in institutions."[54] As a result, despite a proliferation in the number of democracies since World War II (half the world's population live in democracies), and despite empirical evidence that citizens of democracies live longer, healthier lives, a recent Pew Research Center poll in twenty-seven countries found that just over half of all citizens are dissatisfied with the way democracy is working in their country.[55]

A rising tension between liberal, cosmopolitan internationalism and xenophobic nationalism has produced populist leaders such as Donald Trump in the United States, Viktor Orban in Hungary, Mateusz Morawiecki in Poland, Nicolas Maduro in Venezuela, and Jair Bolsonaro in Brazil. These would-be "great men of history" exploit the sense of crisis and uncertainty and people's fears that the system is not working for them.[56] They stoke concerns over immigration, globalization, technological transformation, and changing gender dynamics with nativist pronouncements.[57] Despite not having won the popular vote or perhaps because of it, Trump used his inauguration speech to echo the disingenuous rallying cry of populists down the centuries: "Today we are not merely transferring power from one administration to another, or from one party to another, but we are transferring power from Washington, D.C., and giving it back to you, the people."[58]

FROM RONALD TO DONALD: GOVERNMENT THAT GOVERNS LEAST GOVERNS BEST

The current backlash against the growth of the bureaucratic apparatus and against policy expertise is not new. It began with what political scientists termed Ronald Reagan's "antianalytical" presidency and conservative efforts to privatize public problem solving in an effort to shrink the size of government.

After World War II, the federal government built up new mechanisms and bureaucracies for obtaining information and expertise, for defining problems systematically, and for solving new kinds of problems. During the presidency of Lyndon Johnson, economists flocked to Washington to be part of creating the Great Society programs to combat inequality and poverty. These "Numbers Mandarins" were seen as living up to the Wilsonian tradition of neutral, nonpartisan public managers. In 1965, President Johnson had the Bureau of the Budget (today OMB) issue a directive establishing policy analytic offices in federal departments and agencies.[59]

President Reagan and his circle of neoconservatives sought to reverse this trend—to dismantle the postwar bureaucratic edifice, in particular the creation of Medicare and Medicaid, which had been a watershed in the growth of the nation-state and its powers. Reagan and his allies resented what they saw as overreach and intrusion by the state into every corner of the economy and society. His presidency was, in part, an ideologically driven attempt to outsource the finding of problems and their solutions to think tanks and the private sector.

Under Reagan, public-sector analytical units declined in size. Presidents George H. W. Bush and Bill Clinton continued the trend, despite their personal strengths in policy analysis. Both concentrated and politicized control over policy making in the OMB and rejected the decentralized problem-finding machinery of the bureaucracy—functionaries whose work limited the power and discretion of elected political leaders and whom Trump likes to refer to as the "deep state." As a result, the size of the federal government decreased, reversing the growth since World War II, and has continued to shrink.[60]

The politicization of problem solving has occurred on the legislative side as well. The unique separation of powers between the executive and legislative branches spurred Congress to seek its own sources of expertise, in order to have access to "honest numbers" independent of the White House. Thus, as the administrative side of government grew, so did Congress's oversight power and scope. During the 1970s, Congress established the Congressional Budget Office and the Office of Technology Assessment and reorganized the Congressional Research Service (CRS) in order to support the partisan legislative process with nonpartisan research. These dedicated analytical units complemented the already large congressional staff in the chambers of senators and representatives.

But the Reaganesque small-government push eventually transformed the operations of Congress as well. From 1995, the Speaker of the House of Representatives, Newt Gingrich, in an effort to strengthen the role of the Republican Party, began to dismantle the analytical capacity of Congress, cutting staff, freezing pay, ratcheting up fundraising requirements, getting rid of the Office of Technology Assessment, and limiting Congress's ability, as Congress watcher Daniel Schuman sums it up, to "engage in reasoned decision-making, placing it at the mercy of special interests."[61] Since 1995, Capitol Police expenditures have gone up by 279 percent, and architectural expenditures increased by 131 percent. By contrast, funding for staffing and policy expertise has increased a mere 8 percent over the past ten years. Spending on congressional committees has decreased by 25 percent since the 111th Congress. Committees have lost over one thousand staff positions, and support agencies over twenty-five hundred jobs over the past twenty-five years.[62]

The consequences for the capacity of Congress to research serious issues have been profound. With members needing to raise hundreds of thousands of dollars each year of their two-year term to earn their committee assignments, there is no time for problem solving, especially as they lack capacity to work on issues. Member of Congress Bill Pascrell Jr. of New Jersey writes, "Think about this a second: each of us represents approximately 750,000 Americans, armed with small policy staffs managing portfolios of hundreds of issues. This is the product of fiendish cuts set in 1995 that we have inexplicably never bothered to reverse."[63] In 2010, the House spent $1.37 billion and employed between seven thousand and eight thousand staffers. But corporations and special interests spend three times that number simply to lobby Congress.[64] That lobbying money is, in turn, what funds a member's fundraising totals, so that, in effect, special interests are paying to have members on the committees that matter to them.

Pascrell goes on to say, "Our founts of independent information have been cut off, our investigatory muscles atrophied, our committees stripped of their ability to develop policy, our small staffs overwhelmed by the army of lobbyists who roam Washington. Congress is increasingly unable to comprehend a world growing more socially, economically and technologically multifaceted—and we did this to ourselves."[65]

As the ability to examine issues withers, so does the investment in talent. From 1979 to 2015, CRS's staff has shrunk by 28 percent.[66] Its 421 researchers have to respond to more than sixty thousand questions from members of Congress. It can be dispiriting work, as one former researcher discovered, commenting, "My aspiration was to follow in the footsteps of these great researchers by using my knowledge of government organization to write the kinds of reports that might help Congress fix the USPS [US Postal Service] and other entities. . . . Thanks to growing pressure from a hyper-partisan Congress, my ability to write clearly and forthrightly about the problems of government—and possible solutions—was limited. And even when we did find time and space to do serious research, lawmakers ignored our work or trashed us if our findings ran contrary to their beliefs."[67]

During his tenure, Gingrich had shifted power away from committee chairs to party caucuses, thereby strengthening control by political parties (control lost after the institution of a primary system that enabled the public to select presidential delegates directly). As a result of staffing shortages and political preference, the number of oversight hearings by Congress has decreased dramatically. Committees "have been meeting less often than at almost any other time in recent history," according to the Washington nonprofit Congressional Management Foundation.[68] With exceptions, such as the Trump administration's efforts in its first year to pass laws overturning as many Obama-era regulations as possible, Congress has passed less and less legislation since 1995.[69] Whereas it passed around 700 hundred pieces of substantive legislation every term until the early 1990s, midway through the 116th term in 2020, the number of bills and resolutions was only 140 and 260 by the end of the 116th term.[70]

Government's problem today is not so much having access to expertise and information but the degradation of the processes used to translate available information into solutions. Orderly, reasoned, data-driven practices struggle to survive when every day in Washington is Election Day. As the public policy professors Frank Baumgartner and Bryan Jones write, our political culture has shifted to a "model of decision-making based on hierarchical control, with less concern for analytics, information and contrasting voices."[71]

A hyperpartisan climate imposes constant pressure to shy away from defining problems. After all, if the goal is to "win" by imposing "our" solution, alternative policies are not simply wrongheaded but dangerous. Questioning what the problem is can precipitate an unwanted and deliberative discussion about how to solve the problem that undermines the chance to win and validate one's own views. Increasing partisanship emphasizes elections over effectiveness, party dominance over solutions, winning over working.

All these institutional weaknesses came to a head during the presidency of Donald Trump.

TRUMP: DO NOT SEEK AND YE SHALL NOT FIND

In February 2018, an armed student shot and killed seventeen students and teachers at Marjory Stoneman Douglas High School in Parkland, Florida. In the following week, President Trump held a "listening session."[72] The horrific events had once again spurred a national discussion about gun control. The town-hall-style event was supposed to be a chance for the president to listen and consider the ideas of those who had been affected by gun violence. In fact, the notoriously unempathetic president had to write crib notes of "I hear you" and "I am listening" to remind himself to do just that. His real purpose for the meeting was to float a proposal, originally pitched by the National Rifle Association in the aftermath of the Sandy Hook school shooting in 2012, to arm teachers with guns.[73] "Highly trained, gun adept, teachers/coaches would solve the problem instantly, before police arrive," Trump tweeted afterward, referring to armed teachers. "With such measures in place," he wrote, "ATTACKS WOULD END!"[74]

In the subsequent days, the president continued to press for arming teachers, despite no evidence or data that such an idea would work. His plan had myriad flaws. Even law enforcement officers hit what they aim at just 18 percent of the time; how much worse would teachers be at stopping assailants without injuring themselves or other students? Statistically, more shooters are stopped by unarmed individuals.[75] And since most mass shooters kill themselves, the threat of dying would hardly be a deterrent. No wonder the vast majority of teachers opposed Trump's idea.[76]

The traditional analytical machinery of the White House and the relevant federal agencies played no role in developing, researching, or supporting this half-baked proposal or later uninformed ideas, for example, to cure COVID-19 in 2020 with bleach, hydroxychloroquine, or the flu vaccine or the inane suggestion in 2019 to buy Greenland. Once again, the president bypassed the institutional mechanisms for policy making. His advisers were left to scramble after the fact to develop a plan to bring his idea to fruition.

Similarly, President Trump shut down the federal government in late 2018 and declared a national emergency in early 2019 over his demand for $5.7 billion to fund the construction of a wall on the southern border of the United States—a solution to a manufactured problem, one that the White House had studiously declined to discuss because it was not supported by the facts.

A genuine investigation of the state of immigration and security would have revealed that in 2018 illegal crossings of the southwestern border were at an all-time low. More than 650 miles of border fencing are already in place. The vast majority of those who are deported from the United States have committed no violent crime, and none committed terrorism, despite assertions by Trump while on the campaign trail and as president.[77] Deeper exploration and public discussion of the problem of drug consumption could have pointed to solutions aimed at treating addiction rather than building a wall, but that approach would not have suited President Trump's xenophobic rhetorical aims.

In an administration known for its "undisciplined and reckless" style of decision-making, this slapdash approach to the truth has been the rule rather than the exception.[78] Under President Trump, there has been a profound disregard of government experience, integrity, and competence that has cost American families thousands of lives during the coronavirus crisis. From health care to climate change, the administration violated and even ridiculed evidence-based policies.

None of this should come as any surprise. In 2016 (and again in 2020), the Trump team failed to prepare for a transition to power. Instead, it flouted its legal obligations and a disciplined and systematic preparation for a handover provided by the Obama administration (as President George W. Bush had provided for Obama). In many agencies, no one showed up to get a briefing or learn how the government worked.[79] It was thus no surprise that policies often came verbatim from Fox News scripts—starting with the travel ban against various Muslim-majority countries that Trump put forward without consulting his cabinet.

Trump was the first president since 1941 not to name a science adviser in his first year in office (along with thousands of other positions that went unfilled).[80] In the first year of his presidency alone, the litany of invented policy pronouncements surprised even his closest advisers. He also formally ended the global pandemic response team in 2018. While some of the staff remained and continued to work on global health, the team was disbanded.

Trump's disdain for traditional policy-making processes extended also to appointments. He has chosen advisers on the basis of personal loyalty rather than policy competence. He selected Eric Trump's wedding planner to manage public housing for New York and New Jersey. The twenty-three-year-old tasked with managing the opioid epidemic had no previous employment apart from the Trump campaign; his résumé included a law-firm job from which he had been discharged for failing to turn up and for claiming a master's degree he did not have. The *New Yorker* wrote about a "culture of fealty" inside the Trump White House: "Conformists thrive, and dissenters depart or refuse to join."[81] In the midst of a global pandemic, he fired five agency inspector generals. In 2019, he enacted an executive order (13875) requiring agencies to eliminate a third of their federal advisory committees and in 2020 accorded the President the right to hire and fire civil servants at will (13957).

The culture of personal fealty has further eroded the government's capacity for deep thought. In 2019, the US Department of Agriculture decided to relocate the agency's expert research services—the Economic Research Service and the National Institute of Food and Agriculture—from Washington, DC, to Kansas City, Missouri. In fact, two-thirds declined, thereby gutting the agency of its research staff. Many saw the relocations as an attempt to eviscerate the agency's independent research capacity.[82] "The disregard for expertise in the federal government is worse than it's ever been," says Michael Gerrard, director of the Sabin Center for Climate Change Law at Columbia University, which has tracked more than 450 reports of Trump-administration efforts to restrict or misuse science.[83] During the COVID-19 pandemic, the Trump administration politicized science to an unprecedented degree, manipulating agencies like the FDA and CDC that previously enjoyed sterling reputations for scientific integrity. Knowing, for example, that masks could save lives, they not only made the issue of a mask wearing a proxy for political loyalty but also actively interfered in and canceled a plan for the United States Post Office to send masks to every American.[84]

The hostility to science in the Trump administration, while extraordinary, is emblematic of a growing distrust of credentialed expertise—expertise on tap, not on top—and of the postwar consensus that complex questions of governing need to be managed by technocrats. It amplifies the old debate in US politics over the appropriate size and role of government.

The neoconservatives were right in this regard. Government grew vastly in breadth and scope after World War II.[85] The conservative historian Niall Ferguson takes pleasure in pointing out that the size of the *Federal Register*, the gazette of government, has more than doubled since its original publication in 1946.[86] Similarly, the GAO produced thirty-seven reports in 1966 and over sixteen hundred in 1973.[87]

Even with Republicans' attempts to rein in the scope of the federal government, its remit is huge. Its vast bureaucracies tackle ever more problems in more areas of social and economic life. President Obama made multibillion-dollar investments in everything from green energy to brain science and personalized medicine. Ironically, even President Trump's spending far exceeds that of his predecessor because of his military outlays.[88] Whereas it was once hard to start a government program, today it is hard to stop one.

As Peter Schuck points out, "Today, federal domestic spending is at the highest share of gross domestic product (GDP) since the end of World War II (albeit still well below European levels). A larger share of Americans receives entitlements than ever before; the federal government now backs 90 percent of new mortgages (up from half before the financial crisis). And 93 percent of student loans."[89] The expansion of government bureaucracy seems inexorable. As James Q. Wilson famously said, "Once politics was about only a few things. Now it is about everything."[90]

It is clear that big government will not soon go away.[91]

Critics blame the traditional problem-solving classes, also known as the experts or the best and brightest, for the fiasco of the Vietnam War, for the economic response to the 1970s oil crisis, for failing to foresee and prepare for the economic crisis of 2008, for predicting a Hillary Clinton victory in 2016, and so on.

Ideological supporters of smaller government point out that the more public analysts define and analyze problems, the greater the likelihood of identifying things the government needs to fix. "The more you look for problems, the more you find," write Baumgartner and Jones—hardly ideological supporters of the smaller-government rhetoric—in their book *The Politics of Information: Problem Definition and the Course of Public Policy in America.* "The more you seek to understand the complexity of a given problem, the more complex you find that it is. With each discovery of the nature of a social problem comes at least the possibility (not the certainty) of creating a government program to help alleviate it."[92]

The United States is not alone in witnessing the rise of a pervasive contempt for expertise. "People in this country have had enough of experts," declared cabinet minister and Brexit advocate Michael Gove during the 2016 leave campaign. Gove's comment prompted even a columnist from the *Telegraph*, a conservative newspaper that supported the leave position, to write that a "sinister and pervasive strain of anti-intellectualism" was afoot in British politics.[93]

THE PRIVATIZATION OF PUBLIC PROBLEM SOLVING

Distrust of big government has come not only from the political right but also from the entrepreneurial center. Since the Reagan years, there has been a concerted effort to promote the view that innovation comes from business rather than from government.[94] "No one has told us that government is a good thing for a really long time," writes the journalist Anand Giridharadas in *Winners Take All: The Elite Charade of Changing the World.*[95] From every sector comes the refrain: government officials are failures and dinosaurs. Recent survey data bolster the view that in challenging times people are trusting employers and CEOs more because they perceive government to be failing them.[96]

The success of Silicon Valley has helped to produce a class of hyperrich technology and finance entrepreneurs who see government as too inefficient, too incapable, or too corrupt to solve problems. It should get out of the way and leave it to them. As heartwarming and welcome as it is when generous business and entertainment superstars like former New York mayor Michael Bloomberg, Arnold Schwarzenegger, and John Legend, for example, pay the court fines of the formerly incarcerated to enable them to vote in the 2020 election or when Bill Gates and Warren Buffett fund the development of much-needed vaccines to eradicate tropical diseases, this largesse further reinforces a view that financial success translates into political power.

The myth of the entrepreneur as creative problem solver reinforces the privatization of a "fix the world" mentality and a belief that markets, not governments, will solve societal problems. (While writing this chapter, I was disturbed to receive an email from a UN entity inviting me to a cocktail party for "Slush," which bills itself as a movement of entrepreneurs aiming to make solving some of the grandest global challenges profitable.)

Giridharadas tells the story of an app called Even that charges $260 a year to help workers "smooth out" income swings, ostensibly helping the poor to save more when they make more and have something available for a rainy day. The notion that an app, and an expensive one at that, is the solution to poverty—a personal solution to a public problem—is emblematic of the mind-set of privatized problem solving.[97] It fails to address the causes of poverty and what role the government should play in eradicating income inequality. The notion that impoverished people should pay for an app they can ill afford further suggests that individuals are to blame for—and responsible for fixing—their lack of regular income. Other factors—institutionalized racism, income disparities, inequality of opportunity, the drag of intergenerational poverty, and more—are not considered in favor of this high-tech version of the Christmas Club account.

Companies such as Amazon, Google, Facebook, and Apple promote themselves as organizations for social good. They often tout the entrepreneurial skills of Silicon Valley and the tech sector as the best way to tackle societal challenges.

Universities, too, have embraced the pursuit of privatized public problem solving, creating programs for students to launch venture-backed start-ups (and return revenue to the university). In the past decade, entrepreneurship has been a field of considerable growth in universities, especially in business and management schools.[98] Social enterprise clubs have replaced socialism clubs.[99] Penn, Oxford, Stanford, Yale, Duke, and many more universities have dedicated social entrepreneurship programs. Such teaching often focuses on how to "combine the passion of a social mission with an image of business-like discipline, innovation, and determination commonly associated with, for instance, the high-tech pioneers of Silicon Valley."[100]

But the idolization of entrepreneurship risks putting lipstick on a pig, generating what Giridharadas scathingly calls "personalized theories of change" that do nothing to disrupt the root causes of problems, including politics and power relations. The cult of entrepreneurship favors market-based approaches. Students are taught to launch a nonprofit, start a company, or make an app—in other words, to bypass government, community organizations, and unions in favor of a privatized approach that often intentionally disregards "institutional and organizational norms and boundaries."[101]

The practice and pedagogy of entrepreneurship also suffer from an excessive focus on the ego of the rugged individual and his or her ability to think up an original solution. Besides celebrating the individual leader, the culture of entrepreneurship rewards the spark of an idea rather than the challenging and less glamorous job of implementing and measuring what works.

Whether the tech "solutions" that entrepreneurs create actually respect human rights and dignity and truly aim to uplift and help, ultimately, is a question of individual choice and intentions.[102] To be fair, much good has come of corporate and university investments, especially in socially minded entrepreneurial activities. I devote all of chapter 9 to the benefits of public-private partnerships and the many things that companies are doing, from building civic technologies for social good to sharing data for public benefit. In chapter 12, we look at pathbreaking university programs like the Design for America program at Northwestern University, the Ability Lab at New York University, and the REACH program at University of Toronto, which help students tackle societal problems without the obligation to turn a profit.

Large tech companies like Google have spun off firms like Jigsaw, which describes itself on its website: "We identify emerging technology threats that destabilize the Internet and our society. We develop cutting-edge research and technology to counter these threats, and help defend civil society, journalists, activists and those at the forefront of digital conflict."[103] Facebook Social Good claims that its aim is to "build powerful tools that improve people's lives."[104] Amazon Social Responsibility, too, makes far-reaching public-interest commitments. While these companies are trying to launder bad reputations for perpetuating political polarization and human loneliness, mistreating and underpaying workers, or building discriminatory technologies, it is true that some private entrepreneurs are also inventing transformative technology to extend human lives, improve wellness, reduce the impacts of climate change, and address the impediments to good and safe work. To take one example of such a social enterprise, the US company Bext360 has created a smart contracting platform to administer payments to coffee farmers in Ethiopia, Uganda, and the Democratic Republic of the Congo. Farmers load their harvest into a machine that uses sensors to sift and sort the coffee beans. The crop is then given a grade based on the size and ripeness of the beans, and farmers can receive payment immediately using a mobile application, if their desired price is reached.[105]

Many businesses go through the B-Corp certification process to bind themselves to higher standards of social and environmental performance, accountability, and transparency. There are companies that use market-based approaches to ameliorate societal problems successfully.

But there are no safeguards for the people who might be affected by these initiatives. In the end, B-Corp is only a label. Profit maximization and the financial interests of the firm will always come first for a for-profit enterprise. Because the accountability of business organizations is to shareholders rather than public stakeholders, they all too often give away data for social good, on the one hand, while harming the environment, on the other. They are making an app to help the poor while mistreating their own workers. Facebook donated $10 million to racial justice causes while allowing Donald Trump to post inflammatory content that fueled protests and riots.

In public problem solving, especially in the public sector, many constraints are still present, but motivations are—or at least should be—different.[106] At the very least, we should not limit ourselves to market-based solutions (nor should we exclude them altogether either) and fail to appreciate the power, reach, and resources of public institutions. There are too many limits to the ability and willingness of business to challenge the status quo and the inequitable power structures that cause a problem in the first place to see the private sector as the answer to public problems.

THEORIES OF MANAGERIALISM

In recent decades, especially since Reagan and Thatcher, some scholars and practitioners have argued that the way to fix government is to copy the techniques of the private sector, especially the use of more data to deliver better performance. In line with rising interest in private-sector solutions to public problems, and the concomitant growth of public-sector consulting practices of private management and strategy consultancies, theories of managerialism, total quality management, market-based public administration, entrepreneurial government, and new public management speak of treating government more like a business than a bureaucracy.[107] These approaches value efficiency and cost savings above effectiveness, legitimacy, and equity.

The new public management approach seeks to import business practices into government. It lauds cost-benefit analysis, top-down targets, and data-driven measurement.[108] Public-management classics, such as *Reinventing Government*, criticize a bureaucratic paradigm that prizes process over performance, and rules and regulations over outcomes.[109] Instead, government managers are meant to serve citizens the way businesses serve customers, with greater efficiency designed to increase customer satisfaction. New public management celebrates competition inside and outside government and emphasizes taking personal responsibility and achieving results over following orders. New public management has had a far-reaching influence on public management.

Undoubtedly, these efficiency-focused approaches have helped to improve some outcomes. But widespread resulting failures have led some scholars to declare the new public management mind-set to be "dead in the water."[110] The spread of a new public management mind-set and practices has certainly not increased trust in government.

Whether because new public management's efficiency principles remain at the level of rhetoric rather than real practice or because these entrepreneurial and privatizing techniques are top-down and eschew engagement with citizens, these approaches cast members of the public as customers rather than collaborators. Managerialism's highly quantitative and hierarchical approach, while perhaps useful for improving the efficiency of transactional services, is a poor match for the challenge and uncertainty of complex public problem solving and policy making.

Managerialism works well when objectives are clear and when there is a well-understood problem. But its defenders measure success by cost effectiveness and money saved, avoiding the more fundamental equitable and ethical questions of whether such success criteria make sense. Especially in instances when the problem is not well understood and success demands a more nuanced and deliberative discussion about mission and values, such cost-benefit approaches are inadequate to many contemporary challenges or to a vision of public problem solving as advancing a politics of care and compassion.

Public value theory, another neoliberal classic of public administration, authored in the mid-nineties, also borrows from business to improve government. The idea takes inspiration from the axiom that just as privately owned companies must create shareholder value to survive, government managers must create value for the public through the application of the principles of management.[111] Government managers have to feel responsible and accountable for creating value for citizens. But unlike new public management, value does not derive solely from delivering a service to a satisfied customer. After all, no one is happy about appearing in court, getting arrested by the police, or participating in a contact-tracing program. Instead, value is measured on the basis not of individual satisfaction but of value to citizens as part of a community.

As in the private sector, public-sector managers have to determine how to create public value within the realpolitik context of what is politically and operationally feasible, which might include limiting the role of government altogether in favor of privatization. The rhetorical mantra of public value has had widespread appeal as a description of the enhanced functioning of government and the behavior of managers. But it, too, advanced the largely conservative and antigovernment ethos popular at the time it was penned.

All these managerialist theories elevate the role of business but not of citizens and are devoid of any focus on equity and inclusion. Even if advocates of these approaches do not elevate those who govern into Platonic guardians, who ultimately decide what is best for the public, and ascribe some of that role to politicians, in every case, these managerial approaches lack an adequate normative interest in a truly substantive and equitable role for the public, especially a diverse public, in decision-making. They may define how managers work today—and public value theory does take some account of the role of public deliberation—but the "public" is a largely fictional construct. Although citizens are meant to articulate what "value" means to them, public value theory does not envision the meaningful and robust forms of equitable public engagement we know are possible and imperative today.

These elitist theories all fail to take citizens' expertise seriously or to reimagine how managers could collaborate with the public to become more effective and legitimate, not simply more efficient, problem solvers.

FROM PRIVATE ENTREPRENEURSHIP
TO PUBLIC PROBLEM SOLVING

Private innovators and inventors generally are solving a problem that they personally experience and understand—like the user-inventors whom the MIT professor Eric von Hippel famously identified as being the source of breakthrough ideas in the scientific-equipment market. Public entrepreneurs and public problem solvers more generally, by contrast, are usually trying to solve *other people's problems*. They might have some personal familiarity with the issue, but ultimately, they need to be able to spot, assess, shepherd, and implement the ideas of others, rather than invent new ones, using highly collaborative and participatory methods.

Furthermore, while private entrepreneurship revolves around secrecy and competition, by contrast, collaboration is vital at every stage of public problem solving. Public entrepreneurs must be more democratic and less focused on individual ego. They must define and solve a problem in collaboration with those who are most affected by it.

These changemakers are not "24-year-old male engineers parachuted in from Silicon Valley, but often a diverse range of people who have worked in or around government for years, who are invested in their communities, or who simply like intractable problems."[112] Whereas "moving fast and breaking things," to quote the motto Mark Zuckerberg used to adorn Facebook's walls in the past, may exemplify the entrepreneurial ethos, those who are working in the public interest need to move fast and *fix things*, for real people in the real world.

By solving problems and making decisions *with* rather than *for* the public, public servants can create government that is neither bigger nor smaller but better.

This kind of wholesale systems change—from public administration and management to public entrepreneurship and problem solving—requires a transformation of organizational mind-sets and an evolution, even a revolution, of individual practice. Public servants must move from closed-door, siloed governing to a collaborative approach that draws on expertise and insights from across sectors and with the wider public.

For some time, the market has been seen as the only alternative to Weberian or Wilsonian bureaucracy. We need a new mental model for what it means to govern well—a radical and thoroughgoing replacement of outdated governance practices and a better toolkit for innovation that works for different types of problems.

In a famous article in the *Atlantic Monthly* in 1945, the inventor Vannevar Bush laid out his vision for a machine that would transform man's relationship to knowledge. Fifty years ahead of the World Wide Web, he imagined a personal computer equipped with a screen that would give us access to the cumulative knowledge of the ages. He called it the "Memex." Bush provided a concrete mental model that others enacted over the ensuing decades of the information technology revolution. Thanks to him (and to science-fiction stories like *Star Trek*), we learned how computers should evolve. We now expect computers to reduce our workloads, to bring us closer to one another, and to open up new horizons of learning—and to do all this faster and with smaller devices. What was so radical about the Memex was not the technology but Bush's willingness to imagine how it would change our relationship to knowledge and information and the resulting societal consequences.

Government, however, is much less like the computer and more like the umbrella. That is to say, over the past one hundred years, it has hardly changed at all regardless of political party. As a result, there is no popular appreciation for how those who work in government could work differently. We need a Memex for government, and that is where public entrepreneurship comes in.

The new public entrepreneurs borrow the best of entrepreneurial creativity and innovation from their private-sector cousins. They possess a bias toward action, rapid learning, and real-world impact. But they also work differently than either people in the private sector or their own public-sector forebears.

Public entrepreneurs possess a core set of skills, outlined in chapter 1, that enable them to engage in "seeing like a state," in the famous phrase of the political scientist James Scott.[113] However, whereas Scott was concerned about the past failure on the part of public institutions to perceive on-the-ground conditions and the tendency of those who govern toward reductive simplification, today public entrepreneurs use big data *and* human insight to understand a problem as ordinary people experience it and to collaboratively design solutions tailored to achieve the public's desired outcomes.

These new methods, including problem definition, human-centered design, and data-driven decision-making, are enabled by new technologies. Together, the seven skills laid out at the end of chapter 1 reflect a new understanding of the role of the public servant. They disregard the hierarchy and centralized management at the heart of new public management in favor of networked collaboration. Most depend on the expertise of citizens. Incorporating greater openness and collaboration yields innovative thinking and, even more importantly, solutions that work in the real world.

The following chapters set out the skills and methods of the new public entrepreneur and the public problem solver, more generally—how to acquire those skills and methods and how to use them in order to reinvent government and tackle the major challenges of our times.

CHAPTER THREE

From Idea to Implementation

When I got face-to-face with [my problem], I discovered something.
My problem wasn't what I thought it was. I discovered it had something beautiful inside. My problem held an opportunity! It was an
opportunity for me to learn and grow. To be brave. To do something.

Kobi Yamada, What Do You Do with a Problem?

THE ARC OF THE PROBLEM-SOLVING PROCESS

My exposure to public problem solving came well into adulthood. As a
young professor, I worked with my students to design a platform and a
policy to enable volunteer scientists and technologists to supply much-
needed information to overworked patent examiners in the US Patent Office. The patent system was broken, seemingly beyond repair. It had a backlog of a million applications, and examiners had only fifteen to twenty
hours to review and research an invention and then decide whether to provide a twenty-year grant of monopoly rights.

When we began, we did not know whether the real problem was the
lack of quality of those patents granted, the lack of training of examiners, or
the overwhelming number of people applying. We had no precedent for
how to improve the situation. However, through a series of interventions
and innovations, we developed a process—and the technology—to enable
expert volunteers to share information at the right time to help the government examiner determine if an invention had the requisite novelty and in-
novativeness to merit a patent, which requires a thorough search and
knowledge of the relevant scientific literature. This "Peer-to-Patent" project,
which began as a mere idea in 2005, ran as a pilot project in the United
States, the United Kingdom, South Korea, and Japan and ended up changing the law in the United States to allow for greater participation in the

patent process. It also got me hooked on the notion that we can learn how to take novel public-interest solutions from idea to implementation rapidly.[1]

Before we explore specific tools and methods for public problem solving —along with hands-on exercises that you can use—it is essential to discuss the pathway a public problem solver needs to take to tackle a problem. Every project-management or policy-analysis process adopts some kind of scaffolding, which tracks the steps involved in identifying a problem and developing solutions. This framework is sometimes called the "innovation cycle." Just as the job seeker needs to know how to train, apply for, and secure a job, and the entrepreneur needs to reflect on what to do from beginning to end to launch a successful business, the public problem solver and public entrepreneur need to comprehend the science of "deliverology." That means having an overview of what is involved in solving public problems even before you dive into specific methods. Otherwise, you could get sidetracked.[2]

As Benjamin Franklin reputedly said, "If you fail to plan, you are planning to fail." It is, therefore, important to start with a loose and iterative roadmap for getting from idea to implementation—even if you decide to deviate from the path. This map will help you to anticipate what you need to do and plan for it, spot new opportunities and innovative approaches, identify potential risks and needed resources, and ensure that your team is in agreement about the goals.

First, tracing out the arc of the public problem-solving pathway before diving in should maximize chances of success because it will make you more focused on the end result. By surveying our problem-solving process from beginning to end—and from the end to the beginning—we are forced to imagine what we hope to achieve. As Jaykumar Menon, the human rights lawyer and founder of the Open Source Pharma Foundation, explains, we must "work backwards from scale."[3] Menon is also the founder of the India Nutrition Initiative, which develops a salt that is double fortified with iron and iodine to address malnutrition in the developing world. Originally, the India Nutrition Initiative worked with prestigious scientists at MIT to reengineer the salt crystal to incorporate the desired micronutrients. But then Menon realized that by creating an entirely new variant of salt, he would also have to manufacture and distribute the salt himself. Thus, he shifted strategies, forgoing the cutting-edge science and focusing, instead, on how to plug into an existing supply chain. He collaborated with established producers. This led to designing a simpler process to add the micronutrients on the outside of the salt crystal, allowing him to reach tens of millions of people with this innovative effort to combat anemia.

Second, in addition to making you more goal oriented, such a priori reflection may open your thinking to different ways of working without getting too hung up on any one method. This is especially important because many training programs focus on one method for solving public problems to the exclusion of other tools and approaches. For example, Argentina's LabGob design academy focuses primarily and Brazil's WeGov program focuses exclusively on training public servants in human-centered design. While teaching how to test the delivery of services with citizens reflects an important change over earlier closed-door practices, the would-be innovator who only does human-centered design may not learn the importance of consulting experts or doing data-driven research. Human-centered design, while laudable, is not the only method and may, in fact, even be the wrong method to apply at times. For example, parents and students can offer their lived experience as a guide to improving a service providing a free and healthy lunch to schoolchildren. But failing to scrutinize data about the student population's health needs or to consult with experts on nutrition and education would reduce the likelihood of reaching an effective and legitimate solution.

Third, outlining the likely course of action in advance will make it easier to plan milestones and deliverables and to avoid spending so much time on one aspect of problem solving, such as data analysis or evidence review, that there is no time to consult with residents face-to-face or on defining the problem at such length that the opportunity to experiment with different solutions to see what works is lost.

Fourth, having an overview of the process helps to clarify how the methods and tools we discuss connect and flow from one another.

As a New Yorker, I like to think of the problem-solving pathway like a trip on the subway. The journey has major stops. Those key junctures are the primary stages of problem solving: problem definition, solution identification, implementation, and evaluation.

Like the Fourteenth, Thirty-Fourth, and Forty-Second Street stops, at those junctures, other lines branch off. Those branch lines represent the methods and tools we can employ at each stage to leverage data (information gleaned from sensors) or collective intelligence (ideas, insights, and opinions gleaned from people, preferably working together).

Thus, we augment problem definition using human-centered design *and* data-analytical thinking. We identify solutions better using robust open innovation *and* evidence synthesis. We accelerate implementation by virtue of our own hard work *and* of partnerships. We enhance evaluation with the collaborative learning that comes from creating our own experiments *and* taking advantage of social auditing.

But without mapping the journey first, we risk getting lost down a branch line and never arriving at the destination. Thus, this chapter outlines a strategy for "working backward from scale," or moving as quickly as possible from concept to delivery in the real world.

HOW PUBLIC PROBLEMS DIFFER FROM OTHER PROBLEMS

Of course, we are all too keenly aware that the world is awash in challenges that affect us as individuals and communities. But before devising a set of problem-solving heuristics—new ways of working—it is helpful first to define and understand what public problems are and then to outline new approaches to tackling them.

Genrich Altshuller was the Soviet Union's father of "problem science." Altshuller, a scientist, engineer, and journalist, coined the "Theory of Inventive Problem Solving" (*Teoriya Resheniya Izobretatelskikh Zadatch*), or TRIZ—a series of forty problem-solving strategies that he claimed could be applied in any context. The strategies were derived from studying patented inventions and analyzing learners' written solutions to problems. By codifying a manual for the study of problem solving, Altshuller sought to dispel the belief that problem solving is innate and cannot be taught.[4] TRIZ practitioners simply go down the list of problem-solving heuristics until they find the right one to apply to the problem. By the 1980s, TRIZ had become a movement in the Soviet Union and, eventually, globally to encourage the teaching and learning of methods for solving problems. None of this helped Altshuller with his own problem: in 1950, Joseph Stalin sent him to the gulag for criticizing the nation's failure to adequately teach problem solving, and he was not released until after Stalin's death.

One example of the TRIZ method is the trick of "doing it inversely." Altshuller illustrates this concept with the example of filling chocolate candies with liquid syrup. The obvious but unworkable solution of how to pour the cherry cordial inside the bonbon is to heat the liquid and fill the chocolates, but this melts the candy. The counterintuitive but correct approach is to do it inversely, namely, to freeze the liquid and then encase it in hot chocolate.

Can we apply Altshuller's universal problem-solving manual to complex economic, political, or social problems? Not really. With the mechanical problems that Altshuller (or the algebraic problems of Alan Newell and Herbert Simon in their 1972 classic *Human Problem Solving*) sought to solve, the problem is known, the desired solution is clear, and only the method needs to be selected from a menu of tricks and tools. Many problems can be easily solved because the solution is obvious. When something breaks, we replace the part.[5]

But with public problems (what some people call "wicked problems" or "social problems"), the problem, solution, and method may all be *unknown*; even the goal is contested. Demos's Jake Chapman memorably sums up the difference between solving a societal problem using mechanical thinking and a more complex, systems-thinking approach: "One way to visualise the difference between the mechanistic, linear approach to policy and the holistic, systemic approach is to compare the results of throwing a rock and a live bird. Mechanical linear models are excellent for understanding where the rock will end up, but useless for predicting the trajectory of a bird— even though both are subject to the same laws of physics. To the degree that social and organisational systems . . . show adaptive behaviours they are better regarded as similar to live birds than lumps of rock."[6]

The patent backlog problem set out at the top of this chapter is paradigmatic of public problems. Unlike the highly structured problems usually designed for classroom learning, the challenges that social innovators, activists, and public servants confront are often ambiguous, highly context specific, and difficult to solve. There may be no clear guidance about the tools or methods needed to address them. Their features are usually not well understood, let alone their solutions agreed on in a highly contested political environment. The solutions may be products or services or processes, but they require a high degree of creativity to design and implement if we are going to satisfy a human need. These are classic public problems.

Public problems are distinct from those challenges that are clear and to which there is a known and uncontested solution and pathway to implementation (and we only have to choose the cheapest option). No wonder that the word "problem" derives from the Greek word *problema*, meaning "obstacle." These obstacles are where we focus because overcoming them will have large and beneficial impacts on communities and people.

The development professionals at Harvard's Building State Capability program explain the concept of public problems by comparing getting from St. Louis to Los Angeles in the nineteenth and twenty-first centuries. Today the trip is easy. But in the early nineteenth century, travelers lacked modern means of transport, roads, maps, and knowledge of the terrain.[7] The journey was fraught with perils and unknowns. That is public problem solving.

While many people would call ill-defined yet compelling challenges such as income inequality, social exclusion, or climate change "policy problems," more relevant to our understanding of public problems is the label—and explanation—given by the late educational philosopher David Jonassen, who called them "design problems" or "dilemmas." To Jonassen, design problems are what he termed the "universal form of problem." Design problems usually have vaguely defined or unclear goals. They also "possess multiple solutions, with multiple solution paths."[8] In other words, we cannot agree on a solution, and we would not know how to implement it effectively even if we did. In Jonassen's definition, design problems have no clear metric for success. What makes them unique may be the need to grapple with both the problem and the solution, using one of myriad approaches taken from different disciplines. Thus, design represents what the cognitive scientists Vinod Goel and Peter Pirolli call the "quintessential cognitive task," which helps to explain why tackling such challenges can be so professionally rewarding.[9]

Jonassen distinguishes dilemmas as a distinct category of problem that capture another element of public problem solving: its contested setting. Jonassen writes, "Dilemmas may be the most ill structured and unpredictable, often because there is no solution that will ever be acceptable to a significant portion of the people affected by the problem. . . . That does not mean that there are not many solutions, which can be attempted with variable degrees of success; however, none will ever meet the needs of the majority of people or escape the prospects of catastrophe. Dilemmas are often complex, social situations with conflicting perspectives, and they are usually the most vexing of problems."[10]

Public problem solving is hard because there are no simple set of TRIZ-like tricks, no single, linear method or foolproof set of tools that work for design problems and dilemmas. But there is a process and a set of approaches that make success more likely.

Thus, our goal is to develop this new repertoire—a common toolkit of creative problem-solving approaches that borrow from a variety of disciplines like design, engineering, and policy and apply new technology to yield creative solutions that are both effective and also legitimate.

TACKLING PROBLEMS TOGETHER

Every project-management methodology has a process. For example, the US Government Digital Service created a "Playbook" with thirteen "plays," each of which is accompanied by a checklist of questions. The thirteen plays, such as "understand what people need" and "assign one leader and hold that person accountable," combine to create a process for agile software development.

Stanford professors Jeremy Weinstein and Francis Fukuyama illustrate the process of problem solving in their recently created Engineering Policy Change clinic at Stanford. They show a path that begins with not one but several steps to generate insight about a problem, followed by a stage for solution identification and then implementation.

Nesta, an innovation think tank in the United Kingdom with a large public-sector practice, offers its own version of a problem-solving pathway, which it calls the "innovation spiral." The spiral begins with initial steps for delineating a problem and then separate stages to deliver, implement, grow, and scale a solution. These steps deal with the difficult task of getting something done in practice. They start with simply making the case for the problem and progress toward systems change.

However, these processes fail to acknowledge that public problem solving is *not a solitary process* to be undertaken alone by the clever problem solver. Problem solving is not a skill of the lone leader or policy analyst who must define the problem, devise the responses, and select the right one from among them.[11]

These illustrations fail to mention that no amount of erudition or leadership skill will substitute for the robust analysis of data using new tools like machine learning and predictive analytics, far-reaching collaboration and coalition building that is needed, not once, but at *every step* along the way. We cannot be as smart alone as we are together. Many disciplines have

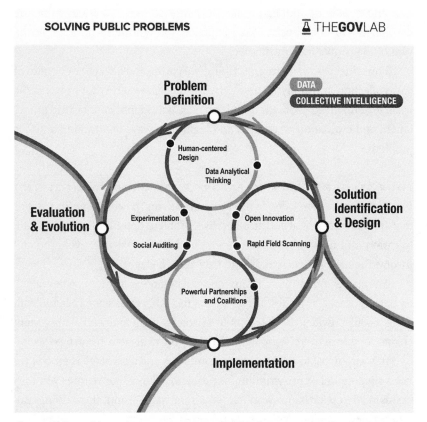

The arc of the problem-solving process (Courtesy of Beth Simone Noveck / The GovLab)

concerned themselves with looking at collective or group intelligence and studying how groups and teams, from armies to orchestras, collaborate and problem solve together, often aided by new technology.[12] That literature on collective intelligence helps to inform how to organize collaborative problem solving.

Engaging with data and with others to understand and define a problem, tapping their intelligence and expertise to design solutions, building partnerships and coalitions to implement those solutions, and distributing the labor of measuring what works—these are all collaborative processes. Deciding on the course of action—both understanding the problem and its contexts and deciding on the optimal outcomes—is no longer something the policy analyst or entrepreneur does alone but must be done in concert with those whom the problem most affects. Done well, collaboration sharpens, and speeds up, public problem solving. Moreover, solutions that are developed with the benefit of participation will be more legitimate in the eyes of the people they most affect.

Thus, the process I am prescribing is a continuous, real-time system of data collection and analytics and networked collaboration that provides the basis for enhanced problem definition, solution identification, implementation, and evaluation of rational and legitimate ways of attacking a public problem.

FOUR STAGES OF PARTICIPATORY PUBLIC PROBLEM SOLVING

For simplicity's sake, I divide the problem-solving process into four stages that are both sequential and also iterative: problem definition, solution identification and design, implementation, and evaluation and evolution. All involve the use of participation and data at each stage.

The stages sometimes contain repeated iterations, so they can be considered tasks as well as stages. Let us look at the skills each stage calls for, with more detail provided in subsequent chapters. This and each subsequent chapter end with exercises to help you apply the skills to your own projects.

It is important to note that these four steps and associated methods are not a rigid model or prescription for problem solving. Sometimes you may evaluate what is or is not working—the final stage—and, in so doing, uncover a new problem to solve. Sometimes you start with a solution and work backward to define the problem you are solving.

In addition, not all methods set out here are obligatory at every step. And each method contains potential traps. For example, while human-centered design helps to make the process more effective and legitimate by testing one's understanding of the problem with real users, too much testing can lead to paralysis. For example, the team I have the honor to lead in the Office of Innovation in the state of New Jersey talks to real people to obtain a much-needed perspective on how people experience a problem like long-term unemployment. In early 2019, when the Office of Innovation launched a project to create a virtual coaching platform for the unemployed, we invested a great deal of effort to meet and collaborate with job seekers in libraries and church basements. But we almost ran out of time and opportunity to complement that ethnographic, human-scale research with macro-level analysis of data about education, training, employment, and income outcomes as well as to talk to academic experts on coaching. It is too easy to go down a rabbit hole.

Testing with the wrong people can lead to misleading conclusions. Too much discussion can get in the way of decisive leadership. The availability of big data can strengthen the evidence base in policy making, but endless research, especially with the wrong or incomplete data, can snuff out the spark of inspiration.

This is why we connect the dots and look at the arc of an agile problem-solving process, rather than innovative methods on their own.

Stage 1: Problem Definition—Human-Centered Design and Data-Analytical Thinking

Of all these stages, defining the problem is the one most likely to get short shrift. But a great deal of time must be invested in defining and refining a shared understanding of the problem using both human-centered design and data-analytical thinking. Never jump straight to the solution. It is always tempting to define the problem as the absence of the solution you have hit upon. No matter how appealing you find your immediate answer—whether it is a website, algorithm, training course, funding mechanism, crowd-sourcing exercise, or new legislation—your stakeholders may reject it as quickly as you have embraced it. They may not yet buy into your goals. Or they may be quite right: your quick solution is solving the wrong problem.

The problem-definition stage is intensive and iterative. It seeks to expose the root causes of a problem. It requires a determination to discover the nature and sources of the problem through the use of data and the intelligence of others—both those who live with the problem and those who have credentialed experience and know-how. Success lies in finding a concrete problem that you have the motivation, energy, and ability to solve, that is neither too big to be tackled nor too small to be worth doing.[13]

What if an issue seems too large or amorphous to tackle? Solutions to growing obesity rates or stagnating incomes, let alone climate change, may seem beyond the grasp of any one community. Yet a community will only tackle problems that are both compelling enough to need fixing and can be fixed. Without both commitment and capacity, a public entrepreneur will not make much headway.

But that simply means you must work with the community to break down seemingly intractable challenges into smaller, more manageable problems. If their causes are so grand and global that no interventions appear capable of making a dent in them, that may mean the problem has not yet been adequately defined and scoped (or we need to keep looking for tractable solutions).

I am not saying there is no place for ambitious goals or grand projects. Such challenges and the language that often accompanies them create momentum and the possibility of creative responses. Public entrepreneurs with the right skills can accomplish goals far beyond their individual limitations. They can inspire a crowd to participate in a global citizen science project. They can forge a coalition of formerly divided actors or use crowdfunding to raise money to support a goal that extends beyond the community. They can elicit engagement from a wide variety of organizations that they might not have known before.[14] Take the example of Safecast. What started as a handful of concerned individuals after the Fukushima Nuclear Power Plant disaster in Japan in 2011 has grown into a network of activists who measure radiation and air-quality levels in 150 countries.[15]

As the next three chapters on defining the problem, human-centered design, and data-analytical thinking explain in depth, it is essential to define a problem with empirical data and in collaboration with those who experience it and who have studied it. Consultation with only one affected party, such as government, is unlikely to succeed.

The policy maker's understanding of the problem may differ considerably from that of the people who live with it. Professionals are also essential. People who have extensively studied similar problems and know the research and grey literature on the topic will deepen the discussion through their informed and learned understanding of the challenge. Even the most ardent public problem solvers, with the best of intentions, are unlikely to understand the problem's cause and roots as well as they might with the help of those who have lived experience and expert know-how. This kind of human situational awareness complements new tools for obtaining and using big data to define the problem.

Defining a problem online offers a democratizing opportunity for more members of the public to contribute expertise and information and increases the likelihood of developing solutions that work. For example, in Taiwan, hundreds of thousands of citizens are translating broad challenges into

specific problems using vTaiwan, a four-stage online and offline deliberative process for reaching consensus around the definition of a problem and
the formation of a legislative proposal in response. vTaiwan begins with a
proposal stage, with offline and online discussion of problems using a series of different tools for deliberation and frequent polling. The second
opinion-gathering stage uses an artificial intelligence tool known as Pol.is
to collect and visualize participants' views. These become the basis for determining the extent of consensus about the problem. Participants post their
views and can vote to "Agree," "Disagree," or "Pass" on statements written
by others or indicate whether the statement is important to them. This collaborative problem-definition process, which can last from a few weeks to a
year, helps a large number of people to agree on and define which problems should be tackled.

Subsequent chapters will explore methods for describing a problem
and its root causes, why it exists and persists, and whom it affects. These
methods are designed to produce results in politically fraught and contested environments because they leverage citizens' engagement to add legitimacy to the process. This stage uses both qualitative (human-centered
design) and quantitative (data-analytical thinking) approaches in order to
find out how different stakeholders understand the problem, why they
might disagree on the solution, and how that disagreement might be managed or resolved.

Stage 2: Solution Identification and Design—Open Innovation and
Rapid Field Scanning
Once public problem solvers have developed a shared definition of a problem supported by data and human insight, they must devise effective and
workable solutions, again taking advantage of available evidence as well as
the collective intelligence of populations that the problem immediately affects, along with distributed expertise and know-how.

Open innovation techniques like crowdsourcing, cocreation, and collaboration are a few of the tools that can mobilize the collective intelligence
of both professionals and stakeholders. Engaging people and their collective wisdom in designing and implementing solutions makes problem
solving more democratic and thereby more legitimate. A diversity of participants also enhances the likelihood of obtaining expertise that is far more

innovative, creative, and varied than the traditional means of public input, such as occasional hearings. Advances in online technology make such deep consultation possible and efficient.

For example, an online platform called Better Reykjavik is enabling the capital city of Iceland to crowdsource solutions to urban challenges and crowdsource decision-making around spending public money (known as participatory budgeting). Many suggestions revolve around the common urban themes of transportation, construction, and environmental issues. Reykjavik residents submit proposals or vote on proposals submitted by others. In 2012, for example, a poet and novelist by the name of Sjón proposed a solution for addressing homelessness in the city. The proposal resulted in a public meeting about the status of the city's homeless people. Then the budget for the issue was increased, and Sjón's idea was combined with several other proposals into the city's new homelessness strategy, involving better city shelters, moveable housing, and permanent residence facilities. Importantly, every month, Reykjavik's Mayor's Office reviews the best ideas from the platform for implementation. The platform has grown in popularity because of its relevance. Now more than half the city's population has participated in proposing or voting on solutions, and 20 percent of the population regularly use the site. Since 2011, twenty thousand registered users have submitted more than sixty-eight hundred proposals, of which more than six hundred have been implemented. On the spending side, Reykjavik citizens determine how the city will spend 450 million Icelandic króna (more than €3 million) each year to implement crowdsourced ideas from the citizens to improve the various neighborhoods of Reykjavik.[16]

Solution identification requires *deep listening*, in which one asks regularly of others, What ambitious goals should we be aspiring to, and how do we get there?[17] This kind of collaborative imagining of workable solutions requires one to look beyond the boundaries of one's own office, party, or agency and to eschew the need to invent the solution oneself, which may necessitate a tremendous shift in both mind-set and skill set.

In addition to using crowdsourcing and open innovation, as we shall explore, solution identification is also the stage at which to use robust data and evidence to learn what else is out there and think more broadly about the range of feasible solutions old and new. The public entrepreneur needs to be able to synthesize the available evidence, and this requires doing three things quickly. We need to know what possible solutions are. We need to evaluate whether they have worked. We need to know how to make them work for our own context and community.

As with other problem-solving steps, we can use data and collective intelligence to enable us to accomplish these three tasks more quickly and effectively. So, for example, we want to conduct a rapid field scan of available solutions using the best available documentary evidence. But we also want to engage experts to accelerate our search for solutions. To evaluate what has worked, we want to look at data from randomized controlled trials that tell us when a treatment succeeded. But we also want to ask knowledgeable and creative entrepreneurs—both public and private—what has gained traction in the field. Finally, we need to know if what worked in one jurisdiction can work to solve the problem we are confronting in our own community, and that requires a rigorous process of analyzing the supporting contextual factors but also deliberating with affected communities to answer that question collectively.

Stage 3: Implementation and Getting Things Done—
Partnerships and Coalitions
Having found a solution through a collaborative process that incorporates data and expertise, you now need to persuade stakeholders to adopt your solution and bring your proposal to fruition. The latter is critical. As Simon Willis writes, innovation without implementation is merely hot air. Failure to plan to implement a policy or service will produce nothing more than pilots and one-offs, a form of showmanship that has no regard for sustainability and makes no impact on real people's lives.[18]

After the global fiscal crisis of 2007–2008, the US Conference of Mayors presented President Obama with a list of 11,391 infrastructure projects that it said were "shovel ready." So did the American Association of State Highway and Transportation Officials. Governors and cities wanted the federal government to pass the $787 billion in stimulus funding it eventually did pass.[19] But the president discovered belatedly that when it comes to public works, there is no such thing as shovel ready, and the initiatives that people were touting were not ready for implementation.[20] The result? Slow-starting projects were sluggish to yield the much-needed and hoped-for economic gains and job growth.

Beyond infrastructure, even much innovative and entrepreneurial ac-

tivity is guilty of poorly conceptualized implementation. Over the past fifteen years of working with public, social, and civic entrepreneurs, I have
seen thousands of good ideas, but rarely are those ingenious solutions tied
to a strategy for making them happen. Innovators love the spark of the creative idea, but the dull and difficult work of assessing feasibility in the context of real-world institutions gets overlooked. Even public policy schools,
where one would assume implementation is taught, says Fukuyama, "train
students to become capable policy analysts, but with no understanding of
how to implement those policies in the real world."[21]

Public problem solvers, by definition, pursue a goal of measurable improvements rather than merely ticking a "mission accomplished" box. The
best of them are concerned with how to *implement* their big idea and to
improve outcomes for real people—and quickly. More than clever ideas
and novel gadgets, our ability to solve problems depends on devising a strategy, including the steps needed to bring solutions to fruition. We must
ensure that an innovative policy or service is ready for delivery in the real
world.[22] Again, approaches, specifically coalition building and partnerships
—learning to collaborate with others to accelerate implementation—are
key methods to ensure success.

Stage 4: Evaluation and Evolution—Experimentation and Social Auditing
Policy evaluation seeks to understand the effects of a policy or other intervention, what worked and what did not. Yet traditional problem solving
often ends with implementation, wrapping up the project without this critical last step, and traditional policy analysis stops even before that.

In an International City/County Management Association survey of
more than five hundred local governments in the United States, 59 percent
reported that they do not collect performance data on service delivery.[23]
Once again, there is a need for data to improve evaluation, and we will discuss how to introduce agile experiments to generate data in real time. Public entrepreneurs need to know how to use experiments when they roll out
a project rather than waiting to study something after the fact.

The strategic use of a randomized controlled trial, for example, is one
of several ways to learn efficiently what is working so that we might iterate
and improve. So many public problems are today addressed with strategies
that are more guesswork than science, and we fail to realize the desired results. For example, we spend billions of dollars in aid to alleviate the condi-

tions of poverty with little understanding of which strategies are working and which are not. This was the dilemma addressed by the three 2019 Nobel Prize winners in economic sciences who garnered the prize for the modest yet profound idea of taking the guesswork out of policy making by using randomized controlled trials to measure the success of specific interventions using simple experiments.[24] By comparing immunization rates in the state of Rajasthan in India, they found that absent any intervention, rates hovered at 6 percent. The creation of an immunization camp boosted participation to 17 percent. Adding the incentive of a kilogram of lentils for every family that comes in for an immunization increased participation to 38 percent.[25]

Collective intelligence, too, can enhance this stage of the process by making it easier to distribute the work of assessing what is working and why.

Evaluation provides an opportunity for public engagement. With the help of online technology such as web platforms and mobile phones, the public can be asked how to gather and monitor evidence, how to measure impact, and what data to use to measure it. Citizens can take pictures, gather data, and submit other "evidence" of on-the-ground conditions. Stakeholders can provide real-time monitoring and feedback on policy issues through the use of surveys and polls, reporting via a web platform or via social media such as Twitter messages collected by a tweetbot. Challenges can inspire participants to design new reporting mechanisms. This approach is known as "social auditing" or "civic auditing," and many governments and nonprofit organizations are using online technology to undertake it. Enabled by new technology, a watchful community can improve problem solving by collectively evaluating outcomes and impact.

TO DO

It can be very helpful to lay out the project from start to finish. Two exercises for planning a public-interest project are described here.

Exercise 1: Fill Out The GovLab Public Problem-Solving Canvas
Use The GovLab Public Problem-Solving Canvas; worksheets are available at https://solvingpublicproblems.org. to develop a pathway for a public-interest project. A canvas is a checklist that you can fill out first on your own and then with others to arrive at a common view of the project. In the online version, others who have access can comment on your answers. The canvas is

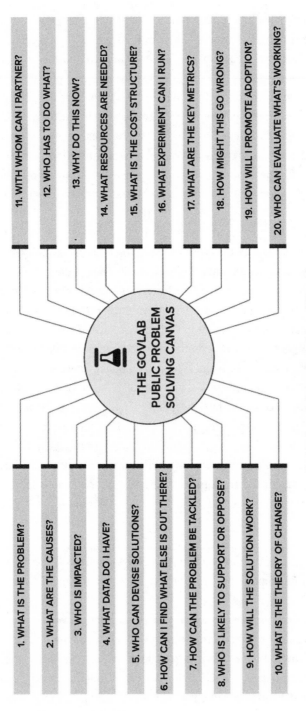

THE GOVLAB
PUBLIC PROBLEM
SOLVING CANVAS

11. WITH WHOM CAN I PARTNER?
12. WHO HAS TO DO WHAT?
13. WHY DO THIS NOW?
14. WHAT RESOURCES ARE NEEDED?
15. WHAT IS THE COST STRUCTURE?
16. WHAT EXPERIMENT CAN I RUN?
17. WHAT ARE THE KEY METRICS?
18. HOW MIGHT THIS GO WRONG?
19. HOW WILL I PROMOTE ADOPTION?
20. WHO CAN EVALUATE WHAT'S WORKING?

1. WHAT IS THE PROBLEM?
2. WHAT ARE THE CAUSES?
3. WHO IS IMPACTED?
4. WHAT DATA DO I HAVE?
5. WHO CAN DEVISE SOLUTIONS?
6. HOW CAN I FIND WHAT ELSE IS OUT THERE?
7. HOW CAN THE PROBLEM BE TACKLED?
8. WHO IS LIKELY TO SUPPORT OR OPPOSE?
9. HOW WILL THE SOLUTION WORK?
10. WHAT IS THE THEORY OF CHANGE?

For blank worksheets, see solvingpublicproblems.org

The Public Problem-Solving Canvas (Courtesy of Beth Simone Noveck / The GovLab) divided into the four steps outlined in this chapter: problem definition, solution identification, implementation design, and evaluation and evolution.

The following twenty questions are designed to help refine your understanding of the problem and the people whom it affects. They also enable you to express your Big Idea and to turn that idea into a strategy that can be implemented and that will improve real lives.

The Public Problem-Solving Canvas is modeled on the Business Model Canvas introduced by the professor and consultant Alexander Osterwalder to capture a business plan in a single diagram. The original business canvas consists of the nine elements of a business model: problem, solution, unique value proposition, unfair advantage, customer segments, channels, key metrics, cost structure, and revenue streams. Many variations on the canvas idea have emerged to encourage private entrepreneurs to articulate their plan of attack in a single go and thereby to spot the gaps in their plans.

Work on public-interest projects also requires iterative planning and thoughtful consideration of the problem. But it also demands consideration of additional issues not captured by the Business Model Canvas or its progeny. For that reason, I developed the Public Problem-Solving Canvas, an interactive and collaborative worksheet to help public entrepreneurs have a stronger impact.

Identifying Problems
1. What is the problem? [need]
2. What are the causes? [causes]
3. Who is impacted? [people]
4. What data do I have? [evidence]

Identifying Solutions
5. Who can devise solutions? [open innovation]
6. How can I find what else is out there? [evidence synthesis]
7. How can the problem be tackled? [big idea]
8. Who is likely to support or oppose? [champions]

Designing for Implementation
9. How will the solution work? [experience]
10. What is the theory of change? [theory of change]
11. With whom can I partner? [partners]

12. Who has to do what? [roles]
13. Why do this now? [events]
14. What resources are needed? [resources]
15. What is the cost structure? [cost]

Evaluation and Evolution
16. What experiment can I run? [testing]
17. What are the key metrics? [metrics]
18. How might this go wrong? [risks]
19. How will I promote adoption? [marketing]
20. Who can evaluate what's working? [social audit]

Exercise 2: Employ the Heilmeier Catechism
The Defense Advanced Research Project Agency (DARPA) uses a worksheet similar to the Public Problem-Solving Canvas to assess what projects to take on and what grants to give. George H. Heilmeier, a DARPA director in the 1970s, crafted a set of questions as a checklist to help DARPA program officers decide which research programs to fund. The "Heilmeier Catechism" goes as follows:

- What are you trying to do? Articulate your objectives using absolutely no jargon.
- How is it done today, and what are the limits of current practice?
- What is new in your approach and why do you think it will be successful?
- Who cares? If you are successful, what difference will it make?
- What are the risks?
- How much will it cost?
- How long will it take?
- What are the mid-term and final "exams" to check for success?[26]

Now consider what questions you would ask, if you were the boss or funder or politician, in order to understand the project and how it will work and to define the course of action. Anticipate those questions and write down your own answers to create a map of your project trajectory.

As Heilmeier looked back on his career as an inventor and someone who inspired other innovators, he offered a few words of advice that are helpful to consider in conclusion.

- Never be afraid to explore something entirely new. Treat intuition as real.
- Don't be deterred by judgments based on "incomplete information" claiming that it can't be done.
- Do the difficult experiments first. Don't substitute research for insight. Review older concepts periodically in light of progress made in other areas that might change earlier views.
- Approach problems from an interdisciplinary point of view. Remove barriers to exploiting the viewpoints of other disciplines, and do not be afraid to be called naïve when venturing outside your own professional discipline.
- Have a clear view of what you are trying to do but be prepared to modify this view in light of new information.
- Understand the limits of current approaches. Understand what is new in your approach and why you think it might succeed.
- Understand the implications of success. Build prototypes so that others can begin to share your vision.[27]

CHAPTER FOUR

Defining a Public Problem

A simple openness to alternative definitions of problems . . . ought to be the preeminent mode of liberalism, and yet somehow it is not.

Daniel Patrick Moynihan, Coping: Essays on the Practice of Government

I once led an innovation training session for state public officials. Over the course of a day, I listened to teams of selected civil servants present projects they were working on. A pair of young, eager public officials got up before the audience to explain that they had recently learned about applying social and behavioral insights—so-called nudges that leverage human psychology to change human behavior—to improve the delivery of social services. They wanted to develop their own nudge-based program to improve student attendance at school.

Taking a page from earlier experiments that used mail, web, or text reminders to prompt people to pay a traffic ticket or comply with a court judgment, the two public servants proposed sending an email to parents of high-school-age children.[1] The reminder would tell parents that attending school was mandatory and that taking vacations during school periods was not an excuse for failing to show up at school. To be more rigorous, they planned to use a randomized controlled trial to compare the efficacy of sending an email over sending a letter.[2]

But when I asked the officials what problem their novel social-behavioral experiment was solving, they earnestly replied that parents were taking their kids out of school off season to get cheaper rates at Disney World and other vacation hot spots. I pushed a little harder: Did they have any data to support this contention? No. Had they identified which schools, neighborhoods, and kids were most affected? No. Had they done research to understand what other interventions had been tried and what worked? No. Were the children concentrated in one place? Was there any chance that there might be a connection between drug or alcohol abuse and truancy? They did not know. It was painfully clear that they had jumped to the solution. Without doing the hard work of first rigorously defining the problem, the right solution will not be found.

By contrast, in 2018 a team of development practitioners at Innovation for Indonesia's School Children (INOVASI), a partnership between the governments of Australia and Indonesia, set out to tackle the fact that early-grade teachers are having difficulties in assessing students' learning progress in literacy. The problem is urgent. In places like East Nusa Tengara, Indonesia's southernmost province, only 19 percent of students grades 1–3 could pass a basic literacy test.[3] The team assumed the problem was bad teaching, in which case training would be the best solution. However, after patiently investigating the problem, listening to the people involved, examining data, and approaching the challenge with an open mind, the team found that budget allocation was the more proximate cause. The slow process of problem definition "lit a candle for us in the very dark place," members of the team write. They were able to uncover that best-performing districts allocate more money toward library development, book acquisition, and extracurricular activities, whereas worse-performing districts spend more on teacher salaries and school management, illuminating a pathway to more effective change.[4]

To take an example closer to my home, during the coronavirus epidemic outbreak in spring 2020, rather than just start handing out loans, the Economic Development Authority in New Jersey sent out a questionnaire and heard from over five hundred small and medium-sized businesses about the impacts of the pandemic and the kinds of support people actually needed. Thus, when the authority released its first grant program, it was tailor-made to respond to real needs. Sadly, it also meant it got ten thousand applications in the first seventy-six minutes!

A century ago, John Dewey wrote that defining a problem by delimiting its root causes is the most important step in developing a good solution. Reflective thought connects the perceived problem and its resolution.[5] A felt difficulty, he explained, must be translated into a clear, specific, and accurate statement of that which needs to be solved.

In *How We Think,* Dewey argued that narrowing an issue down to a solvable problem reflects the essence of how complex thought develops.[6] Dewey was not alone in championing the importance of problem definition.[7] Albert Einstein wrote that "the formulation of a problem is often more essential than its solution, which may merely be a matter of mathematical or experimental skill. To raise new questions, new possibilities, to regard old problems from a new angle, requires creative imagination and marks real advance in science."[8]

The sociologist Robert Merton defined a problem as a discrepancy between what is and what ought to be—hence the need for a process of problem definition that bridges the difference between the current and the future state.[9] Unmasking a problem—just as a sculptor reveals the statue from within the hunk of marble—distinguishes the work that public problem solvers seek to do.

Thus—and this is another way of describing a public problem—innovators are engaged in a process of defining and discovering a problem rather than working on a problem that someone else has already presented to them.[10] Similarly, the psychologists Jacob Getzels and Mihaly Csikszentmihalyi write in their now-classic work, *The Creative Vision: A Longitudinal Study of Problem Finding in Art,* "Some individuals, like the copyist in art, the technician in science, the pedant in scholarship, the bureaucrat in government, deal with problems that have already been identified," but "the fine artist, the inventive scientist, the creative scholar, the innovative statesman, the self-actualizing person, are in addition aware of unformulated problems potentially present in the conflicts of their own experience."[11]

For our purposes, "the innovative statesman" can stand for our public entrepreneurs. Single-mindedly uncovering and laying bare a problem and its root causes, even when they have long worked in a given domain, is core to their work. Difficult public problems require them to follow this process repeatedly while taking advantage of available tools and bringing in perspectives from other disciplines.

It is hardly only inexperienced students of public policy, engineering, or other disciplines who struggle to define a problem. Nearly everyone has a hard time with the methodical and research-intensive process that is problem definition. Even those who are well schooled in policy analysis or management—and who have learned to ask Sakichi Toyoda's "5 Whys"— are often not skilled in defining problems collaboratively, drawing on insights from other people's disciplines, perspectives, and experiences.[12] Even when we know how to do so, steeling ourselves for the discipline of defining the problem is difficult for anyone.

Problem definition has long been recognized as the first and essential step in any rational policy-making process.[13] Yet despite its importance, policy makers rarely pay enough attention to the art and science that lie behind it.[14] In our 2019–20 survey of innovation skills, problem definition was the most widely used skill and even then only among sixty percent of respondents in the United States and eleven percent in Paraguay. Most of us, if we are honest, do not define problems rigorously, preferring instead to jump to the solution and lobby for its implementation. Too many entrepreneurs, in government and the private sector, are too excited by creating a new project, founding a nonprofit, creating a website, launching a program, establishing a financing mechanism. But when we fail to define the problem adequately, we end up developing solutions that do not work.

Einstein famously said, "If I had one hour to save the world, I would spend fifty-five minutes defining the problem and only five minutes finding the solution." He went on to say that detectives solve a known unknown. The crime is given to them. But real scientists—or, in our case, public entrepreneurs—"must commit [their] own crime as well as carry out the investigation."[15] They must first define the problem they want to solve. That is not easy.

WHY PROBLEM DEFINITION IS SO HARD

There are many reasons why the skill of problem definition is not well developed or widely practiced. Policy or public administration schools, where problem solving should be central to the curriculum, often do not teach it.[16] Textbooks stress the importance of correct definitions of public problems yet remain vague as to how exactly one arrives at them.[17] Most problems in case studies that students are exposed to are predefined and taken out of their real-world, value-laden, contentious, and politically fraught context.[18]

Policy sciences, like other disciplines, focus on the study of the solutions —the policies and services that government delivers—but not on the cognitive process by which the problems are discovered and refined. The political scientist David Dery sums up the issue well: "A student of public policy who consults a variety of disciplines pertaining to problem solving will not find straight answers to such direct questions as: What is a problem? What is problem definition? How does one go about formulating a problem? How can one tell good from bad problem definition?"[19]

Reinforcing Dery's point, one experimental class in problem-based learning with thirteen students at the University of Limerick required students to grapple with a real-world problem. They aided a nearby town to run a community engagement process designed to produce a new local socioeconomic plan. The class was considered so unique for political scientists that it merited a write-up in a leading journal of the American Political Science Association.[20] Similarly, a workshop on problem definition where I taught two dozen state officials from Victoria, Australia, on behalf of the Australia New Zealand School of Government in July 2019 was a first of its kind. The workshop addressed how to use data and collective intelligence to define the problems underlying the officials' assignments at work to "fix Melbourne's transit system" or "improve domestic violence support." A training in 2017 for the UN Leadership Program in New York was the first time anyone asked thirty new resident coordinators to pinpoint problems they could solve in their new roles. In 2020 to 2021, I taught problem definition to 200 students at NYU, forcing learners to slow down and narrow broad and overwhelming issues such as pollution in Hanoi or violence against women in Afghanistan to localized and specific problems they could actually tackle. My colleagues at The GovLab took leaders from cities in Mexico, Paraguay, and Argentina and in several cities across Africa on a similar journey of learning the painstaking process of defining a public problem and its root causes.

While it may be more common to engage in a literature review to evaluate the efficacy of different solutions, all too rarely do our habits involve a systematic study of the problem. The absence of problem definition from the public policy and public sector training curriculum is not the only challenge to developing this habit. Both government and other sectors have strong incentives to offer solutions rather than to take time to define problems. Agencies and programs are generally set up to administer solutions, often under the auspices of a prescriptive statute. "Once an organization has assembled the right set of functional capabilities, and organized them around its core operational processes, the bulk of its routine operational practice is established," writes Harvard University professor of public management Malcolm Sparrow.[21] That is to say, even when one recognizes the need to define a problem in a new way, a rigid organizational context and limited solution set constrain one from pivoting away from the standard definition. It discourages staff from articulating problems in a way that might lead to innovative and new solutions.[22] It encourages them to remain hammers in search of nails.

In a hierarchical environment, without contrary incentives, bureaucrats and politicians have to deliver "the solution" rather than spend time defining a problem. No one wants to appear to lack answers. The duty of public officials is to achieve their mandated purposes as efficiently and effectively as possible.[23] In the hierarchical and rule-bound culture of government, one has to convince stakeholders and managers of the value proposition of taking action. In that setting, the innovator, who wants to employ novel ways of working or creative but untested solutions, may have an especially difficult job of convincing others to say yes. The need to climb a mountain of approvals creates pressure to drive toward solutions with great certainty.[24] Taking time to define and redefine a problem can inevitably open up unanticipated solutions, which can be alarming.

Public bureaucracies are not the only ones reluctant to confront the problem. Thomas Wedell-Wedellsborg writes in the *Harvard Business Review* that corporate managers do quite a poor job of *defining* problems. In surveys of 106 C-suite executives across seventeen countries, he found that "a full 85 per cent strongly agreed or agreed that their organizations were bad at problem diagnosis, while 87 per cent strongly agreed or agreed that this flaw carried significant costs."[25] The tendency to jump to a solution before truly defining the problem crosses all sectors.[26]

Because most bureaucracies implement specific types of solutions, be they subsidies, grants, or direct service programs, the ability of individuals to define the problem inside a bureaucracy with settled organizational boundaries, historical practices, and political constraints may be limited. The usual solutions will always be preferred. For example, an agency that is used to tackling a public-health problem such as diabetes by funding treatment may lack the capacity and the mind-set to focus on prior interventions that encourage individuals to change the ways they eat and live regardless of evidence of efficacy.

Furthermore, public officials invariably have too much to do and too little time in which to do it. As purpose-driven individuals working in the public interest, they are eager to dive in and make change happen. Their desire to enact new policies, create programs, deliver services, and help people gives them an incentive to accept the definition of the problem provided to them by stakeholders, think tanks, and interest groups, with all their biases, or at the very least to give short shrift to this process in an effort to be able to report that they are taking more rapid action.

WHAT IS THE PROBLEM WITH NOT DEFINING THE PROBLEM?
James Anderson of Bloomberg Philanthropies provides a powerful explanation of why defining the problem matters. When the foundation launched its first urban innovation challenge, Bloomberg Philanthropies exhorted mayors to come up with good solutions to hard problems. In an interview about participants in the Bloomberg Mayors' Challenge—a competition among cities to receive funding for an innovative project—Anderson explained,

> Well over half the applications we received were not up to
> snuff. The solutions were not matched to well-defined problems.
> That is to say, the solutions were out of sync with the problem
> statements. They didn't consider the evidence base, nor did
> the proposals build on what had come before or reflect knowl-
> edge of what else was out there. In the second iteration of the
> challenge, we realized you couldn't just ask cities for solutions
> because the problem definition piece was a huge gap in compe-
> tency. So we started training people in problem definition and
> problem reframing, and this year the first three hundred cities
> that signed up for the challenge got training in problem
> definition.[27]

The Right Problem Produces the Right Solution
As managers and leaders, we have to create the incentives and structures to engage our staff in regular problem definition.[28] We, and those who work with us, need the flexibility and freedom to pivot away from the original problem and the proffered solution, in order to discover a compelling problem definition supported by data and evidence and developed in conjunction with those who are affected by the problem. When we wrongly champion a method or solution based on a perceived but inaccurate understanding of what the problem actually is, we end up solving the wrong problem and reduce the likelihood of developing solutions that actually

work.[29] Public entrepreneurs, like the officials tackling school truancy whom I introduced earlier, want to act fast and avoid roadblocks. They may be eager to champion behavioral insights, the latest technology, or other innovative methods. But that very inventiveness and agility run the risk that we develop a solution without having a clear understanding of the problem.

The Right Problem Is Narrow Enough to Be Solvable
As one project-management expert says, failing to define the problem creates a "headless chicken" that runs around without a clear sense of direction.[30] Without taking the time to stop and carefully define the problem, we tend to define it too broadly or not at all, wasting time and resources and further contributing to the creation of ineffective and distrusted government policies and programs. But issues like climate change, inequality, and poverty are so broad as to be overwhelming and paralyze the would-be problem solver.

The popular economist Stephen Dubner says that if you define the problem too broadly, you later pay a price by sapping people's optimism and energy. Rather, one should think small—like a child—in order to solve problems more quickly. Thinking narrowly leads to a better chance of getting something done.[31] Dubner tells how providing a simple intervention, giving $15 eyeglasses to children with poor vision in a rural province in China, dramatically improved test scores. There are high payoffs from low-cost, simple interventions like wearing eyeglasses.[32] But identifying those narrow solutions—like adding iodine to salt—requires greater discipline and more work than trying to "solve" illiteracy or malnutrition wholesale.

At The GovLab, I worked on the Zika crisis in Latin America in 2016, when the virus was mysteriously causing tragic birth defects in newborn babies. It would have been easy to try to grasp too big a problem, since "solving" Zika was the order of the day. But it is also an impossibility. To avoid thinking too big, my team and I broke down the challenge of mosquito-borne diseases into sixteen smaller, clearer, better-defined, and more-solvable problems. For instance, we started from the relatively simple question of how to improve the collection of trash in Buenos Aires. At the base of the Zika problem—among other things—a failure to pick up garbage led to an accumulation of standing water and mosquito breeding. Once we were able to articulate more manageable problems, we were able to crowdsource help from global experts to devise solutions such as developing adaptive vehicles for improved pickup, using drones to conduct trash surveillance, and working with companies to change popular packaging to reduce the incidence of water accumulation.[33]

Similarly, we had no cure-all for COVID-19 in 2020 and could not "solve" the pandemic. Jurisdictions that mitigated the effects of the crisis were those that bit off bite-sized chunks and rapidly executed on well-defined problems that lent themselves to practical solutions. New Jersey, for example, reduced transmission by providing people with better information crowdsourced from a network of expert scientists organized by the Federation of American Scientists.

When Thinking Small Fails, Think Differently

While cutting the problem down to size is often the best way to find an efficient and implementable solution, occasionally the simple becomes simplistic and does not work. There are too many apps littering the floor that are failed solutions to problems that are too complex to fix with a software platform. In such cases, collaborators need to think together from differing perspectives. This opens up the opportunity to solve the problem in new ways. Russell Ackoff, in the 1978 classic *The Art of Problem Solving*, offers a trenchant example of the opportunity provided by bringing in different disciplines.

As more British homes started buying freezers, a fish producer started freezing his catch and marketing frozen fish to the British market. After initial success, purchases dropped off, and investigation revealed that the cause was the flat and anemic taste of the frozen fish. The company tried myriad solutions, from freezing the fish on the boat to keeping them alive until they were brought ashore for processing to putting them in tanks before killing them. Nothing worked. In the tanks, the fish were so densely packed that they remained inert, and the resulting frozen filets tasted flat.

Then the managers, instead of calling in the engineers to redesign the tanks at great expense, turned to a biologist, who immediately suggested introducing a predator fish into the tanks. Unsurprisingly (albeit gruesomely), the fish moved about, and the taste improved.[34] By investigating the problem with people from different disciplines and perspectives, its true cause became clearer, and the solution came into view.

The Right Problem Is a Reframed Problem

Sometimes the problem needs to be redefined not narrowly but differently. Ackoff illustrates this with the example of the "slow elevator problem." Office workers complain to the building manager that the elevator is too slow. He consults an engineer, who defines the problem mechanically and proposes the obvious but expensive solution of replacing the elevator engine, at great expense. The manager digs deeper and hires a psychologist, who reframes the problem: the elevator is not too slow; the wait is too annoying. It suddenly becomes obvious that adding mirrors to the outside of the elevator for people to gaze at will reduce frustration more cheaply. The mirrors do not, of course, make the elevator go faster, but they solve a more practical challenge—the annoyance of the wait.[35] A different framing of the problem produces an innovative and workable solution.[36] This insight applies well to societal problems: it is easier, for example, as they are doing in Bogotá, Colombia, to enhance children's school commute with educational games that address the long ride rather than to decrease traffic.[37] Or, for another example, it is easier to rethink the overwhelming and unwieldy problem of flooding in Accra, Ghana, as an issue of efficient waste management or drainage infrastructure instead. In a training session on problem definition with the city of Hermosillo, Mexico, in 2020, public officials reframed the problem of urban mobility that they were asking citizens to solve in a codesign challenge that The GovLab organized known as the MultiCity Challenge (http://multicitychallenge.org). Instead, reframing helped them realize that the more tractable problem was, in fact, the lack of shade. It seemed people wanted to bike and walk, but the lack of canopy prevented them, leading to the overuse of cars.

The Right Problem Emerges from Positive Deviance

In Vietnam, the development professionals Jerry and Monique Sternin of Save the Children were seeking to reduce hunger among local village populations in Than Hoa province, some four hours south of Hanoi. At the time, malnutrition affected 65 percent of Vietnamese children under the age of five. International food aid was both expensive and not as effective as hoped. The Sternins, upon examining the situation, chose to turn the problem on its head and ask why some village children, despite living in the same abject poverty, were well fed and healthy. Focusing on the "positive deviance"—the children who thrived—they asked local volunteers to find the answer. They rapidly learned that healthy families were adding tiny amounts of scavenged tiny shrimps, crabs, or snails to their children's food and feeding the children exactly the same amount of rice, but in smaller portions, throughout the day.[38] Thinking about the problem from different angles and with fresh eyes—in this case, those of the local community—made it possible to identify the right problem and therefore the right solution.[39] Had the Sternins not first reframed the problem, they would have wasted time, gathered a lot of redundant data and information, and not produced better results.[40]

Eric Schadt's lab at the Icahn School of Medicine at Mt. Sinai Hospital is another great example of positive deviance. His team of data scientists and clinicians do not ask why a person is sick but why another person with double recessive DNA for a particular disease is not sick. In 2014, Schadt and his collaborators launched what they called the Resilience Project to cure 170 rare childhood diseases such as cystic fibrosis, sickle cell anemia, and Tay-Sachs. Researchers set out using large-scale data to find individuals who carried the recessive genes for each disease but did not have the disease.[41] By looking at why these people are not sick but by the laws of genetics should be, they are helping to unlock clues to understand the causes of these ravaging diseases.

The Right Problem Enables Collaboration

Clear problem definitions are essential to recruiting the right people to solve the problem *together*. To collaborate, to bring the diverse know-how of others to bear, one has to take the time to define the problem and to do so together. Otherwise, those who are outside one's institution—in other agencies, in the private sector, in the academy, or among the public—have little idea how to help. Clear problem definition fosters common understanding. It also prevents people from interpreting the problem in different and incompatible ways. Just as a failure report saying "this thing doesn't work" is the bane of the engineer's existence, the statement "we have a problem with guns in this country" leaves too much room for different interpretation.[42] Thus, in order to bring collective intelligence to bear, there needs to be a well-articulated and specific problem to solve. To contribute productively, people have to know what an appropriate solution looks like and what would define success.

In a project for the Inter-American Development Bank and the government of Mexico, my colleagues at The GovLab and I wanted to crowdsource solutions from over a hundred global experts to the challenge of corruption in Mexico. To do so, we had to start by defining the problems we wanted people to solve. "Corruption" would have left our audience paralyzed or, worse yet, led to useless suggestions. But by narrowing the broader issue to focus on the smaller (but still challenging) problems of inability to track money flows, ineffective prosecution, and lack of a whistleblowing legal framework, we were able to identify and invite experts to collaborate with us to develop practical approaches. In a similar project for seven governments in Latin America in 2020, we ran an online advisory session on how to solve the problem of people not wearing masks or practicing social distancing during the pandemic. The narrow focus led to a robust debate with specific solutions. The next week, we ran a second conference on the broader topic of helping vulnerable populations without specifying the problems or the populations, and the collaboration was a bust: unfocused and unproductive.

The Right Problem Leads to the Right Job Description

Good problem definition is also useful for attracting good collaborators. How much more compelling is it to undertake to solve a problem like increasing childhood literacy or decreasing homelessness than to apply for a job as "assistant deputy" or "deputy manager"? Instead of postings with vague titles, those job listings that describe problems to be solved attract passionate candidates who are attracted by the prospect of getting things done. Whether one seeks to hire a full-time colleague or a consultant or to crowdsource the answers from volunteers, problem definition is crucial, especially if the goal is to spur collaboration across sectors or to involve private-sector actors, including universities, companies, and individuals. Especially when the public problem solver is simply a passionate individual who may lack convening power, a persuasive problem definition is what makes it possible for anyone to become a pied piper for change, attracting an army of helpers. A compelling problem is what attracted a thousand talented technologists to volunteer with the United States Digital Response (USDR). Founded by former US deputy chief technology officers and seasoned tech-industry veterans in 2020, USDR is a nonpartisan effort that connects technologists and designers to public officials to respond to specific challenges relating to coronavirus response.

PARTICIPATORY PROBLEM DEFINITION

Now that we have explained why problem definition matters and the potential pitfalls and benefits, we need to outline a process for doing it right. This section and the exercises that follow offer a guide for applying problem definition to your own work.

Defining a problem includes a concise and clear statement of its essence and the people it most affects; an analysis of the root causes; and an explanation of why the problem is compelling and worth prioritizing, supported by data and context.[43] The goal is to construct a problem that can be solved and a problem that the solution ultimately addresses.

Most project-management approaches begin with problem definition regardless of the discipline.[44] Eugene Bardach, in proposing how to do policy analysis in public administration, describes a process he calls "The Way of the Eightfold Path." Whether or not it leads to enlightenment, it begins with seizing the problem.[45] Similarly, the Engineering Design Process and the curriculum on Design Thinking from Stanford's Hasso Plattner Institute of Design (the d.school) begin with heuristics for defining the problem. Engineers, too, should begin with a problem statement that articulates the challenge to be solved.

The term "problem definition," however, can be quite misleading because it suggests an initial state, a goal, and a well-defined information-gathering process for arriving at B from A. But problem definition is an iterative and often circuitous journey. It involves peeling back the layers from a vague statement of an issue until a precise statement of the problem is laid bare, together with a statement of the root causes—why the problem is occurring—and a hypothesis about why these are the likely causes. For example, when we undertook the Zika project, we started with the broad issue of Zika and then identified the smaller problem of standing water, which led to zeroing in on the accumulation of trash, which, in turn, became the problem of failure to pick up the trash. Finally, we asked why the trash is not getting picked up and uncovered that too many people in Buenos Aires take their trash to the roof instead of to the curb out of frustration regarding the lack of collection. Such a multistage exercise involves going successively deeper, abetted by research and inquiry of data and people, to find the cause that needs to be addressed, rather than a mere symptom.[46]

The four phases of problem solving set out in chapter 3—problem definition, solution identification, implementation, and evaluation—need not be perfectly distinct. Problem definition, solution, implementation, and evaluation often blend into one another. Iteration is useful for refining and deepening the problem definition. It takes several steps to formulate the problem in a solvable manner, often because the real problem may be deeper than or different from the original statement of the issue.[47] As we have seen, it is important to arrive at a definition that is narrow enough to act on, so that solutions can be implemented.

In the private sector, the innovator is often also the inventor. The pilot who created the first roll-aboard wheeling suitcase was solving a problem of his own that he understood well.[48] In the social and public sector, by contrast, those who are charged with solving problems are not always those who are most affected by them. They must rely on conversations and collaboration with others, especially those affected, to understand the problem, to define it in compelling terms, and to come up with solutions. For example, in the city of Torreón, Mexico, which also participated in The GovLab's 2020 MultiCity Challenge, officials initially defined the problem they were trying to solve as suburban sprawl, assuming that people were chasing the dream of a picket fence. When they actually surveyed and talked to residents, it turned out that they were moving because of safety and security concerns, enabling the city to identify a more relevant and important root cause through collaboration with the public. In public problem solving, innovators do not rely on themselves alone but know how to discover new solutions through better uses of data and conversation with others.[49] That conversation about the root causes, who is affected, what are the solutions, and what is wrong with the way the problem is being addressed depends on a concise articulation of the problem to jump-start collaboration.

Writing a Concise Statement

Succinctly put, the problem definition is a clear and concrete statement of a problem that can be acted on. It should answer (1) what the problem is, (2) when and where it occurs, (3) whom it affects, (4) why it occurs, and (5) why it matters.

For example, you might define a problem around the absence of adequate behavior change, such as wearing masks and adhering to social distancing, in the population (what the problem is). Maybe you have identified specific communities and segments of the population that are at greater risk. For example, Republicans or young people or people in a specific neighborhood or people going out to dinner behave in ways that increase the risk of infection and community spread (whom it affects and when). Then you need to articulate an initial list of root causes (why). One reason might be lack of access to personal protective equipment. Another root cause may be a misguided fear that changing behavior might signal contagion. A third reason may be people's inability to afford a mask. Another might be misunderstanding that masks are only worn if you are experiencing symptoms. You might surmise that people do not wear masks and socially distance because of strong family pressure. They might fear that wearing a mask could signal that they are sick and cause them to be quarantined and lose their job. Do not be content until you have repeated the process of reviewing all possible root causes. As I explain in the exercises at the end of the chapter, make a "list of whys" that describe why the problem is happening. Try to write down at least five. This is your initial list of root causes.

Now ask why *those* problems are happening and see if you can break the root causes down further. This will help you to arrive at a more specific and concrete problem and one that, should you tackle it, will more likely lead to real change. It is very common for the ultimate problem at issue to be different from the problem you started with at the outset. Beware the common pitfall, however, of solutions masquerading as problems. The lack of regulation of Craigslist is not the root cause of the problem of human trafficking. Lack of social and economic opportunity, social instability, conflict and war, poverty, and discrimination are all root causes, and we have to interrogate why those are happening before we jump ahead to the assumption that regulating a website will fix them.

Always Ask Why
In one sense, the process of problem definition is nothing more than a childlike exercise of repeatedly asking "why" something is happening. That simple sky-is-blue question forces a deeper reflection. Professor Michael Barry uses the following example in his need-finding class at Stanford d. school.

If I asked you to build a bridge for me, you could go off and build a bridge. Or you could come back to me with another question: "Why do you need a bridge?" I would probably tell you that I need a bridge to get to the other side of a river. Aha! This response opens up the frame of possible solutions. There are clearly many ways to get across a river besides using a bridge. You could dig a tunnel, take a ferry, paddle a canoe, use a zip line, or fly a hot-air balloon, to name a few. You can open the frame even farther by asking why I want to get to the other side of the river. Imagine I told you that I work on the other side. This, again, provides valuable information and broadens the range of possible solutions even more. There are probably viable ways for me to earn a living without ever going across the river.[50]

Coming back to our previous example about mask wearing, asking why *again* may reveal a more underlying root cause than those initially articulated. Upon further reflection, the real root cause may be systemic misinformation. Bad actors may have capitalized on fear and confusion to promote fake news, spread misinformation, and perpetuate myths and stereotypes. Political leaders may encourage constituents not to follow guidance.

Finally, it is helpful to ask why the problem matters. In this case, the failure to wear a mask may increase the risk of infection, disease, and death.

Another way to tackle the problem statement is by articulating the problem definition as a hypothesis in the form, "If [cause], then [effect], because [rationale]." The cause is the independent variable that changes and whose impact we are measuring. The rationale is another way of saying root causes. While using the hypothesis formulation might simplify the process of articulating the problem, it is important to continue to be specific, rather than reverting to general causes. For example, to stick with public health, we might say that if mask wearing decreases, then COVID rates will increase because deliberate misinformation is perpetuating the false view that masks are only worn by those who are Democrats. To take another example, if the long-term unemployed have increased access to mental health services, then they would suffer from less anxiety and depression and be able to get a job faster because depression makes it harder to search efficiently for work. Or let us take a different example from another domain: if we had better measures of social and emotional well-being, then high schools could more effectively teach their students because they would be able to evaluate their overall learning outcomes.

The more you seek to reveal the root causes, the more you can find a cause that is both correct (there will be more than one of those) and that you can and want to act on. For example, you might be concerned about pollution of your local waterway. The pollution is caused by sewage disposal into the river; tourist boats plying the river with dirty, leaking engines; and a lack of popular understanding and appreciation for the impact of pollution on public health and the environment. While all of these might be genuine root causes, you might be more excited and eager to investigate the role played by tourist boats because of a relationship you have to the industry. You, therefore, choose to dig deeper and understand whether the companies are skimping on repairs, have the wrong equipment, run too many routes, or lack awareness. The definition needs to be realistic about what is possible for you both because of your capacity and because of your enthusiasm. Keep in mind that "actionable" by you—that is to say, pertaining to something you can do something about—includes your capacity to work with potential collaborators and partners.

Again, do not work on this alone. Discuss what is doable with a group of stakeholders and potential partners, since there is no precise answer or science behind these questions, and indeed the root causes may be contested.

This process of asking why, both alone and in concert with others, is an iterative process leading to a more precise problem definition that articulates the underlying causes of the problem.

Describe the Problem Upstream

The process of problem definition also requires asking whether the problem has a cause further "upstream." In other words, ask not how to fix the issue as defined but how to prevent it from arising in the first place.[51] It is easier to prevent someone from falling into a river than to fish out a drowning man. It is less expensive to prevent someone from developing heart disease than to treat it after the fact.

Wedell-Wedellsborg uses the example of Lori Weise's work on dog adoption. Weise, the founder of Downtown Dog Rescue in Los Angeles, is a pioneer of an approach that seeks to keep pets with their original families so that they never enter shelters in the first place. When she realized that about a third of dogs that end up in shelters are "owner surrenders," it became obvious to her that addressing owner surrender might be more effective than trying to increase new adoptions. After further investigation, she realized that, far from being heartless, surrendering owners were often simply poor. "We're talking about people who in some cases aren't entirely sure how they will feed their kids at the end of the month. So, when a new landlord suddenly demands a deposit to house the dog, they simply have no way to get the money. In other cases, the dog needs a $10 rabies shot, but the family has no access to a vet, or may be afraid to approach any kind of authority. Handing over their pet to a shelter is often the last option they believe they have."[52]

By the same token, trying to solve the problem of how few women are in STEM, for example, has been addressed by creating preschool content with positive images of women scientists in addition to trying to change admission practices in graduate schools. The problem of air pollution may be addressed by enhancing public transportation so that people never buy a car in the first place, rather than trying to change how cars are designed. The deep-seated problem of systemic racism starts with changing how we teach children about slavery in elementary school. It is better to change the source of Flint, Michigan's water supply than to try to truck bottled water to all its residents.

Use Reframing and Positive Deviance

In addition to defining the problem and looking upstream for the root causes, it is important to apply both principles of reframing and positive deviance: namely, to ask where a problem is *not* happening. In Chicago, temperatures in 1995 topped 106 degrees; but the city dismissed the danger, and more than seven hundred people died. When the sociologist Eric Klinenberg studied the heat wave, he discovered that the problems of race and income did not determine who died, as most people assumed. Rather, his research revealed that the presence or absence of community and social networks made the difference between life and death. Where neighbors knew one another (as in certain neighborhoods in New Orleans after Katrina or Fukushima after the tsunami), people survived at a higher rate because they had someone to check on them.[53] Using a positive deviant example and then reframing the problem as one of community cohesion rather than poverty leads to a new set of policy prescriptions, namely, investments in parks, libraries, and community centers, which would otherwise be thought irrelevant.

Find Diverse Collaborators

Finding a different frame, identifying upstream problems, articulating root causes, and pinpointing causes that can be acted on all require public problem solvers to treat problem definition as a collaborative exercise that includes participants with different roles, disciplinary backgrounds, and perspectives. Collaboration brings in more diversity of opinion, expertise, and experience.[54]

This is why the city of Philadelphia asked policy makers across government agencies to enter an open process of problem definition. Working with Citymart, a commercial vendor that specializes in innovation in the area of municipal procurement, the city gathered thirty participants from nine agencies to frame priority problems. They asked for input on better ways to use underutilized city infrastructure such as cell towers and telecommunications fiber.[55] Using this problem-based approach, they were then able to turn to vendors and interest groups and get over one hundred responses. Detroit copied the model and received ten times as many creative responses.

In the public sector, it is vital to consult the public and other relevant agencies. Their input is important because often the problem that agencies address is not the problem that citizens are most concerned about. Today it is common for officials to devise problems of their own invention or in response to the request of interest groups or their political party or the "feed" of a lobbyist.[56] According to officials in New York City, as elsewhere, a city council member proposes legislation based on what he or she has heard from listening to the news or perhaps to a constituent or an interest group. The fifty-one council members lack any systematic way to divine the most urgent and important issues for their constituents or diverse segments of the population within their districts. As a result, the concerns of the people with the greatest need may often, despite good intentions, be ignored because they never come to anyone's attention and the squeakiest wheel ends up getting the highest priority.[57]

But it is key to involve the public that is affected by a problem through face-to-face or online communication in order to arrive at a consensual understanding of the problem.[58] Since 2016 in San Pedro Garza de García in Mexico, public officials define problems in collaboration with residents. The process is designed to ensure that the problem definition resonates with real people's experience and at the same time is rigorous, not merely a complaint.[59] Following the model, in 2020 five cities in northern Mexico have begun to replicate the model and undergo a process of defining challenges with residents in order to focus attention on the urgent and important ones.[60]

Finally, a problem-definition process provides an opportunity to articulate criteria for success. A properly defined problem has indicators to determine when the frequency or the severity of the problem has been reduced.[61] By explaining clearly what the problem is, we are developing a metric for what will define victory if our project succeeds. This helps to explain why over 60 percent of U.S. survey respondents to our original survey expressed a keen desire to get trained in problem definition.

TO DO

The six exercises in this section are intended to help you undertake an iterative and collaborative process for defining a problem. Blank worksheets are provided online (https://solvingpublicproblems.org). Have fun! The best problem definition is the one that results in a problem you are excited and passionate about solving.

Exercise 1: Articulate the Problem
The first step is to craft a clear initial description—not a vague statement but a specific statement that can be acted on. A well-formulated challenge is already half solved.

Write a one-paragraph problem definition. It should address the basics, including the following:

- What is the problem?
- When and where does it occur?
- Who is impacted?[62]

First, take care that the problem is not a solution in disguise. For example, "we lack a good website" is not a problem.

Second, avoid vague generalities as responses. The answer to who is affected should not be "the public." Try to be specific, where possible, about geography, time, demographics, or industry.

Third, avoid complex jargon and technical terms, because further defining the problem and developing solutions will depend on collaboration with laypeople who have no in-depth knowledge of the field. The language in which the problem is defined can be specific, detailed, and even technical, but it must not be jargon and excluding of those who are external to the discipline.

Exercise 2: Articulate the Problem Together
Discuss your problem with others and get their reactions. Go through the same list of questions in exercise 1 as a team, talking through and compar-

ing individual responses to see what insights are revealed. The conversation may lead to identifying different problems for members of the team to work on and investigate.

As part of the group work, try retelling the problem as a story, with characters, plot, and timeline. As Karen Schrier explains, providing a story context for a problem can help in a number of ways. Stories can offer people new perspectives.[63]

Creating a story together helps people reach a shared and common understanding of the challenge, especially when participants come from different fields and backgrounds and have different levels of experience. It can also shake up fixed assumptions, by enabling participants to create, inhabit, and better understand the world that they are dealing with, rather than seeing the problem as abstract. After all, those who are affected by a given social condition are best placed to know if what appears to be a problem really is.[64] Thus, it can be particularly useful to make the problem come alive by creating a story about real people, uncovering how and why they experience the problem.

Exercise 3: Identify Root Causes: Five X Why
The next step is to break down the problem into smaller units by diagnosing its root causes.[65] Every big problem has small challenges associated with it, and those are more easily acted on.

Root cause analysis is a structured approach to identifying and articulating underlying causal factors in order to spur a conversation about real causes, as opposed to perceived causes or effects.[66] Although most of us find root cause analysis intuitive in daily life, it emerged formally in engineering in the mid-twentieth century as a way to diagnose manufacturing failures after the event in an effort to seek and remedy the ultimate source of a mechanical breakdown.[67] The task can usefully be applied to social and policy challenges with multiple, interdependent, and complex causes. To do this task, do the following:

Make a "list of whys" that describe why the problem is happening. Another way to ask this question of yourself is to ask, Why has this problem not been solved yet? Try to write down at least five root causes. This is your initial list of root causes.

Now ask why *those* problems are happening and see if you can break down the root causes further.

Repeat this exercise five times or until you can go no further. If you get stuck at any point describing the root causes, ask yourself, "Have I failed to identify a cause, or do I simply need more research to finish this?"

It is helpful to ask "why" this problem is occurring at least *five times* to make sure you have identified the most granular cause of the problem.[68] This exercise will reveal at which level of granularity to tackle the problem. It may also reveal multiple problems, each of which merits its own problem-definition process. Depending on your resources and collaborators, you may decide to tackle one or more of these more specific problems.

Exercise 4: LASSO Your Problem (adapted from Alpheus Bingham)
Now determine whether the description of the problem and its root causes is sufficiently rigorous by subjecting them to the five criteria that come under the acronym LASSO: limited, (capable of being) acted (on), specific, supported, and owned. Go through each of the following questions and use the five criteria to redraft the problem definition as needed:

L: Have I *limited* the scope? In other words, have I narrowed down a large problem to more readily definable smaller problems?

A: Have I described something *capable of being acted on*? Have I made the problem clearer by describing a problem we can realistically do something about?

S: Have I described something *specific*? Have I made the problem more capable of being acted on by being concrete and detailed in my description?

S: Have I described a problem that will be *supported*? In other words, will my organization care enough about the problem to take action and invest in an evaluation process to determine whether the solutions will work?

O: Have I identified a problem *owner*? Someone needs to manage the problem-solving process and communicate back to collaborators. In a well-authored problem definition, someone has responsibility to manage the solution process.[69]

What is crucial about this exercise is that it helps to determine whether you can act on this defined problem. Inchoate causes (such as man's inhumanity to man) may indeed contribute to the problem, but neither you nor your organization can act on them.[70] Which of the problems and root causes that you have identified are solvable by you or your agency?

Therefore, in addition to avoiding vague generalities, you also want to focus on those causes that are within your jurisdictional purview. Some problems are simply going to be either too big or too far outside your jurisdiction to be subject to your impact. Eliminate those. For a given problem definition to be supported, you need to make sure that you have the authority, acceptance, and ability to act on that problem.

Capacity constraints, political and cultural constraints, and other challenges make it difficult to act, which is why it is important to identify and prioritize those causes over which one has ability and authority—but also the passion—to act.[71]

Exercise 5: Define Your Hypothesis

Having defined a problem, try refining your definition by stating the problem as a hypothesis that explains why the problem is happening.

Start by doing the following:

- Do background research on the problem to enable you to formulate the hypothesis.
- Do an initial problem definition, identifying root causes.
- Formulate the problem definition as an "if . . . then" statement. The common format is: "If [cause], then [effect], because [rationale]."
- Do further targeted background research on both evidence and practice to refine the hypothesis (see chapter 8 for more on how to do such rapid evidence reviews).
- Use both data-analytical and human-centered approaches to test your hypothesis (see chapters 5 and 6).

Exercise 6: Reframe the Problem

Before completing the definition of the problem, determine whether it can be reframed rather than simply diagnosed. Are there other ways of looking at the issue from different perspectives to yield new insights? Is the problem really the slow elevator or the boredom of waiting?[72] Is it possible to think about the problem from a different angle?

These reframing exercises might, for example, redefine the problem of crime more narrowly as the perception and fear of crime or the lack of jobs or activities for young people in their spare time.[73]

In a problem definition exercise I did with public officials from Kampala, Uganda, in 2020, participants started by defining the problem as loss of revenue due to unregistered, black-market businesses. Upon reframing, however, low literacy levels proved to be a more actionable root cause driving the failure to comply with regulations. The change in framing also allowed for the definition of a more compelling and hospitable problem to which citizens could contribute solutions. The shift is vital to opening up the solution space. If the cause of auto accidents is bad drivers, the solution is driver education. However, if the problem is unsafe cars, as Senator Patrick Moynihan shifted the frame of one argument in the 1970s, the solution becomes seatbelts.

At Stanford's d.school, students are taught to change the frame of reference by shifting the perspective to that of another person.[74] Instead of looking at a problem from your own point of view, look at it from the point of view of a member of the public or from the perspective of a whole class or group of people. In particular, considering the viewpoint of the population experiencing the problem can lead to unanticipated epiphanies and greater understanding, as we shall see in chapter 5.

CHAPTER FIVE

Human-Centered Design, or Understanding Problems with Help from People

It is one thing to understand the principles, and another thing to understand the forms of government. The former are simple; the latter are difficult and complicated. . . . Who understood the principles of mechanics and optics better than Sir Isaac Newton? And yet Sir Isaac could not for his life have made a watch or a microscope.

Benjamin Rush, Observations upon the Present Government of Pennsylvania (1777)

Otto Wagner's Church of St. Leopold, built in Vienna in the first decade of the twentieth century, is an art nouveau masterpiece. The famous Viennese Secessionist architect incorporated features into his design to serve the particular needs of the church's users. In other words, he was not simply designing for aesthetics; he was practicing design thinking, creating a place to meet the needs of the church's mentally ill congregation. The eight-hundred-seat Church of St. Leopold, also known as the Kirche am Steinhof, is part of the Steinhof Psychiatric Hospital.

To adjust to the patients' needs, the church has very few sharp edges. The corners of pews are rounded to avoid injury. The chancel, where the priest stands to deliver his sermon, is both elevated and inaccessible to the congregation (the entrance is from the vestry in the back) to protect the safety of the priest from possible attacks by the mentally ill. Rather than still basins of holy water, water flows continuously like a fountain, for better hygiene. The floor slants downward for easier cleaning, while the bathrooms are easily accessible. The original design contained pews of different widths to accommodate different types of patients. There were also more side exits to make it easier for patients to leave the building.

The Kirche am Steinhof was pathbreaking, not only for its beauty but because it embodied a radically different view of mental illness. Previously, most asylums had been designed like jails to keep their inmates incarcerated and apart from the public. Wagner's design carefully considered how patients and those who cared for them would use the church. It sought to create a restorative environment.[1] The departures from traditional church architecture exemplified Wagner's approach to the principle that form follows function and his attention to adjusting the design to the requirements of those who would use the space. Today Wagner's design process is both standard practice in architecture and synonymous with the careful research, collaboration, and iteration that have come to be associated with the (sometimes much-hyped) methods of design thinking.[2]

Design thinking enriches our problem-definition process by providing insight into how people actually experience a problem. It is a strategy for gathering evidence to test a problem definition and for bridging the gap between those who govern and those who are governed. Private inventors come up with creative solutions to a vexing problem that they know firsthand, turning a thought for how to fix it into a tangible new product, process, or service. Public problem solvers and entrepreneurs, by contrast, bear responsibility for improving life within a larger community. They are usually taking on problems from which they do not uniquely suffer or may not even suffer directly at all.

Aware of this challenge, the human-centered practices of design thinking impose a series of metaphorical "hurdles" in order to force public entrepreneurs to pause and to talk, empathize, and ideally to collaborate with the public they are trying to assist. These practices of discovery and evidence gathering help to refine an ill-defined and inchoate problem. They make it easier to select among myriad root causes and select the ones that are most at issue, informed by insights from real people in the field who are experiencing the problem.

We live in a time of rising and, in some places, rampant inequality. Many citizens feel a powerful sense of alienation from the practices of government. These realities make human-centered design all the more important— not only for the people affected by government policy but for the public servants who must implement it. Research from social psychology and management shows that when employees seek to benefit others and consider their perspectives, they are likely to be more creative problem solvers who develop novel and useful ideas.[3]

This chapter argues that human-centered design, when used as part of the problem-definition process, leads to more effective and legitimate service design and delivery.[4] It is an important next step in the public-problem-solving journey that seeks to obtain and validate evidence about the nature of the problem to solve. The problem-definition process is not complete without it. The best public servants listen and observe and, above all, ask questions. They invite residents to participate in the diagnosis of the problems.

A BRIEF HISTORY OF HUMAN-CENTERED DESIGN:
FROM DESIGNING FOR TO DESIGNING WITH PEOPLE

Architecture and urban planning have always sought to design structures and spaces to meet people's needs. Over time, these fields inspired the spread of a design mind-set into other disciplines. In the 1950s and 1960s, two polymaths, Buckminster Fuller, architect of the geodesic dome, and Herbert Simon at Carnegie Mellon, worked across fields to create a systematic design science built on greater empathy at a human scale and therefore intended to advance human well-being.

Ultimately, design proposes manmade, technological, or other kinds of interventions that respond to human challenges and transform an existing situation into a preferable one.[5] "Design science," or what we now call "design thinking," refers to the set of practices by which designers seek to understand the people whose problem they are trying to solve—what people do, how they act, and their point of view.[6] The design mind-set revolves around these people's perception of a problem: their perspective, context, needs, wants, and desires at a human scale. Design thinking puts considering the needs of others first. Its approach to problem solving does not see people in conflict with public problem solvers but worthy of our care and concern.[7] (It is worth noting the distinction from professions like law and medicine that, while they serve a client, tend to celebrate the professional as expert-who-knows-best.)

More participatory design methods began to emerge in the 1960s and 1970s, in reaction to the modernist, top-down planning of the 1950s, which was often criticized for emotionally cold artifacts that did not embrace or appeal to ordinary people. Among other movements for change, Scandinavian cooperative design sought to democratize design by going beyond the designer's expertise and intuition to create designs in partnership with ordinary people.[8] It sought to add anthropological and observational practices and, eventually, more participatory approaches to standard bench research. At the same time, architecture and urban planning in the United States began to move toward more participatory practices, inspired by scholar-activists such as Jane Jacobs, who saw involving people in the design of their own communities as critical to making cities human scale and livable. The emergence of environmental psychology, which studies the relationship between human behavior and the spaces and places we inhabit, has further helped to make humans the center of inquiry, rather than simply objects of study.[9]

As the practices of all design evolved over the twentieth century to include intangible products such as computer interfaces and eventually services, the practices of human design have been adopted across industries in product design, technology development, planning, and practically every other field. User-interface and human-computer-interaction studies have become popular in engineering as a way to design products that the consumer should not have to spend much time deciphering.[10] The process of listening to the needs and observing the behavior of customers encompasses what should be the self-evident idea that technology products should be designed based on users' needs and that the best way to ascertain those needs is to involve users in the design and development process.[11]

Of course, any technology user who has ever struggled with a website or gadget knows the reality is far from this ideal. The design-thinking pioneers Don Norman (father of the badly designed and eponymous Norman doors we do not know whether to push or pull) and Jan Stappers write, "There is a tendency to design complex sociotechnical systems around technological requirements, with the technology doing whatever it is capable of, leaving people to do the rest. The real problem is not that people err; it is that they err because the system design asks them to do tasks they are ill suited for. Unfortunately, there is a tendency to blame people for the error rather than to find the root cause and eliminate it."[12]

The growing popularity of the discipline of design thinking owes much to the brothers Thomas and David Kelley, who founded the IDEO design firm in the early 1990s. Their work and sponsorship of the Hasso Plattner Institute of Design (d.school) at Stanford University, along with funding from the German technology magnate Hasso Plattner, have been critical to developing design thinking as an academic field and a practice. Design thinking is now part of countless educational curricula, especially human-computer interaction, engineering, and business. The design mind-set promotes an other-focused way of thinking and working and describes a set of specific qualitative methods and tools for understanding people.

A vital change came in the late twentieth and early twenty-first centuries, when design thinking evolved from a set of research practices for studying users as subjects into practices for designing *with* them as stakeholders and participants. There is a tension between more social scientific approaches of studying problems at arm's length and contemporary design-based approaches that emphasize going beyond disinterested research to embrace normative practices of intervention and partnership. Thus, today, design thinking includes both older approaches of empathizing with users through listening and observing and more contemporary practices of conversation and hands-on codesign. It includes new forms of engagement with communities and individuals. "Co-design is an approach to design that actively involves all stakeholders in the design process," writes the Ohio State professor Liz Sanders, "to help ensure that the result meets their needs and is usable. Also referred to as participatory design, at the heart of this understanding is the notion that we should therefore not be designing for people, but rather, designing with them." She advocates for invoking the imaginations and dreams not only of designers but of everyday people.[13] Human-centered designers, like good researchers in any field, observe, talk to, and listen to those for whom they are designing, but, increasingly, they also collaborate and take direction from the stakeholders they are seeking to help.

In New Zealand, for example, when public officials talked to parents of newborn children, they learned about their frustrations with government services as apparently straightforward as obtaining a birth certificate. Parents were struggling to find the information they needed across a variety of different government websites. In response, officials brought all relevant services into one website called Smart Start, designed to provide one-stop shopping for new parents.[14] Without talking to new parents, public officials would not have understood the problem, the intensity of their frustrations, or how to address them.

In Memphis, Tennessee, in an effort to reduce commercial vacancies, city officials worked with young entrepreneurs to determine how to entice businesses to lease vacant space. They also worked with residents—their end users—to determine the community's needs and what storefronts might best serve them. One outcome was the MemFix project, in which the city cleaned up and decorated streets, added bike lanes, and undertook other forms of small-scale, temporary neighborhood revitalization. MemShop matched new and interested businesses or entrepreneurs with vacant commercial spaces on the basis of the community's needs. Businesses were allowed to sign an extremely short lease (for example, a "pop-up" store that would run for as little time as a few days or weeks), with the option to extend to a long-term lease. MemFix would then throw a massive block party so that residents could see the revitalized area, complete with new storefronts. The change would, in turn, attract more businesses and private partnerships to join the revitalization effort. As a result of these design-thinking-driven practices, Memphis was able to cut the number of commercial vacancies by more than 30 percent.[15]

WHY DESIGN THINKING HAS BEEN MOSTLY ABSENT FROM GOVERNMENT

Of course, policy analysts and public servants have always had to engage in "design"—to come up with solutions to problems. Yet in the main, they have not engaged in participatory human-centered problem-solving practices —the careful ethnographic study of and deliberation with intended users— that have characterized the work of the most sensitive architects and engineers for the past fifty years. To varying degrees, law, regulation, and professional custom have kept public servants at arm's length from the public.

This is no accident. The professionalization of public administration in the late nineteenth and early twentieth centuries was designed to apply scientific principles to governing while reducing the corruption, patronage, and inefficiency that might come from too much contact with the public. Inadvertently, this attitude excluded the public from meaningful participation in government. It was shaped by, and in turn shaped, a belief that people are either unwilling or unable to contribute to governing themselves, except through partisan politics and the pursuit of individual interests.[16]

Reliance on professionals to govern developed in parallel with three social trends that became dominant in the mid-nineteenth century: industrialization and the emergence of organizations, especially bureaucracies, to accommodate the scale and complexity of modern life; the standardization of tools for controlling social conditions; and the rise of professional training in universities. These three trends did much to shape the modern design of closed political institutions. They made professionalism the prevailing ideology and central to the legitimacy of government actions. They also made public participation the exception rather than the rule.[17]

The top-down and professionalized model of public service extolled by Woodrow Wilson, often described as the father of public administration, assumed that university-based education would suffice to understand and find solutions to any problem. Elite credentials equaled effective decision-making. That explains why a twenty-seven-year-old Yale Law School graduate, in his first year of working for the Justice Department and with no other real-world experience, would end up developing the process by which sitting presidents could be investigated after Watergate and Whitewater.[18] It is not uncommon to have junior staffers just out of school afforded massive policy-making responsibilities, whether as a judicial clerk, congressional staffer, or executive-branch intern.

But, as we have come to understand during the course of the first decades of the new millennium, this approach to governing fails adequately to consider public needs or to benefit from public expertise stemming from lived, situational, and academic experience.[19]

Pete Buttigieg, the mayor of South Bend, Indiana, and 2020 Democratic presidential candidate, poignantly illustrates the dangers of the top-down approach in his memoir, *The Shortest Way Home*. Buttigieg tells how, in 2009, Indiana's then-treasurer, Richard Mourdock, sued to block the bankruptcy of Chrysler, which would pave the way for its bailout and the saving of thousands of jobs. Instead, Mourdock pressed (unsuccessfully) for the car company's liquidation on the manifestly ideological ground that government should not interfere in the economy. Buttigieg wonders whether Mourdock ever talked to any of the families who would have been affected: "To me, the whole episode was about what happens when a public official becomes obsessed with ideology and forgets that the chess board on which he is playing out his strategy is, to a great many people, their own life story. Good policy, like good literature, takes personal lived experience as its starting point."[20]

It is quite likely that the failure of the political class to consider people's views and engage them in problem solving also partly explains why so many citizens feel that government is something perpetrated on them, unresponsive to their needs.

In James Scott's pathbreaking book *Seeing Like a State: How Certain*

Schemes to Improve the Human Condition Have Failed, the Yale anthropologist offers a functional explanation for why governing became so removed from the people. His theory predates the rise of professionalism in the late nineteenth and early twentieth centuries. "The pre-modern state," he writes, "was partially blind; it knew precious little about its subjects, their wealth, their landholdings and yields, their location, their very identity. It lacked anything like a detailed 'map' of its terrain and its people. It lacked, for the most part, a measure, a metric, that would allow it to 'translate' what it knew into a common standard necessary for a synoptic view."[21]

As a result of this blindness, the flow of information between government and the governed was fitful and imperfect. Tax collection, for example, was highly uneven, with most communities paying only a fraction of what they owed, if that. Governments, unable to control or predict revenues in a consistent way, resorted to a whole range of measures, including military campaigns, in order to extract rents. But the development of new technologies for regularized measurement and time keeping offered the means for government to manage its affairs more rationally. Engineers, scientists, planners, and other professionals—what Max Weber called the "personally detached and strictly 'objective' *expert*"—were trained to carry out measurement and management on behalf of the modern state.[22] A newly industrialized world offered new tools for controlling what was previously immeasurable and unpredictable, while delegation of authority to university-trained professionals offered a better, more efficient way to bring expertise to governance on a large scale than did the aristocratic or political patronage of earlier times.[23]

But Scott argues that in the effort to streamline and simplify understanding of on-the ground conditions, bureaucratic management has done a poor job of accommodating social and ecological diversity and specificity. As a prime example of this rigid, high-modernist worldview, he points to Le Corbusier's midcentury urban-planning models, such as those on display in Brazil's capital city, Brasilia, with their orderly, rigid, and right-angled grids that obliterate the winding, narrow, and human-scale streets of earlier neighborhoods. To Scott, as to Jane Jacobs, whose book *The Death and Life of Great American Cities* celebrated the bottom-up diversity and community that made some cities so vibrant, such efforts to impose artificial simplicity from above created lifeless cities by failing to take on board local, tacit knowledge.[24] This form of governing, at best, misunderstood complex social and natural systems and, at worst, reinforced authoritarianism and racism. Western governments' twentieth-century embrace of "scientific" and rational models of planning, administration, and governance, while a welcome advance on the cronyism and corruption that marked previous centuries, generated its own forms of waste and discontent by ignoring their citizens' point of view.

HUMAN-CENTERED DESIGN AND THE PARTICIPATORY TURN

Despite all the ink spilled on human-centered ways of working, the tension between designing *for* versus *with* people persists. The traditional celebration of designers as creative actors and instigators of change conflicts with their role as stewards and facilitators of a broad, participatory conversation. This tension has led some of design thinking's leading proponents to question the field itself, even calling it a "failed experiment" that perpetuates the supremacy of the designer at the expense of more democratized problem solving.[25] The habit of designing for, rather than with, users is especially, but surely not exclusively, entrenched in government, where solving problems behind closed doors has been the norm. Heralded as one of the greatest designers of all time, Apple's Steve Jobs was famous for saying he did not listen to his customers: "If we'd given customers what they said they wanted, we'd have built a computer they'd have been happy with a year after we spoke to them—not something they'd want now."[26]

Engaging with people as full participants in a deliberative codesign process is the essence of participatory democracy. It also simply is not possible to define a problem adequately without talking to those who are affected by it to gain a genuine understanding of the root causes. Especially because it is tempting to define a problem broadly, by looking at climate change or violence against women writ large, participatory practices are necessary for gathering the evidence needed to understand a solvable problem. By humanizing the problem definition process, human-centered design forces us to focus on a specific geography, narrow community, and limited time frame and thereby increases our chances of developing practical solutions.

But most governments have rarely governed with, rather than for, the people. Whereas today modern policy making is done largely by elites, ancient Athens developed extraordinary institutional innovations to enable some of its citizens. Citizenship was exclusively male and did not extend to slaves. For the rest, service was a normal part of life in fifth-century BC

Periclean Athens, and some citizens were able and expected to contribute to the government of a population of a quarter million people spread across twenty-five hundred square kilometers. Athens overcame the challenges of coordinating public policy making at scale with institutional designs that made it possible to aggregate and distribute knowledge across the realm. Fourteen unique Athenian governing institutions, such as the Council of Five Hundred, annually chosen by lot, all incorporated amateur citizen participants. Management of the polis engaged a large portion of the population on a regular basis. In a funeral oration in honor of those who died in the Peloponnesian War, Thucydides quotes Pericles as saying, "For we have a system of government that does not emulate the institutions of our neighbors, making us more an example to some rather than leading us to imitate others. It is called a democracy because power is in the hands not of the few but of the many. . . . In accordance with each man's recognition, he is singled out for public service; and never on account of poverty is someone who can do good for the state prevented from doing so by the obscurity of their background."[27] The city's economic and cultural success, coupled with its openness and opportunity, attracted a bounty of talented people from across the Mediterranean to populate these new institutions.[28]

In the twenty-first century, the emergence of human-centered design as the modus operandi for designing policies, services, and platforms is producing a democratic turn (despite some notable regression in political leadership) that revives participatory democracy. For example, California's food-stamp program allowed people to apply online, but the application was fifty web pages long, with more than one hundred questions. Most families that started the process ended up abandoning it. By using human-centered design—namely, analyzing the process from the perspective of the person using it—the nongovernmental organization Code for America was able to reduce the time it takes to complete the application to fewer than ten minutes, substantially increasing enrollment. By involving citizens in design and delivery, Code for America improved the service and, arguably, strengthened democracy.[29]

Many professions, including policy making, are still largely hierarchical and closed, but there is growing interest in the idea of talking to end users.[30] Known as "design thinking" rather than "participatory democracy," these methods emphasize engaging with the public by a different name. However, according to the 2019 survey of local public officials in the United

States, the practice of human-centered design—like other problem-solving skills—is not widespread. Forty-seven percent of American officials said they had used the skill. In Australia, while a full 62 percent were aware of the skill, only 45 percent said they or their teams had used it. But a large percentage in both jurisdictions were eager to learn more.[31]

THE EMERGENCE OF EQUITABLE HUMAN-CENTERED DESIGN IN GOVERNMENT

Thankfully, the top-down approach is changing in some places. More and more universities are training future leaders in ethnographic design-thinking approaches. For example, Northwestern's Design for America is a design-thinking-based learning program in which interdisciplinary teams of students work on prosocial challenges, applying human-centered methods to develop innovative solutions.[32]

Changes in education are also prompting new forms of professional training and leading to a new generation of public entrepreneurs who embrace the lived experience of ordinary people as an asset in problem solving. In the US federal government, the Office of Personnel Management (OPM) has established The Lab at OPM to teach human-centered design to public employees. Australia's BizLab Academy trains public servants in human-centered design in small group classes.[33] WeGov trains thousands of Brazilian public servants in human-centered design at every level of government. Argentina's Innovation Academy offers programs on human-centered design that reach thirty-six thousand public servants. Canada has rushed headlong to embrace design thinking, with teams popping up across the country: Alberta CoLab, Ontario Digital Service, British Colombian Digital Experience Division, the Canadian Digital Service, Calgary's Civic Innovation YYC, and Nova Scotia's NS CoLab are just a few examples of new units focused on bringing design approaches to government.[34]

Perhaps the best-known example of human-centered design in government is Denmark's MindLab, which helped public servants in Denmark to learn and practice the skill for sixteen years. MindLab adopted human-centered design as its core methodology, applying it, for example, to help the country transition from a half to a full day of elementary school, which resulted in teachers spending less time preparing and more time teaching in the classroom. For this project, it solicited the input of four hundred teachers to redesign the country's school curriculum.[35] MindLab worked with teachers to see how they balanced their time and cocreated solutions with them, like "speed sharing," a type of "speed dating" so teachers could exchange lesson ideas with one another.[36] MindLab's work started with documenting and understanding citizens' and public servants' experience, in order to understand the shortcomings of that experience and how those shortcomings affected people.

Today when governments hire design professionals (they come with diverse titles like interaction, strategic, systems, service, or policy designer), they are recognizing that, in addition to deep subject-matter, technical, and legal expertise, public problem solving needs to include those people who know how to take a human-centered approach to designing public policies and services.[37]

Since the beginning of the new millennium, those who inquire into the needs of diverse stakeholders and end users have come to form a new profession known as "service designers."[38] The National Health Service (NHS) in the United Kingdom hired the service design consultancy USCreates (now called FutureGov) to manage its consultation with citizens in a UK community in order to find innovative solutions to the problem of childhood obesity.

FutureGov's professionals, like community engagement specialists and deliberation consultants, are intentionally not experts in health care, obesity, or the NHS. Instead, in collaboration with those subject-matter experts, they teach how to work with communities in order to help an institution like the NHS get smarter about the needs of the people it serves. As service designers, they enable rather than lead. They identify affected, interested, and knowledgeable parties; elicit their expertise; and maximize their incentives to drive change. FutureGov conducted ethnographic research in order to codesign solutions for childhood obesity with thirteen UK communities. Some of those solutions focused on banning advertising for sugary foods, while others concentrated on the role of religious institutions in promoting healthier behavior. FutureGov is working with five cities on rapid pilots of the most promising ideas.[39]

The emergence of the Black Lives Matter movement has sparked greater interest in and emphasis on equity and inclusion in governing, which means giving voice to the needs and desires of those who are traditionally excluded, especially people of color, the poor, and other systematically excluded groups. Calls for greater racial equity further invigorate the embrace of human-centered methods and techniques.

An equity-centered design approach that takes special account of the impact of race on who participates, how we design, and the resulting outcomes of service delivery represents a major shift away from cost-benefit approaches, which evaluate a program at an economic macro-level, or traditional policy analysis that evaluates the outcomes of a policy or service at a meso-level but without regard for social justice. Instead, human-centered equitable design seeks to put the individual at the center, assessing the delivery of a policy or service from the human perspective of someone waiting in line at the Department of Motor Vehicles or receiving job counseling at the unemployment office and does so by engaging that person in the design process. Theo Keane, a senior manager in the innovation skills team at the UK innovation foundation Nesta, explains that in government we must humbly "communicate, interact and empathize with the people involved, stimulating them and obtaining an understanding of their needs, desires and experiences."[40]

HUMAN-CENTERED AND PARTICIPATORY DESIGN METHODS
There are many practical strategies for ethnographic research. Bruce Hanington and Bella Martin's *Universal Methods of Design* offers 125 different methods, from participant observation to interviews to artifact analysis to service blueprinting.[41] Many of these call for designers to "empathize" with the subject by putting themselves in the subject's shoes. Many designers create personas, or fictional archetypes of the people who will be affected.[42] Others call for observing human behavior, the way a zoologist studies an animal in the wild, by watching how people behave in a given context, such as online or in their workplace. Some practitioners even call for meditation as the best way to empathize with others. But because we are focused on strategies of engagement that help to make problem solving legitimate as well as effective and that take seriously the lived experience and expertise of ordinary people when defining the problem, we caution against such approaches and advocate for *talking to* and *designing with* actual humans.

Observing people, while useful, misses out on the wisdom and insight that people can share and perpetuates discrimination and exclusion. It is harder to know how people feel about a problem without engaging them more directly and therefore too easy to make assumptions that the root causes are something other than they are. Talking about fictional personas or archetypes can lead one to miss important categories of relevant people, such as university experts, businesspeople, philanthropists, or staff of local government agencies, any of whom might have important information to share.

Qualitative social research has always involved speaking with people, usually through an interview or a survey. The digital age creates new opportunities for talking to more people more quickly and in new ways that are easier and less time-consuming (and, therefore, potentially more equitable for the participants). Just as the telephone transformed the survey, the Internet, too, and the prevalence of big data will create a multiplicity of new ways to ask questions.[43]

I discuss five methods for engaging with people to define a problem: interviewing, the related technique of service blueprinting, and the three online methods of smarter crowdsourcing, wiki surveys, and AI-based collaborative problem identification. But there are literally dozens of additional ways you can structure a conversation to elicit people's lived experience and know-how to inform the problem-definition process.

Interviewing
Interviewing is common to all human-centered design methods. Talking to outsiders invariably probes, sometimes challenges, our assumptions about the root causes of a problem. It allows us to collect firsthand accounts of people's experience of a problem. Such interactions may turn up memorable detail that enlivens the problem statement. But good interviewing produces much more than just stories. By exposing the visceral, lived experience of people affected by a problem, it can cast light on the strength or weakness of our problem definition and help us pinpoint the most important root causes. The challenge is to impart meaning to the detail and explain why something is taking place while respecting and honoring what others have told us.[44]

Design-led innovators, as the OECD calls them, use ethnographic interviewing practices to uncover the needs of people using a service or affected by a policy.[45] This form of research complements the traditional bench research that policy analysts do in the library or at their computers.

Yet, while interviewing is a time-honored form, even some of the most empathetic adherents of design thinking do not use it, preferring to trust their observation or meditation skills. Although it may seem easier to simply empathize and more challenging to find "real people" with whom to talk, the handbook *Designing for Public Services*, coauthored by Nesta, IDEO, and Design for Europe, emphasizes that "people like to share, and you may be positively surprised by just how much! If you approach the activity in an open and transparent way, and are clear about your objectives, then you will be able to unlock invaluable insights."[46]

Interviewing people, either as individuals or in a group, about their understanding of the problem and its root causes involves developing a plan of attack, which I discuss here (and summarize in exercises at the end of the chapter). Of course, interviewing individuals and interviewing groups have different benefits—the former is more intimate, while the latter may produce useful and interesting deliberation and reveal contradictions.

Project goals. Bearing in mind that ethnographic research aims for deep understanding, but not prediction, of patterns of behavior, what do you need to know to inform your problem definition? How can ethnography help you to learn that? What kinds of things do you want to know to confirm the problem and its root causes? Have you articulated the hypothesis that you want to test with people?

Research and sampling design. If your goal is to study people who use a particular government service or suffer from a given problem, you still need to select diverse users and nonusers of the service, identifying an average and an extreme user. You want to ensure that your participants are of varied racial, ethnic, and demographic backgrounds. How many is enough? Ideally, you will keep observing or interviewing until you are no longer surprised by what you learn.[47] Your sample size is big enough when, having included diverse participants, what you hear still starts to repeat. If you are iterating and evolving your work in an agile fashion, then you will talk to people early and often throughout the problem-solving process.

Recruiting participants. This can be the hardest step. If you are focusing on face-to-face recipients of a government service, you might go to the office where they receive that service. But finding willing participants can be hard. This is where third parties come in. For example, you might find participants with the help of interest groups and industry associations that regularly convene their members or have membership lists.

Conducting research. Fieldwork should be undertaken in collaboration with participants, not perpetrated on them. Thus, coming up with conversation starters—ice breakers to help build trust and intimacy with participants—ahead of time can be useful, along with a written description of the research to share with participants, informing them about the purpose of your research and the information you plan to collect, to obtain their consent.

Interview and observation guide. Interviewing can be combined with other techniques such as questionnaires or participant observation.

Service Blueprinting and Journey Mapping

Another technique that builds on good interview skills is *service blueprinting*, also known as *journey mapping* (an exercise for this technique is provided at the end of this chapter). Service blueprinting involves developing a step-by-step rundown of a process. It is frequently used in business to document a customer sales experience in order to improve it. In the public sector, this approach refers to documenting how a government service, such as applying for a benefit, is provided. Journey mapping is often used to capture the experience from the individual citizen's perspective, whereas service blueprinting documents the entirety of the process from the institutional perspective.

This method, especially when done in collaboration with affected citizens and civil servants, can help to lay bare "just how complex and uncomfortable the customer experience" is and how much it deviates from expectations.[48] Documenting the process from start to finish—from the perspective both of residents and of those who serve them—helps to make the problems more readily visible. "A blueprint," writes one commentator about the practice in the *Harvard Business Review*, "encourages creativity, preemptive problem solving, and controlled implementation. It can reduce the potential for failure and enhance management's ability to think effectively about new services."[49]

An example of service blueprinting comes from a project that my students and I undertook (together with collaborators at Pompeu Fabra University in Barcelona) for the Colombian Constitutional Court during a class in 2019. The court receives fifty-five thousand appeals on paper every month from lower courts, making it all but impossible to select the handful of fundamental and human rights cases it will hear on any basis other than random selection.

The first step in addressing the problem was to document how paper moves through the appeals process, interviewing staff of the court, lawyers, and litigants, in order to detail how an appeal arrives at the court and is reviewed. Only by recording the process in detail and describing every interaction between people and paper could we uncover nonobvious but fixable problems, including the lack of a cover sheet summarizing each case, the absence of training for clerks, and the failure to group the cases by topic. The research helped to inform the court's awarding of a small grant to the University of Buenos Aires to begin to address the challenges quickly and design a new electronic filing system.

In another project, for the Aspen Institute on nonprofit tax returns in 2013, my coauthor and I documented the pathway of a nonprofit tax return from filing through processing by the Internal Revenue Service (IRS). By doing so, we discovered that the IRS was taking electronically filed returns, printing them out, and scanning them back in, thereby rendering a useful digital file into a useless image.[50] Revealing this almost-unbelievable inefficiency played a part in an eventual decision by the IRS to digitize all nonprofit tax returns and in a law from Congress mandating electronic filing.[51]

Smarter Crowdsourcing

Smarter Crowdsourcing (http://smartercrowdsourcing.org/) is a method developed by The GovLab for convening a large number of global experts online to develop rapid problem statements and implementation plans informed by high-quality expertise.

"Crowdsourcing" refers to the use of the Internet to solicit help from a distributed audience, or crowd. But crowdsourcing can be hit or miss, since it relies on the happenstance of having the right people learn about the opportunity to participate and wanting to do so. It may not attract the people with the right know-how quickly enough. Typically, crowdsourcing works well when small tasks without a high degree of complexity need to be performed—situations in which it almost does not matter who participates. Conversely, traditional methods of obtaining expertise, whether through conferences, traditional policy advising, or think-tank report writing, are too slow, especially when we need innovative and diverse ideas quickly to respond to the crisis at hand.

In the case of serious and time-sensitive challenges, it is necessary to marry the scale, agility, and diversity of crowdsourcing (also called "open innovation") with curation to target people with relevant know-how and

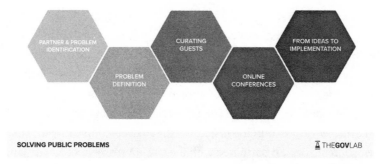

The GovLab Smarter Crowdsourcing process (Courtesy of Beth Simone Noveck / The GovLab)

bring them together in a format designed to produce effective and implementable outcomes. Instead of a handful of people meeting once at great expense in a conference room, you can use technology to get hundreds to lend their time and know-how and bring them into conversation with one another to identify, design, and refine good ideas.

Smarter Crowdsourcing enables ongoing, systematic, and useful exchange of expertise among dozens or even hundreds of global specialists. The goal is to solve policy and/or strategic challenges by combining rigorous problem definition, research, and curation with crowdsourcing in order not only to attract diverse ideas but also to render them useful and implementable. This more targeted form of crowdsourcing makes it possible for institutions to get more diverse help systematically and for more members of the public to participate in problem solving, by sharing their rare knowledge, skills, and experience.

Following the initial problem identification, Smarter Crowdsourcing involves convening a series of online deliberative conversations with invited, self-selected, or recommended participants to discuss the problem and sometimes to identify new ones and their root causes. This can be done using a web-conferencing platform such as Zoom.

The process is more than just an online dialogue. Participants are asked to recommend other invitees, making it possible to grow the group beyond the "usual suspects" who bring similar viewpoints and reinforce each other's biases.

You can use your convening power to ensure participation by a wide variety of individuals from industry, civil society, government, and academia. In Smarter Crowdsourcing, each online discussion lasts two hours and is focused on a specific problem. After the conference, we typically post videos, transcripts, and postconference briefings of each discussion online for comment. The insights are extracted and expanded on with further research and interviews. Following those conversations, ideas are fleshed out with interviews and research into implementation plans.

For example, in 2016, the Inter-American Development Bank (IADB) used Smarter Crowdsourcing to address the Zika epidemic (https://smarter crowdsourcing.org). It partnered with the city government of Rio de Janeiro in Brazil and the national governments of Argentina, Colombia, and Panama to find solutions. Working with The GovLab, the team broke down the issue into fifteen more specific problems. Partner governments selected six to address: assessing public awareness; communication and behavior change; predictive analytics; trash and standing water; information collection/data governance; and long-term care. The team organized six online dialogues over two months in response to each problem—attracting more than one hundred global experts, who deliberated online to deepen understanding of the problems and their root causes and to identify solutions. The team then created a "Playbook" of twenty implementable solutions to these six problem statements.

In a variation on the method in 2019, The GovLab used smarter crowdsourcing to invite hundreds of "bilinguals"—people with data-science and subject-matter expertise—to map the world's most pressing, high-impact questions that could be answered with the right data. Thus, for migration, air quality, future of work, gender, and disinformation, the 100 Questions Project (https://the100questions.org) sought to identify the problems that need to be addressed and the data that would be needed to do so. The experts suggested the problems, and the public voted on and prioritized among those problems. In 2020, The GovLab convened diverse global experts to help seven governments in Latin America respond to the challenges of the pandemic. In 2021, the GovLab repeated the process to find practical solutions to improve vaccine uptake.

Using Wiki Surveys to Define the Problem
Wiki surveys provide another way to elicit popular input into the definition of a problem. Designed by the Princeton sociology professor Matt Salganik, the open-source All Our Ideas wiki-survey tool (https://www.allourideas

.org) allows anyone to create a no-cost, collaborative survey to learn which problems people feel are most salient or to suggest alternative problems and root causes.[52] Wiki surveys combine the advantages of closed- and open-ended questions.[53] The tool was originally called "which do you want more?" because it presents the viewer with a choice between two responses (or "I can't decide") from a longer list of statements. Respondents receive exactly two randomly generated options from which to choose. They can respond as many times as they like or stop at any time. They can also select "View Results" to see how other participants are responding.

Participants can submit their own answer choice, such as an additional root cause or problem statement, using 140 characters or less, and submit as many ideas as they choose. The survey creator monitors submitted ideas for appropriateness, and those that are approved will start appearing as an answer choice under the corresponding question.

All Our Ideas has been used for 18,245 surveys with thirty-four million "votes" cast. It seeks to combine "the scale, speed, and quantification of a survey while still allowing for new information to 'bubble up' from respondents as happens in interviews, participant observation, and focus groups."[54]

You can use All Our Ideas to interrogate your problem definition and its root causes by explicitly asking people, "Which of the following are the root causes of this problem?" and offering them a series of answer options.[55] You can also ask, "Which of these problems are most urgent to address?" This is what the state of New Jersey's Future of Work Task Force (which I chaired) did in 2020. Over a six-week period, over four thousand workers told us which the most pressing problems are relating to the impact of technology on workplace safety, worker rights, and lifelong learning for workers.

AARP (formerly the American Association of Retired Persons) used the tool in December 2019 for three weeks, and over six thousand participants cast sixty-seven thousand pairwise "votes" about the biggest problems involving use of big health data, or the ability to gather and analyze large quantities of information about health, wellness, and lifestyle. Big health data include information from health-care providers as well as data from sources such as apps that track our sleep and exercise habits and the purchases we make. Doctors, medical researchers, health-care organizations, insurance companies, financial service providers, product and service companies, and governments at every level are keen to use such data.

Using All Our Ideas, AARP solicited people for their views, asking them to choose between sixty-five-plus statements of possible problems. Participants prioritized such concerns as "Big health data may reveal personal information about me without my control or consent" or "Companies can use big health data without having to tell anyone what they are doing with it or being accountable for it."[56] In 2021, the GovLab helped the Gates Foundation use the tool to ask students which are the most urgent educational challenges.

Using AI to Identify Problems

Among newer methods for defining problems with constituents are artificial intelligence (AI) tools to seek online input from large numbers of people with relevant firsthand experience. One exemplary use is Virtual Taiwan, which has engaged two hundred thousand people in helping to define problems as complex and difficult to solve as Uber regulation and online alcohol sales. As a result, the Taiwanese legislature has been able to formulate twenty-six bills, using the process to reach "coherence" (rough consensus) among stakeholders about the nature of the problem in order to devise more legitimate solutions.

Taiwan uses Pol.is, an open-source AI platform for "crowdsourced consensus-mining." Designed to show areas of consensus and division, Pol.is uses an artificial intelligence technique known as "principal component analysis" to visualize participants' opinions and see how many people agreed or disagreed with an issue. According to Pol.is, the software makes it possible to obtain information about the "dynamics of the issue, the facts of the matter, what is at stake, and who is involved" with a large number of participants.[57]

The process proceeds in multiple phases. In the first round, organizers create sample problem statements to prompt discussion. In the second round, participants are asked to "agree," "disagree," or "pass" on these statements or simply answer, "Is this statement important to you?"

Statements are shown to all participants on the basis of a comment routing system that gives each statement a priority score based on the responses it has received so far. To avoid bias, every person who enters the conversation sees a random ordering of the statements. As voting progresses, the algorithm finds the underlying structure of the conversation using unsupervised machine learning. The software analyzes the votes, and participants are placed into an opinion landscape on the basis of their vote. Aufstehen, a German collective movement comprising members of left-wing political parties, ran a large-scale Pol.is conversation with more than thirty-three thousand people who cast nearly two million votes on what the new platform of the movement should be.[58]

Pol.is is not the only tool that uses artificial intelligence to create conversations in order to understand a problem. One large financial services institution, for example, used a commercial AI tool called Remesh to conduct a real-time focus group about gender inequality. Previously, the company used email, surveys, web conferencing, community sites, chat rooms, in-person events, and other methods to collect views on the subject. However, by using so many different tools and having disparate conversations, it was very difficult to efficiently and meaningfully synthesize the outputs into comprehensive insights. To address these inadequacies, the organization employed an AI tool to organize a large-scale conversation with twelve thousand employees to understand the problem.

In 2019, in order to make a discussion about problems more usable for civil servants, CitizenLab, a Belgian software company that designs software for citizen engagement in use in twenty countries (disclosure: I am on the board), incorporated natural language processing (NLP) and machine learning to categorize and cluster the text submitted by citizens.

CitizenLab's algorithms identify the main topics and group similar ideas together using a common machine-learning method known as "topic modeling." It works by grouping content that shares similar words, both in meaning and in form. For example, the words "trees" and "forest" are similar in meaning; therefore, two ideas with these words are more likely to be grouped together. With regard to word form, for example, "bicycle" and "cyclist" are also considered similar.

Such clustering, according to CitizenLab's CEO, happens in real time and takes between five and fifteen seconds. This makes it easier for the people running a consultation to see what the comments are about and understand priorities. If organizers require people to log in, then the comments can also be sorted by demographic groups and location, making it possible to cluster topics, for example, by location as well. An engagement on youth climate action in 2019 elicited seventeen hundred contributions, which CitizenLab grouped into fifteen concrete issues. This helps decision-makers to make sense of the content gathered through citizen participation and better understand the priorities and ideas of the public.

RISKS OF HUMAN-CENTERED DESIGN

Human-Centered Design Is Still Not Participatory Design
It is a risk to assume that one knows what others want and need and to substitute that assumption for the hard work of actually designing in true partnership with people. Many methodologies of design thinking are not more participatory or democratic than other methods. Other methods may call for observing human behavior but treat people as lab rats to be studied rather than as experts to be consulted. "Human-centered design," writes an editor at IDEO, "is premised on empathy, on the idea that the people you're designing for are your roadmap to innovative solutions. All you have to do is empathize, understand them, and bring them along with you in the design process."[59]

IDEO's definition of "empathy" here perpetuates the passive rather than participatory approach to human-centered design. As we have seen, it is too easy to substitute "empathy" for real engagement. For example, the Age Lab at MIT has created AGNES, or the Age Gain Now Empathy System. AGNES is a suit that experimenters put on, containing yellow glasses to mimic ocular degeneration, a boxer's neck harness and bands around the joints to decrease movement, and foam coverings for the extremities to reduce tactile sensation.[60] AGNES is a wonderful way for an MIT millennial student engineer to mimic the aging process. But it can also be a way to avoid speaking to the elderly about their experience. Consultants just have to don the suit and they will magically know what barriers others are facing. Many design-thinking methods, such as the creation of personas, preach empathy by asking people to imagine the circumstances of others.[61] But they do not involve actual interaction with those other people. Design thinking has the potential to perpetuate elite and closed-door problem solving.

As the Yale psychologist Paul Bloom cautions in his book *Against Empathy,* the assumption that you can put yourself in the shoes of someone else is based on hubris. More than that, he asserts, empathy preferences emotional rather than rational forms of decision-making, and Bloom argues that when governing, in particular, it is dangerous to base decisions on how others may or may not feel, as opposed to on reason and facts, especially if "how others feel" is something I assume rather than ascertain.[62]

Human Centered Is Not Bureaucracy Centered

Human-centered design is currently so popular that there is a risk that its benefits will be oversold and its shortcomings ignored. The way processes work often fails to match, or even conflicts with, how things should be, and starting a human-centered process creates the expectation of shifting from the current state to the desired state, which might be hard to accomplish.[63] If we study how entrepreneurs set up a business, we know that they have to form and register the business, apply for the necessary permits and comply with appropriate regulations, seek investment and funding such as tax incentives, and search for employees.

But in many US states, oversight of these tasks is dispersed. The state secretary of state oversees business formation, financing is the domain of economic development authorities, the Department of Labor manages training and apprenticeship programs, and countless agencies have jurisdiction over regulatory compliance. A human-centered approach would suggest making all this information available in one place—a so-called Business One Stop website—as San Francisco, Los Angeles, and New Jersey have created. Yet what makes sense for humans does not make sense for how government works, and changing the website might not cut across institutional silos and well-worn boundaries between different agencies and authorities. Such reengineering can be difficult to accomplish, and when it is not, the insights developed through problem-based inquiry may go unused and then create greater frustration.

One stark example was the case of long-term-care facilities during the COVID-19 epidemic. Qualitative and quantitative analysis revealed the alarming rates of death in long-term-care facilities. Research at one long-term-care facility in King County, Washington, found that, by the time the first case of COVID-19 was identified in a staff member, 30 percent of residents already tested positive. Despite infection-control measures being put in place after case discovery, 64 percent of residents had a confirmed COVID-19 diagnosis within twenty-three days, 26 percent of whom had died. Nationally, limited US government data (only 80 percent of facilities reporting) showed that nearly twenty-six thousand nursing-home residents died from COVID-19 and more than sixty thousand fell ill.

But pointing out the problems to a largely for-profit industry did not lead to solving them fast enough. Quarantining and isolating patients is challenging in facilities with limited space. Staff members serve multiple residents often with limited access to personal protective equipment. Knowing the problems, even with the insights provided by human-centered design, is only the beginning of the process and not enough![64]

Privatizing Problem Solving Based on Human-Centered Design
The philanthropist Melinda Gates has spoken of human-centered design as the innovation that is changing the most lives in the developing world.[65] But while the idea of asking end users what they want seems intuitively right, there is another risk. The process is not without the risk that right-wing ideologues or probusiness libertarians will argue that governments (and even social innovators) should surrender the field to companies like IDEO, the design consultancy, or McKinsey, the management and strategy consultants, because these private firms are better suited to practice design thinking and solve the world's problems.

At the philanthropic behest of the family foundation of Amazon founder Jeff Bezos, for example, IDEO conducted extensive interviews with low-income parents, pediatricians, and child-development experts in order to develop approaches to encourage reading to young children and to strengthen early-childhood neurological and emotional development.[66] IDEO devised strategies, piloted in King County, Washington, and now in use in fourteen states, including exercises, activities, and an app, to help parents build reading skills during quotidian tasks like teeth brushing or laundry. Of course, we want to democratize the solving of public problems, and every sector should take on the challenge of bettering society; but some parts of the design-thinking movement display an antigovernment and proindustry undercurrent that threatens to replace public servants or even nonprofit public problem solvers with profit-maximizing consultants. "All too often," writes Eric Nee, editor in chief of the *Stanford Social Innovation Review*, "social innovation leaders have given up on creating positive social change through public sector institutions, and instead focus their efforts on creating nonprofit and for-profit organizations. . . . Government agencies often deserve criticism, but 'they will still be here after advocacy organizations lose their champions and philanthropy moves on to different priorities.'"[67]

Among the myriad risks of doing an end run around public institutions is that human-centered practices have to be equitable and sustained. That means talking with diverse citizens, not only those who are easy to find and engage with but those who are reluctant, and doing so both before and after a policy is crafted. If engaging with residents depends on someone paying the bill, there is a danger that human-centered design will be a limited and one-off response rather than an ongoing dialogue. For example, when the New York City Corrections Department hired McKinsey to help reduce the population at Rikers Island Prison, it did a round of interviews with corrections officials but did not speak to inmates, their families, or interest groups with deep knowledge of the situation. Relying only on consultants, especially management consultants, runs the risks that the problems defined, and the solutions adopted, will reflect what has been proposed elsewhere and the preferences of those who are paying the bills without taking the expertise of communities, especially communities of color and the poor, into account.

Human-Centered Designs Risk Being Everything and Nothing
If design thinking has been applied to everything from supporting democratic transition in Libya (unsuccessfully) to building an all-terrain wheel chair for under $200 (more successfully), and if all the people who seek to reshape cities, solve water crises, redo websites, and fix all the world's problems are now known as "designers," what does "design" really mean now? Has it become a catch-all for any form of problem solving?

A standard from the International Organization for Standardization, ISO 9241-210 (2010), claims to define human-centered design methods formally. After shelling out 138 Swiss francs for the document, you learn that a human-centered approach is based on an explicit understanding of users, tasks, and environments and that design is driven and refined by user-centered evaluation—in other words, vague and obvious observations.

Lucy Kimbell, a writer on design thinking, comments, "Even on a cursory inspection, just what design thinking is supposed to be is not well understood, either by the public or those who claim to practice it."[68] Kimbell may be right that trying to define and measure design thinking's processes and methods, or name its practitioners, is what Germans describe as "trying to nail a pudding to the wall." The confusion may help, ironically, to perpetuate a view that professional designers must run human-centered design practices instead of owning up to the fact that nondesigners can and do use these techniques quite regularly.

Bastardizing Qualitative Research

While treating human-centered design as the exclusive domain of professionals risks disenfranchising participants, relaxing standards also creates a different risk. Ethnography is fraught with challenges, especially if one attempts it without rigorous training in social scientific methods. After all, ethnography has its roots in academic anthropology, where practitioners like Margaret Mead and Branislaw Malinowski conducted multiyear studies in situ, amassing vast collections of notes.

University-based researchers are also trained in and required to comply with ethical rules on conducting research with human subjects. They learn how to seek informed consent, what is off-limits to do, and how to store and handle private information securely. Public problem solvers and public entrepreneurs are under no such constraints. They can interview and observe without any ethical guardrails or the oversight and accountability provided by a university institutional review board (IRB). A university IRB generally reviews and approves any research designs to ensure that they comply with ethical guidelines. But what is standard practice in the academy is not in other domains, creating the risk that well-meaning public problem solvers may behave irresponsibly in the name of human-centered research.

The popularization of human-centered design and short training courses in its practices risk giving short shrift to the process, whether by compressing the time or forgoing asking people in favor of observing them, and increases the ethical risk of overreliance on the results. There is also the danger that human-centered practitioners, unlike trained social scientists, will be content with interviewing a handful of people and call it quits. Compressing a method intended to unfold over time with a high degree of detailed work into a short project without regard for equity and inclusivity gives rise to the danger of ascribing meaning inaccurately.

Human-Centered Design Is Not Enough

The wild enthusiasm for design thinking may weaken attention to other forms of evidence gathering, especially the use of data-driven analysis to gain insight. Effective public entrepreneurs combine both individual-level, human-centered design and population-level data, as they are doing in Argentina to combat teen pregnancy.

As teen pregnancy rates rose over the past decade, despite increasing investment to keep them down, the Laboratorio del Gobierno team in Argentina used data analysis to identify, predict, and geotarget areas of the country with the highest risks. The team combined these data with user research, public consultation, and cocreation with teens from vulnerable populations in order to understand their perspective and bring their voices and expertise into program design. The team then convened all relevant ministries (social, education, and justice) to ensure that the insights would be shared.[69]

But many places only teach and practice human-centered techniques to the exclusion of other important, complementary methods. There is no empirical evidence yet whether those people who have taken WeGov's design courses in Brazil or the BizLabAcademy training programs in Australia but who have not learned other innovation skills like data-analytical ways of working are any better at solving problems.

Because design thinking is a core discipline in the program in which I teach at New York University, I regularly encounter students who consider the process of showing their website design to a few classmates for feedback to be both academically rigorous research and adequate evidence of a product's viability in the marketplace or in society. As I write this, I have just finished reading a master's thesis that proposes an app to solve a societal problem on the basis of the "evidence" of user testing with a handful of similarly situated classmates. Superficial ethnographic practices have substituted for any rigorous bench research. Human-centered design undertaken without regard for whom one is observing does not add up to real research, let alone predict the viability of a solution. Without complementary data analysis (chapter 6) and evidence review (chapter 8), the designers have not defined a problem adequately.

Especially in the context of a public sector that lacks numeracy and data-science skills, the hype about human-centered design can prompt a rush to embrace talking to ordinary people at the expense of using data or consulting with experts.

Bloomberg Philanthropies programs, for example, teach human-centered design to every level of government official, because the skill is both widely applicable and more easily learned than data science is. In contrast, it teaches data science to just a few people in certain roles in government, people whom the nonprofit has assessed to have the capacity and willingness to develop these analytical skills. While not everyone needs to know how to do both data analysis and human-centered design, everyone does need enough familiarity to be able to collaborate with those who possess the complementary skill one lacks.

Human-centered design can also fall short of its goals because the evidence that comes from interviewing those who are directly affected by a problem is often idiosyncratic, unreliable, and hard to interpret. Those who study how to use human psychology to change how people behave challenge the very notion that people know what they want and are able to articulate what either the problems or solutions are. After all, as Henry Ford famously said, "If I had asked people what they wanted, they would have said faster horses." Given the irrationality of human behavior, ethnographic methods may be necessary but not sufficient.[70]

Done right, user-centered design must usually be coupled with an analysis of relevant data.[71] For example, to design an intervention intended to improve educational outcomes, one wants test scores and demographic, health, and employment data, along with what one can learn from talking to teachers, parents, and students about what is wrong with their school district. The qualitative and quantitative complement each other, and to gather evidence effectively, it is essential to use both.

It Is Easy to Get Human-Centered Design Wrong
I cannot overemphasize that it is far too easy to talk to some people and call it human-centered design but to miss talking to the most marginalized, underrepresented, and needy, without which your problem definition is not complete. To start, it is essential to identify who the audience is and whether it is the right one. To design better services for business, one needs to talk to big *and* small companies, different professionals within those companies, businesses in different regions of the state, and the lawyers, accountants, and other professionals who serve them, as well as the frontline government workers involved in providing these services.

Doing a focus group or two with a few dozen people, especially if they are self-selected, may not be systematic or legitimate enough to gain real insight about the locations and intensity of a problem. Yet doing more might be unreasonably time-consuming and difficult to organize.

Furthermore, to make both design and delivery of a service equitable, we need to also observe and talk to those who do not receive the service. Finding those who are usually invisible to the administrative system can be difficult and require unusual tactics. When Policy Lab in Brooklyn works with the families of high-needs children in New York's school system to improve uptake of services, it has to go into schools and homes to figure out who is not getting served and why.[72]

Also, it is not enough to talk to people only at the outset of a project. For example, Philadelphia city officials talked to 221 people in an effort to redesign 134 forms and signs. But because the agencies did not go back and ask people using the forms after they were changed, we do not know how effective the changes were.[73]

Human-Centered Design Can Frustrate and Mislead

Finally, observing people and asking them about their problems says nothing about who decides. If, in the end, managers still decide how to spend money, wield power, and exercise control, human-centered design is window dressing that merely substitutes for participatory democracy.

Furthermore, human-centered processes can generate frustration by sometimes promising more than what can or even should be done. They can unduly raise expectations that what people say will be translated directly into policy. For example, talking to subway riders could create an unrealistic expectation that they will be provided with faster, more frequent, and better trains. They will learn soon enough that modernizing old infrastructure, if it happens at all, often requires taking tracks and trains out of service for a time or raising taxes on gas or other commodities to pay for such investments.

Asking people for problems or solutions that never get addressed or implemented may serve to produce more frustration and less trust in government—the very opposite of the purported goals of human-centered design. If you are going to learn from ordinary citizens, you must use what you learn.

Also, before starting, one has to decide whose perspective to adopt. Are you focusing on the citizen's experience in relation to a policy or to the use of a public service, or are you focusing on the experience from the perspective of the institution and its officials? The answer may be both. Being explicit about the distinctions between these inquiries will be key to interpreting what you are observing.

It can be difficult to get permission to conduct ethnographic studies. Once students in a class I taught at Yale Law School sought to design a computer tablet for use in connection with adult education among prisoners. They struggled to get approval to interview or observe either prisoners or prison staff. Department of Corrections officials were reluctant to let incarcerated individuals speak for themselves or to participate in the design process.

Having begun to define the problem to solve in chapter 3 and devoted this chapter to testing our assumptions about the problem with real people using face-to-face and online techniques, now chapter 6 will look at the use of data to round out our definition of the problem.

TO DO

There is no shortage of user-centered design methods and tools. Here we focus on a few of the participatory strategies for qualitative research, saving quantitative approaches for the next chapters. In order to refine the definition of a problem and begin to uncover solutions, we offer five approaches: developing a plan, identifying stakeholders, interviewing and observing, service blueprinting, and creating a wiki survey. Additional techniques, including Smarter Crowdsourcing, are discussed in the body of the chapter and online at https://solvingpublicproblems.org.

Exercise 1: Develop a Plan

1. *Articulate project goals.* What do you need to know to inform your problem definition?

2. *Research and sampling design.* Whom do you want to study? How many will be enough so that you are no longer surprised by what you learn?

3. *Recruit participants.* Who can help you talk to the people you identify in exercise 2?

4. *Conduct research.* What is the description of your research? How will you build trust?

5. *Interview and observation guide.* What are your questions? What are your activities?
6. *Collect and document.* How will you document your interviews?
7. *Draw insights and analysis.* What have you learned?
8. *Develop recommendations.* So what—why does what happened matter?

Exercise 2: Identify Stakeholders (adapted from The GovLab)
Which communities, organizations, and individuals have the know-how to define the problem statement? Brainstorm who needs to be asked. Make sure to include diverse kinds of people, including both average users and

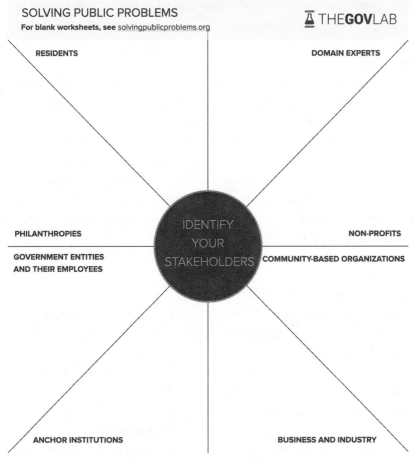

SOLVING PUBLIC PROBLEMS
For blank worksheets, see solvingpublicproblems.org

THE**GOV**LAB

RESIDENTS

DOMAIN EXPERTS

PHILANTHROPIES

NON-PROFITS

GOVERNMENT ENTITIES AND THEIR EMPLOYEES

COMMUNITY-BASED ORGANIZATIONS

IDENTIFY YOUR STAKEHOLDERS

ANCHOR INSTITUTIONS

BUSINESS AND INDUSTRY

Identifying stakeholders worksheet (Courtesy of The GovLab)

outliers, focusing in particular on those who are least likely to have been heard. Make sure you are hearing all viewpoints.

What follows is a nonexhaustive list of categories of people and groups to interview, observe, and consult with when seeking help identify-, ing, defining, and prioritizing among problems.[74] It can also be reused at other stages of problem solving, including solution finding and implementation.

This exercise is adapted from an older exercise by The GovLab on people-led innovation; however, it has been rewritten to better reflect real-world usage. Adapt it to your own needs to identify whom you need and want to consult. Use this list to build up a network of people you can turn to both for specific projects and on an ongoing basis to offer quality control and help gut-check your instincts.

Residents

These are inhabitants of the neighborhoods who are or will be affected and whose expertise is rooted in the experience of living in the community.

The experience of residents is particularly important for defining and prioritizing problems that will have the greatest impact on the community. Residents are also crucial to the effective implementation of any plan; their buy-in can help to ensure that solutions will have maximum impact.

How do you choose different types of residents? Consider segmenting between those in different places, those who are longer- and shorter-term residents, and those of differing economic classes, genders, races, ethnicities, and sexualities.

Domain Experts

This category includes researchers, consultants, and other specialists. See the discussion of Smarter Crowdsourcing in this chapter for a method for engaging with them.

Tapping into domain experts' knowledge can accelerate the ideation process and deepen understanding of the problem. These individuals possess in-depth knowledge that could be brought to bear for problem solving. It is vital to maintain a Rolodex of such people to help you over time when you need to know whether an idea is worth pursuing. You need to talk to several experts when doing due diligence in order to ensure that your understanding of the problem, as well as a proposed solution, reflects an up-to-date understanding of current research and practice.

How do you choose among them? Social scientists such as sociologists and anthropologists often have background on communities and their residents, as do urban planners and political scientists. Depending on the nature of the problem, technologists, designers, and data scientists might be of greater relevance. And of course, each problem can draw on expertise on specific subjects. Experts can be found in many places, and turning to nearby universities is one way to find them. The Provost's or President's Office can usually help identify experts on campus. See chapter 8 for other ideas for identifying experts. Trade-industry associations often have a research arm that employs experts, albeit with a distinct point of view. Consultancies are another avenue for sourcing experts.

Nonprofits

Nongovernmental organizations and not-for-profits are a distinct source of know-how.

NGOs bring extensive knowledge of and experience with a given problem area that would require years to piece together. Some organizations may be working directly in the problem area, and consulting them might accelerate understanding of the problem. They may also have direct relationships with the residents you want to reach.

How do you choose among them? Possible segmentation criteria include topical distinctions: economic development, legal, workforce training, research/academia, environmental, health, human rights, state, city, charitable, and faith-based. But more important is to assess which organizations are deeply embedded in the community, which have values that align with the agency, and of course, who will make a lot of noise and derail a project if they are not included.

Community-Based Organizations

Organizations that work in specific communities provide a uniquely relevant category.

Community-based organizations, like NGOs, have extensive knowledge of a problem area, but their expertise is focused on the needs of smaller geographic areas. Members of community-based organizations provide a unique perspective on the problem. They also have ties to other stakeholder groups, such as transient residents, who may be difficult to access.

How do you choose among them? As with nonprofits, there are different types (educational, economic [commerce], economic equality, environmental, human rights, health, faith-based) with differing levels of community involvement and interest.

Business and Industry

Small, medium, and large companies may also be worth consulting. The relevant audience could be owners, managers, or employees, depending on the issue.

Many policies and services affect the businesses that create jobs and economic growth in a community. Also, businesses employ people with domain knowledge that may be of great use. Enlightened companies will share a sense of vested self-interest in the well-being of the communities in which they are located, and involving them might help to bring more resources to bear on a problem.

How do you choose among them? These might be geographically based businesses (such as companies in a given place) or companies in a particular industry, depending on the nature of the problem. A company or set of companies might have particular influence over the region's economy (tech companies in Silicon Valley or coal companies in Lackawanna, for example), or companies might provide services that are relevant to the problem (such as those that sell to affected individuals).

Anchor Institutions

In this category, which overlaps with businesses and nonprofits, are institutions or businesses that play such an outsize role in the affected community's economy that they deserve special consideration. For instance, one community may be dominated by a single factory or served by a single hospital.

These *anchor institutions* are often the largest hiring entities in a given community, creating a big impact on workforce development and job growth. Policies that affect them will, in turn, deeply affect residents and other businesses. In addition, these anchor institutions often know the lay of the land and can advise on who's who regarding a particular issue.

How do you choose among them? These can be for- or not-for-profit employers or service-delivery entities, such as the major business in a company town or a university in a campus town. Other examples of potential anchor institutions are libraries, museums, hospitals, churches, and key nonprofits.

Governmental Entities and Their Employees

Often as important as talking to residents is talking to those who serve them, because they have firsthand understanding of the challenges of service delivery. Other jurisdictions are likely to have grappled with the same problem your jurisdiction is facing and have experimented with policies and services that will be of use to you.

How can they provide value? Not only are public officials immediately concerned with improving their communities, but they often know the constraints that determine what is feasible and meaningful, as well as how to translate solutions into policy. Career public servants, as distinct from shorter-term political appointees, often know what was previously tried, what worked, and what did not, and they have a clear sense of the organizational landscape within government, including who is working on what issue.

How do you choose among them? They might be elected officials and their staff, appointed officials and their staff, or civil servants in an executive, legislative, or judicial capacity.

Philanthropy

Foundations and charities have an interest in funding responses to the problem at issue.

These organizations often possess deep expertise about the project and have a good overview of who is doing what in the same space. They can also provide additional resources to fund solutions, and they may be open to more experimentation than are other participants in the project.

How do you choose among them? They might be foundations, philanthropies, corporate social responsibility officers from the private sector, or religious leaders.

Exercise 3: Responsible Interviewing and Observation

Before Bill Stumpf and Don Chadwick designed their famous Aeron chair, they asked office workers about their day. They also observed them sitting in chairs and discovered that they fidgeted a lot, not because their chairs were uncomfortable but because they were hot.[75] This insight led to the chair's unique mesh design.

Write down a series of questions and activities for your interviewees to last about an hour. Some of these might involve direct questions and others simply silent observation or an activity, such as narrating while the partici-pant does a task. Use a combination of short and long answer formats. Consider yes/no questions followed by open-ended questions about why people have that view. Evaluate each question, asking yourself, "What am I hoping to learn by asking this?" Make sure to test your questions with a few people to help you improve the questions.

Interacting with people. Ask people to be specific and elicit more detail by asking them to tell a story or give an example. Be sure to tell people how you plan to use the information they share with you. People are more likely to give their time and respond to questions if they know their input will be relevant and have impact on decision-making.

Collecting and documenting. You will need to be equipped to gather data. You will need a notebook or a laptop but perhaps also a digital pen that automatically transcribes your notes, a digital camera, and an audio re-corder or phone, as well as programs such as Evernote for managing and later sorting observations. When interviews are conducted online, they can be automatically recorded to a remote cloud or to your computer.

Drawing insights and analysis. Throughout the process, endeavor to summarize and unify your observations. The methodologists Barney Gla-ser and Anselm Strauss lay out a four-part framework to describe what you are learning: (1) interactions among actors, (2) conditions of these interac-tions, (3) strategies and tactics actors employ, and (4) consequences.[76]

Developing recommendations. In the end, your analysis is not designed to answer the question "What happened?" but "So what—why does what happened matter?" Drawing those conclusions and using them to rewrite your problem definition is valuable to do both alone and in groups together with those you are interviewing as well as other public entrepreneurs. Hav-ing to talk through the evolution of the problem statement helps with refin-ing and improving it.

For additional suggestions on how to conduct user research, check out the UK government's User Research Service Manual, at https://www.gov.uk/service-manual/user-research/.

Exercise 4: Make a Service Blueprint Collaboratively
To create a process map of the service experience, use interviews and sur-veys of individuals and groups to record the following:[77]

1. Customer actions: the steps a customer must take in chronological order to receive the service
2. Employee actions: the steps an employee must take in chronological order to deliver the service
3. Face-to-face contact: any live interactions that are part of that process
4. Virtual contact: any phone calls or web-based interactions that need to take place
5. Support processes: additional interactions, including interaction with anyone who is not a contact employee but is necessary for the service to be provided
6. Conditions: the conditions under which the service is provided, for example, the physical condition of the office

Use this process map or blueprint to find the points of failure and to engage in preemptive problem solving.[78]

Exercise 5: Create a Wiki Survey Using All Our Ideas
Matt Salganik, a Princeton sociology professor and the designer of All Our Ideas (http://www.allourideas.org), offers a few recommendations for how to use a survey wiki successfully.[79] Here is an amalgamation of his advice and my own about setting up a good wiki survey. An expanded version is available online.

1. Make Sure You Have Enough Ideas

Try to come up with at least fifty ideas. Without enough content, the process is not engaging or dynamic enough for participants. Make sure content is in a common format. In other words, if the goal is to get help defining the problem, then make sure all the statements describe problems.

2. Advertise

If you build it, people still will not come unless you advertise the opportunity to participate. When we worked with AARP to run a wiki survey on big health data, the organization sent notices to millions of people through its newsletters. If you do not have that kind of reach, however, you can still get the word out. Consider using a newsletter, an email, online ads, offline fliers, word of mouth through other leaders in your community who could announce or tweet, or an op-ed or media coverage to raise awareness. When the Office of Innovation in New Jersey wanted to reach out to workers in the state to inquire about their concerns about the impact of technology on the future of work, my colleagues convened a group of over forty interest groups for a call, asking them to help spread the word. We reached four thousand people in three weeks.

3. Make It Relevant

Whether using All Our Ideas or setting up your own site, make sure to explain to people why you want their feedback and how you plan to use it, along with directions for what to do. For example, here is what we wrote for AARP:

> Your voice matters. AARP wants to hear from you! The ideas below are opportunities and challenges arising from the greater use of data in healthcare. AARP wants to know what you think about how health data should be used and protected.

> Share your opinions and help us learn the priorities of people 50 and older when it comes to big health data. We will use this information to inform our thinking and to serve as the basis for developing solutions that can address challenges and take advantage of opportunities.

> You will be presented with a series of two-option questions. Tell us which, between the two options, is your greater concern. These options might be dangers from the use of data or from the failure to use data.

> Answer as many (or as few) two-option questions as you like . . . or add your own option! The more you tell us, the better we can understand the possible challenges of big health data together.

4. Test first

Testing and iterating can be valuable. Therefore, before launching a large wiki survey, create a test version and have a small number of people participate.

CHAPTER SIX

Understanding Problems Using Data

Not everything that can be counted counts, and not everything that counts can be counted.

William Bruce Cameron, Informal Sociology

DATA-ANALYTICAL WAYS OF WORKING

At a press conference on April 6, 2020, Governor Phil Murphy of New Jersey spoke about the central role that data played in responding to the coronavirus pandemic in the state.

> When we began our first discussions for responding to this emergency as far back as January, well more, by the way, than a month before our first case of COVID-19 was ever confirmed, we knew that our best chance of getting out in front and staying in front would require a data-driven approach. . . . We would not leave anything to chance, or rely on anecdotal evidence, to the very best of our abilities. We knew that only an objective, fact-based and as I said, Moneyball approach, would get us through this. And it is through this approach that our aggressive stance on social distancing has taken shape. That's an important point to note here. We didn't just pick social distancing because it seemed like it might be a good idea to try. We did it based on the facts, based on historical and current facts. . . . We have built a strong modeling program that we can use with great and increasing confidence.[1]

Lacking employees trained in data science except a handful of (albeit very talented) individuals in the state's epidemiology unit, the state turned to a network of volunteer data scientists from universities to complement the existing team.

Publishing and visualizing data and predictive analytics made it possible to see in stark relief the differences between those jurisdictions that responded swiftly and early to the outbreak and those that did not. Seeing the curve rise or flatten drove home the ability to understand the impact of social distancing on infection rates. Modeling viral prevalence and spread made it possible to decide when and how to reopen businesses and public places and where to send ventilators and respirators. Collaborating with university-based data scientists and machine-learning experts with the skills to analyze large quantities of raw data made it possible to appreciate the disparate impact on communities of color and long-term-care facilities and to tailor responses (and to recognize how much data we lacked to be able to understand on-the-ground conditions).

The ability to make decisions, such as where to put testing sites or how many contact tracers to hire, required the availability of data. The asset of accurate data made it possible to target interventions, improve policy responses, and minimize preventable illness and death.

It is not enough, however, to have access to data; one must be willing to use good data and sound models as part of a broader problem-solving process that also takes on-the-ground conditions into account. Data-analytical techniques are a vital way to develop the evidence base to define and understand the problem with specificity. Whether it is quantifying the impact of period poverty (being too poor to afford menstrual supplies) in Jaipur on the education of girls or measuring the public-health impact of child labor in Mexico City or tracking COVID infection rates in New Jersey, without data (combined with engagement) you cannot measure if you are solving a problem.

While states eventually stepped up to lead a data-driven charge against COVID-19, initially they took their cue from the federal government, which ignored the data. Although President Trump received his first COVID-19 briefings in January, he did not act on them until March. In fact, a study from Columbia University in May 2020 found that had social distancing policies been enacted a week earlier, it could have saved thirty-six thousand American lives, and two weeks earlier would have saved fifty-four thousand.[2] The federal government also cooked up spurious predictions to justify its positions. The Council of Economic Advisers even developed a "model"—debunked by economists and epidemiologists alike—predicting incorrectly that deaths would drop to zero on May 15.[3] There were widespread allegations of data doctoring by the White House throughout the pandemic.

Thus, although COVID-19 drove home the importance of evidence-based decision-making—that action without evidence is worthless—it also highlighted the fact that numbers, by themselves, are not a panacea. Evidence without action, too, is worthless. Even in New Jersey, for example, where we have the data about disproportionate deaths in long-term-care facilities, the industry and public-health officials did not take adequate actions, and people may have died needlessly. Thus, data analytics must be viewed as one extremely important, but only one, asset in a problem-solving process that combines (legitimate) analysis of (good) data with human-centered approaches. There are good examples, especially on the part of cities, of combining participatory and data-analytical strategies to solve problems.

New Orleans has one of the highest murder rates of any city in the nation. Determined to change this dismal statistic, the then-mayor, Mitch Landrieu, in 2012 created a unit in city government that was called the Innovation Team, or i-Team. Using more than fifty years of data grouped by neighborhood and by rates of murder, crime, educational attainment, unemployment, and recidivism, the team uncovered a significant correlation between unemployment and violent crime (and thus recidivism). The data showed that a small and identifiable set of people in a few neighborhoods committed a majority of murders, usually as the result of petty disputes.[4]

That knowledge produced significant change. Municipal agencies instituted various programs to train and hire ex-offenders in an effort to reduce the likelihood of reoffending among those who had been incarcerated.[5] A range of strategies was used, from more social services and job opportunities to threats of prosecution, using data to know where to target which approach. The first year saw a 19 percent reduction in the murder rate from 2012. Two years in, the rate declined by 25 percent. Between 2018 and 2019, the rate fell another 18 percent. New Orleans murder rates in 2019, though still among the highest in the country (30.7 per 100,000), were at their lowest level in almost fifty years.[6] (Unfortunately, most major cities saw an uptick in 2020.)

In 2015 in Boston, ambulance response times were unacceptably low. As in New Orleans, public officials looked at data in order to understand the problem and its causes. After analyzing types of emergencies, routes, and response times using 911 calls, they found that a 20 percent increase in call volume over the past ten years had pushed up the median first-responder response time for the most serious cases from 5.5 minutes in 2009 to 6.8 minutes in 2015.[7] To reduce times, Mayor Marty Walsh launched a data-driven initiative to change the way ambulances were deployed. The number of ambulances was increased, and a Community Assistance Team was created to take the load off ambulances by connecting substance abusers and other people in crisis to social services, rather than simply transporting them to a hospital.[8] Within just a year, response times had dropped to 6.3 minutes.[9]

Adding quantitative research allowed these cities to improve outcomes. These examples are among thousands of recent stories of how governments are turning to quantitative analysis and mining newly available data in order to improve how policies are crafted and services are delivered. Governments, non- and for-profits, and public problem solvers are using data to spot inefficiencies and to spot positive deviants—those examples of what is working particularly well—that they can replicate.

Government has always collected data, and even Article I of the Constitution mandates the collection of census data. Nevertheless, the adoption of data-driven practices reflects a relatively new way of working that seeks to collect, analyze, use, and share data not simply to comply with requirements but to effect rapid change and performance improvement.[10]

When our goal is problem solving, we recognize the important role that data can play in helping us to define the problem. When we are public entrepreneurs and we use data, the "result is a smarter and nimbler government that better employs its resources and attention," write the Harvard professors Stephen Goldsmith and Susan Crawford in their book *The Responsive City: Engaging Communities through Data-Smart Governance.*[11] The process of problem solving increasingly depends on continuous collection and analysis of big data to enable more accurate problem definition.[12]

However, while data-science programs are proliferating across universities, the traditional training academies for public administration—public affairs and public policy schools—do not regularly train graduates in data science. Of the top twenty-five public policy schools as ranked by *U.S. News and World Report* in 2019, none required students to take even basic coursework in data science.[13] In a proposal to create a data-science curriculum for prospective public administrators at Cornell University's Institute for Public Affairs, authors Elizabeth Day, Maria Fitzpatrick, and Thomas O'Toole argue, "If policy analysts cannot work with data scientists to create systems adequately designed to address policy needs, those systems will never be created. To create and implement policy effectively will require all public servants and people in public affairs–related occupations to truly understand data's promise and pitfalls, and how to use it effectively."[14]

It is not surprising, therefore, that in a 2014 survey of 283 federal employees, 78 percent of respondents said that data were integral to their roles, but more than 60 percent reported that their agencies were either ineffective or only somewhat effective at using data.[15]

In a 2019 survey that my colleagues and I conducted of four hundred local officials in the United States, *only a third said they had used the skill of data-analytical thinking in their work.* A further third said they could explain what it was but had not used it. I also worked with an Australian colleague at Monash University to survey public servants in Australia. We found that while 59 percent said they had used the skill of data-analytical thinking and 25 percent said they had received formal training in it, only 60 percent of those who claimed to use the skill said they knew how to formulate a hypothesis, the first step in data analysis. A further 68 percent said they knew how to identify the data needed to test a hypothesis.[16] In other words, there are questionable gaps in people's knowledge. This shortcoming in data literacy is not unique to the public sector. A 2018 LinkedIn Workforce Report found that the demand for data scientists was "off the charts" and that there were more than 151,000 data-scientist jobs going unfilled across the United States.[17]

In this chapter, we dive in to explore how to use data critically and in a responsible way as part of your problem-solving process.

GETTING SMART FROM DATA AND PEOPLE: WHY DATA ARE NOT ENOUGH

While we want to get away from defining problems on the basis of anecdotes or impressions, we must take care not to assume that big data is somehow "better" at portraying the problem. Data analysis must always be complemented by "talking to humans." Becoming evidence based cannot be an excuse for avoiding people's lived experience, especially as we all too often lack data about those who are most in need. Complex problems benefit from the use of both kinds of data. We need the "thicker" data that come from human-centered design and assessment of individual experiences, combined with the bigger data that come from population-level analysis. Together, the two sources tell us more about why a problem is occurring than one source does by itself.

In both the Boston and New Orleans examples, responsible officials combined data-driven approaches with human-centered and participatory initiatives in order to develop a more robust evidence base for defining the problem. The New Orleans i-Team sat down with law enforcement, social services agencies, educators, and above all, residents themselves.

In Boston, the analysts did not just crunch numbers but also rode with paramedics and found that "modeling data alongside the people whose work it represented led to some impactful insights."[18] The data modeling along with observations and interviews—officials talking and working with the public—generated the proposal to create the successful Community Assistance Team discussed earlier.

Chapter 5 focused on how to observe, talk to, and collaborate with experts, namely, residents, academics, and business leaders, using ethnographic and human-centered practices in order to better understand a problem. This chapter examines how quantitative methods—data analyses—are also essential to understanding the problem we are solving, especially when done in collaboration with others.

Because not every public problem solver has sophisticated data-science tools and skills, we emphasize simple techniques as well as participatory and collaborative approaches for working with others to collect and analyze good data, lest those who work in and for our own communities be at a disadvantage to large nonprofits, consultancies, and others who can afford to employ an army of data scientists.

By working together and involving distributed groups of people in data analysis, public problem solvers and public entrepreneurs can leverage data as much as any private company can. Former US chief performance officer Shelley Metzenbaum points out that the delivery company UPS uses the data it collects from its truck drivers to give insights back to truck drivers to "enable front-line drivers to deliver packages quickly, affordably, courteously, and in good condition." But, Metzenbaum asks, "Who does the equivalent in government? Who reviews and packages analytics, and the findings of well-designed pilots, so that the second largest group of government workers—those working in hospitals and health care—can learn from their own and others' experience how to improve health and reduce health-system-acquired illness and injury? Who helps front-line Social Security, Veterans Administration, and social workers in every level of government learn from data, analytics, and measured trials so that they can provide continually better services and benefits?"[19]

Of course, data analysis does not weave magic, and its promise of objective certainty can mislead. Only when it is combined with human-centered design and participatory practices can it produce a well-rounded and realistic picture of a problem and its causes. People are as essential as numbers to data-analytical methods. They offer an on-the-ground perspective to complement abstract graphs and charts. And, of course, sometimes we need people power to collect or analyze data.

For example, Mapaton CDMX was a program that sought to map Mexico City's system of twenty-nine thousand microbuses (*peseros*). In two weeks in 2016, *pesero* riders mapped almost the entire system using a specially created app. Participants who mapped the most *pesero* routes earned cash and other prizes. With the data in hand, innovators were able to create an SMS-based service that allows a commuter to enter an origin and destination and get route information. Collaboration with the community and among the thirty-five managing NGOs that analyzed the information is what made the data so useful.

Similarly, residents of Flint, Michigan, worked with the city to gather data to produce the city's land-use map. The population had fallen by more than 50 percent from its peak in 1960, leaving the city with many vacant homes and empty lots. Nearly 40 percent of properties are blighted. The city developed a plan to address urban blight, but Flint public servants did not have the resources or data to carry it out. Instead, the city created the Flint Property Portal, a website that allowed residents to collect and report data about blighted properties. Community groups have completed a census of all fifty-six thousand properties in Flint. This information helped the city to apply for and receive a $60 million blight-elimination grant from the US Treasury's Hardest Hit Fund.[20] Perhaps most importantly, this collaboration between government and citizens produced a transparent picture of conditions in the city and empowered residents by involving them in solving a serious problem.

DATA, DATA EVERYWHERE

Digitization has made it dramatically easier for an ever-wider range of people, with or without extensive technical skills, to collect, analyze, and use information. Even individual social innovators and nonprofits, as well as small towns and cities, benefit from the use of data. And the quantities of data do not need to be enormous to be of use. Even small and nonrepresentative data sets can shed light on a problem, as we shall discuss.

However, before we explore the transformation toward more evidence-based institutions and practices, we need to understand why this transition is happening now and why many media headlines have described the current decade as the era of big data.

"Big data" refers to extremely large data sets that are too big to be stored or processed using traditional means. Over the past decade, new technologies of collection, storage, transmission, visualization, and analysis have generated a huge proliferation of data sets collected by public and private entities about everything from health and wellness to phone and purchase records.

These data provide powerful raw material for problem solving and the creation of tools that can further the public interest. The "big" in "big data" comes from the "3Vs"—increasing *volume, velocity,* and *variety,* credited to the Gartner consultant Doug Laney from a 2001 report; Laney wrote, "Big data is high-volume, -velocity and -variety information assets that demand cost-effective, innovative forms of information processing for enhanced insight and decision making."[21]

First, the term "big data" reflects a huge rise in data volume. In 2015, 12 zettabytes—that is, 12×10^{21} of data—were created worldwide. By 2025, that number is forecast to reach 163 zettabytes. For comparison, the entire Library of Congress is only 15 terabytes, and it takes 1 billion terabytes to get to 1 zettabyte. It is no wonder that data volume is increasing when Tinder users swipe the app 1.6 billion times and 1.59 billion people log onto Facebook every day.[22] These are among the many sources of data that are collected continuously and thus provide not only quantity but a high degree of granularity.

Second, data velocity—the speed at which data are generated, analyzed, and utilized—is increasing. Today, data are generated in near real time, created by humans in credit card sales, social media interaction, and so on and captured by machines using different types of sensors. People are interacting thousands of times a day with data-collecting devices. Much of these data are *designed data*, meaning that they were collected for statistical and analytical purposes. But large quantities of data are also *found data* (also known as *data exhaust*) that were collected for something other than research but have proven susceptible to analysis.[23] Of course, all data were collected for a purpose, but the eventual use may be quite different from the original reason for which they were collected. For example, JPMorgan Chase Institute uses financial services data, including credit card purchase records, to analyze and comment on the future of companies that are part of the online platform economy, such as Uber and Lyft.[24]

Third, big data are varied. Data come in many formats including numbers, text, images, voice, and video. Some data are organized in traditional databases with predefined fields such as phone numbers, zip codes, and credit card numbers. However, more and more data are unstructured— they do not come preorganized in traditional spreadsheet-style formats but helter-skelter as Twitter postings, videos, and so forth. According to some estimates, unstructured data account for more than 95 percent of all data generated today.[25] Nevertheless, contemporary analytical methods make it possible to search, sort, and spot patterns in unstructured data, even without a predefined idea of what to look for.

Another important characteristic of diverse data is that they are collected without people's knowledge. When I conduct a traditional survey or poll, respondents are aware that they are being studied and may change their behavior, responding to what they think the pollster wants to hear. But much digital data collected from diverse sources can be studied without people self-consciously biasing the results. For example, Seth Stephens-Davidowitz's work on racism reuses search-engine queries to get a picture of racial animus across the United States. By studying where such racially charged search queries occurred, Stephens-Davidowitz found that this indicator was a robust predictor of President Obama's 2012 election results in those places.[26]

THE VALUE OF DATA COLLECTION AND ANALYSIS

Data collection can be focused on the past, present, or future. Each viewpoint offers useful insights about us, our workforce, our society, and the economy. We measure what we value and value what we measure.

By analyzing data, policy makers can understand *past* performance of public policies and services, evaluating both their efficiency and impact on different populations. The economists Raj Chetty, Nathaniel Hendren, and Lawrence Katz studied twenty years of income records from families that moved to new neighborhoods using the Housing Choice Voucher Program. They discovered that these families earned significantly higher incomes, completed more education, and were less likely to become single parents than were peers who stayed in their neighborhoods. Citing this research, the Department of Housing and Urban Development overhauled the formula that it had used for four decades to calculate rental assistance and increased opportunities for families to move to low-poverty areas from high-poverty areas.[27]

Larger quantities of data also enable the delivery of more tailored interventions in the *present* by helping governments to match people to benefits to which they are entitled or to assistance they need. For example, Louisiana's Department of Health uses Supplemental Nutrition Assistance Program (SNAP) enrollment data to sign up people for health benefits. Of nearly 900,000 SNAP recipients, Louisiana has enrolled 105,000 in Medicaid without a separate application process, relying on a four-question, yes-or-no survey. This approach has helped some of the state's poorest residents get access to benefits, while saving the state about $1.5 million in administrative costs.[28]

Better access to data even helps with forecasting *future* outcomes, such as who is likely to be a frequent visitor to the emergency room, thereby enabling more targeted interventions and treatment. In New York, the Fire Department and the city's first-of-its-kind analytics team under the leadership of Mike Flowers created the FireCast algorithm to use data from across the city government to help the FDNY identify buildings with the highest fire risks.[29] Predictive models also help governments to slow the spread of disease by identifying how many people a disease will potentially infect, how far and how quickly the disease will spread, what areas and people are at highest risk, and when they are most at risk. During the COVID-19 outbreak, many jurisdictions started using "symptom trackers," simple software tools to enable people to report their symptoms and share that data with public-health officials. Especially in the absence of effective testing data, a symptom tracker provides an early-warning mechanism, signaling where people are complaining of coughs and fevers. This enables emergency officials to anticipate the need for equipment, supplies, and hospital beds in the not too distant future.

DATA ARE CHANGING HOW WE DEFINE PROBLEMS

Truths that policy makers have taken for granted for decades are now being overturned or confirmed by new data. The result is often stronger policies, programs, and interventions.

Spotting Mistakes with Data

Data enable us to spot mistakes, outliers, and rare events. It is not necessary for data to be a representative sample of the population. If we are looking to generalize about a large group on the basis of a smaller group, then we might need a representative sample. But if the goal is simply to measure and spot problems in a given group, then nonrepresentative data may be wholly adequate.

Pittsburgh has equipped municipal vehicles with data-gathering sensors to provide the raw material for spotting potholes—a big improvement on the current practice of having public-works personnel search for them.[30] In New York, by examining some of the city's taxi data, the analyst Ben Wellington was able to identify a radical disparity between two different types of cabs that led to one set of drivers being paid a much-smaller amount in tips. One taxi company's on-board computer was calculating tips on the basis of the base fare of the ride, while others were calculating the tip on the basis of the gross fare, including fees and tolls.

Wellington also looked at data on parking tickets and discovered that a handful of hydrants were earning the city a huge chunk of revenue each year, as drivers parked too close to them. One plum spot was the result of bad markings that made the spot seem legal. Wellington pointed out the problem to the city, and officials, to their credit, changed the markings to clarify the rules, even if it meant losing revenue.

Improving Effectiveness with Data

Ultimately, the goal of using data is to produce a more precise definition of a problem that will enable us to craft better policies, design more effective services, and save money.[31] If our plan of attack is based on data, it is more likely to solve the problem because it addresses the problem's empirical root causes.

For instance, rat infestations in large cities are difficult to tackle because rats travel in virtually unpredictable ways. In 2011, Chicago's rat problem peaked when it received more than twenty-five thousand rodent complaints via 311 calls (notifications from residents about problems needing attention) in that year alone. This call-center information generated a novel database that offered a deeper understanding of the day-to-day patterns of rat infestations.[32]

In search of a new strategy, the city partnered with Daniel Neill, a computer scientist at what at the time was Carnegie Mellon University's Event and Pattern Detection Lab (now at NYU). Together, they gathered twelve years of 311 citizen-complaint data, including information on rat sightings, along with related factors such as overflowing trash bins, food-poisoning cases, tree debris, and building vacancies. The 311 system "constructs a collaborative relationship between city residents and government operations," writes the public affairs professor Daniel T. O'Brien. "Residents act as the 'eyes and ears of the city,' reporting problems that they observe in their daily movements."[33]

The city and the university quickly discovered that 311 calls related to food (prevalence of restaurants) and shelter (indications of population density) were the strongest predictors of rat infestations. Areas where residents called about sanitation violations or tree debris were good predictors of rodents. They then built a model to predict spikes in rodent complaints days before an infestation would happen. The model was shared with Chicago's sanitation department, and targeted rodent-baiting services trialed in 2013. After running Neill's model that year, the city of Chicago claimed this method to be 20 percent more effective than traditional baiting methods for catching rats. In July 2013, Mayor Rahm Emanuel announced that residents' requests for rodent-control services had dropped by 15 percent in the previous year.[34] Chicago continues to encourage citizens to make 311 calls to report infestations, which helps to improve the accuracy of the model.

Given the prevalence of data collection, how do we now make use of it? How do we think about data to define the problem better, especially if we are not trained data scientists? How do we define our question, identify what data are available to us, and draw inferences from the data that we can rely on?[35]

Telling a Story with Data
As the blogger and medical doctor John Byrne writes, "The ability to tell stories likely led to tremendous survival advantages for those early human groups that achieved it. . . . A tribe whose members could relate their indi-

vidual experiences about the location of food or predators would be expected to survive in greater numbers."[36] Yet while good stories about individual journeys and struggles naturally move us, they are not so good for explaining the problems of our complex society. We need to be able to see the trends and patterns that emerge when we compare whole populations.

Although some people might consider data dry and abstract, whether the data set is big or small, entrepreneurial individuals and organizations are turning to data, especially with the benefit of data visualization, to tell a more informed story about the problems they are trying to solve. Both the US gross domestic product (GDP) and the national unemployment statistics, while hopelessly flawed measures, tell an important story about national economic well-being. On a more local level, the data scientist Ben Wellington, explaining his work analyzing New York taxicab data, tells a story about on-the-ground conditions in Manhattan. The city collects data about each taxi trip, including start and end time and location, fare, and tip. Just after 5:00 a.m. on a weekday, cabs are traveling at an average of twenty-four miles an hour. But by 8:30 in the morning, they are going at eleven miles an hour, and the speed stays that way all day. The task of a public entrepreneur is to solve the problem of "rush day," not rush hour.

Similarly, if we want to learn where tourists go in New York, we can try using data from parking tickets. By looking only at out-of-state license plates, we can look at where people tend to go—midtown Manhattan, not surprisingly. However, Californians rack up more tickets in Williamsburg and other hipster parts of Brooklyn.

Data storytelling does not depend on high tech. In India, the civil-society group Mazdoor Kisan Shakti Sangathan (MKSS) turns such statistical data collection into a storytelling opportunity. The group paints government budgets on the walls of villages in the state of Rajasthan and holds theatrical readings of the information to define a problem of "bridges built to nowhere."[37] Its work enables these communities to point out wasted public investment. Ultimately, data collection is vital to life in a democracy because it allows us to be counted and therefore represented.

Enhancing Equity with Data
Increasingly, data can play a role in promoting equity and fighting inequality. Rashida Richardson, director of policy research at the New York University's AI Now Institute, comments that inequality and bias persist because

discrimination is "embedded into our social and legal systems and structures. Thus, it is difficult for most people to see and understand how bias and inequalities have been automated or operationalized over time."[38] Data can help to lay bare what is hidden in plain sight, such as disparate rates of police violence, incarceration, or economic outcome based on race, gender, or other protected categories.

Looking at local government data about public works in Zanesville, Ohio, revealed a fifty-year pattern of discriminatory water-service provision. While access to clean water from the city water line spread throughout the rest of Muskingum County, residents of the predominantly African American area of Zanesville were only able to use contaminated rainwater or to drive to the nearest water tower and truck water back to their homes. Opening and visualizing the data laid the truth bare and led to a successful civil rights lawsuit against Zanesville in 2008.[39]

Groups like Data for Black Lives (http://d4bl.org) use data science to improve the lives of Black people. EqualHealth (http://www.equalhealth. org) uses data to measure disparate public-health impacts on the basis of race. Organized by the Urban Institute, the National Neighborhood Indicators Partnership (https://www.neighborhoodindicators.org) connects partners in more than thirty cities to share neighborhood-level data to the end of advancing equity in communities. The Human Rights Data Analysis Group (https://hrdag.org/) uses data to study human-rights violations. Our Data Bodies (https://www.odbproject.org/) works on data privacy and digital data collection in marginalized neighborhoods in Charlotte, North Carolina; Detroit, Michigan; and Los Angeles, California.

Data-driven journalists and researchers are using new sources of information to report on systemic racism and disparate impacts. The *Washington Post*'s "Fatal Force" project documents fatal shootings by police. ProPublica's "Documenting Hate" project is a collaboration between two hundred professional newsrooms, college papers, and journalism schools to document hate crimes around the United States. The National Institutes of Health and the community of Jackson, Mississippi, are using environmental and genetic data to study cardiovascular disease and health disparities among African Americans.[40] The Centers for Disease Control of the federal government is reporting widely disparate impacts of COVID-19 on the basis of race. Blacks are 4.7 times more likely than Whites to be hospitalized, and Latinos are 4.6 times more likely, with Blacks also more than twice as likely to die. But even these data are still very incomplete.[41]

DEFINING A HYPOTHESIS

Using data analytics to address a policy starts with defining a problem that is capable of being acted on and that matters to the community and those who are working on the project. As I also discuss in chapter 4, from the statement of the problem, we can formulate a hypothesis: a testable proposition that something is caused by one or more of the root causes outlined in the problem definition, which that data can help us to validate.[42] Although you should also talk to relevant audiences to ascertain whether the hypothesis expressed in the problem statement is true, you can also use data to prove or disprove the definition of the problem.

Before trying to determine what data to use, it is essential to "establish a clear understanding of the problem to be addressed by a given analytics project," argues the Civic Analytics Network, a community of urban chief data officers organized by Harvard University's Ash Center for Democratic Governance and Innovation. "Data-driven policymaking is not data use for the sake of data use. After working with departments to identify a mission-critical problem, analytics experts or data scientists can proceed with identifying data readiness, scoping and piloting the project, and so on."[43]

Having identified a problem, therefore, try defining it as a hypothesis by writing down why you think it is happening. You may hypothesize that children are skipping school because their parents are taking them on off-season holidays to Disney World, that unemployment is increasing because robots are replacing workers, or that the rate of starting new businesses is decreasing because interest rates are increasing and therefore the cost of capital is going up. A hypothesis can be formulated as an "if . . . then" statement: "*If* parents are taking their children to Disney World, *then* they are skipping school."

The analyst needs to work closely with stakeholders and the relevant implementing agency to make sure the hypothesis is well defined and compelling.[44] Both public and private stakeholders are more likely to share data needed to prove a hypothesis when they are presented with a well-defined, important, and agreed-on problem to be solved. Arriving at a shared and consensual definition of the problem requires both public entrepreneurs and stakeholders to define the hypothesis together. Thus, try to be specific with regard to who is affected, when, and how.

Often a hypothesis includes a theory about the best way to solve the problem. Because the root cause of poor health is a lack of attention to lifestyle choices such as diet, smoking, and alcohol consumption, perhaps we hypothesize that we can improve health care by spending more on preventive medicine, such as annual checkups, than on after-the-fact procedures. Indeed, analysis by the Centers for Disease Control and Prevention shows that each diabetic patient whose condition receives preventive treatment reduces health-care costs by $6,394 (in 2017 dollars) because of fewer hospital admissions.[45]

A well-formulated hypothesis helps to define the search for data, and at the same time, background research and data can make defining a hypothesis easier. Getting familiar with the relevant data can make it easier to formulate the question. For example, coming up with a hypothesis about preventive medicine depends, first, on knowing the statistics about preventable diseases and the relationship between diet and morbidity. That is why formulating the hypothesis often needs to be done and redone after data have been gathered and analyzed. Identifying what data to use to test a hypothesis is essential to defining a specific and concrete problem, to which we turn next.

IDENTIFYING THE DATA

A plethora of data is available to assist us in defining a problem. The data may not always be clean, current, or complete, but more information becomes accessible every day. One kind is information collected by government and then openly published for free reuse.

Among the government's many roles, it gathers information from companies, universities, hospitals, and more in its role as regulator; it tracks statistics about the economy and society in its role as policy maker, and it collects data from citizens in its role as a provider of public goods and services and administrator of the decennial census.

For example, the United States routinely collects large amounts of information about national weather patterns, demographics, and geography. There is no single statistical agency in the United States. Rather, multiple departments collect, analyze, and increasingly share data. To increase transparency and accountability, governments also generate and sometimes publish data about their own operations—such as budgeting and spending data.

Open Data

Governments, companies, universities, and other organizations are all increasingly making their data available to the public. Although government has always collected data, what distinguishes open data from other types of data, such as health, police, or other individual records, sometimes known as "administrative data," is that open data are publicly available, can be freely accessed and used, and are capable of being processed by a machine. Unlike administrative data, open data are generally population-level, whole data sets such as census records, environmental safety records, or workforce data.

To be open, data must be technically accessible—available in a form that a computer can access and use—and legally accessible: licensed in such a way that anyone can use and reuse the information without fee or restriction.

When these conditions are satisfied, anyone with the right tools, whether they are the data owner or not, can create sophisticated and useful tools and conduct analysis across data sets, with the potential to increase the public good.

For example, Mejora Tu Escuela (Improve Your School) is an online platform that publishes government data about Mexico's schools. Created by the Mexico Institute of Competitiveness (IMCO), the website provides parents with comparative academic data so that they can compare their school's results to others, thereby empowering them to demand better-quality education. It also publishes expenditure data, giving activists, administrators, policy makers, and journalists the means to dig deeper, to spot fraud and corruption, and to advocate for change.[46]

This is exactly what happened in 2014, when a report by IMCO revealed that more than fourteen hundred teachers on the public-school payroll were supposedly older than a hundred years old (with most having the same birthday) and that many earned more than the president of Mexico, revealing that money was being embezzled through the creation of these fictional teachers.[47] The story illustrates the power of open, free, and downloadable data.

Federal authorities had required states to provide information about the condition of schools, payrolls, and other expenditures. Civil-society activists at IMCO then created the platform to make that information accessible to citizens. They also scrutinized that information, ultimately exposing hidden and rampant malfeasance. Although the government initially prevaricated, claiming clerical error, a media frenzy over the website helped to prompt reform and a shift of responsibility over education from states to the federal government. Ultimately, the activists and the federal bureaucracy worked in parallel, addressing this local-level corruption and acting to improve Mexico's schools.

Now the phenomenon of open data is everywhere. All fifty US states and hundreds of cities release some data and have some form of open-data portal.

Since the Obama administration's Open Government Initiative pioneered the opening up of government data in 2009, open-data policies and practices have been broadly adopted. "The advent of open data portals across cities, states, and federal departments is creating a two-way conversation between residents and their government," writes analytics expert Carter Hewgley. "So, if you're in the market for external data about your municipality or your peers, start by looking at the open data portals of your state, local, and federal partners. There's so much out there about demographics, the economy, crime, and transportation—there's really no excuse for not leveraging the open data all around you."[48]

Open-data portals often contain spending data at the local, state, and federal level; federal grant and contract data; census data; and crime, housing, and utility data.[49] The catalog of national data available on http://data.gov was launched with forty-seven data sets and now houses a quarter of a million. It also offers a metacatalog of local data portals from around the country. The Open Knowledge Foundation publishes a census of open data.[50]

The United Nations has a data catalog at https://undatacatalog.org/, and the World Bank has one at https://data.worldbank.org/. The US Census Bureau and national statistical agencies in other countries disseminate data as well.[51] The Humanitarian Data Exchange hosts four thousand data sets such as country-by-country stats on food prices and undernourishment.[52] In the United States, the National Neighborhood Indicators Partnership and the Urban Institute both offer additional gateways to data sources and offer tools and visualizations that make other sources of demographic, economic, and spending data more intelligible and useful.[53] As examples in this book have shown, larger cities frequently publish data from their 311 complaint hotline, offering a granular picture of life in the city. Social media data offer another source of real-time information, especially about social movements and sentiment on a topic.[54]

You can use open data to quantify problems. Engie Impact is a software program that analyzes energy-consumption data to allow utilities, energy service providers, and building owners to identify buildings with high energy savings potential. In Argentina, the Ministry of Justice and Human Rights' open-data portal publishes aggregate crime and prosecution data that are sortable by gender. The ministry then uses these data to visualize the disparities between men and women, for instance, in the violent crime rate. And data collected from universities have been transformed by the federal Department of Education into a calculator—the College Scorecard—to help parents and students understand the costs of education and make more-informed decisions about college.

Administrative Data

Another source of data is that which government collects but does not openly publish. Federal, state, and local governments collect and process troves of personally identifiable data in order to administer public programs, fulfill regulatory mandates, and conduct research.[55] Government agencies provide driver's licenses, passports, welfare benefits, and food subsidies; collect taxes; administer the census; record crimes; and release prisoners who have served their time. These activities generate data. Hospitals, schools, and employers also collect data about us that are reported to the government. All this information allows the state to know a great deal about us as individuals and across the population, making it possible to analyze the outcomes of interventions, for example, by measuring whether my income goes up, how fast I get a new job, or how long I stay out of prison.

Prudent restrictions may be imposed on personally identifiable information that government collects while administering services. Such data should not be published as open data but may be accessible in aggregate to a policy maker or accredited researcher. For example, the state of New Jersey maintains the Education to Earnings data system (NJEEDS) in collaboration with Rutgers University. Within its secure infrastructure, the system houses education, employment, and earnings data about individuals that can be used to inform state decision-making and measure the impact of new policies and services.[56] For example, New Jersey is building a project known as Data for the American Dream that enables a person seeking up-skilling to search for information about the cost of training programs. This "smart disclosure" tool allows job seekers to compare training opportunities and outcomes.[57] That website (https://training.njcareers.org/) is powered by an open data set of information about the cost and content of training programs collected by the state's Department of Labor and Workforce Development from providers. Eventually, using anonymized administrative earnings data from NJEEDS, the goal is to be able to tell searchers, without disclosing any personal information, whether people who took a training program saw their incomes go up or down and, thus, whether a training program imparts skills that translate into a better job. The combination of open data and administrative data will make it possible to go beyond the usual subsidies and tax breaks for training and tell workers, researchers, and policy makers whether training offerings actually create economic improvement.

At the federal level, the Social Security Administration (SSA) collects and manages data on social, welfare, and disability benefit payments to nearly the entire US population, as well as individual lifetime records of wages and self-employment earnings. The SSA uses these administrative data to analyze policy interventions and to develop models to project demographic and economic characteristics of the population. State governments collect computerized hospital discharge data for both government (Medicare and Medicaid) and commercial payers. The Centers for Medicare and Medicaid Services analyzes such billing and payment data to improve services and reduce costs.[58] The Department of Justice (through the Bureau of Justice Standards) collects prison admission and release data to monitor correctional populations and to address several policy questions, including about recidivism and prisoner reentry.[59]

While administrative data are private, there are ways you can use them for your project. Many public institutions make private data available for use while protecting privacy by creating so-called data labs, policy labs, or data warehouses. These organizations store data securely but, in many cases, also employ small groups of data analysts to make administrative data usable for evaluation and research. And while data labs vary widely in their configuration, they have all developed models to tap into the skills of highly talented data analysts and to responsibly and securely access valuable government data sets.

For almost thirty-five years, Professor Fred Wulczyn and his team at Chapin Hall Data Center at the University of Chicago have worked with states to help them build what he calls "research-valuable data" from the administrative records that states maintain in collaboration with the public sector.[60] The cornerstone of the center's offerings is the Foster Care Data Archive and associated web tool that support access to data that can generate evidence to support analysis of foster-care programs and inventions. By harmonizing the data across jurisdictions (states and counties), the archive makes comparative research between and within states possible. Harmonization enables data collected from different state agencies operating under different guidelines to be integrated in a coherent framework.

Similarly, at the University of Pennsylvania, the Actionable Intelligence for Social Policy initiative works with state and local governments to develop and maintain an Integrated Data System (IDS) that links administrative data across government agencies, making the data from multiple states accessible to policy makers and researchers to improve programs and practices. Thirty-five different data-sharing arrangements enable this evidence-based collaboration.[61]

In the United Kingdom, the Justice Data Lab (JDL) provides organizations working with offenders with access to reoffending data.[62] The information helps organizations to assess the impact of their work on reducing recidivism. It also provides evidence to funders and clients of which programs are actually effective. The Ministry of Justice set up the JDL in 2013 following a presentation by New Philanthropy Capital (NPC), which surveyed criminal-justice charities to understand the difficulties in evaluating reoffending.[63] The vast majority of charities found it difficult to access recidivism data. NPC proposed the idea of the JDL to improve access to the data, particularly for charities, and since that time has worked with the Ministry of Justice to make greater access a reality. The JDL was confirmed as a permanent service in 2015.

The JDL makes valuable administrative data available to those outside government who do not have the skills or capacity to transform the data into information. As well as charities, many public- and private-sector organizations have also used the service. The data are highly personal and sensitive, but to ensure privacy, the model stipulates that all queries about personally identifiable data must go through qualified JDL staff. By using administrative data from the Police National Computer (PNC) and other linked data sets, the JDL evaluates the impact of a service using up to fourteen measures, dependent on the nature and sample size of the intervention.[64] Core measures provided for every analysis are whether offenders reoffend, how often, and how long before they do so.

To use the JDL, an organization needs to submit information on a minimum of sixty individuals who were provided its service and details of the program. A team of statisticians calculates the reoffending statistics of this group and uses statistical matching techniques to create a comparison group with similar characteristics. JDL staff then perform comparative analysis of the reoffending rates of the two groups and write it up in a plain-English summary for the ministry website.[65]

In the United States, Recidiviz, a not-for-profit organization supported by various philanthropies, is seeking to build a nationwide administrative data warehouse that will integrate the criminal justice, policing, and other data needed to test interventions that reduce recidivism.[66]

Crowdsourcing and Citizen Science

When desired or needed but not yet collected or publicly available, data may need to be gathered through your own survey, crowdsourcing, or citizen science exercise. There is a growing movement involving the use of community-driven data collection. After the 2011 Fukushima Daiichi nuclear disaster in Japan, citizens who were distrustful of government-published information began collecting data of their own using handheld Geiger counters. The data were compiled, monitored, and openly shared through a project known as Safecast.

Safecast now coordinates citizen engagement to monitor nuclear safety and air quality around the world. It describes its mission as "provid[ing] citizens worldwide with the tools they need to inform themselves by gathering and sharing accurate environmental data in an open and participatory fashion." All of Safecast's 150 million data points are openly published.[67]

When there are data that residents can reasonably be asked to collect, such as data about air or water quality in their own backyards or the conditions of their schools or neighborhoods, public entrepreneurs should consider making the most of this distributed capacity.

Obtaining Data Using FOIA

As a last resort, you may also need to take advantage of the Freedom of Information Act (FOIA) to demand data from government that should be open and are not. All US government entities post instructions about how to file a request for records under FOIA. For example, in 2013, the transparency activist Carl Malamud began coordinating an effort to use FOIA to force the IRS to publish nonprofit tax returns as open data.[68] Malamud used the act to request nine nonprofits' tax returns from the IRS. After the agency refused to make them available in digital form, he sued in federal court to compel the agency to disclose.

Although the law requires disclosure of the returns of nonprofit organizations, and the filers had submitted those returns electronically, the IRS wanted to send Malamud image files of the returns.[69] As we uncovered in our service blueprinting section in chapter 5, the IRS typically took electronically filed returns, printed them, scanned them into their system, and sold DVDs with the images on them. Our documenting of this practice, along with Malamud's successful suit and campaign, caused the IRS both to turn over Malamud's nine requested returns in a digitally readable format and also to begin to make all electronically filed nonprofit tax returns—which represent about 60 percent of those filed since 2011—downloadable as open data.[70] While an FOIA request may be slow, when added media pressure is brought to bear, governments may be more forthcoming in turning over information.

VALIDATING THE DATA

Regardless of where a data set comes from, you need to be sure that what you have measures what it is supposed to measure and is the right data to help you define your problem. This involves three steps: first, make sure the data set comes from the most authoritative source. For example, get census data directly from the Census Bureau. If you need student test scores, go directly to the Department of Education or national testing bodies and, when necessary, generate your own, original data through surveys, questionnaires, and other means.

Second, take a look at the data and make sure the data sets pass the basic sniff test: Does the data make sense based on what I know about the problem? Data often suffer from quality problems, such as gaps in the data, lack of timely reporting, and even mistakes. When we first started analyzing the use of personal protective equipment in New Jersey, for example, we were getting wildly disparate entries. One hospital reported 400,000 gloves; another reported 250. Obviously, one hospital entered the number of individual units, while another was reporting the number of palettes. It is important to scrutinize the data for those inconsistencies.

Third, even when you have the most authoritative source for the data, you also want to try to triangulate the data by looking at multiple sources to verify accuracy and capture different dimensions of the problem.[71] Ideally, it is a good idea not to rely on any one data set and to get more than one person reviewing the data to spot mistakes and outliers.

Different data may need to be combined to answer the research question. For example, the city of Chicago, which has more than fifteen thousand food establishments but only three dozen health inspectors, wanted to create an algorithm to predict food-safety violations.[72] Officials started by analyzing historical data on food inspections to predict which establishments were more likely to reoffend. In time, they expanded their analysis to consider three-day average high temperatures, nearby garbage and sanitation complaints, who the inspector was and the length of time since last inspection, and the length of time an establishment had been operating, among other factors. A breakthrough came when officials analyzed customer complaints. This project increased the effectiveness of the city's inspections by 25 percent.

Although one does not have to be a computer scientist to adopt data-analytical methods, it can help to include those who have some social- and data-science expertise when figuring out which data sets to use. Thus, when the city of London sought to identify unregistered houses with multiple occupants—homes that are most at risk of fire—the data-science consultancy it engaged worked with borough officials to identify available data sets relevant to the problem. As a report from the mayor of London points out, "These included physical property features as well as records on anti-social behavior, noise complaints, council tax bands, housing benefits recipients, and improper waste disposal, among many others."[73] As will be addressed further in chapter 9 on collaborations and partnerships, governments frequently turn to universities to do research and analysis that they find difficult to do themselves.

Finding the data needed to solve a problem starts with a conversation across relevant programs and departments, writes Beth Blauer, executive director of the Center for Government Excellence at Johns Hopkins University:

> Most conversations in governments occur in those ubiquitous silos, and employees rarely get the chance to talk horizontally; but governments who only communicate vertically are missing huge opportunities to identify data that might be useful across programs. For example, create a conversation between your finance department and your building inspection program to see if data on tax delinquency can inform your code-enforcement strategies. Does your Water Department have information that the Public Health Department should use to better target outreach for lead-poisoning prevention? As you create these conversations between programs, listen for evidence that public servants are unnecessarily flying blind. You'll be surprised how quickly you can identify opportunities to leverage data across programs.[74]

DOING THE DATA ANALYSIS

Once the problem is defined and the data identified, the next step is to decide what kind of analysis to do and what technique to apply. Knowing whether the goal is description, detection, classification, prediction, or behavior change will help with choosing the statistical or data-science techniques to develop the analytical or predictive model. The purpose of this section is not to offer a comprehensive substitute for a statistics or data-science book or course. There is a proliferating number of those online, including the free course Solving Public Problems with Data (http://sppd .thegovlab.org/) that The GovLab put online in 2016. Rather, the goal here is to illustrate that anyone familiar with data-analytical thinking, with or without computational skills or formal research-methods training, can collaborate with others to exploit relevant data to define a public problem.

Counting Things

Some fairly simple and straightforward things can be done with data, such as counting. "Simple counting," writes the Princeton sociologist Matt Salganik, "can be interesting if you combine a good question with a good idea."[75] On the one hand, anyone who has studied the results of complex machine-learning experiments tends to be in awe of what can be accomplished with big data and sophisticated computation. But sometimes what is needed most are the simplest functions, such as adding up.

As an example of the value of tallying, Salganik points to another piece of research involving New York City taxi data (who knew that one open data set could go such a long way?). A 2014 study by Salganik's Princeton colleague the economist Henry Faber used the taxi data to address a fundamental question in economics—whether taxi drivers would drive more often on days on which they could earn more, as neoclassical economics would suggest. Or would the data reveal what behavioral economics would assume—that drivers would simply seek to earn a certain amount and stop driving when they had earned it? Supporting the neoclassical optimizing model of labor supply, and contradicting earlier work by behavioral economists, the study revealed that drivers would drive more when they could earn more.[76] It was an important finding that Faber arrived at by doing little more than adding up taxi drivers' earnings.

Natural Experiments

Natural experiments try to find correlations and causes through rigorous comparisons of targeted populations. They involve comparing groups that occur naturally in daily life, instead of assigning people to groups in a formal experiment, as randomized experiments do. (Chapters 8 and 9 will talk more about randomized controlled trials and experiments.)

Natural experiments, which rely on observation, are another way to use data without the need to design an experiment or build an algorithm. Usually dependent on data that have already been gathered, they simplify the process for the policy maker, who wants the insight but does not have the need or ability to do original research or construct a designed experiment. In many contexts, it may not be ethical or practicable to construct an experiment such as a randomized controlled trial, and instead we must trust the evaluation of natural experiments.[77]

Federal government systems, such as those in the United States, Australia, and Germany, create the conditions for observing naturally occurring outcomes, because similar or different policies can be compared across jurisdictions. In order for the Mexican government to study the effects of its antipoverty interventions, especially the use of direct cash transfers, it trialed them in some states and not in others.[78] In the United States, experiments occur naturally in cities that do or do not have free, universal pre-K education, easy access to abortions, or legalized medicinal or recreational marijuana use.

In a natural experiment, we look for an event that is naturally occurring from which meaning can be gleaned. A grocery store or a bus stop might open in one neighborhood and not in others; one jurisdiction might differ from others by introducing a tax on cigarettes or a ban on abortions. These differences make it possible to infer the effects of the intervention.

For example, in 2001, Norwegian tax records became easily accessible online, making it possible to compare one's income to others. The UCLA economist Ricardo Perez-Truglia used the transparent income data, along with survey data from 1985 to 2013, to test whether enabling people to see a wealth gap that had previously been hidden affected their happiness and satisfaction. He found that transparency made the rich more satisfied and the poor less satisfied with their lot in life, with implications for the policy debate on tax transparency.[79]

Because so many activities have moved online, it can be even easier to draw comparisons between different interventions. For example, with hundreds of cities conducting citizen engagement, such as participatory budgeting, online, those exercises are generating so much data that we do not have to engineer artificial experiments to draw comparisons.[80]

Although it can be difficult to isolate cause and effect in messy, real-world conditions, natural experiments can help to answer the question, Are we investing our scarce resources in a way that works? Are we solving the problem? When the answer is that we are not, then it helps us to understand where the problem lies and what its root causes are.

Machine Learning

The big-data analytical techniques of machine learning are a transformative innovation for problem solving. Machine learning (a subset of artificial intelligence) offers a powerful way to build and design a model based on earlier data in order to predict future occurrences.[81]

Machine learning is the science of teaching computers to learn using big data and helps to make processes more autonomous, efficient, and effective using training data sets. Machine learning has become so popular that it is now practically synonymous with AI. Familiar home assistants like Siri, Alexa, and Google Home are all powered by machine learning. They learn from earlier questions to be able to understand and answer new questions. In other words, with machine learning, a computer learns by example rather than through explicit programming instructions.

Machine learning takes many forms. The most common, *supervised machine learning*, is akin to how a teacher trains a child in arithmetic. The conclusions are known, and the teacher shows the child how to arrive at them. Similarly, in supervised machine learning, the outputs are known and used to help develop an algorithm to reach that conclusion. Using large quantities of data, machine learning can uncover patterns and inductively create general rules. The learning in machine learning occurs when the machine turns the data into a model.

To take an example of how one researcher trained a machine-learning algorithm using supervised machine learning, Joshua Blumenstock, a researcher at the University of California, Berkeley, called a random sample of one thousand residents culled from a database of one and a half million mobile-phone users in Rwanda to interview them about their level of wealth. His research team used what they learned from the phone survey—the "supervised" input—to develop and train a machine-learning model to predict wealth. It applied the model to the complete calling data of one and a half million users to create a detailed map of the country's wealth levels, then compared these results to those from the government's national demographic and health study previously created through manual surveys. Blumenstock's approach achieved the same results as the surveys did ten times faster and fifty times more cheaply, paving the way to apply machine-learning models to accelerate demographic research.

Machine learning is especially useful with data that are difficult to analyze, such as human speech and language or images. It gives us a model for making sense of big data. Models make us smarter, writes the political scientist Scott Page:

> Without models, people suffer from a laundry list of cognitive
> shortcomings: we overweight recent events, we assign probabili-
> ties based on unreasonableness, and we ignore base rates. With-
> out models, we have limited capacity to include data. Models are
> formal mathematical representations that can be applied to data to
> help us make sense of it. With models, we clarify assumptions and
> think logically. And we can leverage big data to fit, calibrate, and
> test causal and correlative claims. With models, we think better.[82]

In head-to-head competitions between models and people, he says, models win. Machine learning offers a powerful means for both spotting and solving problems.[83] In an effort to improve food security across sub-Saharan Africa, the Rockefeller Foundation has partnered with the Alliance for a Green Revolution in Africa (AGRA) and Atlas AI to fund a predictive-analytics project to anticipate damage to agriculture.[84] Using satellite imagery, Atlas AI has trained a machine-learning algorithm to study crop growth in relation to changing weather, diseases, and pests. By predicting perturbations in agricultural production, it can help government and philanthropy to anticipate and prevent losses. The challenge is part of YieldWise, a Rockefeller Foundation $130 million initiative aimed at reducing food loss by at least 50 percent by 2030, one of the United Nations' sustainable development goals.[85]

Be forewarned that it takes training in data science to design machine-learning algorithms. However, familiarity with what AI and its analytical techniques of machine learning and predictive analytics can do can make you a better collaborator and consumer of data-science advice from university or industry professionals.

However, you must also be a critical consumer. There are serious risks and challenges inherent in using machine learning precisely because of the way it creates generalizable rules. If a machine-learning algorithm is "fed" with bad data, it will encode bias into the model.

Thus, absent specific intervention to counter the bias, the increasing use of machine learning in hiring is leading to major problems.[86] For example, a prominent video-interviewing company, HireVue, reduces the costs of screening potential employees by recording video answers from job applicants. The software uses machine learning to compare responses with interview answers provided by current, successful employees. Given that "speech recognition software can perform poorly, especially for people with regional and nonnative accents" and "facial analysis systems can struggle to read the faces of women with darker skin," the public is right to be concerned that such uses of machine learning end up encoding biases.[87] Generalizing from historical examples requires providing the algorithm with good examples. If all current job applicants are White and American born, then the algorithm will "learn" that diverse, foreign-born applicants should be included.[88]

Another example of the risks of machine learning is illustrated power-fully by the example of FindFace, a Russian-made app. FindFace works by comparing photographs to profile pictures from Vkontakte, a popular so-cial media outlet in Russia with more than two hundred million accounts. FindFace founders Artem Kukharenko, Alexander Kabakov, and Maxim Pellin amassed five hundred thousand users shortly after launch. The app was first marketed as a means of revolutionizing dating: take a picture of a movie star, use the app to find ten people who look similar, and then mes-sage them through their social media networks.

Even putting to one side the disturbing perpetuation of gender-biased body-image issues, the problems went even deeper. In 2016, the Russian photographer Egor Tsvetkov took pictures of St. Petersburg and Moscow subway riders and was able to match around 60 to 70 percent of the pic-tures to social media profiles for people between the ages of eighteen and thirty-five.[89] Russia's FSB security service also used the app to find suspects and witnesses for long-abandoned cases (and who knows what other ma-lign purposes). While displaying the potential to solve several identification problems, FindFace quickly became a bête noire of the privacy community.

In September 2018, FindFace was taken down because of the privacy brouhaha and later relaunched as a paid service to help shopping com-plexes identify shoplifters.

WHAT MIGHT GO WRONG

Expanding on the risks discussed in connection with machine learning, this section may help you stay alert to potential problems and be better consumers of data-science help. At every stage of the data life cycle, from collection to processing to analysis to use, the risks must be weighed against benefits when using data to define and solve problems.[90]

Relying on a Single Model

"To rely on a single model is hubris, it invites disaster," warns Scott Page. "To believe that a single equation can explain or predict complex real-world phenomena is to fall prey to the charisma of clean, spare mathematical forms."[91] Because no one model, method, or data set can explain reality, especially in a complex and interdependent world, we continue to need a diversity of approaches to understanding a problem. Especially if the model is based on biased data, then it is especially problematical.

Suppose we're building a model for scoring resumes for a programming job. What if we simply withhold gender from the data? Surely the resulting model can't be gender biased? Unfortunately, it's not that simple, because of the problem of proxies. . . . In our culture, the age at which someone starts programming is well known to be correlated with gender. This illustrates another problem with proxies: they may be genuinely relevant to the decision at hand. How long someone has been programming is a factor that gives us valuable information about their suitability for a programming job, but it also reflects the reality of gender stereotyping.[92]

To repeat a point made throughout this book, ideological adherence to one method, quantitative or qualitative, risks oversimplifying one's understanding of the problem. It is vital to look at a problem from a variety of angles using both data and human-centered design and to test different hypotheses in order to arrive at an approximation.

Privacy Violations and Other Misuses

As the FindFace app example shows, increased collecting and linking of data accelerates the risk of reidentifying individuals in violation of the principles, and perhaps the law, of privacy.

The number of US data breaches in 2018 increased by over 45 percent from the previous year, explaining why much ink has been spilled on the challenges of big data for privacy.[93] The Harvard researcher Latanya Sweeney has built her career on pathbreaking work demonstrating how little anonymity we have in our data. Using public anonymous data from the 1990 census, she found that 87 percent of the US population—216 million of 248 million—could probably be uniquely identified by their five-digit zip code, combined with their gender and date of birth.[94] On the one hand, anonymous data are a boon for problem identification. On the other, writes the security issues blogger Bruce Schneier, "in the age of wholesale surveillance, where everyone collects data on us all the time, anonymization is very fragile and riskier than it initially seems."[95]

Beyond the harm that big data presents to individuals, collective analysis of data can be used to distort the processes that society has put in place for decision-making. Nowhere is this risk more evident than in the most sensitive and fundamental decision-making process, democratic elections. The British consulting firm Cambridge Analytica has been at the center of an accelerating scandal involving massive data theft and manipulation at the behest of the Trump organization prior to the 2016 presidential election.[96] The firm Psy-Group, an Israeli private intelligence agency (now closed), boasted about their success in swaying public opinion toward views or candidates who paid them to manipulate public sentiment. (Some observers express skepticism about how much of an impact they have had, but the danger is clear.) The debacle reminds us of our ethical obligations in connection with the use of data.

Missing and Uncollected Data

When designing a machine-learning algorithm, data and computer scientists train the algorithm with available data. But if data are not available, an algorithm is likely to overrepresent the behavior of those who generate the most data exhaust, at the expense of those who leave fewer digital footprints.

For example, if I am trying to use Twitter to measure popular sentiment on an issue, I am measuring only the sentiment of those people who use Twitter. The elderly, the poor and homeless, and others who rarely use social media—people who are what Justin Longo calls "data invisibles"— may go undercounted. And since not all tweets are geolocated, I might be looking at data from people who are not part of my target population. I might also double count the views of people who have multiple Twitter accounts. "The empiricism of policy analytics," writes Longo, "is impressive but still represents an incomplete view of the world when considering the digitally invisible."[97]

Furthermore, data that are not collected will have no influence on policy development. Broadband policy is one example of an area that suffers from an absence of accurate data. For years, inadequate reporting by Internet service providers (ISPs) to the US Federal Communications Commission (FCC) has stymied the efforts of policy makers and advocates to set better broadband policy.[98] The FCC's methodology considers an entire zip code as "served" with broadband if just one home in an entire census block has it. It is very difficult to diagnose problems when we do not know who has service. Whether the misreporting is intentional, as in this case, or accidental, FCC policy hampers efforts to collect data and improve the system.

The absence of data can have life-or-death consequences. Health-care systems use algorithms to identify the sickest patients and allocate care. But a study in *Science* shows that Black patients are deemed to be at lower risk than White patients. "The magnitude of the distortion was immense," the authors write. "Eliminating the algorithmic bias would more than double the number of black patients who would receive extra help." The problem is that the algorithm measures "sickness" using the most readily available data: health-care expenditures. "But because society spends less on black patients than equally sick white ones, the algorithm understated the black patients' true needs."[99]

The problem of incomplete or low-quality data is exacerbated by the fact that at least fourteen billion data records have been lost or stolen since 2013, according to one estimate.[100] Gartner, a corporate research and advisory company, estimates that a quarter of Fortune 1000 companies have information that is inaccurate, incomplete, or duplicated.[101]

But beyond theft, if we fail to ask the right questions, we will not collect the right data in the first place. Despite a statutory requirement to collect data relating to shootings and deaths in police custody, those data are practically nonexistent. It has taken nongovernmental actors concerned about systemic bias and police brutality against communities of color to start mapping police violence or creating a fatal-force database.[102]

Because we value what we measure, government does not always keep track of the data needed to assess discrimination. US federal crime data provide a good example of how certain data are collected while other relevant information is ignored. Although the FBI's Uniform Crime Reports show estimated monthly aggregates of instances of eight major crimes (murder, rape, assault, robbery, arson, burglary, larceny-theft, and motor-vehicle theft), no similar data store exists for white-collar crime.[103] As the authors of the National Academies crime-statistics reports, Janet Lauritsen and Daniel Cork, say about crime in the United States, it is, "arguably, at least as much about corporate fraud as about armed robbery, harassment via the Internet as about breaking and entering, and endangering health through environmental pollutants as about assaults and muggings."[104] Yet early twenty-first-century information infrastructure tracks only data about "street crime" to the general exclusion of other types of offenses.

Bias

Data convey a sense of impartiality and infallibility. Machine-learning algorithms are sometimes introduced to reduce human bias in decision-making.[105] Because an algorithm undertakes a small range of tasks, in contrast to humans, who must sleep, eat, and work, many people believe that machines can achieve more optimal performance and less-biased decision-making. "The additional constraints under which humans must operate manifest themselves as biases," write Oxford's Carl Benedikt Frey and Michael A. Osborne.[106]

But, as discussed earlier in the examination of machine learning, there is no such thing as unbiased machine learning making impartial decisions.[107] Biased inputs lead to biased outputs, and a machine-learning algorithm simply learns from the historical data that it has been fed, potentially leading to discrimination in the prediction of recidivism, educational assessment, and employment and hiring.[108] Gideon Mann, the chief data scientist of Bloomberg, explains the point with an example: "If some of your population are not represented in your training data, the algorithm that you are going to come out with is not going to perform well or be accurate on that part of your training data sample."[109]

The data may be inaccurate due to a lack of comprehensiveness caused by a failure to collect data from representative sources. But it also might be problematic because changes in policy change the behavior of those whom the policy affects. When that occurs, "models estimated with data on past human behaviors will therefore not be accurate," writes Page. "Models must take into account the fact that people respond to policy and environmental changes."[110]

Two books, Frank Pasquale's *Black Box Society* and Pedro Domingos's *Master Algorithm*, tell horror stories of bad algorithms, and there are many more. Especially troubling is the reliance on opaque and privatized algorithms to deprive people of their rights and liberties. Algorithms used in Florida's criminal courts, for example, produced biased risk predictions; African American defendants were 77 percent more likely to be considered "higher risk" of committing crimes than were their White counterparts.[111] A White House report on algorithms expressed concern about "unintentional perpetuation and promotion of historical biases, where a feedback loop causes bias in inputs or results of the past to replicate itself in the outputs of an algorithmic system."[112] After the killing of George Floyd in May 2020 and the outbreak of protests against police violence across the country, IBM, Amazon, and Microsoft halted development and deployment of facial recognition systems that could be used to surveil and racially profile people in Black and Brown communities, especially.

Bad Interpretation

It is easy to make mistakes when doing data analysis. For example, we can draw conclusions that are not supported by the facts at hand. The terms "p-hacking" or "data dredging" describe the problem of inferring statistically significant findings in data when none exist. In p-hacking, researchers massage and play with data until they arrive at results that appear to be significant. They do so by being selective in their choice of data, stopping an experiment early, looking only at a subset of the experiment, or simply doing the analysis over and over until they find something.

Ideally, we define our research question and hypothesis prior to analyzing data, which we then use to prove or disprove the claim. If the first hypothesis does not bear out, we might try to analyze the same data differently in order to look for a new hypothesis. By itself, this is not p-hacking. Iteration is always necessary.

There is a fine line between evolving a study and redoing an analysis and manipulating the results.[113] Repeated analysis designed to generate a result where none exists is poor practice and can be unethical. A Cornell food-science professor was forced to resign for a scandal involving bad data practices and misreporting.[114] His lab set out to study the effect of buffet prices on how much people eat. When the study did not pan out, he had his team slice the data in different ways. He looked at male and female diners, lunch- and dinner-goers, and how close or far they sat from the buffet. The professor, trained in marketing rather than social science research, was probably well intentioned in his efforts to figure out what worked. But he fell afoul of the high standards of peer-reviewed academic research by claiming to be doing social science.

In the right context, digging around to find a result might be exactly the right thing to do—public entrepreneurs and problem solvers need not be professors. But taken to an extreme, data dredging can be dangerous.

After the Boston Marathon bombing in 2013, the FBI opened its investigation by calling on spectators to provide any media they had in relation to the marathon in order to look for clues to the identity of the bombers.[115] But what started as a crowdsourced, intelligence-gathering request quickly became a digital witch hunt. Redditers and 4Chaners falsely identified over a dozen suspects on the basis of clothes and appearance. Users of these channels posted images and social media profiles of people who looked similar to the potential suspects identified by the FBI. Because Reddit and 4Chan users were acting in real time in parallel to the official FBI investigations, these false accusations spread to the national news and via social media and led to false arrests.[116]

To ensure that insights can be gained without harming individuals or groups, it is essential to establish principles and processes for *responsible* sharing, analysis, and use of data.

Failure to Use Data

Perhaps the greatest risk, however, is the failure to use data to solve public problems. It was estimated in 2012 that 90 percent of the digital data ever created in the world has been generated in the past two years (a number that has only grown since), but only 1 percent of that data has been analyzed.[117] Organizations, especially governments, are collecting, storing—even hoarding—data but failing to analyze and share data for social good. The costs of gathering data are far outweighed by the opportunity costs of not using it, especially to make chronic problems like inequality and systemic racism more visible.

A story told by Beth Blauer from her time leading Maryland's StateStat performance-management team starkly illustrates the dangers of failing to use data, whether for legal, cultural, or technical reasons:

> I had a meeting with our juvenile justice agency, and we also had our social services agency and our public safety agency. We were talking about our most violent and dangerous offenders in our state, and I asked a very innocent question about how often were our agencies taking our foster-care locations—our registered statewide foster-care locations—and overlaying it with where our most violent and dangerous offenders lived and matching those addresses. And what I thought was a very innocent question turned into a very serious problem because the answer was that

information is not shared because by law, we are prohibited to exchange that information interagency. And my head nearly exploded. I couldn't imagine a scenario where we weren't thinking about this on a regular basis as we're placing children into our own care.[118]

However, it turned out that what Maryland officials thought was a law preventing the sharing of data turned out to be only custom and practice. Once they realized their mistake and looked at the data, they were able to identify where foster children were living with or near the most dangerous and violent offenders, including registered sex offenders. This discovery allowed Maryland child-welfare officers to visit every foster child over the course of forty-eight hours to make sure they were safe.

Underinvestment in data for public problem solving is probably the biggest challenge, especially when the same data sets can be used and re-used for different purposes to answer many different research questions.

Today we can use a vast array of data to help us understand problems, but we need humans to ensure that our data-analytical processes yield results. We need people to collect and interpret the data just as much as we need machines and algorithms to understand what the data tell us about the problem and its root causes. Too many projects are handed off to data scientists and statisticians, when collaboration remains core to the process. Data-analytical thinking is one step along the continuum of public problem solving, which begins with defining the problem and accelerates by using both data *and* human-centered design to test and refine our problem definition.

TO DO

Please see https://solvingpublicproblems.org for worksheets.

Exercise 1: Identifying the Data
In the era of big data, you need to understand what information you are looking for in order to define your problem.

To Think About

- What is the problem that I want to study, and what data can best represent this problem?
- What format do I want these data to be in?

- What could be some good sources to find the data I am looking for? If the data are not publicly available, whom should I contact to get access to them, or what steps should I take to collect the data myself?

To Do

- Conduct a data audit: compare existing open data sets from across agencies with the types of information needed to answer priority questions.
- Talk to those who hold the data: take political considerations into account and be sure to articulate how the data will be productively used to justify the effort required to collect and/or publish the data.
- Engage with data and domain experts: partner with relevant staff inside and outside government to ensure you have the data expertise needed to use the data.
- Prepare and clean the data: work with data experts to ensure that the data are timely, complete, and relevant.

Exercise 2: Open Data Availability

Where can you find data to define your problem? Does an agency of government—your own agency or another—collect data that would be useful for solving your specific problem?

While you can start with your state's open-data catalog, often these catalogs are not comprehensive sources of available data, and relevant agencies need to be engaged to identify available data sets.

There are numerous aggregators of open data, including the following:

- Data.gov
- US Census Bureau
- European Union Open Data Portal
- Google's Public Data Explorer
- Urban Institute
- World Bank
- World Health Organization
- Dataverse
- UN Data
- Enigma Public Data
- Depending on your field of interest, different federal agencies such as

the EPA, the US Department of Labor, and the FBI, offer access to free and machine-readable data
- The Lens (world's largest open database of patents)
- OpenCorporates (world's largest open database of companies)

Exercise 3: Validating Your Data

First, make sure the data come from the most authoritative source. If you need census data, get them directly from the Census Bureau. If you need student test scores, go directly to the Department of Education or national testing bodies.

Second, take a look at the data and make sure the information passes the basic sniff test: Does it make sense based on what I know about the problem?

Third, try to triangulate the information by looking at multiple sources to verify its accuracy and capture different dimensions of the problem.

Exercise 4: Assess Your Readiness to Use Data (adapted from The GovLab)

- Are the data fully open and/or accessible to you in a machine-readable form enabling you to readily use the information, or do you need additional resources?
- Do factors such as staffing limit your organization's ability to make use of data?
- Is there a clear commitment to using the data to solve the problem as defined?
- Are the right people available to act on insights generated through the data? If not, can you identify external or internal partners with the relevant expertise to help you clean and prepare the data for use? (One strategy for cleaning the data is to organize a "hackathon" or "data-thon," also known as a "data-dive." Data-dives are high-energy, marathon-style events in which teams of volunteer data scientists, developers, and designers help mission-driven organizations to organize, manipulate, clean, or visualize their data.)
- Even if you have the data, do you have access to the expertise necessary to make use of the data? Again, reaching out to partners, especially in universities, can be one way to obtain the necessary expertise.
- Can you use novel approaches such as data labs, data collaboratives,

open innovation challenges, or competitions to enhance your organization's readiness to use and analyze data? New York City, for example, hosts the BigApps competition to attract data-savvy individuals to analyze its data.

Exercise 5: Consider the Risks
Working with data brings many risks. To name just one, you can be handed sensitive material or data that are not representative of your area of interest or data that are incomplete.

Consider the following:

1. Is what is represented in my data enough to understand the problem at hand? (If not, you need more data!)
2. What biases might underlie what is present in the data I am seeing? (There are always biases!)
3. How can I ensure these biases do not impact my analysis or are at the very least addressed? Do I need more or different data? Or do I need another set of eyes to review the data?
4. Is there any sensitive information in these data I should be aware about? If so, how can I protect its confidentiality?

Exercise 6: Working with Your Data
Now that you have the data, how do you use the data to tell a story? Consider the following:

- Do the data need to be manipulated in any way for better understanding? (This might be as simple as removing columns or retitling entries.)
- Are there any visualizations I can create to improve understanding of my data? (Examples include mapping information geographically or creating charts that visualize trends.)
- Is there anything out of the ordinary I notice from my visualization? (Sometimes, outliers are the biggest indicators of things going wrong, but you should also pay attention to general trends and counts.)
- What more specific insights about my problem does this information point me toward?

CHAPTER SEVEN

Using Collective Intelligence to Solve a Problem

CROWDSOURCING, COLLABORATION, AND CODESIGN

Children growing up in the twenty-first century take it for granted that they are surrounded by sensors and social media, and their participation in overlapping group minds—hives, crowds and clubs—makes the idea that intelligence resides inside the human skull into an anachronism.

Geoff Mulgan, Big Mind

COLLECTIVE INTELLIGENCE AND PROBLEM SOLVING

To prepare for military expeditions, Napoleon needed better ways to preserve the food his troops would need to survive long winters in the field. Unable to rely on local populations for food, his soldiers had to carry their own, and the common techniques of pickling, smoking, or drying were impractical and unappealing. After all, as Napoleon was wont to say, "an army marches on its stomach." The French government turned to the "wisdom of the crowd," and, in 1795 offered a 12,000-franc reward to anyone who could improve methods for preserving food. In 1809, a confectioner and brewer, Nicolas Francois Appert, won for a method he had developed for heating, boiling, and sealing food in airtight glass jars. That is pretty much the same process we use for conserving canned goods today.

The food-preservation competition is an example of what we might call "collective intelligence." The term "collective intelligence" is but one of many ways to describe how groups work together to create or analyze information, deliberate, collaborate, and make decisions. The term is often used interchangeably with other terms, including "public engagement," "swarm intelligence," "wisdom of crowds," and "crowd science," as well as with collective intelligence methods like open innovation and crowdsourcing, but whatever the lingo, many institutions are turning to the use of collective intelligence to solve problems. By posing the question to a distributed network of solvers, the French government was able to develop a solution faster than had it attempted to solve the problem on its own. Thus, as we progress from idea to implementation, we examine how new technology can help us identify and refine *solutions* with a broader community just as we previously explored how to define a *problem* with collective intelligence and engagement. This chapter addresses why and how to mobilize collective intelligence and collective action to *solve* problems, tapping distributed and diverse intelligence and expertise to design better and more critically aware interventions than we could do on our own.

Today, new technology is making it faster and easier to organize collaborative problem solving online. Thanks to the Internet, humans, aided by machines, are able to become smarter acting together. For example, they are able to collect and share the information needed to solve problems better. In 2012, the Metro Government of Louisville, Kentucky, and the digital health firm Propeller Health (then a research project known as Asthmapolis) used the Internet to gather data from more than one thousand residents about environmental triggers of asthma and chronic obstructive pulmonary disease (COPD). The city provided participants with inhalers fitted with sensors that recorded where and when they used their inhalers and the dosage. The Metro Government then used the data collected to design actions, such as new zoning policies and planting trees in at-risk areas. Over a twelve-month period, the pilot program reported an average of 82 percent reduction in the use of asthma rescue inhalers among participants.

Together, we can also brainstorm solutions. Across the globe, in Africa, five cities—Accra (Ghana), Bahir Dar (Ethiopia), Kampala (Uganda), Kano (Nigeria), and Mutare (Zimbabwe)—are collaborating to launch an open innovation challenge in 2020, inviting their over twelve million residents collectively to devise solutions to three contemporary urban challenges: digitizing the informal economy, building urban resilience, and improving waste management.[1] Similarly, aimed at the billion global farmers who produce 70 percent of the world's food, WeFarm boasts 1.9 million farmers as part of its online community in Africa. To date, farmers have asked over 4.6 million questions and given 10.6 million answers.[2]

Collectively, we can also take action on the solutions we envision. In 2013, the documentary filmmaker Amalia Zepou approached the then-mayor of Athens, George Kaminis, with an idea: create a central hub within the city's government that would connect citizens' projects in various neigh-borhoods to share resources and learn from one another. Now 449 groups have posted 4,129 activities on synAthina, the city's one-stop website for setting up and finding civic-engagement projects of all kinds and enabling residents to collectively revitalize their city. SynAthina won the Bloomberg Mayors Challenge prize in recognition of its central role in fostering civic engagement in Athens. The project has even survived a transition in politi-cal leadership, signaling its enduring relevance.[3]

As with other skills that we have learned about, however, it is not obvi-ous or intuitive how to accelerate the solution-identification stage of prob-lem solving using collective intelligence. That is why, in response to the COVID-19 pandemic, my colleagues and I used collective intelligence to create a course about using collective intelligence to address the pandemic (http://covidcourse.thegovlab.org). Fourteen different organizations rang-ing from UNDP to Safecast to RiskMap that have successfully mobilized groups of people online to solve problems present the basic concepts and tools for assembling effective collective-intelligence projects and leveraging mutual aid to engender more legitimate design.

This chapter focuses on how to proceed from defining to solving prob-lems by working together with those who have diverse skills and back-grounds, whether from lived experience or working in the field or academic credentials. People are knowledgeable about so many things, from cancer to software to how garbage is collected in their neighborhood. Given the opportunity, they can go far beyond deliberating about the nature of prob-lems; they can be activated to solve them.

People are hungry for such meaningful opportunities to participate in problem solving, especially those who are ordinarily disenfranchised. Half of respondents surveyed by Pew Research said they had participated in a civic activity in the past year.[4] But more want to do so. Americans think that innovative approaches to problem solving would help their communities. But people would be more attracted to community problem solving if they could apply their skills, someone they respect invited them, and public offi-cials were listening. About three-quarters of those surveyed by Public Agenda in 2019 said they would participate if they knew that participation was relevant and if they could contribute their skills and experiences.[5]

Whereas chapters 4–6 have focused on the importance of defining a problem in a way that is precise, clear, and compelling by engaging with others, now we shift to looking at how to take advantage of distributed intelligence and expertise to design interventions and "solve" the problem.

OPEN INNOVATION METHODS

To take advantage of collective intelligence as a way to solve a problem, you first have to decide on an open innovation process for identifying and devising solutions. In other words, you have to determine how you want to work with a broader network of individuals.

Of course, groups are dynamic, living, changing organisms. Studying them is a hard and imperfect science. The late Harvard organizational psychologist J. Richard Hackman and his coauthor Nancy Katz argue that there will never be a "definitive" study of groups, given the different ways that success for them might be defined, the different tasks groups perform, and the diverse ways they work.[6]

One way to distinguish group work categories is in terms of *the task* the group is asked to do (e.g., brainstorming, collecting data, sharing opinions, giving money). Or we can focus on *the domain of the problem* the group is trying to solve (e.g., air quality, education, traffic). Alternatively, we can understand collective-intelligence practices by *the level of group collaboration* called for, which can range from highly individualistic to intensely collaborative.

Hackman and Katz have fleshed out a typology for group work by likening groups to sports teams. These might perform "disjunctive tasks," in which the performance outcome is as good as the contribution of the best member. Then there are "conjunctive tasks," such as a roped-together group of climbers, who perform at the level of the least competent member. "Additive" tasks are like a tug-of-war, where the result is the sum of people's contributions, which is typical of many crowdsourcing projects.

Technology enables more additive and networked collaboration, in which the work of individuals contributes to a hive mind but without any particular sense of shared or group agency. For example, the traffic application Waze aggregates reports from individual drivers about accidents and traffic congestion in order to offer everyone on its network better driving directions. In this model, participants interact with the platform rather than with each other. "Compensatory" tasks are specific kinds of crowdsourcing projects that modify member contributions by averaging the results, in the way a prediction market works to set a price on the likelihood of an event.

"Complementary" tasks involve the assembly of smaller parts into a whole, such as we find on Wikipedia or in the Flint city property portal, where individuals entered smaller bits of data to create the bigger map with the intention of being part of a collective project.

Drawing a distinction between more and less purposive group work helps us to understand different types of choreography and levels of intensity through which we can engage with others. Simplifying Hackman and Katz's taxonomy, let us look at three ideal types of group work: crowdsourcing, collaboration, and cocreation.

In crowdsourcing projects like Napoleon's food-preservation challenge, individuals do not interact with one another; instead, their activities are coordinated by a process like a contest, which today usually involves a software program, and they compete to provide one or more solutions to a challenge. Collaboration, by contrast, may involve more interaction and shared agency between people, but they are working toward a common project. Cocreation, by contrast, involves working closely with other people to develop many solutions to the same problem. Of course, my definitions are fluid, as both the public and academics use these and other terms in place of one another and indistinguishably. But it is helpful to recognize that groups can be enlisted to solve problems in more and less competitive ways and in ways that implicate a greater or lesser sense of shared agency and purpose.[7]

CROWDSOURCING

In 2006, the journalist Jeff Howe blended the words "crowd" and "outsourcing" to create a new term, "crowdsourcing." Howe defined "crowdsourcing" as "the act of a company or institution taking a function once performed by employees and outsourcing it to an undefined (and generally large) network of people in the form of an open call."[8]

Although "crowdsourcing" is used almost interchangeably with "engagement," regardless of how big the crowd or how collaborative the project, a paradigmatic demonstration of crowdsourcing involves a large audience of volunteers guessing the number of jellybeans in a jar and averaging the results. With a large-enough number of guesses, the average converges on the right number. That does not require much collaboration among participants.

Crowdsourcing often comes in the form of a challenge, contest, or competition (also called "open innovation") that usually involves soliciting responses from a large group of people and picking a winner. Challenges generally offer a well-defined statement of a problem and invite solutions from a broad public. Contests work well when it is not obvious which combination of skills, or even which technical approach, will lead to the best outcome. Because they rely on the crowd, including unusual suspects who may be unknown to the organizers, to come up with the best solution, they are intended to stimulate greater innovation than if the organization had to come up with the solution for itself or awarded a contract to a single individual. The use of a prize ensures that the organization only pays for successful results. For example, in 2009, the online DVD-rental and video-streaming service Netflix offered a grand prize of $1 million in a competition to create the best algorithm to predict user ratings for films, based on previous ratings.

The X-Prize Foundation is famous for running crowdsourcing competitions to tackle social and environmental challenges. Recently it announced winners in a $7 million competition to advance technologies for rapid, unmanned, and high-resolution ocean exploration and discovery. In 2019–2020, the MacArthur Foundation ran a $10 million competition to improve economic opportunity for low-income individuals in the United States. Proposals must identify a specific barrier to progress and offer a solution to overcome that barrier. In 2020, W. K. Kellogg Foundation announced a $90 million challenge aimed at advancing racial equity by 2030. The challenge seeks ideas to transform the systems and institutions that uphold inequity.[9]

Government has widely used crowdsourcing over the past decade. The Obama administration's Open Government Memorandum, issued on the president's first day in office (disclosure: I drafted it), declared, "Public engagement enhances the Government's effectiveness and improves the quality of its decisions. Knowledge is widely dispersed in society, and public officials benefit from having access to that dispersed knowledge."[10] Subsequently, after changes to the 2011 America Competes Act, the federal government authorized the use of federal money for prize-backed challenges.[11] The change enabled the Health Resources and Services Administration to launch a competition offering $300,000 in prizes for innovative solutions to address the "word gap" that can occur for low-income children due to limited early exposure to language. The 2015 Bridging the Word Gap Challenge run via the website Challenge.gov sought to identify existing technology and expertise to spur the development of low-cost, scalable, technological interventions that drive parents and caregivers to talk to and engage in more back-and-forth interactions with their young children.[12]

The challenge unfolded in three phases. The first called for ideas to be expressed in five pages or less. Ninety participants were winnowed down to ten teams, which each received $10,000 and mentoring to develop and present their intervention after six months. From these teams, five semifinalists were selected for a $25,000 cash prize and further coaching. The final winner received a cash prize of $75,000 for Hablame Bebe, a dual-language app that promotes "language nutrition." Hablame Bebe launched on the Apple and Google app stores in March 2018. Since 2010, more than one hundred federal agencies have run nearly one thousand such challenges via Challenge.gov. This profusion of open innovation and crowdsourcing challenges in the public sector may help to explain why of those public servants surveyed in the United States in 2019, one-third said they had used the skill of crowdsourcing and open innovation.[13]

NASA has regularly used prize-backed challenges to spur crowdsourcing of innovative solutions from the public. The Asteroid Grand Challenge, for example, was focused on finding all asteroid threats to human populations. NASA collaborated with existing crowdsourcing communities like InnoCentive and Top Coder to devise solutions to a variety of scientific and computational challenges.[14]

But prize-backed competitions that search for one or a few solutions are not the only way to take advantage of the wisdom of the crowd. Depending on your problem, it may not even be the best way.

COLLABORATION

Crowdsourcing generally aggregates the separate responses of individuals working across a network on their own. Collaboration, as we loosely define it here, by contrast, aspires to a more intentional peer production and shared group effort that has produced, for example, Wikipedia, in which volunteers sign up to peer produce encyclopedia entries.[15]

There is a large literature on the diffuse concept of collaboration. What we call collaboration refers specifically to members working together, whether in the same room or at a distance on a common, rather than a competitive, project. While crowdsourcing activities like competitions or prediction markets aggregate individual preferences across a network, collaboration implies more robust and diverse coordinating structures that enable people to divide and assign tasks and roles as part of a common whole.

The collaboration of thousands of volunteers who submitted words and their etymologies to editors created the *Oxford English Dictionary* in the nineteenth century. Collaboration works well when a community can be marshaled with a common vision, getting many hands on deck to develop something together.[16]

The case of Dana Lewis, who was diagnosed with type 1 diabetes at the age of fourteen, offers a compelling example of collaboration. Dana never got used to the various hassles of managing her condition: toting a portable glucose monitor to measure her blood-sugar levels, then calculating with a second device whether and when to inject herself with the insulin that she also carried. She set alarms overnight, lest her blood sugar should drop to fatally low levels. In 2013, dissatisfied with the lack of innovation by conventional medical-device firms, she created an artificial, do-it-yourself pancreas system that administers the right amount of insulin automatically. Later, she decided to make the technology available to everyone with the illness who was willing to build his or her own system. The resulting Internet community now has four hundred "DIY diabetics" who share readings online and collaborate to improve the device over time. They are collectively focused on making this product the best it can be.[17]

Sometimes collaboration centers around a process that distributes efforts to collect and map data. In a pilot project in 2000, the Connecticut Policy and Economic Council engaged local residents to collect information that would evaluate local government projects to clean up derelict land-use sites. Residents took photos of graffitied buildings with broken windows, trash mountains accumulating on front stoops, yards pock-marked with land degradation, and rodent infestations. From the project's origins in Hartford, CityScan was extended to half a dozen other cities. Equipped with what was then state-of-the-art technology, including handheld computers, wireless modems, and first-generation digital cameras, citizens were trained to collect and map data to assess whether city agencies were doing their jobs: scrubbing paint, picking up trash, cleaning yards, and boarding up broken windows. Connecticut's introduction of citizen-based performance assessment made CityScan one of the earliest examples of technology-enabled collective intelligence.[18]

COCREATION

Cocreation, also called codesign, is a process that generates many diverse responses to a question and uses these contributions in order to go beyond a single solution. The Lakewood, Colorado, sustainability network is an example of it. The city of Lakewood supports its residents to design and deliver workshops and events to get more residents engaged in the process of designing and implementing sustainability to enhance the livability of their local neighborhoods. Since the program launched in 2012, almost thirty thousand residents have participated in more than five hundred events, workshops, and projects, which have increased the city's tree-canopy coverage, reduced waste, conserved water, and improved energy efficiency.

Local Motors, founded in 2007, is another example. It uses the ideas of customers to design and manufacture new cars, coordinating the work of many people to design and then manufacture a plethora of automotive designs. A recent creation is Olli, a 3-D-printed, 100 percent recycled materials, autonomous minibus powered by the latest IBM Watson artificial intelligence but still capable of being "printed" in nine hours.[19]

In 2018–2019, the Royal Society for the Arts in Britain (RSA) created the Future of Work Award to elicit innovative and inspiring ways to generate quality employment. Far from seeking a single solution, the RSA wanted to build a movement for innovation in the future of work. Among the twenty-eight new technologies recognized by the award was Bob Emploi, a French open-source application that uses big data to give job seekers a personalized assessment of their unemployment situation and automatically recommends viable strategies to reenter the job market. Portify, another entry, helps freelancers to understand, manage, and plan their finances, in order to improve their financial security and well-being.[20]

While few people will disagree with the importance of cocreation, that does not mean we know how or when to use it. For this reason, The GovLab collaborated with Nesta, the innovation think tank of the United Kingdom, to produce thirty case studies along with a report and guide on solving public problems with collective intelligence to showcase the how-tos of codesign, available at https://www.thegovlab.org/collective-intelligence.html.

All of these explanatory materials exist because government, in particular, stubbornly maintains its culture of working behind closed doors and shielding its "deliberative work product"—how it marks documents to keep them confidential—from public view.[21] Private companies, too, are secretive about proprietary work products, reluctant to invite customers or suppliers to collaborate, lest they lose control of their intellectual property. Whereas once the Lego Group threatened legal action against Lindsay Fleay, the Australian creator of one of the earliest Lego "brick films," *The Magic Portal*, the company later came to embrace customer crowdsourcing and cocreation through such programs as Lego Mindstorms and Lego Ideas. Inviting fans to participate in designing Lego sets has been credited with turning around the company and catapulting it into first place as the world's largest toy manufacturer.

But despite the varieties of group work available and the success stories, engagement too frequently becomes an empty promise without a clear plan to take advantage of the power of the crowd efficiently. Examining more closely the different ways that groups can function—crowdsourcing, collaboration, cocreation—and the benefits helps us to understand how to design options that enable groups to participate in different problem-solving tasks, especially solution identification.

WHAT IS THE VALUE OF USING COLLECTIVE INTELLIGENCE?

Collective intelligence unlocks the potential for innovation by exposing institutions to new and different ideas and perspectives from "outside." We know that customers are a vital source of innovation for firms like Lego. The MIT professor Eric von Hippel coined the term "user innovation" to explain customers' contribution to the design of products and services they use. In "The Dominant Role of Users in the Scientific Instrument Innovation Process," von Hippel documented more than one hundred examples of the most important scientific and commercial innovations inspired by customers rather than firms.[22] He found that approximately 80 percent of those new products had been invented and field-tested by customers who were end users, rather than by the traditional process of manufacturers trying to guess a market gap. Von Hippel says customers have the real "expertise" about where problems lie and are better placed than anyone else to drive the product innovation that meets their needs.

Building on von Hippel's work, in 2003, Henry Chesbrough, a professor at the Haas School of Business at the University of California, Berkeley, popularized the term "open innovation." This term describes the distributed process in which people work across organizational boundaries in order to accelerate innovation.[23] Crowds of problem solvers can outperform a company's internal R&D unit, if one knows when—and how—to use them.[24]

Plenty of subsequent research has borne out the findings of von Hippel and Chesbrough about the creative power of groups working together in an open innovation process, whether it is crowdsourcing, collaboration, or cocreation. Research has taught us that when we distribute a problem to a broader audience to help us solve it, it increases the diversity of the people who participate and improves, in many cases, the solutions that get developed. In other words, collaboration helps to improve the effectiveness of problem solving.

When we turn to a larger community of people, whether from our own or a different workplace, from another sector like government, academia, or business, from our own community or around the globe, we are, in the first place, getting more hands on deck, making lighter otherwise hard work. Federal agencies have sponsored one thousand crowdsourcing challenges (like the Word Gap Challenge) since 2010, engaging the public in tackling such hard problems as improving methods to find asteroids, because they are looking for more people to help solve hard problems. Private platforms such as InnoCentive or Kaggle similarly offer additional problem-solving people power.

But involving a greater number of people is only one reason to prefer an open innovation approach. A greater diversity of people, with various skills and perspectives, can be just as important, especially when care is taken to go beyond the usual suspects for expert input. For example, the Intelligence Advanced Research Projects Activity (IARPA) invests in high-risk, high-payoff research programs to tackle some of the most difficult challenges confronted by the US intelligence community. IARPA's former director Jason Matheny explains that managers are encouraged to use prize challenges, alongside traditional research grants and contracts, to broaden IARPA's research and to engage nontraditional researchers.[25] The story of the Argentinian car mechanic who revolutionized childbirth is perhaps the most illustrative example of the value of attracting unusual suspects. Inspired by a YouTube video about how to extract a cork that has fallen into a bottle of wine, the car mechanic invented a pathbreaking improvement on forceps that is designed to be much safer for the baby and that is now in widespread use. He had no formal medical training yet had the insight precisely because he approached the problem differently.[26]

The pooled intelligence of groups can draw on lived experience in order to identify fresh insights and innovative ideas. In Colombia, the Supreme Court judge Carlos Bernal wanted to better understand the circumstances under which the proceedings of a trial might legitimately be closed to the press in order to decide whether he should expand a legal ruling to make all proceedings open. He crowdsourced information from journalists, prosecutors, and judges to learn more about conditions in courts across the country, receiving thirty-five submissions in writing and via video.[27] No amount of studying could have taught him what he learned from the distinct lived experience of these diverse audiences.

Pooled intelligence also helps to catalog what is being done and what works well in a given area of policy and practice. In my home state of New Jersey, for example, our Office of Innovation created a "policy and practice catalog," a searchable open repository of policies and programs relating to the impact of technology on the future of work, in order to bring to bear the collective experience of other jurisdictions, think tanks, activists, and experts to inform our work.[28] At The GovLab in 2021, we used the Smarter Crowdsourcing method (described in chapter 5) to gather global expert practitioners from a wide variety of fields, from education to neuroscience to artificial intelligence to video-game design to policy, in order to canvass solutions to the challenge of administering nonacademic measures of student performance, such as grit, curiosity, and social and emotional intelligence, without bias. We also convened parents, students, and teachers. Without bringing people together across fields and from diverse perspectives, it would have been extraordinarily difficult to come up with as many effective solutions as quickly.[29]

Finally, and most important, encouraging others to participate and invest in solving a problem helps to build legitimacy for an initiative. Those who are most affected by a familiar problem can be readily engaged and are often excited to help devise solutions for it, unlocking their potential for buy-in, trust, and loyalty. It is especially important to engage broader communities in the design of solutions to reduce bias and discrimination, to promote equity, racial justice, and equality. Using collective-intelligence methods like crowdsourcing, collaboration, and cocreation can lead to new partnerships among civil society, government, business, and academia—partners that may not otherwise have met or recognized their interests in common or the potential they have to work together as equals. When we design solutions with, instead of for, people—working in tandem with communities—as we saw with human-centered problem definition, we respect the people we are aiming to serve.

HOW TO USE COLLECTIVE INTELLIGENCE

Engaging with others is useful at every stage, from defining a problem right through to project evaluation (to be covered in chapter 11). Yet to succeed, crowdsourcing, collaboration, and cocreation must be intentionally designed and choreographed if they are to be efficient and effective. Just as one would decide on the moderation process for any meeting—the most recognizable form of collective intelligence—success in organizing collective intelligence requires designing the rules of engagement. You need to be able to articulate which audiences you want to involve, what you want people to do as part of the process, and how you will communicate with them. Creating a detailed plan with well-defined milestones may help you persuade others of the need to go outside your own organization for input. Most importantly, it will help you convince yourself.

Before designing the process for working with your "crowd," however, you must be able to articulate the reason you want to work with others. This is a necessary condition of your ability to listen openly. It requires the groundwork to define the problem. If you have not gathered some initial data, and if you cannot yet articulate your goal to the crowd you intend to approach, you may not be ready.

There are nine key design decisions you must make to develop a collective-intelligence project.[30]

1. Can you articulate the project's goals?
2. Can you identify the right participants?
3. Can you reach the participants you have identified?
4. Can you pick the right owner?
5. Can you select the incentives to encourage participation?
6. Can you clearly define the tasks?
7. Can you clearly design the process?
8. Can you evaluate inputs?
9. Can you use what the group creates?

Defining and clearly articulating your *goals* is the first prerequisite (see exercise 1). The most successful examples are those where the organizers clearly define for participants and for themselves what the project seeks to

ASSEMBLING YOUR COLLECTIVE INTELLIGENCE PROCESS

For blank worksheets, see solvingpublicproblems.org

ARTICULATE THE GOALS

Define a clear and compelling goal and write it down so it can be clearly articulated to others?

CHOOSE PARTICIPANTS

Decide when you want to mobilize the crowd during your problem-solving process

CONDUCT OUTREACH

Advertise the opportunity to participate via multiple channels.

SELECT THE OWNER

Make sure the owner and coordinator of the process has the resources and ability to manage the process, respond to and implement what users propose.

SELECT INCENTIVES

Decide on the incentives by asking "what will motivate people to contribute. Decide whether to use financial or non-financial incentives (or a mix).

DEFINE THE WORK

Chunk the work you want people to do into manageable tasks.

DESIGN THE PROCESS

Clearly communicate the workflow from start to finish.

EVALUATE OUTPUTS

Design a judging and evaluation process. Use tools to help you make sense of voluminous inputs.

USE THE GROUP'S WORK

Make the process relevant by devising and communicating a plan to make use of the output.

🏛 THEGOVLAB

SOLVING PUBLIC PROBLEMS

How to design a collective-intelligence process (Courtesy of Beth Simone Noveck / The GovLab)

accomplish. You must confirm that using a collective-intelligence process fits the context and that you are using the group to solve a clearly delineated problem.[31] CityScan, described earlier, was so successful in its day because its aim was clear and well understood by all involved: to get cities like Bridgeport to clean up eight derelict land-use sites every month.

Second, you must *identify who participates* and determine whether the "crowd" you want to engage will be selected or self-selected or both (see exercise 2). There have been many recent experiments with sortition, the random selection of a representative sample of the population as participants.[32] However, the most successful collective-intelligence problem solving generally involves some opportunity for audience members to self-select to participate and leverages their passion for the work. This may be because it speaks to their interest or experience. Self-selection is what made the Word Gap Challenge a success, for example. In other cases, though, a representative sample of the public would be more appropriate, to guarantee diversity or strengthen the legitimacy of the process and its result. Targeting rather than randomization is also more important when, for example, you want to hear from doctors or residents of a particular neighborhood or people of a specific age. In some cases, you might want people to participate together. The 2020 Administration for Community Living Challenge required a team comprising "state leaders across aging, disability and Medicaid programs, community based organizations in the aging and disability networks, health IT developers, health care providers, health plans, and others with expertise in technical standards and data analysis" to apply for its $500,000 prize-backed challenge to design solutions for data sharing between health-care and social services organizations.[33] The right answer to who should participate is whoever will add to the effectiveness *and* the legitimacy of the project. Therefore, keeping equity in mind, always consider how you will include diverse members of the community, especially marginalized voices and vulnerable populations.

Third, you must *decide who will inform people about the opportunity to participate and how will they find out* (see exercise 3). A robust outreach strategy is needed to advertise the opportunity to participants. The Governor Asks program in Brazil deployed two "voting vans" equipped with laptops, tablets, and Internet access. The vans traveled more than fifteen hundred kilometers around Rio Grande do Sul to engage the state's offline population in devising and prioritizing solutions to a policy problem. This in-person outreach was key to recruiting the one hundred thousand participants of what would become the largest digital consultation in Brazil's history. In 2020 in New Jersey, when we wanted to consult workers about their views on the future of worker rights, health, and lifelong learning, the Office of Innovation partnered with more than forty interest groups to invoke their assistance in spreading the work and advertising the engagement.[34]

Advertising to the desired audience the opportunity to participate will yield innovative and diverse solutions. In Iceland, one in five of the citizens of Reykjavik use the city's codesign platform in part because the Mayor's Office invested in mailing an announcement about the platform to every resident. Your intended audience will not become aware or involved without a deliberate strategy. Rahvakogu, an Estonian initiative to crowdsource proposals to reform the country's political financing system, was weakened by inadequate investment in attracting diverse participants. The initiative found that a disproportionately large number of participants were middle-aged males with a higher level of education, potentially skewing the nature and range of proposals.

Fourth, you must *decide on the owner of the process*: who will do the organizing, ensuring that the entity turning on the machinery of crowd participation is in a position to use what it learns from participants and that governance of the process is legitimate. Therefore, partners need to discuss how the project will be managed. Choosing the owner may also be a question of whether the initiative should be managed from the top down by the convening organization or from the bottom up by the crowd or third-party organization, be it a government, NGO, university, or interest group. The crowdsourcing researcher Daren Brabham explains that "crowdsourcing entails a mix of top-down, traditional, hierarchical management process and a bottom-up, open process involving an online community."[35] As a result, there are many options for ensuring an efficient yet inclusive process.

Fifth, you must *identify the interests of the participants and design the incentives*—intrinsic or extrinsic—that will motivate their participation. This is not easy to do, and there is no right answer (see exercise 4). The literature is almost equally divided between research arguing the merits of intrinsic or extrinsic incentives.[36] We saw with the food-preservation challenge or the Word Gap Challenge how the financial incentive of a prize can spur engagement and get people to develop innovative solutions. By contrast, one meta-analysis of 128 studies found that offering rewards causes participants to feel that the activity is less valuable.[37] Intrinsic rewards like public recognition can also be a powerful incentive. Citizens of Lakewood, Colorado, earn credits for sustainability initiatives. Those communities that earn sixty credits achieve Sustainable Neighborhood certification. Lakewood also celebrates a community's accomplishments through public events with city leaders and in local publications. Given that there is no one way to do this, you can ask people what they would prefer and experiment with different approaches.

Sixth, you must *define the tasks* that the group will undertake (see exercise 5). What type of participation will elicit the input you need? You may have to "chunk" or break down a bigger project into smaller, more discrete tasks such as data collection, fundraising, generating solutions, commenting on other people's ideas, or, as we saw with the Pulsepoint program, performing CPR. Thus, gathering data, analyzing data, and visualizing data might usefully be separated because different people are good at these tasks. Some of the most successful collective-intelligence projects have clearly defined the participants' tasks.

In the Carbon Neutral Helsinki 2035 Action Plan, residents of the capital city use the Climate Watch website to hold city officials to account for accomplishing the 147 targets to which civil servants and citizens have collaboratively agreed. Both citizens and government officials have clearly assigned tasks. Ordinary people serve as real-time monitors of progress. Each department also designates specific "contact persons" who are responsible for reporting on the progress made toward each measure on the Climate Watch website.

Whatever you ask people to undertake, be sure that the people involved understand clearly what is being asked of them and have the capacity, tools, and know-how to participate. You should develop good documentation that explains how each task should be done and by whom. The National Institutes of Health's All of Us research program provides instructions through a series of online modules, which explain how to participate in this big-health-data-sharing initiative using explanatory videos with brief text. All content is targeted at a middle-school or lower comprehension level. As the All of Us program crowdsources medical records and bio-samples from participants to inform scientific research, clear instructions are crucial to ensure the accuracy of the information collected and that people clearly understand their rights and obligations.[38]

Seventh, related to defining the task, you must *design the process and the associated workflow from start to finish* and choose a platform that makes that process possible in practice. In use in Indonesia, India, Japan, and the United States, PetaBencana, also known as RiskMap, is a collaborative mapping platform that integrates Twitter and text messaging to produce shared flood maps. The system is programmed to react when, for example, a Jakarta resident tweets the word *banjir* (flood) and tags @PetaJkt. PetaBencana.id automatically replies via Twitter, requesting visual confirmation with geo-tagged photos. The platform combines incoming reports with official data from the city government to build an up-to-the-minute, online flood map. The process is designed to be simple enough to understand and use by anyone with a smart device.[39] Because the tool explains and documents exactly what the resident needs to do and what the response will be, it is in widespread use. Since 2015, more than 761,746 unique users have accessed PetaBencana more than 1,554,913 times. On New Year's Eve 2019 and into 2020, Jakarta experienced torrential rain. As floodwaters rose, thousands of residents submitted reports to PetaBencana and used the online map to avoid flooded areas and make decisions about their safety. This led to an increase in activity on the platform of 24,000 percent.[40]

Eighth, while not all collective-intelligence projects are competitions, *you want to be able to evaluate inputs to ensure that they are helping you to achieve your goal* (exercise 6). The evaluation method depends on the desired outputs. For instance, the state of New Jersey ran an open innovation competition called the ENJINE Challenge in 2019 to source ideas from state employees to improve the delivery of services by state government in a two-stage competition. In the first round, other state employees voted to select the twenty most important and feasible ideas to advance to the second stage. Importantly, the evaluation system was not a thumbs-up and thumbs-down scale that would have turned rating into a mere popularity contest. Many software platforms offer vague rating schemes that lead to inconsistent evaluations and often the selection of the funniest or most outrageous submission. Having the wrong evaluation mechanism is what led during the Obama administration to ideas such as "build a Death Star" (the fictional *Star Wars* space station and superweapon) or "deport Justin Bieber back to Canada" receiving the most votes on the White House's "We the People" electronic petition website.[41] By contrast, the open-source "Your Priorities" tool used in the ENJINE Challenge customized the evaluation criteria—importance and feasibility—and invited participants to rate sub-missions using these two scales. Then a panel of five expert judges deliberated and chose the five winning proposals. This approach helped build legitimacy in the first round while ensuring that the winning proposals were practical.

Where necessary, you may want to use technology to evaluate a large number of responses. For example, in 2016, the US State Department sought to improve its passport application and renewal process in anticipation of an increase in the number of applications. It ran an online public-engagement process to ask people what improvements they wanted. In order to make rapid sense of the one thousand ideas received, it used a commercial software platform called Insights.us to scan the text and create summaries. A human team then grouped the summaries into nine categories.[42]

Ninth and finally, you must *plan ahead how to use the input and actions* you have gathered or activated. Using the input effectively provides a powerful incentive for people to participate, yet too often, open innovation efforts are launched into the world without a clear strategy to convert contributions into operations. This not only leads to the waste of resources but can deter citizens from wanting to participate in future efforts. There is no need to use collective intelligence for its own sake. Rather, you want to engage a broader community if you are going to use its work.

Challenges arise when the information received is too voluminous, underdeveloped, or irrelevant. During the planning period following President Obama's election in 2008 and before his inauguration in 2009, the president's transition team (of which I was a member and made the suggestion to do this) asked the American public to suggest actions for the first one hundred days of the administration. This "People's Briefing Book" process yielded eighty-four thousand suggestions, a volume so great that it was impossible to read or consider them all. Though the project was designed to make it easy for individuals to participate, without enough attention to how the information would be used, it became more of a publicity stunt.[43]

When designed well and executed properly, collective intelligence is an efficient and effective way to tap into the wisdom, expertise, and lived experience of the crowd. The array of new technologies available makes it easier than ever for you as a public problem solver or public entrepreneur to extract useful insights and contributions from people who have traditionally

gone unheard. Doing so allows us to create better solutions to public problems and more effectively serve the public.

TO DO

Now that we have outlined three types of group work at the root of collective-
intelligence practices—crowdsourcing, collaboration, and codesign—and
explained the process for using collective intelligence, let us look at some
exercises for choreographing a successful project. For additional help, see
the free online course on designing collective-intelligence projects in response to a crisis: http://covidcourse.thegovlab.org and The GovLab's collective-intelligence case studies at https://www.thegovlab.org/collective-intel
ligence.html, which offer detailed design instructions and advice from
those who have run successful projects.

Exercise 1: Assemble Your Collective-Intelligence Process

1. *Articulate the goals.* Define a clear and compelling goal and write it
   down so it can be clearly articulated to others. What constitutes
   success? What outputs and outcomes are you seeking?
2. *Choose participants.* Decide when you want to mobilize the crowd
   during your problem-solving process. You have the option, for
   example, to incorporate "the crowd" at a foundational stage to help
   define the problem at the outset or, later, to refine a definition already
   crafted. (See exercise 2 for more on choosing participants.)
3. *Conduct outreach.* Advertise the opportunity to participate via multiple
   channels.
4. *Select the owner.* Make sure the owner and coordinator of the process
   has the resources and ability to manage the process, to respond to and
   implement what users propose.
5. *Select incentives.* Decide on the incentives by asking, "What will
   motivate people to contribute?" Decide whether to use financial or
   nonfinancial incentives (or a mix). Incentives do not have to be
   financial. In fact, research shows that intrinsic, namely, nonfinancial,
   incentives often work better than cash prizes do.
6. *Define the work.* Chunk the work you want people to do into manageable tasks.
7. *Design the process.* Clearly communicate the workflow from start to
   finish.

8. *Evaluate outputs.* Design a judging and evaluation process. Use tools to help you make sense of voluminous inputs.
9. *Use the group's work.* Make the process relevant by devising and communicating a plan to make use of the output. If you are not going to use the input, do not wind up the machinery of participation.

Exercise 2: Identify Stakeholders and Participants
You will need to define whom you want to participate in your project, considering what input they can provide to help you better define or solve the problem. Here we refer back to exercise 2 in chapter 5, where we laid out in much more detail the types of participants you may want to ask, keeping in mind that academic experts, government colleagues, local residents, and global citizens may all have something to offer.

Do you need to access domain experts with detailed knowledge of a specific field?

Or do you need to get a better insight into the problem by getting input from people with the lived experience of it?

Do you need to engage stakeholders in other agencies or in the wider public who may have important information?

And are there eligibility criteria such as age or location or other qualifications that will help you to target the people you most need to hear from?

Do not forget that you can use open innovation with your own colleagues across agencies as well as with local residents and global citizens. The sky's the limit!

Exercise 3: Develop a Timeline for Outreach
Once you have the design finalized, it is time to create a timeline for the exercise and launch it. Create a detailed plan, including dates and responsibilities, and stick to it. You will want to determine the following:

- What needs to be done prior to launch and how long that period will take
- How long the actual exercise will be open for participation
- How long the results will take to analyze and publish
- Who will support and organize the process and who will implement and use the outputs
- What platform will be used to undertake this activity

Additionally, in most cases, whether you are trying to attract participation from a broader audience or you simply want to promote the work you are doing, it is ideal to have a communications strategy throughout the process to share your work. This can include the following, for example:

- Posting on social media
- Engaging key stakeholders, interest groups, and other partners
- Contacting partners
- Contacting publications
- Distributing information via mailing lists

Exercise 4: Determine Incentives
Determine appropriate incentives. Incentives you can consider include the following:

- *Knowledge building.* Asking people to contribute to a specific field of knowledge
- *Skill development.* Helping people to build a range of useful skills while they are participating in the challenge
- *Community building.* Asking people to contribute to a large project of common interest
- *Civic responsibility.* Encouraging people to do things that benefit the community and fellow citizens
- *Public recognition.* Offering public acknowledgment and networking opportunities
- *Competition.* Appealing to those who are enthused by being challenged with a tough problem
- *Making a difference.* Offering the satisfaction of seeing their work implemented
- *Financial incentives.* Offering people money, prizes, and free stuff

It is important to understand your target audience, so that you can choose the combination of incentives that you believe will be most likely to motivate them to act or engage.

After thinking through potential motivation to participate, you want to think about the communication technology or platform that will best enable participation. To maximize participation, it is usually desirable to use multiple platforms or channels. Some to consider are the following:

Mobile applications (or apps)

SMS texts

An ideation or brainstorming platform

A commenting or collaborative editing platform

Social media like Facebook, Twitter, or Twitch

In-person meetings or discussion forums

Exercise 5: Defining the Tasks

What tasks are you asking people to perform? Note those here.

Broadly speaking, tasks might include the following:

- *Brainstorming and idea generation.* For example, Estonia's Rahvakogu process invited people to suggest ideas for how to reform the nation's political system.
- *Budgeting.* In Helsinki, the city's government uses the open-source Decidim platform to undertake participatory budgeting.
- *Collective action.* In the United States, United States Digital Response coordinates thousands of volunteer technologists and designers nation-wide to work on civic tech projects in collaboration with local government.
- *Commenting.* Since 1946, Americans have had the right to comment on draft regulations. Now they can do that online via http://regulations.gov.
- *Crowdfunding.* Go Fund Me is a well-known platform for soliciting and tracking contributions. Space Hive is a UK-based platform that helps local communities coordinate contributions to pay for things like renovating the park or starting a community garden.
- *Data analysis.* Kaggle is a commercial platform for crowdsourcing data-analysis projects.
- *Data gathering.* The Cities of Antwerp and Barcelona distribute straw-berry plants to residents. People test the leaves as a way to gather data about air quality.
- *Deliberation.* In South Australia, the government asked residents to debate the merits of major issues like nuclear power both on- and offline.
- *Drafting.* On Mudamos, Brazilians can draft proposals and invite signatures. With enough support, the legislature will review.

- *Predicting.* Unanimous is a platform to help groups organize a prediction exercise.
- *Surveying.* The proliferation of mobile phones has opened up new opportunities for conducting surveys in developing countries. Data about people's lives can now be gathered more cheaply and quickly. The World Bank's Listening to Africa initiative is now collecting household data through mobile-phone surveys in African countries.
- *Tasks.* Oxford University's Galaxy Zoo and NASA ask distributed volunteers to label pictures of galaxies taken by the Hubble Space Telescope in an effort to categorize them.
- *Voting or making decisions.* The crowd makes either binding or nonbinding and advisory opinions.

Exercise 6: Decide on Assessment Criteria
Whether this is a competition, collaboration, or cocreation exercise, you need to determine how you will evaluate people's contributions. What is your plan for evaluation?

Some possible methods are the following:

- Using expert judges to verify the quality of submissions and decide which to pursue. This is usually a good course of action when the submissions are less plentiful—so government staff can manage the workload—and when selecting the best inputs is more reliant on technical know-how or knowledge of government capacity to carry out projects.
- Asking the crowd itself to verify the quality of the activity performed by voting for the best choice or ranking submissions. This is common for e-petitioning or proposal-submitting platforms such as New Jersey's Innovation ENJINE Challenge, where, for Stage One, participants rated the top ideas submitted by simply "liking" proposals. This method works best for open innovation processes in which the volume of proposals or ideas and the number of participants are both high and when maintaining transparency, participation, and representativeness is crucial.
- Creating a peer-review mechanism through which a self-selected group of peers will verify the quality of the activity performed, similar to the way Wikipedia users and editors maintain the quality of the

crowdsourced content on the site. One approach involves a "double-verification" process in which, if you are asking the crowd to classify an image, for example, the response is not officially recorded until a minimum number of other people give the same response. This is a useful method when you want to ensure that the quality of contributions is high and when the outputs are critical, such as an open innovation project in which the decisions are binding.

- Seeking supporting evidence, for example, requiring people to upload a picture that verifies their submission or other data that back up what they are claiming or asserting.

Whichever method you use, it is good practice to be clear and up front about who will decide and the criteria for assessment.

The last thing you want is to have the evaluators picking the funniest proposals when what you need are the most feasible ones.

This transparency builds trust in your process and enables people to provide you with better-quality inputs.

CHAPTER EIGHT

Fast Field Scanning

You seek truth. You build trust. You practice service. And we love you for that.

Yo-Yo Ma

IDENTIFYING SOLUTIONS THAT WORK

In 2019, California passed legislation that required high school classes to start no earlier than 8:30 a.m. and middle schools no earlier than 8:00 by 2022.[1] A newly elected state senator championed the California law against significant opposition. Although failed federal legislation, the "ZZZ's to A's Act," had been introduced a decade earlier, state senator Anthony Portantino originally got the idea to sponsor the legislation from a 2016 *Los Angeles Times* opinion piece laying out research in support of later school start times.[2] The article explained that, while teens should get at least eight hours of sleep each night, a US Centers for Disease Control study found that only a quarter actually slept that much. The American Academy of Pediatrics found that "insufficient sleep represents one of the most common, important, and potentially remediable health risks in children, particularly in the adolescent population, for whom chronic sleep loss has increasingly become the norm."[3]

Practice in other states confirmed these findings: in schools where the school pushed back the start time, students got more sleep. Teens at two Seattle high schools got thirty-four minutes more sleep each night after the district delayed school start from 7:50 to 8:45. When sleep went up, so did educational performance.[4] While it remains to be seen whether the Start School Later measure in California will have the desired impact, many people are heralding the new law as a pathbreaking step toward putting the interests of children first and investing in their future.

Portantino's bill took advantage of scientific research in order to devise a new approach to an old problem. He was able to do so thanks to a preponderance of evidence—enough to combat pressure from those who feared giving up local control over schools or the disruption or inefficiencies the change might cause.

Portantino came across the evidence by chance, while reading the newspaper. But what if he had never seen the article? Or, more likely, what if he had read a slapdash article, full of opinion but no good research?

Solid research is essential to the work of public problem solvers. Before championing an intervention such as later school start times, they need to know whether it is likely to improve educational outcomes. Will the results be worth the investment it will take to bring about this change? What alternative solutions are out there? How do they know what the right—or at least the likely—answers to these questions are?

Too many leaders today outsource this process of finding evidence to a consultancy like McKinsey, paying exorbitant rates (a single junior consultant runs clients $67,500 per week, or $3.5 million annually) for research that could and, arguably, should be done by those who are working in the public interest, whose goal it is to uncover the most innovative solutions and reuse what has been tried elsewhere rather than to sell such solutions to governments at the taxpayers' expense. If nothing else, everyone on your problem-solving team should have rapid evidence review skills.

As public problem solvers proceed from defining a problem to defining its solution, they need systematic strategies for identifying what works, rather than chancing upon an idea in a newspaper or accepting a proposal from a lobbyist or a consultant. There is a great risk to starting with a preconceived solution rather than a method for searching for and arriving at the best solutions. While private-sector entrepreneurs want to invent the newest app or product, public problem solvers need ways to expand the Overton Window to find the most innovative ideas and also to know which among them are practical and tested and contain less risk. We would rather "steal" a page from a successful playbook than invent a new playbook—if for no other reason than it is easier to persuade others to try something that is proven to work elsewhere. But we do not want the desire to avoid risk to lead to settling for "the solution" or accepting what is presented on the consultant's PowerPoint deck and to short-circuit a thorough but rapid process for researching innovative alternatives.

Just as with problem definition, we want to use both data and collective intelligence—participatory approaches—to research solutions as a complement to inventing solutions through collective-intelligence methods. While we may start by looking at university-based empirical studies of effective policies and services, to de-risk the choice of solution, we have to go beyond academic publications and engage with communities. Efficacy cannot be judged by studying only those interventions that have been the subject of a small number of controlled experiments or other formal evaluations.

Rather, we need to use collective know-how to learn what is working in practice. There is an exploding attention to practical pilots, social innovations, civic technology, entrepreneurial experiments, and positive deviance (people whose success against the odds makes it possible to spot unusual solutions).

These innovations also merit review because they work in the real world for real people who use them. As one public official said to me, you cannot saddle an entrepreneur with having to do a randomized controlled trial (RCT), which they do not have the time or know-how to do. They are busy helping real people, and we have to allow them "to get on with it." Ultimately, whether people use the innovation is the real test and more important than any study.

While the movements around formal evidence-based policy making and open innovation may be engaged in their own methodological debates, these communities are not sufficiently in conversation with one another. The risk is that any consultant will use one approach or the other. Policy makers need approaches for canvassing a broader range of solutions, evaluating what works, and making an informed decision. That is why this chapter examines the skills of fast field scanning and rapid evidence review from both these movements and how to use them. It outlines sequenced and, above all, participatory methods for scavenging for solutions, evaluating solutions, and adapting solutions using blended research.[5]

We start with exploring randomized controlled trials, which are considered the gold standard for what works, as well as systematic reviews of RCTs.[6] But there are limits to using only RCTs or academic standards to evaluate evidence.[7] Thus, we move on to explore how to canvass nonacademic sources to learn what works. We start by looking at generic solutions (tools in our toolkit of change) for models and then identify methods for using "documents" (that is to say, written sources) and "people" (talking to social innovators and communities who have evidence of what works).

In combining these diverse sources of evidence, we are updating the definition that David Sackett—the father of evidence-based medicine— suggested: "Evidence based medicine is the conscientious, explicit and judicious use of current best evidence in making decisions about the care of individual patients. The practice of evidence-based medicine," he argued, "means integrating individual clinical expertise with the best available external clinical evidence from systematic research."[8] Similarly, the public problem solver needs to use all relevant research, broadly understood, to learn what works.

We need to go beyond finding solutions. We also need to evaluate them, and we need to engage with others to know how to assess what we are finding. Finally, we need to explore strategies for determining if that which worked elsewhere might work in our own context. The chapter ends with a series of practical exercises in fast field scanning.

Bill Clinton famously said, "Nearly every problem has been solved by someone, somewhere. The challenge of the 21st century is to find out what works and scale it up."[9]

THE SKILLS OF FAST FIELD SCANNING

Good evidence is the cornerstone of public problem solving. Public entrepreneurs need a systematic search strategy for finding solutions. This requires knowing three things:

1. How to scavenge for solutions
2. How to evaluate whether a solution worked "there"
3. How to determine whether a solution will work "here," in our context and community[10]

At each stage, you will want to canvass both academic *and* practical sources—use the right methods and tools to learn from documents and from people.

However, problem solvers risk drowning in information. We can spend too much time reviewing one promising source or chasing one expert interview, not realizing there is better information elsewhere. This is why it is vital to have a strategy for allocating time appropriately and pragmatically to

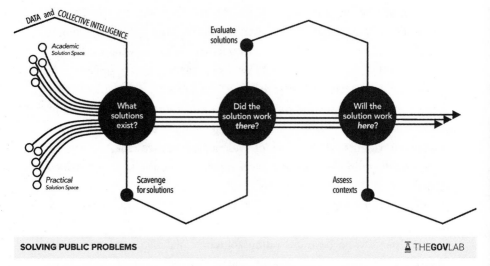

The skills of fast field scanning (Courtesy of Beth Simone Noveck / The GovLab)

potential sources both from the academy and from social innovators and methods for efficiently gathering evidence of what works.[11]

The first step involves developing efficient ways to learn how others have responded to the same problem. This book explores methods to canvass the "solution space" and do a rapid field scan to learn what has already been tried. Since we are committed to participatory problem solving, we want both to conduct a traditional paper-based evidence review and also to ask scholars and practitioners, in order to accelerate and legitimate our learning.

The second step is to know, Did those solutions work, and is the evidence of success reliable? If we are state senators or other nonexperts reading an op-ed about later school start times, what mechanisms do we have at our disposal to make sense of the studies cited in the article? What else has been tried, and did it succeed? Can it be reproduced here?

Third, we need tools for answering this last question. Even when a study is high quality, and there is strong evidence that the intervention it measures worked where it was tried, the intervention might not work in another place. For example, Street UK copied the idea of microcredit lending pioneered by the Grameen Bank of Bangladesh and subsequently replicated by Poland's Fundusz Micro. Yet the microlending experiment that was so successful in Bangladesh and Poland failed in the United Kingdom.

This was because microlending "there" depended on lending to individuals from more homogeneous groups, which provided greater peer accountability because they occupy the same social circles. That was not the case in Britain, where recipients were more diverse. Also, even poor people in the United Kingdom have access to credit cards, making the need for microlending lower than in Bangladesh and Poland and preventing the project from achieving the necessary scale.[12] We will explore some strategies for evaluating why an intervention worked in order to make a more educated guess about whether what worked "there" will also work "here."

The three steps that the twenty-first-century public entrepreneur uses to conduct rapid field scanning differ from those of the twentieth-century policy analyst. Whereas the policy analyst also searches for evidence, the public entrepreneur takes advantage of new technology to connect with data and with people in order to scan for and evaluate solutions. Especially for those public problem solvers who are outside of government, such as community leaders, activists, students, and others without access to institutional resources, technology makes a huge difference in rendering rapid field scanning cheaper and easier.

Using technology to make sense of large quantities of information helps to ensure that reviewing the evidence works within the time and resource constraints of the busy public entrepreneur, especially one who works within the tight constraints of government—which, of course, are numerous.

Because evidence is only part of the picture, we need ways to get smart quickly so that we can focus on investing the extraordinary level of effort required to convince others in order to get our solution implemented. The level of research rigor expected of a graduate student with several years to sit in cafes and write a dissertation is an unaffordable luxury for an activist, social innovator, or public servant who may only have a few days, especially in a crisis, and yet must avoid reinventing unnecessary wheels.[13]

Before we turn to strategies for rapidly identifying relevant research, solid evidence, and effective experiments and solutions, it is important to understand the background against which we discuss reviews of evidence.

A BRIEF HISTORY OF EVIDENCE-BASED POLICY MAKING

Leaders have used evidence from the time of William the Conqueror recording all ownership of land and livestock in the Domesday Book in order to determine tax policy—and probably earlier than that.[14] Yet it is a relatively new and increasingly popular idea to use what is considered "best evidence" in order to lessen the risk of bias in governing.

The concept of evidence-based policy making emerged in the 1990s in the United States and United Kingdom following the rise of evidence-based medicine a decade earlier (although its true origins are much older).[15] The idea represents a high point in the professionalization of governing that evolved over the course of the twentieth century with the rise of university-based training programs for public servants, the concomitant spread of scientific positivism, and the growth in the size of government.[16] Interest in more rational strategies for public management arose at the same time, as the emergence of network technologies created more pressure to modernize government.

As a movement, evidence-based (also called "evidence-informed" or "evidence-influenced" or "research-based") policy making has sought to replace ideologically driven policy making with rational, fact-based practices that purport to tell us that if we do X, Y will result. Advocates push for proof of what works to avoid harms and help accomplish greater social good. As the social policy professor Eileen Munro explains, this effort to predict the impact of a given intervention "embodies a positivist epistemology," that is to say, the assumption is that we can ascertain objective truths that can inform politicians and other policy makers about how to solve problems.[17] The Obama administration, in particular, put the development of evidence front and center in the design of key social programs in employment, training, K–12 education, and more.[18]

Critics worry, however, that the idea of evidence-based decision-making is deterministic to a fault. They are concerned about cherry-picking of evidence obscuring political decision-making. Where many people see evidence as helping to overcome corruption and bias, others see the language of evidence as obfuscating the political. As the saying goes, we measure what we value and value what we measure. The choice of evidence—among competing evidentiary bases—is an inherently value-laden decision cloaked under the language of rationality and science and subject to misuse.

Albeit contentious, inherent in the argument for evidence-driven policy making is the notion that values, and therefore politics, should and could play less of a role in problem solving. As the political scientist Deborah Stone explains,

Inspired by a vague sense that reason is clean and politics is dirty, Americans yearn to replace politics with rational decision-making. Contemporary writings about politics, even those by political scientists, characterize it as "chaotic," "the ultimate maze," or "organized anarchy." Politics is "messy," "unpredict-able," an "obstacle course" for policy and a "hostile environment" for policy analysis. . . . Policy is potentially a sphere of rational analysis, objectivity, allegiance to truth, and the pursuit of the well-being of society as a whole. Politics is the sphere of emotion and passion, irrationality, self-interest, shortsightedness, and raw power.[19]

Thus, notwithstanding the current assault on science and the willing-ness of many leaders to engage in fact-free decision-making altogether, the longer-term trend since the end of World War II has been toward a stronger embrace of scientific positivism.[20]

The Cold War era marked the beginning of federally funded research and development centers such as RAND and the National Laboratories such as Lawrence Livermore. According to the National Academies, a mile-stone in the emergence of evidence-based policy making was the 1966 Coleman Report, which surveyed six hundred thousand students across four thousand public schools in response to a congressional request to in-vestigate "the lack of availability of equal education opportunities for indi-viduals by reason of race, color, religion, or national origin."[21] The late 1960s was the golden age of quantitative approaches to policy making, with increasing uses of data modeling, statistical and cost-benefit analysis, sim-ulations, and other highly theoretical and quantitative approaches.[22]

As new sources of data and experiments, especially in the social sci-ences, become more available, the cry to use them to measure the effects of social and economic policies has grown ever louder.[23] In 2016, following a bipartisan call to "improve the evidence available for making decisions about government programs and policies," Congress established the Com-mission on Evidence-Based Policymaking.[24] Its mission was to "develop a strategy for increasing the availability and use of data in order to build evi-dence about government programs, while protecting privacy and confiden-tiality." A year later, the commission unanimously endorsed a final report, *The Promise of Evidence-Based Policymaking*, which outlined a vision of "a future in which rigorous evidence is created efficiently, as a routine part of government operations, and used to construct effective public policy."[25]

As the British psychologist and civil servant David Halpern, a leader of the global movement in evidence-based policy, writes, "We take it for granted, when a doctor writes a prescription, that there are good grounds to think it might make us better. But what makes us think that, when we drop our kids off at school, that the way they are taught is effective? Or when we report a crime, that the way that the Criminal Justice System responds is likely to lead to less crime in the future?"[26]

Halpern's comment explains the appeal of studies like the one undertaken by the University of Chicago's Crime Lab scholars, who tested the anger-management practice of teaching kids to stop and think before acting out. Their 2009–2010 study showed that participation in a Chicago Public Schools program called Becoming a Man reduced violent-crime arrests by 44 percent and improved schooling outcomes. A subsequent study of Becoming a Man of 2013–2015 showed reductions in arrests of 50 percent. A third study of the program, carried out in the Cook County Juvenile Temporary Detention Center, showed that participation in the program reduced recidivism rates to the center by 22 percent.[27] No wonder there is tremendous appetite for more such empirical work!

Interest in evidence-informed policy has also been fostered by the growth of new institutions dedicated to introducing social science experimentation into governing. Several governments are founding behavioral insights teams (as well as the "What Works Centres" discussed later in this chapter).[28] The term "behavioral insights" refers to the practice of using what we know about human behavior from experiments conducted in psychology, cognitive science, and social sciences such as economics in order to develop policies and services that encourage individuals to make better decisions. These teams focus on designing policies and services informed by empirical experiments in the social sciences. They either undertake experiments themselves or seek out successful experiments done by universities in order to inform the interventions they recommend to policy makers.

The British government was the first to create such a public entity. Established in 2010 by David Halpern, the Behavioural Insights Team (also called the BIT Team or Nudge Unit) starts with an insight from university-based social science research and then designs and scales a policy or service based on that learning. For example, research by the Austrian economist

Doris Weichselbaumer involved sending out fifteen hundred job applications to German companies with identical qualifications. She gave one applicant a German name, "Sandra Bauer," and two applicants a Turkish name, "Meryem Öztürk." One of the Meryems was shown with a head scarf. The results showed that the scarfed applicant had to send out four and a half times as many applications as "Sandra Bauer" to get the same number of interviews.[29] The study replicated 2003 US research by Marianne Bertrand and Sendhil Mullainathan, who sent out job applications using the names Emily, Greg, Lakisha, and Jamal. They found that the names that were more likely to be perceived as "White" received 50 percent more callbacks for interviews.[30] On the basis of her research findings, it created a software platform called Applied to change how public and private institutions recruit and hire and to overcome implicit biases.[31]

Today, more than two hundred public-sector agencies use behavioral insights in their work, according to the OECD.[32] In the United States, what began as a White House initiative under President Obama has been institutionalized (and depoliticized) in the General Services Administration as the Office of Evaluation Sciences (OES), which works across government to help agencies build and use evidence. To date, OES has completed over seventy randomized evaluations with dozens of agency partners.[33] Washington, DC, set up The Lab@DC to conduct behavioral-science research, including randomized evaluations, on issues of importance to residents, such as the use of police-worn body cameras or discounting public transit to improve mobility for low-income residents.[34] The Australian government set up BETA, its own social and behavioral economics team (originally established in the state of Victoria as the Behaviour Change Initiative), which coordinates a network of such units across government.[35]

The 2019 survey of innovation skills that I conducted with Monash University of the Australian public service showed that of the skills asked about, behavioral insights was the most well-known. More than 43 percent of public servants said they could explain the skill (although only 28 percent said they had used it in their work). By contrast, in the United States, only 35 percent said they could explain the skill, and 24 percent said they have used it.[36]

Finally, a general decline in trust in institutions and professions over the past few decades has fueled the movement for evidence-based policy making.[37] Doubts about government performance, coupled with fiscal austerity, are driving a demand for more empiricism in how policies are made and delivered and for connecting government to academia to learn what works. As political fights grow ever more partisan, research-based governing is also seen as a way to create a value-neutral and demilitarized battleground.

SCAVENGING FOR SOLUTIONS

Randomized Controlled Trials
The rationales for more evidence are driving greater use of RCTs in order to generate data about the impact of behavioral interventions.

An RCT takes its cue from John Stuart Mill's principle of the "method of difference" for making causal inferences.[38] A method-of-difference study aims to compare two things that are the same in all respects except one. If they then differ on that one element, the qualities of that element must explain the difference. The key to this measurement is randomization—ensuring that the groups being compared are alike in all other key characteristics except the intervention.

In an RCT, one group of individuals (called the treatment group) receives an intervention, and the other (the control group) does not. People are randomly assigned into one of the two groups, and ideally, neither participants nor researchers know who is in which group. As the science philosopher Nancy Cartwright and the economist Jeremy Hardie write, "By randomly assigning people to groups we can eliminate the possibility of external factors affecting the results and demonstrate that any differences between the two groups are solely a result of differences in the interventions they receive."[39]

For example, in Tennessee, an RCT was used to test the impact of reducing class size on students' test scores. Over four years, teachers in eighty schools with 11,600 students were randomly assigned to classes of smaller sizes (13–17 students per teacher) or to a control group of regular-sized classes (22–25 students with an aide). The study found that, on average, students in small classes performed four percentage points better in test scores than those in the larger classes in the first year of the experiment and one percentage point better every year thereafter.[40] Because similarly situated teachers and students were randomly assigned, we can infer that class size explains the improvement in test scores.

By comparing two identical groups chosen at random, we can control for a whole range of factors that enable us to understand what is working and what is not.[41] This is why many people consider RCTs to be the gold standard of evidence.

The standing of RCTs perhaps reached its apex with the awarding of the 2019 Nobel Prize for Economics to Michael Kremer, Abhijit Banerjee, and Esther Duflo for their experimental work alleviating poverty. They won the prize not for any particular policy intervention but for the experimental methods they used for testing the efficacy of interventions.[42] The three behavioral economists are the most prominent of the many development researchers and practitioners who use randomized evaluations to validate small interventions designed to reduce poverty in places like Kenya and India. The Nobel committee wrote, "This year's Laureates have introduced a new approach to obtaining reliable answers about the best ways to fight global poverty. In brief, it involves dividing this issue into smaller, more manageable, questions—for example, the most effective interventions for improving educational outcomes or child health. They have shown that these smaller, more precise, questions are often best answered via a series of carefully designed experiments among the people who are most affected."[43] (This needs careful strategic planning so that multiple RCTs are designed specifically to be meaningfully compared.)[44] The youthful trio's prize win also put to rest the long-standing notion that we can test the efficacy of drugs but not of social policies.

The Nobel Prize has elevated the importance of testing interventions using empirical field experiments based on RCTs and connecting that evidence to policy decisions. Rather than evaluate programs after the fact, RCTs enable promising approaches to be tested—and therefore scaled—more rapidly.

Where to Find RCTs and Their Reviews
A number of open repositories have emerged to make it faster to find solutions backed up by RCTs. These evidence clearinghouses produce what are known as "systematic reviews" of primary studies.[45] A systematic review is a review that attempts to collect all empirical evidence according to defined criteria. Systematic reviews "sit above" RCTs with regard to confidence in findings, as they consolidate multiple RCTs.[46]

Those criteria are intended to reduce bias, systematize and organize the evidence, and provide reliable findings on which to base decisions.[47]

There are now tens of thousands of systematic reviews, and using what the evidence-based policy expert Peter Bragge calls this "chronically underused asset" as your entry point can take much less time than scouring the eighty million individual research studies published since 1665, let alone billions of web pages indexed by Google.[48]

There are a number of organizations (see exercise 1) that produce systematic reviews or databases of studies or also conduct RCTs.[49] In education, the American What Works Clearinghouse (WWC) provides reviews of interventions in education and evaluates whether the research was credible and whether the policies were effective. The WWC, created in 2002 within the Department of Education, catalogs more than ten thousand studies of educational interventions.[50] It reviews the studies of programs (not the programs themselves), using a consistent set of standards. Hundreds of trained and certified reviewers evaluate these research studies according to set standards and then summarize the results. The WWC also publishes practice guides for practitioners, developed by an expert panel. Similarly, in the United Kingdom, the Education Endowment Foundation provides evidence syntheses about educational interventions aimed at teachers.[51] In Australia, the education clearinghouse is called Evidence for Learning.[52] The Clearinghouse for Labor Evaluation and Research (CLEAR) in the United States does the same for workforce-development topics.[53]

In the United Kingdom, the What Works Network comprises ten similar centers that review studies of social interventions and create a systematic way to find evidence.[54] Centers include the National Institute for Health and Care Excellence (NICE), founded as early as 1999, and the Centre for Homelessness Impact.[55] In addition to rating and ranking studies, they help UK policy makers with their searches and create toolkits and other accessible products designed to make solutions more easily findable.[56] Unlike What Works Clearinghouses in the United States, they also support the running of RCTs and have funded more than 150.

The Campbell Collaboration, based in Philadelphia, also puts together systematic reviews of interventions from around the world. It describes itself as "an international social science research network that produces high quality, open and policy-relevant evidence syntheses, plain language summaries and policy briefs."[57] While not all the studies it reviews have to be RCTs, studies are meant to be highly trustworthy and based on best available evidence. Campbell does systematic reviews on social welfare, disability, education, international development, crime and justice, training, knowledge translation and implementation, and business and management topics. It studies such interventions as Scared Straight programs, welfare-to-work strategies, mindfulness-based stress reduction, conditional cash transfers in education, school-based programs to prevent bullying, school-based feeding programs, parenting programs, and kinship care.[58] It also provides "policy briefs" (shorter reviews of reviews). It has an Oslo outpost and a branch in India founded in 2019.[59]

Campbell was meant to parallel the originator of systematic reviews, namely, the Cochrane Collaboration. Launched in the United Kingdom in 1993, Cochrane produces systematic reviews of medical research to speed up and enhance review of the clinical research literature by practitioners. Its work has led to significant changes in health care. For example, work on corticosteroids for women at risk of giving birth prematurely has demonstrated the benefits of this treatment and influenced clinical practice around the world. Other reviews of anti-arrhythmic drugs for atrial fibrillation have raised important doubts about the effectiveness of interventions in common use.[60] In addition to experimental studies, Cochrane looks at comparative and descriptive observational studies.[61] These alternative methods are important for considering "the effects of large-scale public health interventions or organizational change."[62] Intervention reviews may also address patients' experiences of the intervention.

In New York, Ideas42 (named for the meaning of life, the universe, and everything in Douglas Adams's *Hitchhikers Guide to the Galaxy*) is a nonprofit consulting company founded by the University of Chicago professor Sendhil Mullainathan. Ideas42 sells evidence reviews and related advice in order to push governments toward a more evidence-based approach. It trains people in how to use evidence, especially from the behavioral sciences, and it designs and runs dozens of social and behavioral experiments with public institutions in order to improve public-service delivery.[63] Bloomberg Philanthropies' What Works Cities also offers training to help cities of three thousand or more people use data and evidence.[64]

In Australia, BehaviourWorks Australia at the Monash (University) Sustainable Development Institute combines evidence reviews with searching for broad solutions and doing experiments.[65] Established in 2011 at one of the country's leading universities and among the more pragmatic of the what-works institutions, BehaviourWorks is the largest applied-behavior-change research unit in Australia. Its website states, "By using insights from the behavioural sciences, organisations can avoid making misguided assumptions about the influences on behaviour (what matters to people) and the types of interventions that are likely to work."[66] BehaviourWorks conducts evidence and practice reviews at the request of public entities. Rather than have a politician or public servant search studies in a database, it prepares jargon-free summary reports in plain English to help government scan the solution space. It also does rapid evidence reviews in time frames of three to eight weeks by drawing on an in-house database of five thousand studies.[67]

BehaviourWorks does not limit itself to searching for reviews but examines a wider body of evidence. It collaborates with specialist librarians to frame the search strategies and draw on grey literature such as government reports. It also contextualizes the evidence and practice review by interviewing a small number of practitioners and citizens.[68] When the Australian state of New South Wales was deciding whether to implement a container deposit law (ten cents back for every can or bottle returned), Behaviour-Works reviewed research and data from forty-seven examples of such schemes around the world. It found that on average, the programs recovered three-quarters of drink containers.[69] In 2017, New South Wales rolled out its Return and Earn deposit scheme.

Staffed by researchers based at Monash University, BehaviourWorks also conducts trials. However, it always conducts an initial evidence review to establish what experiments it will then test with government partners and combines this with structured stakeholder consultation to determine the local context for trials.[70]

Massachusetts Institute of Technology's Abdul Latif Jameel Poverty Action Lab (JPAL), home to the three Nobel Prize winners cited earlier, works in a similar way, blending original research and reviews of research. Its 194 affiliated faculty conduct evidence reviews and are also conducting or have completed 986 randomized evaluations in eighty-three countries.[71]

Two of the newest sources for searching experiments are open databases searchable by everyone: Health Systems Evidence (HSE) and Social Systems Evidence (SSE) from Canada. The first is run by McMaster University in Ontario and by the Cochrane Collaboration.[72] HSE provides an "access point for evidence to support policymakers, stakeholders, and researchers interested in how to strengthen or reform health systems or in how to get cost-effective programs, services and drugs to those who need them." It accomplishes this by providing "a synthesis of the best available research evidence on a given topic that has been prepared in a systematic and transparent way."[73]

While HSE primarily provides systematic reviews and evidence briefs for policy makers, it also contains a repository of economic evaluations and descriptions of health systems and reforms to them. Searches can be narrowed with a variety of filters based on the issue, the location of interest, or the type of document, among other variables. A "guided search" feature offers various tips on navigating the repository.

HSE's sister project, Social Systems Evidence, expands access to evidence reviews in twenty areas of government policy, including climate action, social services, economic development, education, housing, and transportation, in an effort to accelerate finding solutions to the problems outlined in the Sustainable Development Goals. Monash University, home of BehaviourWorks Australia, has partnered with McMaster to curate the SSE database. Monash University is the Australia, New Zealand, and Pacific Regional Centre of the UN Sustainable Development Solutions Network and therefore positioned to make this resource available to the broader sustainable development community. SSE identifies synthesized research by conducting weekly electronic searches of online bibliographic databases and manual searches of relevant websites.[74] As a result of such initiatives, the Minister of Health in Ontario, Canada, for example, now requires any policy memo proposing a new intervention to include a search of one of these two databases in order to demonstrate that the proposal is grounded in evidence. McMaster, like BehaviourWorks, also provides decision-makers with help finding evidence and creating rapid learning and improvement in health organizations, in particular. The university will prepare rapid evidence syntheses in three, ten, or thirty days and assist with conducting evaluations and training leaders in evidence review.[75]

RANDOMISTAS VERSUS CONTESTISTAS: THE LIMITS OF RCTS
In the hierarchy that has emerged in evidence-based policy making, the RCT is the gold standard and top of the evidentiary pyramid. Social scientists and social science methods experts who either run experiments or conduct systematic reviews—as noted earlier, studies that gather known research on a particular topic and summarize both the findings and quality

of the research—tend to be fervent proponents of the value of RCTs. But that evidentiary hierarchy—what some people call the "RCT industrial complex"—may actually be dangerous and blind us to research challenges from which RCTs are not exempt, cause us to overlook important other sources of evidence, or lead us to discount workable solutions just because there is no accompanying RCT.

However, exclusive focus on RCTs can lead to other important sources of solutions being overlooked. A trawl of the solution space shows that successful interventions developed by entrepreneurs in business, philanthropy, civil society, social enterprise, or business schools who promote and study open innovation, often by developing and designing competitions to source ideas, often come from more varied places. Uncovering these exciting social innovations lays bare the limitations of confining a definition of what works only to RCTs.

Unfortunately, advocates of evidence evaluation, especially RCTs—what I nickname the *randomistas*—diverge from the *contestistas*, who focus their enthusiasm and energy on the use of incentive prizes to spur social and policy innovations. Both groups are growing but growing apart.

There are significant limitations to RCTs. For a start, systematic evidence reviews are quite slow. Not only do experiments take time to conduct and often over a year or more to publish in a peer-reviewed journal, but the curation and collection of a systematic review adds another year to the time frame—assuming that a standard for how to evaluate the evidence has already been agreed on. A Cochrane review takes upward of two years, and despite published standards for review, there is a lack of transparency.[76] Faster approaches are important.[77]

In addition, many solutions that have been tested with an RCT clearly do not work. Interestingly, the first RCT in an area tends to produce an inflated effect size. Many more entrepreneurial and innovative solutions are simply not tested with an RCT and are not the subject of academic study.

For example, MIT Solve describes itself as a marketplace for socially impactful innovation designed to identify lasting solutions from tech entrepreneurs for the world's most pressing problems. It catalogs hundreds of innovations in use around the world, like Faircap, a chemical-free water filter used in Syria and Mozambique, or WheeLog!, an application that enables individuals and local governments to share accessibility information in Tokyo. Every year, Solve issues four "Global Challenges" to attract teams developing socially impactful projects. It then provides the winning teams with money and mentoring. There is little formal research about the fourteen hundred grassroots community innovation projects from which Solve selected thirty-two teams, yet these solutions are working in the field.[78] Solve is just one example of a prize-backed approach to find innovation.[79] You will recall from chapter 7 that Challenge.gov has over a thousand posted challenges with an enormous variety of solutions, not all of which are the subject of an academic article. As such challenges proliferate, and more programs in social innovation spring up, ever more promising solutions emerge.

Research funding is also too limited (and too slow) for RCTs to assess every innovation in every domain. Many effective innovators do not have the time, resources, or know-how to partner with academic researchers to conduct a study, or they evaluate projects by some other means. Social innovation competitions, prize-backed challenges, and government contracts generally do not call for or provide funding to support associated academic research. Also, academic researchers cannot conduct experiments for which there is no grant funding, as they need such funding to hire the PhDs and postdoctoral students to conduct the work with them. Academic faculty are expected to provide such professional opportunities for students.

Moreover, limiting evidence to RCTs may also perpetuate systemic bias because of the underrepresentation of minority researchers and viewpoints in traditional academe and philanthropy. Limiting evidence, too, to that which is developed by academics, instead of by communities (see the discussion in chapter 10 about social auditing as an alternative), is biased. The Nobel Prize–winning economist Angus Deaton points out that RCTs create the risk of discrimination:

> How is informed consent handled when people do not even
> know they are part of an experiment? . . . Even in the US, nearly
> all RCTs on the welfare system are RCTs done *by* better-heeled,
> better-educated and paler people *on* lower income, less-educated
> and darker people. My reading of the literature is that a large
> majority of American experiments were not done in the interests
> of the poor people who were their subjects, but in the interests
> of rich people (or at least taxpayers or their representatives)
> who had accepted, sometimes reluctantly, an obligation to

prevent the worst of poverty, and wanted to minimize the cost of doing so.[80]

Pushing decision-makers to rely only on RCTs could cause them to overlook important solutions developed by communities for communities. This is why organizations like BehaviourWorks in Australia and Project Evident and The GovLab in the United States help public partners find more diverse, nonacademic sources of evidence as well. Looking to non-academic sources may debias one's sources of evidence.

And whereas RCTs answer the question "Did it work?" (and some-times not even that), they do not explain how it worked or how satisfied people are. These are better measured using qualitative techniques such as structured or unstructured interviews. Deaton and the philosopher Nancy Cartwright write, "RCTs would be more useful if there were more realistic expectations of them and if their pitfalls were better recognized. . . . RCTs can play a role in building scientific knowledge and useful predictions but they can only do so as part of a cumulative program, combining with other methods, including conceptual and theoretical development, to discover not 'what works,' but 'why things work.'"[81] But qualitative approaches are often deemed inferior in the evaluative hierarchy.[82]

An intervention might even "fail" an RCT but still be promising. In the 1990s, the US federal government did an experiment in housing policy by giving some families a rental subsidy if they moved from a higher- to a lower-poverty neighborhood.[83] The results of the initial RCT found that "moving out of a disadvantaged, dangerous neighborhood into more afflu-ent and safer areas does not have detectable impacts on economic outcomes four to seven years out."[84] The Moving to Opportunity project would have seemed to be a failure.

But the absence of economic results in the short to medium term did not mean they would not exist ten or twenty years later or that people would not realize other benefits such as reduced violence, lower stress, and im-proved physical and mental health. The evaluation measured only short-term changes in income. In fact, subsequent research a decade later reveals that these relocation programs had profound and positive economic bene-fits for the children of the families that moved.[85] A few extra years of data made all the difference. Yet the initial failed RCT might have wrongly re-duced willingness to invest in social mobility programs like these.

Furthermore, RCTs test only very small and incremental experiments, like whether to give away a kilogram of lentils. Sometimes we need to be radical and try bigger things than we can measure with an RCT. For example, of the thirteen thousand RCTs run by Google and Microsoft on their platforms, 80 to 90 percent have found no significant effects, largely because they are testing trivial interventions. Google tested forty-one shades of blue to determine which hyperlink color to use. Most of those tests were probably inconclusive.[86] RCTs intentionally do not look at broader context. They are designed to be narrow, to say "this" intervention is better than "that" and incrementally build a knowledge base through successive experiments. But the more significant research results may also not correspond to a more practical, palatable, and implementable solution for the real world.

Not all "solutions" lend themselves to testing with an RCT. Traditional RCTs have not previously lent themselves well to studying how institutions innovate. While many innovative solutions relate to the design of organizations, research into how such design influences performance has been slowed by the challenges of running RCTs on such complex questions. Professors Kevin Boudreau and Karim Lakhani, of London and Harvard Business School, respectively, have spent the past decade trying to develop experimental approaches to empirical measurement of how institutions make decisions and solve problems, areas where there is a dearth of empirical literature. Sometimes institutions do not want to randomize participants, especially if the goal is to measure, for example, what kind of innovators participate in open innovation competitions and what they do. As we saw in chapter 7, we need participants to self-select whether to join a prize-backed crowdsourcing challenge. Randomization interferes with the design of that incentive. Second, as Boudreau and Lakhani point out, it is rare that the most important dimensions of an institution can be manipulated in isolation.[87] Given the variety and diversity of new tools in the innovator's toolkit, including creative forms of institutional design, we do not want to rule out such solutions even if they are hard to test with a good RCT.

While successful RCTs, especially as evaluated through a third-party systematic evidence review, are one way to evaluate the quality of evidence, they are not the only way. Evidence can be evaluated using other criteria that place the value on different measures. Take the example of York, England. York measures the effectiveness of its programs using a method called Social Impact Return on Investments, through which it analyzes the anticipated return on investment for every dollar spent with regard to its stated social values and goals. In 2016, York's People Helping People partnership came together to reimagine the approach to volunteering and to explore a people-led approach, embedding social action across the city. Among its initiatives, York enlists neighbors to visit and help the elderly to combat loneliness and social isolation. GoodGym is one such example of thinking locally, acting personally: neighbors form running clubs to get exercise while they run to visit an isolated senior and run back. In the city's people-helping-people approach, it places value on—and hence measures success by—mobilizing the talent and energy of citizens and civil-society organizations and creating a more collaborative and compassionate public service, not only on decreasing loneliness.[88]

Finally, modern machine learning may offer approaches superior to an RCT. It might make it possible to assess more complex context and variables than can be assessed in an RCT. The Dutch data scientist Arjan Haring writes, "We can utilize novel breakthroughs in our understanding of causality; as it turns out, it is strictly not necessary to resort to uniform random allocation as is done in the clinical trial. Rather, as long as we can compute and store the probability of receiving a treatment conditional on the patient characteristics, we can use the collected data to estimate causal effects."[89] The methods by which machine learning can complement or substitute for RCTs are still in their infancy (and beyond the scope of this book or the competence of its author to explain). What is important to note is that big data is leading to new ways of measuring causality and running experiments to measure, and even predict, the success of interventions.

In summary, the existence of so much bottom-up innovation means that we cannot be limited to choosing only solutions that have been evaluated using an RCT. This approach is only one way to spot solutions, and it comes with inherent biases. While some philanthropists demand RCTs, others eager to reward and celebrate community activism and creativity may see academic research as cumbersome and out of keeping with their desire to reward the agile innovator. For example, the Unorthodox Prize rewards unorthodox ideas that are not attracting sufficient attention and resources elsewhere.[90] If an innovation has been the subject of much study and publication, it does not meet the prize organizers' definition of unorthodox and undiscovered. Whereas they want to know how the idea is achieving impact and can be scaled, they impose no evidentiary standard or requirement. Nonetheless, such competitions attract potentially effective solutions with their promise of millions of dollars in prize money.

BEYOND THE RCT: FINDING EVIDENCE IN EXPERIENCE

Despite the strengths of RCTs, they are not enough to ensure that policy is informed by evidence and practice, as will be discussed in "Evaluating Solutions" later in this chapter. Solutions that are not backed up by an RCT or even academic research must also be sought and found. Public entrepreneurs need a strategy for complementing the kinds of reports available from HSE, Campbell, or Cochrane with their own research, using both documents and people, all without drowning in a sea of information. Again, we need to take advantage of collective intelligence to crowdsource knowledge of old ideas: What else is out there? What else has been tried?

Let us explore some of the methods and tools for conducting a rapid field scan that goes beyond systematic reviews of RCTs to include experience-based learning from both documents and people.

Cataloging Generic Solutions

While public problem solvers are seeking creative ideas to solve a public problem, their approaches, however unique, are also likely to fit a familiar paradigm. Reviewing generic responses to typical policy problems can help to improve the search for the solution by zeroing in on those that seem most promising. For each generic solution, it can be helpful to ask, Might this be a useful approach for me? Is there a version of this approach that will respond to my problem?[91]

Generic mechanisms for solving problems include those typical policy responses such as legislation, budgets, grants, contracts, loans, and economic and social regulation.[92] Lester Salamon's *Tools of Government* and Eugene Bardach's *Practical Guide for Policy Analysis* both list these usual instruments of governance. For each, there is a range of common options for what to do, including adding something new, getting rid of something old, changing how people do things, and so on. These generic lists capture the standard solutions—the acceptable Overton Window of options—in response to frequent problems of service delivery. Here are a few examples of typical plays in the policy playbook that may be useful for public entrepreneurs or public problem solvers to consider.

Governments levy taxes to raise revenue or to create a disincentive for a behavior. A tax on cigarettes generates money that can be spent on the public-health consequences of smoking or on something else. Raising the price also reduces the number of cigarettes people will buy. A public entity has the choice to impose a new tax or abolish an existing one, to change the tax rate, or to change who is taxed or how taxes are collected. A tax break or deduction can encourage prosocial behavior. Many jurisdictions are considering a Worker Training Tax Credit (WTTC) to reverse the decade-long decline of employer expenditures on worker training and help small and mid-sized businesses overcome financial hurdles to provide training to workers.[93]

Government also regulates. A public entity can create, abolish, or change a regulation. It can change the standard on which the regulation is based, add or remove an exception to it, or increase or reduce enforcement of it. There are countless examples of government seeking to solve a problem by imposing a regulatory requirement.

Government spends vast quantities of money—the US federal budget was $3.84 trillion in 2015—on contracts and grants.[94] In 2017, the federal government spent $94 billion on information technology alone.[95] These sums provide the government with substantial instruments, such as block or competitive grants, strategies that leverage the state's role as a huge market player, or sponsorship of research and development, which it can use to influence policy.

Finally, government, especially at the state or local level, often faces challenges delivering a service. Thus, public problem solvers can think about which new service to offer and which to abolish, how to deliver the service differently or to a different audience, how to reduce cost or to improve access to the service, how to stimulate its uptake and use, or how to change who delivers the service in the first place.

While many earlier tools were "vertical," in that they leveraged the power of government to impose laws, taxes, or regulations, in recent years, more emphasis has been placed on using "horizontal" solutions. These may be changes in process or method. For example, new kinds of partnerships, voluntary codes of conduct, and new forms of self-regulation may help to change behavior while reducing the burden of regulation.[96]

In addition, there are new strategies enabled by the availability of technology and data. The twenty-first-century public problem solver's and public entrepreneur's toolkit is much more expansive than legislation, regulation, grants, and tax breaks.[97] Thanks to new technology, entirely new instruments have expanded the window of acceptable interventions. The following list of approaches illustrates some of the novel means available.[98]

Create digital tools to enhance consumer choice. In the digital age, problem solvers inside and outside government can and do create and improve websites and other digital tools in order to offer an independent and unbiased source of information or to provide a more convenient service online from driver's license renewal to tourist information. The development of healthcare.gov to give people access to a health-insurance marketplace complemented the legislative strategy of passing the Affordable Care Act (Obamacare). The website, when it worked, was key to increasing the number of insured.[99] During the COVID epidemic, many states and cities built new websites to provide the public with a single place to find information about the virus, where to get tested, how to protect employees, school and business closures, and where to obtain much-needed state services. Like the training search tool that New Jersey is building, the federal Department of Education's College Scorecard has helped millions of parents and students make more informed choices about colleges by giving them better information about the costs of tuition and the value of the education.[100]

Hire people with unique skills who can help to solve a problem in new ways. Ricardo Haussman of Harvard University argues that one of the most effective ways to accelerate innovation and learning in systems is to "move the brains around."[101] Many of the new approaches set out in this book rely on creative personnel strategies and the creation of new roles to attract people with diverse talents that have rarely been seen before in government, roles such as Chief Data Scientist, Chief Technology Officer, Chief Innovation Officer, Chief Behavioral Officer, Digital Services Director, or Software and Product Development, as well new positions that involve the use of design and marketing skills. These roles, which might be short-term fellowships or advisory positions, create the opportunity to bring new talent into an organization. While most organizations are usually deluged with résumés from eager applicants, finding these innovative skills, especially among diverse applicants from underrepresented groups, necessitates a proactive outreach and intake strategy.

In 2016, the Italian government recruited the head of Amazon Europe, Diego Piacentini, to spend two years as Government Commissioner for the Digital Agenda. The team he created, which included people from the private sector with experience in computer science, product design, and big data, were all asked to commit to a one-year stint "on the inside."[102] Mexico and the United States both launched a Presidential Innovation Fellowship to encourage the best and brightest, especially people with computer science, design, and other skills less likely to be found inside government, to serve in the public sector for a year. Because this stint in government is time limited, the short-term appointee has a greater sense of urgency not to waste the opportunity.

Conversely, while places as diverse as France and Korea are experimenting with inviting people into government, the United Kingdom is encouraging civil servants to leave government for a "career break."[103] Scotland and Ireland, too, offer sabbaticals to public servants.[104] London and New York have held "innovation exchanges" to learn from each other about their methods of combating climate change and congestion.[105] As a result, in my own job as chief innovation officer for the state of New Jersey, we set up the office as a nonprofit, rather than as a project of another government agency, to give us more flexibility in hiring new staff.

Public labs. Another play in the public entrepreneur's playbook, especially, is to create a new organization (or reorganize an old one) such as a public lab, behavioral sciences team, or data analytics unit. Singapore created GovTech, or Government Technology Agency, reporting to the prime minister to create a more agile way to create digital services and signal their importance.[106] Changing the rules in these experimental organizations to make it easier to hire or procure or work differently can end up changing practices more broadly. One of MindLab's contributions was to bring human-centered design to the whole of government. Even if you are outside government, civic tech or critical tech labs can play an important role in galvanizing talent in civil society and nonprofits, universities and community organizations.

Create a prize to recruit people who compete to solve a hard problem. As chapter 7 discussed at length, prize-backed challenges are an increasingly popular strategy for promoting innovative solutions. On private platforms such as Innocentive and Kaggle as well as on the federal government's Challenge.gov website, institutions have posted thousands of competitions, from inviting the public to design a next-generation combat suit to asking it to devise a strategy for removing salt from saltwater to improve agricultural yields. Prize-backed challenges are suitable when the desired result, such as saving money or getting children to learn more quickly how to read, is agreed on. In these cases, solutions submitted via a competition can be measured, compared, and evaluated.[107] In one such competition in 2010 (my personal favorite), the Air Force Lab asked for solutions to deal with the problem of an out-of-control vehicle racing toward a military checkpoint. It costs real lives when the driver is shot and killed, with risk of further collateral damage. A retired engineer in Lima, Peru, devised the solution: a remote-controlled car with an air bag attached. Drive the car under the oncoming vehicle, deploy the air bag, and tip over the car. The lab spent $20,000 on the prize, a mere drop in the Pentagon budget. The challenge created the incentive, however, for this unlikely suspect to devise an innovative solution.

Introduce advance market mechanisms. Drawing on the insight that the size of an eventual market dictates the level of effort inventors will invest in innovating, the economists Michael Kremer and Rachel Glennerster have powerfully articulated the case for advance market commitments. An advance market commitment guarantees a certain level of sales to innovators if they invest in R&D that leads to effective solutions. Creating a "pull market," to use Kremer and Glennerster's term, has helped to produce vaccines and cures for otherwise-neglected diseases such as Huntington's, ALS (Lou Gehrig's disease), and muscular dystrophy, which affect fewer than two hundred thousand Americans each. These conditions are so rare that the cost of finding treatments would be too high without government assistance. An advance market commitment, especially on the part of developed countries, can help bring down the cost of making a vaccine available for free or cheaply in developing countries.

The US Orphan Drug Act offered pharmaceutical companies seven years of market exclusivity, when the FDA will not approve another drug to treat that rare disease, creating an incentive to develop such drugs. More than two hundred orphan drugs have been developed since the act was passed in 1983, while fewer than ten were introduced in the decade before that.[108] A key benefit of well-designed pull programs is that innovators get paid only for success, which brings down the cost for those who make the commitment, whether government or philanthropy, while increasing returns for those who solve the problem.

Experiment with algorithms to solve the problem of allocating scarce resources. Professors Atila Abdulkadiroglu, Parag Pathak, and Alvin E. Roth, all experts in game theory and market design, developed a matchmaking algorithm for assigning student applicants to scarce seats in public high schools in New York. In 2004, the first year of the new matching program, the number of students who went unmatched to a school dropped from thirty-one thousand to about three thousand.[109] Roth expanded his work on matching markets to find donors for people needing kidney transplants, as Nancy Shute explains in an article for the National Academy of Sciences:

> In all these situations, which are called matching markets, everyone wants the best possible match, but the parties usually have very different goals and priorities. So it's hard to devise a system that's fair and doesn't get bogged down while people ponder their choices. With kidney transplants, for instance, a patient might be unwilling to reveal details about her health because that information could be used to give her a kidney from an older or a sicker donor, even if a better one was available. For a matching market to work, people have to trust the process and feel safe revealing information that could potentially harm them. In the 1980s, Roth showed that deferred acceptance algorithms and top trading cycles make it safe for people to reveal their true wishes.[110]

With a background in operations research, Roth was able to think practically, not only mathematically, about how to make his algorithms work to address politically complex and value-laden issues. This work on market design earned him and Lloyd Shapley the Nobel Prize in economics in 2012. Designing new types of auction formats is a related tool in the toolbox. In 2020, the Nobel Prize in economics was awarded to two Stanford professors who redesigned the concept of the auction to account for common as well as private preferences. These newly designed auctions are used for buying and selling complex goods, from broadcast spectrum to electricity to carbon emissions.

Use open data. Many of the new tools involve the collection or use of data. Open data, collected and published by governments and other organizations, is a new tool in the twenty-first-century toolkit that affords many benefits, as discussed in chapter 6. These include improving government accountability, improving service delivery, or enabling citizens to make informed choices with the benefit of more information.[111] Institutions also collect personally identifiable administrative data and use them to better understand a problem or deliver a more personalized service or solution.

For example, many health-care and education organizations endeavor to use data about a person in order to target an intervention. Data collaboratives —also known as "public-private data partnerships" and "data-science talent exchanges"—are another tool now available, since the evolution of big data and machine-learning technologies. Opening or sharing data can be a way to solve a wide variety of access-to-information problems.

Use behavioral sciences. Today's public-sector institutions frequently use insights from behavioral sciences to change human behavior. The creation of prize-backed challenges or incentive prizes comes from the insight that offering an inducement will increase people's desire to innovate. "Nudges" —efforts to change behavior by changing the delivery of a policy or service in response to an insight from a social science experiment—are another tool in the expanded policy toolkit drawn from the social sciences. Many examples demonstrate that changing how an agency notifies residents will make them more likely to comply with a mandate. For example, millions more people in the United States and United Kingdom are saving for retirement thanks to a simple change to the way workplace pensions are set up. When employees in large firms were automatically enrolled into pension schemes, participation rates rose from 49 to 86 percent for workers who had been automatically enrolled.[112] And utilities in the United States showing people how their energy usage compares to that of their neighbors has already helped reduce energy consumption by $700 million.[113]

New approaches to policy making are also emerging from branches of behavioral sciences that deal with social judgment theory, heuristics and biases, learning and judgment making in teams, and naturalistic decision-making.[114] The Behavioral Insights team in the United Kingdom has codified these methods using four principles captured in the acronym EAST: make it easy, attractive, social, and timely. The team also developed a playbook of strategies that reflects the new types of tools in our policy toolkit.[115] Nudges are not limited to government. The same psychological techniques are being applied by a variety of actors, trying to change human behavior for good as well as malicious purposes. Whether it is NGOs promoting the use of masks during COVID or organ donation year-round or Cambridge Analytica allegedly manipulating messages sent to African American voters on Facebook to encourage them to stay home on Election Day 2016, these social and behavioral approaches are gaining in popularity.

This expanded repertoire of solutions—a toolbox that is growing in response to crises like the COVID-19 pandemic or the Black Lives Matter movement—offers a useful checklist of possible approaches for you to try in response to your own challenge.

Learning from Documents

Having mapped some of the landscape of generic policy solutions in an effort to identify promising approaches, we now need to get more specific and try to learn which interventions have worked in the real world, going beyond the RCT and the systematic review.

Solutions surface in two ways: from documents and from people. A few methods and tools will help us to make sense of the welter of available memos, white papers, and other literature from which these ideas emerge. After discussing documentary research, we examine how to use collective intelligence—people—to identify possible solutions. In both cases, to guide your search, it is essential to start with the problem you defined in chapter 4 and refined through uses of human-centered design (chapter 5), data analysis (chapter 6), and collective intelligence (chapter 7).

Journals

Web and library databases enable us to search academic journals containing qualitative and quantitative research well beyond RCTs. Google Scholar, Social Science Research Network (SSRN), Microsoft Academic, Research Gate, Baidu Scholar, Scopus, J-STOR, and Web of Science are all (partly) free search engines for finding journal articles. To reduce the need for frequent searches, they also allow you to set up alerts to receive notifications about new publications. Databases such as PubMedCentral for biomedical and life sciences and ERIC for education also provide more focused ways of searching domain-specific literature. The footnotes or bibliography in an article offer other sources: further articles or references to organizations with responsibility for or related to your field of interest.

Statistics and Trends

Organizations that conduct surveys or opinion research and polls can provide helpful context to understand both the problem and potential solutions. The US Census Bureau has a rich collection of statistics and reports with data that can provide helpful context. The Pew Research Center, Gallup, Dalia Research, the American Association for Public Opinion Research, Rasmussen

Reports, Quinnipiac University Polling Institute, and the Roper Center for Public Opinion Research are all survey research organizations that also publish statistics and data. Such surveys often ask how people feel about solutions to specific problems. For example, in a survey about big data, Pew found that three-quarters of US adults say that governments should more carefully regulate what companies can do with customers' personal information.[116]

News

A news search is the most obvious place to begin using an Internet search engine or a news database. Google News at http://news.google.com is a domain-specific search engine for news. In addition to searching popular news sources such as the *New York Times*, the *Atlantic*, or CNN for articles and opinion pieces, setting up a news feed that allows Google to send you the news stories relevant to your query at the frequency you want can be done at https://www.google.com/alerts.

YouTube offers high-quality sources of news and information, such as Vox News. Founded in 2014 by the former *Washington Post* columnist Ezra Klein to offer "explanatory journalism," Vox News provides in-depth videos designed to explain stories found on the website and has won or been nominated for multiple Emmy Awards.[117] Countless evidence-based policies are described in videos on YouTube. Results for America, an offshoot of Bloomberg Philanthropies, exists "to make investing in what works the 'new normal,' so that policy makers seeking to make decisions start with the best evidence and data, then use what they find to get better results."[118] Results for America produces YouTube videos about a range of issues from workforce development to child welfare.[119]

News magazines often write about academic studies, and stories about what works are popular. Just as Portantino learned about late school start times from an op-ed, most of us, especially if we do not work in academia, encounter evidence of different kinds on television, radio, and print and online media, all of which can make scholarly research more accessible and findable than technical databases. For example, *Harper's* magazine publishes a monthly index of fun facts and figures. A recent issue revealed that 38 percent of US heterosexual couples—but 65 percent of homosexual couples—who met in 2017 did so via a dating app or site. The source? A serious academic study by Michael J. Rosenfeld of Stanford University in the *Proceedings of the National Academy of Science*.[120]

The nonprofit start-up SciLine helps to connect scientists to journalists to improve coverage of scientific issues. It also runs bootcamps, such as a 2019 workshop titled "Covering and Communicating the Evidence: Adolescent Health." The goal is to deepen journalists' knowledge about "emerging adolescent health and behavioral issues and build communication skills among scientists conducting research in related fields, while also fostering trust, understanding, and cooperation between these two groups."[121] SciLine also puts out Fact Sheets with impartial discussion of evidence.[122]

The Conversation is an academic journalism platform, funded by sixty-one university partners around the world, that seeks to make academic research more accessible. Its editors help scholars to write about their research in simple language. *The Conversation* puts out nine different editions, including in Australia, Spain, and the United States, and the latter edition enjoys thirty-seven million readers each month. The US *Conversation* edition has published more than eleven thousand openly licensed articles, which are, in turn, distributed by the Associated Press.[123]

While the news is full of stories based on academic research, one has to take care, as journalists are sometimes unreliable reporters of the validity of scientific studies. The prolific food-policy writer Marion Nestle writes about how industry funding of research studies combined with poor journalistic reporting leads to untrustworthy evidence. For example, the Blueberry Association of North America has funded several studies that indicate that cognitive benefits may be found from eating blueberries. As a result, countless media outlets have published stories on the benefits of blueberries for preventing Alzheimer's, dementia, and cancer. But there is a catch, as Nestle writes: "The combination of irreproducible effect size calculations, selective reporting of effects, and general errors in systematic review methodology result in a misrepresentation of the strength of evidence about blueberries and cognitive performance."[124] Stories that tout one food as a cure-all are the same as any story that claims that any single intervention will fix education, reduce the cost of health care, create jobs, or address climate change—unlikely to be true.

Government and Nongovernment Publications

In 2010, the Twelfth International Conference on Grey Literature in Prague produced a long-winded but necessary definition of its subject and purpose: how to use the many reports and white papers in which studies of innovation in governance can be found. The conference defined "grey literature" as the "manifold document types produced on all levels of government, academics, business and industry in print and electronic formats that are protected by intellectual property rights, of sufficient quality to be collected and preserved by libraries and institutional repositories, but not controlled by commercial publishers; i.e. where publishing is not the primary activity of the producing body."[125]

Searching grey literature can be challenging, especially since it encompasses such a wide array of material, but these working and white papers are frequently the best sources of information about your solution space.

Organizations, including government agencies, think tanks, interest groups, and NGOs, frequently publish studies, reports, and position papers, detailing successful interventions. But the United States alone has 1,872 think tanks doing some of the work tracking developments in a policy arena and offering prescriptions for what to do.[126] Reviewing all the relevant think tanks and government agencies at the federal, state, and local level as well as philanthropies in your field of interest is a daunting task.

It helps to start by creating an initial map of the key organizations and reviewing their websites. Many of these organizations publish newsletters, which will arrive in your inbox and remove the need to search for sources. For example, just a few organizations focusing on innovations in governing —the Brookings Institution, the Organisation of Economic Co-operation and Development (OECD), the Institute for Local Government, City Lab, Bloomberg Philanthropies, the Centre for Public Impact, and The GovLab —all publish newsletters with stories about what is working in different communities in a variety of policy domains.

Remember that many of these organizations are advocacy organizations. They may publish helpful and detailed white papers, beautifully formatted publications and websites, and well-edited newsletters. But often they are not disinterested sources providing a neutral or evidence-backed overview of the options. They are pushing a position. As with any evidence, therefore, it is important to consider more than one source and to evaluate it critically.

Some organizations are set up specifically to do the work of summarizing policy solutions. The National Academies and the Congressional Research Service publish reports that collect relevant sources of research. Their reports can either substitute for reviewing scientific journals or provide a useful starting point for navigating the literature. The National Academies Press publishes reports of the National Academies of Sciences, Engineering, and Medicine, along with more than two hundred books a year on a wide range of topics in science, engineering, and medicine. For example, its *Roadmap to Reducing Child Poverty* provides a six-hundred-page overview of policies, programs, and approaches. It is a consensus study, meaning that a committee of experts crafted the report's findings and conclusions, and the report was also peer reviewed.

The Congressional Research Service (CRS) provides policy analysis to members of Congress, and since 2018, that research has been publicly available. Its website states, "CRS is well-known for analysis that is authoritative, confidential, objective and nonpartisan. Its highest priority is to ensure that Congress has 24/7 access to the nation's best thinking."[127]

CRS creates a report on a policy issue at the request of a member of Congress. Those reports do not offer recommendations. Rather, they provide an overview of current law and policy. For example, the report on federal child-welfare policy offers a forty-page explainer about current statutes, agency programs, and their funding.[128] Brief "In Focus" memos help to explain a policy debate, such as the trade dispute with China over rare-earth metals, without taking sides or adopting a partisan position.[129] The memo explains what the seventeen rare-earth metals are used for, China's dominance of exports, how US industry could be affected, current policy, and possible outcomes.

Learning from People: Using Collective Intelligence to Find Solutions
The public entrepreneur should not just ask "What solutions are out there?" but "Who is out there?" Informed people are the fastest shortcut to learning what has been tried and what is working. After creating a map of organizations, you can expand that map by creating a list of knowledgeable individuals. They can help you accelerate your learning and get a handle on the solution space (including pointers to relevant RCTs and grey literature). You can save time and effort by finding people with the experience, knowhow, further suggestions for what else to read and how to obtain those materials, and introductions to other people working in the field.[130]

You want to be able to "take advantage of design efforts made by others before you," as the public policy expert Eugene Bardach writes.[131] You may feel like the first person to confront your problem, but that is unlikely. It pays to see what others have done and learn from their successes and their failures. Talking to people in a comparable role but with more experience might dramatically shorten your search process. What innovations are out there and being tried? What is really working in the field? Who is doing the work that we might connect with to learn about their experiences, steal a page from their playbook, and possibly collaborate?

Professional Experts

Often, we do not know who, or what, we do not know. Combing through relevant documents for links and citations can lead to relevant experts. Asking them is often the best way to find others in the know. The expert heart surgeon and the jazz aficionado are the best people to lead you to others like them.

It was precisely this contention—that people who have special expertise or attributes will tend to know of people who have even more expertise than they do—that the economist Eric von Hippel and his colleagues set out to test. Their work on "pyramiding" (sometimes called "snowballing") showed that asking a known expert who knows more than the questioner about a topic, and repeating the process with each successive recommendation, is an especially good way to learn who has rare forms of expertise within large but poorly mapped knowledge domains.[132]

Identifying lists of relevant conference speakers and people on panels and delivering keynote speeches are other shortcuts for finding experts; so is checking grantee lists from philanthropies funding related work or searching through patent filings as well. I also recommend searching for journalists who write about your topic and who have a bird's-eye view of the field. Another search for lawyers and government-relations professionals who work on the same topic is often fruitful. Finally, you will want to identify experts in related but complementary arenas. For example, if your problem relates to overcoming the lack of consensus about what or how to measure something in your field, those who have worked on GDP or unemployment metrics might have useful insights. Hence, you will want to be on the lookout for "lateral" experts.

Whatever the topic, you want to look broadly across sectors. For example, when New Jersey wanted to develop a suite of workforce-development tools, the Office of Innovation talked to public officials in Singapore, who created the MySkillsFuture training website, but also to private-sector de-

velopers in France, who designed Bob Emploi, the virtual coaching platform, and to UK social innovators at Nesta working on workforce development to benefit from their experience—successes and failures—developing such platforms.

Civil Servants

Looking to other jurisdictions and their institutions can be a useful starting
point. For example, if you are thinking about a problem at the state level,
look both to other states and to organizations that catalog what other states
do, such as the National Governors Association. If you are interested in
what other cities are doing, you can reach out to sister agencies in cities of
a similar size. You can also contact the National Conference of Mayors or
International City and County Managers Association. The association for
the relevant office (such as the police chiefs association) may catalog relevant solutions or at least serve as a pointer to innovative leaders in the know.
Whether you are inside or outside government, public servants in other
agencies, other levels of government, and other governments should be a
go-to resource for expertise about what is and what is not working. Public
servants are as likely as not to be very forthcoming with their time, expertise, and know-how. They know (or can find out) what has been tried in
their city, state, or region. During COVID-19, New York, New Jersey, Pennsylvania, Connecticut, and other states in the mid-Atlantic region regularly
coordinated to ensure they aligned their policies on restaurant and school
closures, quarantining, testing, and contact tracing. Because people regularly crossed their borders, it made sense, for example, for New Jersey to
follow the lead of New York when choosing a contact-tracing platform, not
only to learn from New York's experience but to give residents a consistent
experience. Even if you are a public problem solver in a university or company, public servants are still a useful source of knowledge about solutions.

Social Media

Searching social media is a way to find people as well as content. Social
media sites sometimes measure influence on the basis of retweets or links
back to a person's online postings. These measures of a person's ties, as
calculated by mentions in social media or quotes in articles, drive sentiment analysis, the techniques that network scientists are pioneering to detect patterns in who is talking about whom.[133]

About two-thirds of Americans say they, at least sometimes, get their news from social media.[134] Twitter, Facebook, and other platforms for user-generated content (we could count YouTube here as well) are excellent sources of real-time, albeit not always reliable, news. Because many organizations cannot afford the communications staffing needed to bring attention about their programs to broadcast media, many prefer to advertise their work on social media.

Searching social media is an obligatory way to discover developments in your solution space. But to make the task easier, consider subscribing to existing or creating new Twitter *lists*. A Twitter list is a curated group of Twitter accounts. You can compile a list of the best people on your topic and create a list to monitor relevant conversations.[135] Twitter allows individual users to create up to one thousand lists, each with up to five thousand users on it. While such numbers hardly reduce the volume of information, creating a list of ten to twenty leading voices who write substantively about a domain of interest can be a good way to leverage the collective intelligence of those who are knowledgeable about an issue. In every field, there are people who use Twitter to curate and report news, research, and expertise. For example, if you want a snapshot of developments in citizen engagement, @participatory is great one-stop shopping. For the latest research developments on COVID, @AliNouriPhD at the Federation of American Scientists or @DrEricDing at Harvard School of Public Health cover the field. They are among those who use Twitter as a professional curation tool.

Identifying relevant hashtags can also be another excellent shortcut for finding people and content. Mentionlytics, Hashtagify, and Hashtagit, are three examples of hashtag search tools, allowing you to search social media descriptors in order to identify which descriptors people are more likely to use to tag their postings. When searching by hashtag, you need to know if #education or #edtech or #classroom will be the better way to learn about learning-related interventions.

Another type of popular social media platform is question-and-answer sites. Quora, Stack Exchange, Wiki Answers, and Reddit, as well as tutoring sites like Chegg (think chicken and egg) or Wyzant, are all examples of forums for asking and answering questions, where people engage in online conversations. The company Yext specializes in helping organizations turn their websites into Q&A websites to facilitate the asking and answering of customer questions. These Q&A as well as tutoring sites are another tool worth trying for a rapid approach to solution canvassing.

Expert Networks

Expert networks allow you to search for domain experts through databases that increasingly use data science and machine-learning techniques to source experts from catalogs of publications and other sources. Gerson Lehrman Group (GLG) catalogs seven hundred thousand experts and sells access to them, primarily to banks and financial institutions. Scholars Strategy Network, set up by the Harvard professor Theda Skocpol in 2011, is a nonprofit network of seventeen hundred academics interested in advising policy makers. VIVO is another easily searchable online knowledge network, in this case of scientific experts, primarily from the biomedical sciences. *The Conversation* offers another way to find who's who in academe. Apolitical is one example of an expert network for public servants. In Chile, the Red Innovadores Publicos is a searchable network of ten thousand public servants.

Academic citation services such as Google Scholar are another way to source experts. Citations are simply a special category of the tie between nodes on a network. They measure how many people have viewed, read, downloaded, or cited academic papers. The academic networking site academia.edu uses page views to create its bibliometric (the use of statistical methods to analyze books, articles, and other publications) rankings.

On a competing platform, the Social Science Research Network, scholars upload their papers, and expertise is then quantified (albeit crudely) based on the number of times those papers are downloaded. Google Scholar computes an author's h-index, another measure of publication influence and productivity. Citation, page view, and download scores are variations on a single theme in expert networking: measuring and quantifying expertise on the basis of the strength of ties in a network. These bibliometrics offer a useful (albeit controversial) proxy for locating trustworthy expertise in a field.[136]

As Bardach emphasizes, timing and sequencing matter when we consult experts. "We may divide the 'when' part of the question into 'relatively early' and 'relatively late' in the course of the research project."[137] Early in the project, it is good to consult people who will be good sources of additional information, as well as powerful and connected people who will open doors to others either directly or by virtue of your known connection to them. You will want to make it easy for such people to introduce you to others by writing a draft of the letter you want them to forward.[138] However, very busy or important people should be interviewed late in the process, once you have strong knowledge about your subject. You do not want to risk doing a poor job of interviewing them, since you will only get one chance to do so.

It is also a good idea to contact both friendly experts and those who are likely to object to your project in the early stages of your research. There are those people working in the same domain who may feel aggrieved by your efforts if they are not consulted. There are those who will feel disrespected if you do not inform them of your work. Experts, especially those in government, can be easily insulted if they are not invited to the proverbial meeting and included in discussions that they feel they "own." Contacting potential opponents early will help to reduce political risk or the chance that they will impede the progress of your research.

On the other hand, truly hostile sources who, for whatever reason, such as partisan politics, personality, or personal vendetta, can never be won over should be dealt with later, once you have had time to build up your evidence base and marshal your supporters. You do not want to give them the opportunity to oppose you sooner than you have to in your planning and problem-solving process.

EVALUATING SOLUTIONS

Systematic Reviews

The results of an RCT and of systematic reviews of them are generally seen, often wrongly, as the evidentiary gold standard for causal claims.[139] RCT design gives the investigator confidence that differences in outcome between treatment and control groups were caused by the treatment, since random assignment theoretically equalizes the groups on all other variables. RCTs come at the top in most evidence hierarchies.[140] Control groups are so important that one CEO is rumored to have said (joked?) that there are only three ways for an employee to get fired: for theft, for sexual harassment, or for running an experiment without a control group.[141]

Thus, when you need to evaluate the solutions you have found, determining whether there is academic evidence in the form of an RCT about your intervention helps with evaluation for all the reasons discussed earlier.

Similarly, systematic reviews of RCTs, of the kind that the Cochrane Collaboration has conducted in medicine for the past quarter century and that we discussed at the outset, comprehensively assess studies in a field using transparent and reproducible criteria and help you with evaluating evidence.[142] Rather than cherry-picking among studies for those that support the desired conclusion, a systematic review is supposed to look holistically at all available studies to make it possible to evaluate the strength of a given claim.[143] The review team assesses the validity and relative reliability of studies. It looks at the sample size and the methods employed to assess quality. It looks for potential errors and bias in how a study was conducted. It determines whether the conclusions drawn by the analysis make sense. Finally, it assesses whether the results of a study can be generalized. The great advantage of metareviews is that trained statisticians and subject-matter experts do the evaluative work for you.[144]

Results First, sponsored by Pew Charitable Trusts and the MacArthur Foundation, is an online resource that brings together information on the effectiveness of social policy programs from nine other national clearinghouses.[145] It applies color coding to the clearinghouses' distinct rating systems, creating a common language that enables users to quickly see where each program falls on a spectrum from negative impact to positive impact. The collection of metalevel data on 2,992 programs is intended to help you simply find and evaluate the quality of the evidence base for a variety of programs.[146]

Strong Evidence

While the overwhelming preference expressed by many people in the evidence-based policy community in evaluating evidence is for well-designed experimental studies like RCTs, as I have explained, other evidence is also valid and worthy of consideration, especially practical evidence of what works. The US Department of Education defines four tiers of evidence (strong, moderate, promising, and evidence that demonstrates a rationale). "Strong evidence" is evidence that was validated by at least one experimental study with a large, multisite sample and that has been assessed by the department's What Works Clearinghouse.[147] The department defines an "experimental study" as one "that is designed to compare outcomes between two groups of individuals (such as students) that are otherwise equivalent except for their assignment to either a treatment group receiving the

project component or a control group that does not." In other words, the
agency relies on strong evidence too.[148]

Private-sector funders will also ask for an experimental study like an
RCT in order to improve an investment's chances of success. The Mac-
Arthur Foundation demands at least one external evaluation of outcomes to
qualify for its $10 million economic opportunity challenge.[149] MacArthur
defines an experimental study a little more broadly than some organizations do. It prefers an RCT, but its competition will also consider quasi-
experimental design, contribution analysis, and evidence of collective impact. Contribution analysis is a nonexperimental method to allow managers
to tell a plausible story about impact by inferring causality from a theory of
change. It offers no conclusive proof of effectiveness.[150] Collective impact,
as we shall explore in chapter 9, on coalitions for change, involves a group
of organizations agreeing to a shared set of metrics and collective measurement.[151]

Nevertheless, experimental approaches are overwhelmingly preferred
as an evaluation mechanism. The ideal is to find an RCT that demonstrates
the effectiveness of an intervention, follow it exactly, and get the same results, thereby justifying the expenditure. When multiple RCTs are conducted in different places and then systematically reviewed, confidence that
the policy will achieve the desired result is even higher. The more high-
quality studies that exist, the more we know the intervention worked somewhere and can hope it will work where we are.

The appeal of replication based on successful RCTs may explain why
Bloomberg Philanthropies invested in a program called Providence Talks
and then, once it was shown to work in Rhode Island, funded three years of
replication and scaling of the program across five more cities: Birmingham,
Detroit, Hartford, Louisville, and Virginia Beach. According to an evaluation by Brown University, the program helped three thousand young children
in Providence, Rhode Island, to increase their language development. It
provides families with a "talk pedometer"—a kind of Fitbit that records
words instead of steps and creates an incentive for families to increase the
number of words they speak. It is grounded in earlier research showing the
existence of "word gap," or difference in the number of words a rich and a
poor child hear before the age of four. National data show that children in
low-income households hear approximately 616 words an hour, nearly half
as many words as heard by children in middle-income households and

fewer than one-third as many words as heard by children in high-income households.[152]

The Providence Talks experiment measured the number of words spoken by the adult and the child and the number of "conversational turns," or interactions between the two. The treatment group of adults knew what the voice recorder was measuring and received regular data reports showing progress and free books. The control group (in fact a quasi-control because its members also got a voice recorder) did not know what the recorder was measuring and did not get training or feedback or free books.[153]

The evaluation of Providence Talks showed dramatic improvements in adult conversational behavior as a result of using the voice recorder.[154] Children who were developmentally the furthest behind, on average, showed a huge 51 percent growth in the number of adult words they heard—from an average of eight thousand to over twelve thousand words a day over eight months. This leap put these children on about the average level of words heard.[155] By contrast, the control group showed no improvement, suggesting that without a purposeful intervention, the word gap would widen over time. Once the children receiving the intervention entered formal schooling, all have shown gains in reading skills over time, based on their standardized literacy test scores.

Thus, the presence or absence of an RCT can help you to evaluate the evidence but should be neither definitive nor dispositive when evaluating an approach. Many initiatives that are not the subject of an RCT have significant impact, while many interventions that are the subject of successful RCTs do not translate well from one jurisdiction to another. Keep in mind that correlation is not causation in the process of evaluating solutions.

Using Collective Intelligence to Evaluate What Works
In the absence of a clearinghouse or what-works database—and even with those resources—and in order to evaluate nontraditional, nonexperimental evidence, you can leverage collective intelligence to conduct and evaluate your field scan and determine what worked from the perspective not of researchers but of the people involved. This can help speed up and improve your evaluation. In Sweden in 2020, for example, the nation's lead epidemiologist evaluated the options regarding COVID-19 and advised leaders to eschew lockdown in the hope that so-called herd immunity would kick in

and limit the number of sick. In fact, the strategy failed abysmally.[156] Sweden's death toll ended up (as of this writing) being among the highest globally per capita. Had more people been involved in evaluating the evidence and making the decision, this outcome might have been avoided.

By contrast, in 2019, the United Nations' International Labour Organisation collaborated with The GovLab to do a survey of successful innovations that used technology and data science to improve the regulation and enforcement of worker and workplace protections. The GovLab convened more than sixty professionals, who helped us to identify and assess dozens of promising innovations. We then further evaluated those solutions using a structured interview process.

Another example of collaborative evidence evaluation comes from the UK College of Policing, the What Works Centre for Crime Reduction. When the organization was established in 2013, it began by running a pilot "Evidence Boot Camp" to engage police officers and staff in crowdsourcing evidence and identifying solutions that work. The first two days were devoted to training participants in search strategies and skills and explaining the concept of evidence-based policy making and policing. Participants then divided into five teams to research evidence for interventions that had been effective in the following:

- Supporting individuals during an acute mental health crisis
- Tackling barriers to career progression experienced by under-represented groups
- Preventing or reducing theft from the person
- Supporting mental well-being in the workplace
- Getting people out of prostitution

Each team sifted through an average of 1,133 publications in order to arrive at a collection of about 50 relevant articles and build an initial evidence base.

You can also reuse the Smarter Crowdsourcing and wiki survey methods and associated tools discussed in chapter 5 in order to convene groups online to identify and, above all, evaluate the quality and relevance of evidence. Just keep in mind that you do not need to limit your audience to academic experts. Instead, "experts" can comprise a very diverse bunch, going beyond the randomistas to include the contestistas and other practitioners, stakeholders, community groups, entrepreneurs, and residents. Each of these has different skills and insights into what is working and a helpful lens for evaluating evidence.[157] For example, at The GovLab in 2021, we convened a Smarter Crowdsourcing exercise to bring together dozens of academic and industry experts to assess the evidence relating to effective measures of social and emotional learning. But, in parallel, we also brought together teachers, parents, and students, especially from communities of color, to address and evaluate how those same interventions actually worked in practice from their perspective, paying special attention to issues of bias and discrimination that formal experiments did not measure.

Now that you have canvassed your solution space in order to discover and evaluate possible approaches, you still need to determine whether the solutions you find might apply to your problem.

The Providence Talks example earlier contained two different types of programs. In one, the voice recorder was used at home; in the other, it was used at a play group. Some families spoke Spanish at home, others English. Some were poor but had a college degree, while others never finished high school. There were two-parent and single-family households. While we know that training adults to talk to children can work, we do not fully know why or why in some circumstances it does not. Therefore, we do not know that what worked "there" will work "here." You need to find out.

DOES THIS SOLUTION WORK HERE?

Incontrovertible proof does not exist. This does not mean that we should not take the risk of replicating a promising program. But it is important to acknowledge that high-quality evidence—even many RCTs—will not tell us everything we need to know. For example, while an RCT involving the use of police-worn body cameras in California in 2012 showed that use of cameras reduced incidents of violence, a 2017 experiment in Washington, DC, showed no effect. This was, in part, because the Washington study was much bigger (two thousand participants instead of the fifty-four studied in California) but also because of the context, including additional training, programs, and initiatives aimed at improving community-police relations.[158] Replication is not enough. Even the most successful RCT depends on myriad contextual conditions, making it impossible to execute any intervention exactly as it was tried elsewhere. So we must assess whether a solution is likely to work in our own context.

Assessing Context

Understanding the conditions for successfully reproducing an intervention from elsewhere in our community requires going beyond the RCT. We must know more about our context.

Remember our example of Tennessee's successful experiments to improve reading scores by reducing class size in the 1980s? In the early 2000s, California sought to replicate its success. Not only did reducing class size fail to improve reading scores, but it made things *worse*.

In Tennessee, the project involved only schools that had available space. In California, often there was not enough spare space, and it had to be taken from other programs. Tennessee had no shortage of qualified teachers to staff the smaller classes. But California had to hire an additional twelve thousand teachers so quickly that many were unqualified.[159] Tennessee's policy *might* have worked in California, but the support factors were not present.

To figure out what needs to be present for an intervention to work "here," you need to understand the supporting factors that made it work "there." The social science philosopher Nancy Cartwright and the economist Jeremy Hardie describe the solution as one ingredient in a cake that works with other ingredients to produce the desired effect. Without the supporting ingredients and context, the cake will not rise.[160]

To evaluate whether a potential solution is relevant to our context means interrogating it to identify what support factors must be present, what must not be present, whether all or just some of the conditions need to be satisfied, and what are likely to be the unintended consequences.

Cartwright and Hardie suggest applying four techniques to understand why a solution worked and to determine its relevance for our context. The first technique she calls the "pre-mortem." By imagining that a policy did not exist or did not work, we can begin to unpack why it did. The second is to think step by step to explain how an intervention leads to the desired outcome. Alternatively, to understand the causal pathway, start with the outcome and work backward to arrive at the original policy. Finally, Cartwright suggests making "quick exit decision trees" to map out the factors that will help you to determine if the solution will work for you. Those factors might be questions of context, cost, political acceptability, or organizational priority, the answers to which will enable you to determine if you can translate what worked there to here.[161]

Using Collective Intelligence to Assess What Works Here

Public entrepreneurs can engage with the community they are serving to decide whether an intervention that worked "there" is appropriate for "here." There is no hard-and-fast rule for success in this process. The entrepreneur and the community must exercise their collective judgment and wisdom to decide whether the factors needed for the intervention to be replicated are locally present and whether the risk is worth taking. By making the search for evidence participatory, we triangulate the solution against on-the-ground realities from the vantage point of those who are affected by the problem.[162] There are a variety of techniques you can apply to engage people in this process.

Face-to-Face Deliberation

Deliberative dialogues can be one way to engage people in mining evidence for its relevance to their community. The health-policy expert John Lavis, creator of the Health Evidence Systems Clearinghouse at McMaster University in Ontario, describes an experiment that used small groups of citizens to weigh evidence in Africa.[163] In a pilot project in Burkina Faso, Cameroon, Ethiopia, Nigeria, Uganda, and Zambia, 530 individuals were given evidence briefs to read—systematic reviews covering interventions on seventeen topics ranging from preventing postpartum hemorrhaging to scaling up malaria control. The briefs were used to inform deliberative dialogues between researchers, policy makers, and stakeholders about the use and implementation of evidence in policy making.

Participants were then surveyed before and after a deliberative dialogue in an effort to measure what they learned. Regardless of the country, group, or issue, respondents viewed the evidence briefs and deliberative dialogues very favorably. Kaelan Moat, also of McMaster, and Lavis and their coauthors wrote, "The policy-makers, stakeholders and researchers who had read an evidence brief as an input into a deliberative dialogue all reported strong intentions to act on what they had learnt from this process."[164] The process they describe closely resembles the deliberative Consensus Conference established in Denmark in the 1980s to gauge the views of the public.[165] A consultative group of about sixteen people is selected from among the general, interested public (no one with a direct tie to the issue may participate). The group may meet for three days in a row or for two days at a time over several weeks. It reads background information and receives presentations from a panel of professional experts with whom the participants interact throughout the conference. The process gives ordinary people an opportunity to weigh in on difficult scientific and social issues. The Jefferson Center in Minneapolis, Minnesota, has developed a very similar model, which promotes the use of "citizen juries" to deliberate on specific policy proposals.[166] As in Denmark, jurisdictions like South Australia have turned to using these small groups of deliberating citizens to make binding decisions on such significant issues as nuclear-energy policy. These deliberative and representative minipublics, as they are also known, have become increasingly popular as a way to engage citizens in dialogue. Their small size makes them particularly well suited to this process of evidence evaluation because they are easier to manage and moderate.

Online Evidence Checks

The British Parliament takes a different approach to collaborative evaluation of the applicability "here" of evidence.[167] In month-long online exercises known as "Evidence Checks," parliamentary committees invite experts, stakeholders, and members of the public to comment on the validity of evidence on which a policy is based. The process begins when government departments supply information to their respective committees about an issue. Each committee publishes the information on a parliament.uk web page, and it is scrutinized by a wider pool of invitees. The committee also presents specific questions and problems that it would like participants to address.

In contrast to a representative sample, this process allows a larger and more diverse group of people with relevant experience and expertise to identify gaps in research that require further review. Evidence Checks help parliamentary committees to more effectively hold government to account by employing the collective intelligence of a broader audience. They are one example of legislatures turning to new technology to create a two-way conversation with the public—in this case, to improve the oversight process. Such online engagement in lawmaking is known as "CrowdLaw."

Commons Select Committees have implemented evidence checks via the World Wide Web in varying ways. In 2014–2015, the Education Select Committee used them to help it develop its work program. Initially, the committee requested a two-page statement on nine topics from the Department of Education, inviting public comment via web forums on each, as well as general comments on the department's approach to the use of evidence. Comments in the web forums then informed committee decisions about its areas of focus.

In 2016, an Evidence Check into sexual harassment in schools conducted by the Women and Equalities Committee generated contributions from knowledgeable stakeholders and students with lived experience of harassment. It led to estimates of the incidence of harassment being revised upward.

Assessing the relevance of evidence is not the only consideration. Chapter 9, on implementation, will consider broader issues of political and logistical feasibility that must be considered when assessing whether to implement a given solution.

TO DO

The following exercises offer a series of practical techniques you can use for identifying what possible solutions exist, how to evaluate whether a solution worked "there," and, finally, how to evaluate whether will it work "here," in your own context and community.

Exercise 1: Search the Clearinghouses
Which clearinghouses will you search?

- Abdul Latif Jameel Poverty Action Lab (JPAL), USA
- BehaviourWorks, Australia
- Campbell Collaboration, USA
- Centre for Ageing Better, UK
- Centre for Homelessness Impact, UK
- Centre for Transforming Access and Student Outcomes in Higher Education, UK Office for Students
- Clearinghouse for Labor Evaluation and Research (CLEAR), US Department of Labor
- Cochrane Collaboration, USA, Norway, India
- College of Policing What Works Centre for Crime Reduction, UK
- Early Intervention Foundation, UK
- Education Endowment Foundation, UK
- Health Systems Evidence (HSE), Canada
- Ideas42, USA

- National Institute for Health and Care Excellence (NICE), UK
- Social Systems Evidence (SSE), Canada
- Wales Centre for Public Policy
- What Works Centre for Local Economic Growth, UK
- What Works Centre for Wellbeing, UK
- What Works for Children's Social Care, UK
- What Works Clearinghouse, Department of Education, USA
- Youth Endowment Fund, UK
- Youth Futures Foundation, UK

Exercise 2: Use an Evidence-Review Tool

- *STARR Decision Tool.* The University of Sheffield STARR Decision Tool is designed to help with planning a rapid evidence review of RCTs and can be found at https://doi.org/10.15131/shef.data .7970894.v1.
- *AMSTAR Checklist.* AMSTAR stands for "A MeaSurement Tool to Assess Systematic Reviews." It is another planning tool to aid with RCT-driven research review planning: https://amstar.ca/Amstar _Checklist.php.

Exercise 3: Use a Generic Solution

The search for solutions should begin by considering "generic" solution types, going down a list of traditional and more contemporary solutions that work in other domains to consider if they are promising approaches to tackle your problem. The review of this catalog of approaches can be done collaboratively. As a reminder, Lester Salamon's *Tools of Government* and Eugene Bardach's *Practical Guide for Policy Analysis* both offer extended lists of generic solutions.

Are there one or more generic approaches you can use?

Examples of Traditional Tools

- Budgets
- Contracts
- Executive actions
- Grants
- Legislation

- Loans
- Regulation
- Subsidies
- Taxes

Examples of New Solutions

- Build an app
- Build a chatbot
- Build a coalition or partnership
- Create innovative roles
- Create a prize
- Create a website
- Design a market mechanism
- Develop digital platforms and apps
- Establish a data collaborative
- Establish a public lab
- Experiment with algorithms
- Hire people with new skills
- Introduce advance market mechanisms
- Offer training
- Use behavioral sciences
- Use open data

Exercise 4: Scavenge for Solutions in Social Innovation Communities
What promising ideas do you find?
Search the following examples of social innovation catalogs for ideas:

- Ashoka U Innovation Marketplace: https://ashokau.org/exchange /marketplace/
- Echoing Green (catalogs fellows and their projects): https://echoing green.org/fellowship/issues/
- Challenge.gov: https://www.challenge.gov/
- Innocentive: https://www.innocentive.com/
- InnovationXchange: https://ixc.dfat.gov.au/
- Just One Giant Lab: https://jogl.io/
- Kaggle Competitions: https://www.kaggle.com/competitions

- MacArthur Foundation 100 & Change: https://www.macfound.org /programs/100change/
- MIT Solve: https://solve.mit.edu/
- MultiCity Challenges: https://multicitychallenge.org/
- OpenIDEO: https://www.openideo.com/
- UNDP Accelerator Labs: https://acceleratorlabs.undp.org/

Exercise 5: Learning from Documents—What Is Out There?
Write down your search strategy.

- *Journals.* Search web and library databases. Also search domain-specific databases. Use the footnotes and references to refine your search.
- *Statistics and trends.* Organizations that conduct surveys or opinion research and polls can provide helpful context to understand both the problem and potential solutions.
- *News.* A news search is the most obvious place to begin using an Internet search engine or a news database. Try Google News and establish an alert.
- *YouTube videos.* A video search of news sources provides access to additional sources of news and documentaries.
- *News magazines.* News magazines often write about academic studies, and stories about what works are popular.
- *Online news magazines. The Conversation* puts out nine different editions. Project Syndicate offers policy op-eds from leading lights.
- *Government publications.* Relevant agencies, federally funded R&D centers (i.e., national laboratories), National Academies, Congressional Research Service, Government Accountability Office, Congressional Budget Office, and *Congressional Quarterly* are just some examples.
- *Nongovernmental organizations.* Think tanks, interest groups, and nonprofits frequently publish studies, reports, and white papers, detailing successful interventions. Start by creating a map of key organizations and reviewing their websites.
- *Newsletters on governance innovations.* The GovLab Living Library, the Brookings Institution, the Organisation of Economic Co-operation and Development (OECD), the Institute for Local Government, City Lab, Bloomberg Philanthropies, and Centre for Public Impact all

publish relevant newsletters that cover innovative policy, social innovation, and related solutions.

- *Other jurisdictions.* The National Governors Association, National Conference of Mayors, International City and County Managers Association, and Living Cities are umbrella organizations in the United States with good insight into which public officials are knowledgeable on your topic. There are comparable associations in other countries.

Exercise 6: Learning from People—Who Is Out There?

Write down your people search strategy.

The following is a list of examples of places to look for experts with insights about solutions:

- Identify global scholars using academic citation services like Google Scholar.
- Search evidence clearinghouses to find the people conducting relevant high-quality experiments and RCTs.
- Identify experts by searching speakers at TED or major conference websites in your field.
- Check grantee lists on foundation websites.
- Use social media to identify key influencers in the field.
- Curate a Twitter list of those key influencers.
- Identify relevant hashtags to follow to find more experts.
- Check Q&A sites like Quora.
- Search expert networks like VIVO.
- Check publication download services like SSRN.
- Review global patent filings for innovative solutions at lens.org.
- Identify public leaders (politicians and civil servants) pursuing innovative projects by asking an association of government leaders.
- Identify relevant journalists with a bird's-eye view of the issues by doing a news search.

Exercise 7: Run an Evidence Bootcamp

Remember that to scavenge for or evaluate evidence, you might want to enlist some help. The UK College of Policing set up an "Evidence Boot Camp" to crowdsource review and evaluation of evidence. To do something similar, start with the following:

- Explain evidence-based policy making
- Train people in search strategies and skills
- Sort and divide up evidence to read and review
- Discuss and deliberate about promising approaches

Whom will you invite? When will you do it? What is your plan for the event? Refer back to Smarter Crowdsourcing and wiki survey techniques in chapter 5 for methods.

Exercise 8: Evaluate Evidence (adapted from Cartwright and Hardie)

1. *Pre-mortem.* One very good way to come up with a list of factors that are necessary for your solution to work for you is to imagine that the intervention has not worked.
2. *Thinking step by step.* The technique is to think through how that solution leads to the desired outcome (sometimes known as "crafting your theory of change").
3. *Thinking backward.* You can do this either by starting at the beginning with the policy implementation and ending with the targeted outcome or by thinking backward, from the outcome to the intervention. Try doing both!
4. *Create quick exit decision trees.* Decision trees are a familiar device to help with figuring out what to do. A decision tree starts with a question followed by two branches, one of which leads to NO, the other to YES. The NO is a dead end. "Suppose the first question is 'Have we got the money to do this?' If the answer is NO, you stop. If it is YES, you go on down the branch to the next question. And so on. If fully completed, it provides an unequivocal answer to the question, 'Will this solution be effective here?'"[168]

CHAPTER NINE

Implementing Solutions with Partners

A man may do an immense deal of good, if he does not care who gets credit for it.

Father Strickland, cited by Sir Mountstuart Elphinstone (1863)

POWERFUL PARTNERSHIPS

Around the world, more than 137 million people are exposed to drinking water contaminated with arsenic. In the Vietnamese districts of Kim Bang and Dan Phuong, natural contaminants in the underlying bedrock of the Red River Delta made the arsenic level ten times higher than was safe.[1] This was the kind of problem that in 2017 inspired the Australian Department of Foreign Affairs and Trade to partner with Google to launch a series of prize-backed challenges.

As a result, Sydney University of Technology (UTS) devised a system to provide arsenic-free drinking water and manage arsenic residues produced during the filtration process. The department introduced UTS to NUSA, the Vietnamese NGO promoting safe drinking water. Other countries trialed the technology, prompting UTS to spin off a new venture based on this innovation. The venture attracted significant funding and uptake throughout the Asian region.

The arsenic project is just one emerging from the Australian department's innovation strategy. The InnovationXchange (IxC), created in 2015 to foster fresh thinking across Australia's aid program, has asked companies and not-for-profit organizations from around the world to submit other solutions: for safe drinking water for Timor-Leste, better education in India, and microlending in the Philippines. Between 2015 and 2018, the department partnered with more than one hundred organizations to support one hundred projects operating in more than fifty countries through the launch of eleven challenge prizes.

Sarah Pearson, former chief scientist and head of the InnovationXchange, says that partnering and using open innovation to solve problems were driven both by diplomacy and by commercial necessity. "We want to portray Australia as a progressive country," she explains. "To build both the nation's reputation and its exports, we can help the business sector help Australia help the economy."[2] The challenge program has enabled the IxC to tackle development problems while attracting further funding for start-ups, both in Australia and in other countries. The IxC provides early-stage funding that removes or reduces the risk for the start-up; then other entities supply follow-on funding. Pearson says that "partnerships give IxC access to better ideas because of the passion and commitment of entrepreneurs with ideas we would never had dreamed of." The sense of shared agency created through partnership gets multiple sectors focusing together on solving common challenges.

The IxC has helped to attract more than US$820 million worth of funding opportunities through its eleven prizes targeting social innovations in emerging markets. In one challenge, the department partnered with GSMA, the trade body that represents 750 mobile operators around the world, to call for technology to be applied to development solutions. The partnership offered funding, technical assistance, and the opportunity to partner with mobile operators to help implement and scale solutions in local markets. One winner was eFishery, an aquaculture start-up that developed proprietary software to enable fish farmers to use sensors to manage and remotely control feeding in real time.

Partnerships are not just about money; the department is also able to tap into the brand value and skills of corporate-challenge sponsors such as Google and Atlassian, companies with employees who know how to start and run a venture and who can go beyond spotting a solution to being able to implement it and scale it up. Pearson thinks that using this kind of external expertise enables projects to deliver extraordinary outcomes: "There's a goal, and you can achieve it with other people, rather than holding on tightly to 'my' solution."

Partnership and coalition building are essential for Australia to be able to afford to meet its targets under the United Nations Sustainable Development Goals (SDGs). The seventeenth and last SDG explicitly calls for countries to "strengthen the means of implementation and revitalize the global partnership for sustainable development."[3] As Pearson puts it, "The UN's Sustainable Development Goals are short of $2.5 trillion, so we have to partner."[4]

So far, we have explored steps on the path to public problem solving, examining methods to analyze data and use human-centered design to define a problem. We have described ways to interview people and tap into their intelligence and expertise, both online and offline. We have outlined ways to source solutions, applying the practices of open innovation, as well as diverse techniques to synthesize research and know-how using data and people. Each of these steps in public problem solving calls for creative collaboration.

But no phase of the problem-solving process is more difficult than implementation. Yet implementation challenges rarely receive attention during an innovation process that places so much more emphasis on solution identification. Therefore, in this chapter, we briefly explore the challenges of implementation and then devote our attention to the pros, cons, and how-tos of partnership and collaboration to overcome those implementation challenges. At no time is working together with partners and communities more imperative than when we want to translate a good idea into legitimate and effective practice.

IMPLEMENTATION HURDLES

Implementation may be the most important—yet the most neglected— phase of public entrepreneurship. Entrepreneurship courses and competitions put all the emphasis on coming up with a good idea. But that often misses the point, as Tina Rosenberg writes in the *New York Times*:

> Have you thought of a clever product to mitigate climate change? Did you invent an ingenious gadget to light African villages at night? Have you come up with a new kind of school, or new ideas for lowering the rate of urban shootings? Thanks, but we have lots of those. Whatever problem possesses you, we already have plenty of ways to solve it. Many have been rigorously tested and have a lot of evidence behind them—and yet they're sitting on a

shelf. So don't invent something new. If you want to make a contribution, choose one of those ideas—and spread it.[5]

Similarly, the failed rollout of healthcare.gov in 2013 reminds us that even the most brilliant policy, poorly implemented, cannot succeed. No solution, no matter how clever, can make a difference unless it is successfully implemented. We always need a plan to get something done.

There is a wide range of actions that must be taken into account and planned when moving from solution to implementation. These are not uncommon to any project-management method, which establishes a process for determining milestones for getting from the current state to the desired state. A quick skim of the to-do list for implementation of your intervention includes a variety of considerations that must be addressed.

First, plot the steps that need to be taken to implement. Make a checklist of the tasks to be done. For example, if the goal is to increase organ donations, then legislation or an executive order might be needed to change the default for donation from opt-in to opt-out. Alternatively, the solution might entail a media campaign with strong public-service announcements. Doing the former requires a very different set of steps than the latter, and you will need to lay out those actions, identify the actors, and coordinate among them. For example, rolling out a contact-tracing program for the state of New Jersey required hiring workers, setting up a technology platform for them to use, and establishing guidelines for how they would work. Just the staffing piece alone had a hundred smaller actions, from inking a memorandum of understanding with the state's university to writing a request for proposals to solicit bids from additional staffing agencies. The Department of Health, Office of Innovation, Office of Information Technology, and ninety-nine different county and local entities each had a role to play, and coordinating among them required a great deal of attention. While having multiple partners necessitates coordination, it provides more hands on deck.

Second, there needs to be consideration of resources and assets, including budget, talent, tools, and data that are necessary for accomplishing the project. The desire to solve a problem with citizen engagement will require identifying a platform and ensuring involvement by those who know how to use it. The creation of a new app to address a societal problem necessitates investment in programming but also in marketing and distribution. The absence of a key asset, whether money or data, is another motivator for the partnerships described in the next section.

Third, any project requires a timeline with milestones and deliverables and agreement on realistic deadlines. Many projects fail because they take too long to accomplish and political will is exhausted too soon. Setting aggressive targets might be unrealistic or might be just the fuel needed to light a fire under people, imploring them never to waste a good crisis. The Change@SouthAustralia innovation team of the government of South Australia has a concept of ninety-day projects. Projects come from inside or outside the government and are designed to address complex problems quickly. The benefit of "time-boxing" the project is that projects are narrowed in scope to ensure rapid results. Collective intelligence can be brought to bear to aid in planning and with more rapid execution.

Fourth, agreement on a solution might be vague and high level, opening the door to challenges of interpretation. It is common for legislators to give discretion to agency implementors to work out the details. But this kind of delegation occurs in many contexts where the details of what a solution entails simply do not get worked out, giving rise to challenges of interpretation and increased risk of what software developers like to call "scope creep." These require hammering out a governance process for agreeing on how to agree. R. Kent Weaver of Brookings, who argues forcefully for greater use of implementation analysis by Congress to avoid unaccountable delegation, explains, "In deciding how to implement a new policy or program, policymakers need to consider the mission as well as the organizational capacity of potential implementing organizations, and consider whether it makes most sense to create a new implementing agency or, if they work through existing organizations, changing organizational leadership or structure to send strong, clear signals about the importance of the new organizational task."[6] As we shall explore, having more partners only heightens the urgency for this clarification but can smooth the pathway to implementation.

Fifth, the "no machines" are those actors who impede progress toward implementation. You must assess the risks. They may be lawyers, procurement officers, or others arguing that rules must be complied with that are not on the roadmap. They may be security or law enforcement professionals arguing that the project is dangerous. They may be managers, leaders, or politicians who are risk averse to innovation. They may be bean counters worried about the costs. They may be groups that feel the project is competitive with their own or threatens their funding or status. Whether the objections are reasonable or spurious, motivated by inertia or malevolence, serious consideration must be given to those individuals and groups that stand in the way of implementation.

Each of these considerations creates risks to successful, timely, and frustration-free implementation and gives rise, in many cases, to added benefits from enlisting partners in the job of implementation. In chapter 3's exercises, we prescribe The GovLab's Public Projects Canvas to aid with project planning. It includes questions about implementation analysis that are worth revisiting at this juncture.

COLLECTIVE INTELLIGENCE AND IMPLEMENTATION

The magnitude and urgency of challenges such as climate change, social inequality, and technology-generated un(der)employment call on us to work together. With the right design, and far more effectively than if we acted separately, we can concentrate resources and energy to tackle our problems. Implementing solutions calls for public entrepreneurs to be agile and innovative, a clear difference from the way institutions have typically operated in the past. At the point of implementation, collaboration using collective intelligence and the resources of other individuals and groups might be the *only way* to break out of public-sector strictures in order to convert ideas to impact. It might also be the only way to help public problem solvers cross the chasm and make their ideas a reality.

"Can we afford it?" is inevitably one of the first questions about implementation. We can get so much more done by pooling resources of finance, talent, data, know-how, specialist expertise, digital infrastructure, technology, attention, and influence.[7] Many examples of pooling resources follow, involving well-known institutions such as UN agencies, global foundations, and brand-name product companies. Wherever possible, though, collaboration should involve the deep participation of the less famous: individuals and families, neighborhoods and schools, small organizations and businesses, community organizations and community colleges, all of which have immense capacity for action in our communities and around the world.

As Kofi Annan wrote, "Partnerships have already demonstrated their transformative impact. In recent years, we have seen collaboration between the private sector and international philanthropists leading to significant reductions in malaria deaths. Partnerships between mobile-phone providers and governments have greatly increased access to finance for Africa's poor. And collaboration between civil society and intergovernmental organizations has vastly improved access to credit for smallholder farmers and helped raise agricultural productivity."[8]

Almost ten thousand companies have signed on to the UN Global Compact, a voluntary UN partnership, to encourage companies to align their missions with the UN Sustainable Development Goals.[9] The United Nations is complementing intergovernmental activities by increasingly fostering multistakeholder partnerships such as the Global Alliance for Vaccines and Immunization (Gavi).[10] Established in 2000, the partnership includes the World Health Organization, UNICEF, the Bill and Melinda Gates Foundation, the International Federation of Pharmaceutical Manufacturers Association, and other partners. Gavi has raised $500 million.

Large and complex challenges, such as global vaccination campaigns, demand collaboration. Private companies control access to the pharmaceuticals but require the authority of public institutions to convene and coordinate a vaccination campaign. The Harvard professors Ronald Heifetz and Mark Kramer and the writer John Kania explain why public problems demand collaboration:

> Technical problems are well defined: Their solutions are known
> and those with adequate expertise and organizational capacity can
> solve them. When a foundation tackles a technical problem, it
> knows exactly who to fund, how much it will cost, and what the
> outcome will be. . . . In each case, the problem is clear, the
> solution depends on well-established practices, and, given
> enough money, a single organization can implement the solu-
> tion. Adaptive problems are entirely different. They are not so
> well defined, the answers are not known in advance, and many
> different stakeholders are involved, each with their own perspec-
> tives. Adaptive problems require innovation and learning among
> the interested parties and, even when a solution is discovered, no
> single entity has the authority to impose it on the others. The
> stakeholders themselves must create and put the solution into
> effect since the problem is rooted in their attitudes, priorities, or

behavior. And until the stakeholders change their outlook, a solution cannot emerge.[11]

Partners can always be found. They include members of the public, officials in other agencies and at other levels of government, journalists, funders and investors, faith-based organizations, for-profit and not-for-profit corporations, foundations, and academic and industry experts. All of them can help to put into practice ways to see, share, and solve problems.

Private entrepreneurship, by contrast, emphasizes trade secrecy as the condition of getting a competitive advantage in a private marketplace. Launching a new company or product makes commercial independence paramount, since the focus is on being the first and best. But when the goal is to solve a problem, rather than to advance one's own company or initiative, roping in many actors is often the best way to get it done.

Policy makers, too, are often reluctant to build a broad-based set of partners, because it compels them to share the credit with others. Increasingly, however, many public problem solvers are implementing projects more effectively by sharing roles and responsibilities. "Partnerships are becoming the most effective method of accomplishing large-scale public good in the twenty-first century—dramatically improving programs by sharing responsibility that governments alone are unable to deliver," write Howard W. Buffett, a philanthropist and former Obama administration official, and William B. Eimicke, a former New York State and City official.[12]

A leading-edge example of partnership is Brooklyn's Pathways in Technology Early College High School (P-TECH). This six-year program takes year 9 students through to an associate degree by year 14, to prepare them for a career in a STEM (science, technology, engineering, math) field. There is no entrance exam, and admission is by lottery to improve equity and diversity. P-TECH began as a partnership between the New York City Department of Education, the City University of New York (CUNY), and IBM. Working together, the partners launched the first school in Brooklyn in September 2011, graduating the first class in 2017. The Department of Education identified a location, hired a principal and teachers, and designed the standards. IBM was responsible for identifying industry-specific skills that students would need. It designed and developed workplace internships —over five hundred to date—as part of the curriculum, bringing in other corporate partners. IBM also provided student mentors and paid summer internships. CUNY designed the curriculum and opened up college-level courses and faculty to P-TECH students.[13]

Although P-TECH has sometimes struggled with many unprepared students enrolling too early in college-level classes and partners disagreeing about how to train them, the data show that early college programs like P-TECH are successful.[14] P-TECH has grown into a global education movement, with 220 schools in 24 countries and 11 US states, representing partnerships between 600 companies and 209 universities.[15] The movement shares its work and learning by publishing, for example, a checklist for bringing together public school, university, and corporate partners.[16]

Each collaboration model illustrates the distinctive contribution of its participating partners. Partners can bring talent and skills—in finance, marketing, technology, data, design, and other areas—that the public sector otherwise lacks. Partners might contribute various kinds of information or infotech: raw data or access to technology such as data storage or sophisticated artificial intelligence algorithms that are hard to come by in public organizations. Nongovernment partners can be less constrained by procurement rules or cultural customs such as government's tendency to find "we've never done that before" a reason not to try it now. Other partners can have the courage, passion, and position to get things done, qualities that can be in short supply in politically fraught and partisan government environments.

PARTNERSHIP IS NOT PRIVATIZATION

I want to be clear about how this book defines "partnership." It is a collaboration between two or more entities in different sectors for a public-interest purpose, often with a public or philanthropic partner in the lead.[17] Because this book takes a laser-like focus on the public interest, I am not referring to the privatization of public institutions that became popular in the 1980s and the outsourcing of public services to private contractors to run prisons or schools, for example.

Privatization became government orthodoxy under the administrations of Ronald Reagan and Margaret Thatcher in Britain, although in the United States, most privatizations occurred during the administration of Bill Clinton. Although outsourcing government services to the private sector might in some cases have initially saved money and increased efficiency, it has since emerged that privatization tends merely to replace an inefficient public monopoly with inefficient private monopolies, without improving services and often by degrading them significantly.[18]

Without adequate guard rails, privatization can encourage the worst of rent-seeking behavior, driven by private self-interest. The United States' privatized health-care system is the most expensive in the world. According to the OECD, the United States spends 17.1 percent of GDP on health, greatly outstripping Switzerland (12.3 percent) and France (11.3 percent), the second and third highest spenders.[19] Despite that outlay, the life expectancy of Americans, especially the less well off, is declining.

Similarly, studies also show that private prisons perform poorly with regard to intraprison violence, jail conditions, and rehabilitation efforts.[20] The profit motive is an incentive to put and keep more people in jail, ultimately at greater cost to taxpayers, undermining the argument that prisons-for-profit save money or are better.[21] Private prisons dole out twice as many infractions to justify keeping people in prison longer. Although private prisons account for a small percentage of the United States' incarcerated (and a majority of immigrants in detention), their population increased by 1,600 percent from 1990 to 2005.[22] The Trump administration scrapped Obama-era plans to do away with private prisons, although several states are moving to ban them (and, in turn, facing legal challenges from these companies attempting to protect their sinecure).[23]

That said, there have been successful examples of outsourcing and of government purchasing of innovative products from the private sector, most notably in the domain of technology, such as cloud storage services. This book does not wade into the extensive and well-documented literature on the pros and cons of privatization and outsourcing, but it seems increasingly clear that delegating services to the private sector (as distinct from partnering with the private and other sectors) invariably puts profits before participation in the design of public problem solving.

Instead, I want to address how to use the collective intelligence of diverse participants across government, civil society, and business to perform public undertakings in an accountable and responsible way and to help you accelerate your pathway to implementation. It is important to emphasize this distinction between cross-sector partnerships and privatization. Rather than merely delegating responsibility for design and delivery to the private sector, public problem solvers or public entrepreneurs should maintain a central role in convening partnerships anchored in public purpose. This means sharing information among the parties and maintaining public accountability, public responsibility, and commitment to the public interest.

Challenges can still arise in such collaborations when values diverge. In 2020, TalkSpace, the nonprofit provider of online mental health services, scuttled a partnership with Facebook over the latter's refusal to rein in White-supremacist postings by President Trump: "We at @Talkspace discontinued our partnership discussions with @Facebook today. We will not support a platform that incites violence, racism, and lies. #BlackLives Matter."[24] The year before, art institutions refused donations received from the Sackler family, which also owned pharmaceutical companies responsible for the country's opioid crisis. Universities scrambled to justify donations received from the sex offender Jeffrey Epstein, drawing attention to the relationship between the wealthy and public-purpose institutions. Such scandals reveal the grave ethical risks that arise when corporations seek to forge high-profile partnerships with government, philanthropy, and cultural and civic organizations in order to launder a bad reputation, gained from rapacious business activities, through ancillary social good.

While one must take precautions to be able to unshackle oneself from an unpalatable partnership, as we will discuss shortly, such challenges do not have to prevent the development of successful public-private collaborations. Buffett and Eimicke trace the evolution of cross-sector partnerships going back to the large-scale coalitions that implemented Franklin Roosevelt's New Deal and Lyndon Johnson's Great Society programs. The NYU professor Victoria Alsina Burgués and the Pompeu Fabra University professor Carles Ramió Matas explain how "advanced democracies have evolved towards a model of the relational state, which distributes roles, assignments and responsibilities among the state, the market and civil society."[25] The United States has enjoyed a generation-long transformation by which, in increasingly innovative ways, government has partnered across sectors and across other levels of government.[26]

Cross-sector collaborations have become an increasingly important way to respond to complex problems.[27] The Ohio-based StriveTogether partnership for education began in greater Cincinnati and northern Kentucky and helps organize local and regional partnerships that engage 10,800 local organizations to improve the United States' failing public-education system in twenty-nine states.[28] StriveTogether explains that its cross-sector partners adopt common goals, shared best practices, and mutual responsibility.[29]

In climate-change policy, a good example of a partnership is Connect-4Climate, a collaboration of the World Bank and the Italian Ministry of Environment, Land, and Sea, together with the German Federal Ministry for Economic Cooperation and Development: "The Connect4Climate community connects about 500 partners around the world including civil society groups, media networks, international organizations, academic institutions, youth groups, and the private sector. Connect4Climate interacts with a global audience of more than a million individuals who participate on Connect4Climate's social media channels."[30]

On gun violence, the Prevention Institute in Oakland, California, similarly declares, "In everything we do, we are deeply committed to partnership and collaboration. Our ability to innovate, for example, emerges in our work alongside communities and organizations across the country that are surfacing problems and applying our tools and methods to approach challenges in new ways. . . . We lead and collaborate to advance policy and systems change. And we champion community successes and developments in the public health field."[31]

In New Jersey, in response to the COVID-19 pandemic, the Department of Health partnered with the state university's School of Public Health to train and hire contact tracers, who call those who come into contact with infected patients, from their school and from colleges around the state. The partnership took advantage of the university's superior skill in training and education and the diverse nature of its students and alumni, making it possible to hire local residents from every community to do the hard work of tracing.[32]

Of course, not all collaborations succeed, and not all partnerships are effective. There is little empirical literature on the relative merits of governing through partnerships (versus other forms of governance).[33] However, there is a growing volume of cases and toolkits explaining both why to partner and how to do it.[34] And, again, for many public problem solvers, the choice is not between partnership or another form of governance. Partnership may be the only pathway to implementation.

REASONS TO PARTNER

Before discussing the methods and tools needed to manage complex and diverse forms of partnership, let us first consider more systematically some of the many rationales behind coalition building.

Cost Savings

Cost savings are a strong reason to partner. This chapter has explained how Australia's Department of Foreign Affairs and Trade benefits from opportunities to share expenses or to take advantage of investment from outside entities, propelled by a prize-backed challenge model that is sponsored by private companies.[35] The department simply did not have enough funds to run so many challenges or to implement the identified solutions on its own.

Similarly, for over forty years, New York City has revitalized its parks with private-sector funding. Local residents started the Central Park Conservancy in 1980 to raise funds to renew the park after neglect, mismanagement, and economic decline led to its desolation in the 1970s. By 1995, the conservancy had taken over the care and management of the park, and it signed a formal agreement with the city in 1998.[36] By 2013, the conservancy had raised around $700 million to restore and run the park.[37] Park management has not been privatized or contracted out. The conservancy reports to and works with the Parks Department. It also partners with other cities to promote its partnership model and to help other major urban parks renovate and revitalize.

The Central Park partnership has attracted controversy. Critics say that while parks with wealthy neighbors, like Central Park and the Highline in the western Manhattan neighborhood of Chelsea, attract donations, needier parks in poorer neighborhoods are neglected. Tax deductions enjoyed by donors deplete the public purse, ultimately reducing funding for parks in other neighborhoods. Finally, some argue that a privately funded nonprofit is not as responsive or accountable to the needs of diverse residents.

Improved Service Delivery

Partnering can unlock better ways to deliver services. The Intersector Project has documented forty case studies of what they point to as successful cross-sectoral collaborations. It documents the example of ForcesUnited (formerly the Augusta Warrior Project), which serves veterans in the southern United States. To do so, ForcesUnited develops partnerships with area nonprofits, local businesses, and governmental agencies to improve veteran care in thirteen counties in Georgia and South Carolina by providing a single point of contact to help veterans avail themselves of services such as job training, to help employers find veterans to hire, and to channel donations that government would not be in a position to accept.[38] It also provides convening and governance under the auspices and on the campus of the University of South Carolina. According to the organization, in 2018, it worked with over 2,100 veterans, finding housing for 225 and employment for 319.[39]

No empirical data exist comparing ForcesUnited services with those that Veterans Affairs would deliver or identifying whether the involvement of a coalition of private actors in veterans' job training and placement has led to any groups getting less care or funding or poorer services. But at a time when the public agency is mired in repeated scandals about its failure to deliver care and benefits, it makes sense to involve entities outside government that are able to fund-raise and operate more nimbly.[40]

During the COVID-19 epidemic, partnerships with skilled technologists and designers from the United States Digital Response, a volunteer effort coordinated by former Obama administration officials, lent staff to state and local governments to fix websites and transform formerly face-to-face or paper-based services such as qualifying for food benefits or applying for unemployment into fully digital services for citizens.

Services can also be improved through access to more cutting-edge technology from outside the public sector. In Mongolia, for example, up to 41 percent of all medicines are counterfeit.[41] The country's government has partnered with Farmatrust, a UK-based start-up, to use blockchain and AI to track and trace the pharmaceutical supply chain. This approach uses data and high-end technology to record and store information about the production and pathway of each packet of pills.[42]

Better Expertise

Partnerships for implementation are able to reduce costs and improve service delivery by accessing know-how, expertise, and skills that can be limited or lacking in the public sector. The Rockefeller Foundation writes about this kind of mutual learning in its account of the 100 Resilient Cities partnership, a six-year effort to support resilience in the world's cities: "By establishing partnerships outside of business-as-usual models, and at new scales, cities and noncity actors can invent and advance new solutions to longstanding challenges."[43]

In San Francisco's quest for greater expertise and more talent to strengthen the way the city delivers services to citizens, it taps into the pro bono contributions of tech-sector companies. The city cannot compete with

Silicon Valley salaries in hiring and retaining good programmers, designers, and data scientists; while one-off "hackathons" and similar events generate ideas and get people excited, they do not produce a clear roadmap for
implementation. Instead, the Mayor's Office created a new way to partner
with the private sector. Civic Bridge is a sixteen-week program that pairs
city staff with technology companies to improve city services using technology, data, and design. Companies find it easier to partner with the city
through this single entry point, while city agencies find a formal program
and a process that is easier than working with individual volunteers.

An early challenge taken on by Civic Bridge was to change the application process for affordable housing. Thousands of economically insecure
residents had to make different applications for each development, leading
to excessive paperwork, extra stress, and missed opportunities. Google volunteers brought in user-centered design skills, and to understand the problem better, the Civic Bridge team—tech-company volunteers and city officials
working together—did some "secret shopping," pretending to be residents
looking for housing. What they learned informed the specifications for a
new web portal through which residents could submit a single reusable
application for all public housing. Now 85 percent of applications are processed through the portal.

Since Civic Bridge began in 2015, it has generated pro bono contributions to the city worth an estimated $3.9 million, and more than 250 volun-
teers have worked on forty-nine projects. These include ways to better manage
nonemergency 911 calls, to improve the efficiency of street cleaning, and to
make services for transgender communities more accessible. In 2017, Civic
Bridge added twelve additional projects, and in 2019, the Office of Innovation in San Francisco launched a new one-day model called Day of Service.
During the course of one day, ten public-private partnership teams worked
on ten challenges.

City leaders attribute the success of Civic Bridge to a mind-set that con-
ceives of companies as partners and codesigners of solutions with the
city, rather than as vendors of services to the city. A fifty-page template of
checklists and process diagrams sets out the terms and makes it possible to
choreograph the work of the partnerships, which always focus on public
priorities defined by the Mayor's Office.

A lasting benefit of the codesign process has been skills transfer, according to the former San Francisco chief innovation officer Krista Can-

nelakis. Corporate volunteers demonstrated user-centered design skills to city staff members, who were able to apply them to other projects.[44] At the same time, tech-company volunteers developed a new appreciation for the complexity of city problems, inspiring some to volunteer more of their time to support civic goals.

Working Differently

As the Civic Bridge program demonstrates, working with partners brings all the benefits of good teamwork, enabling people to contribute their diverse and complementary skills. Problem solving can be highly complex, and not every public entrepreneur knows how to collect and assess data, think analytically, and engage with citizens and experts at the same time. The person who is gifted in the ethnographic practices of human-centered design may not be able to develop data-driven mathematical models. Another, who knows how to synthesize evidence from randomized controlled trials, may not know what is working in the space of open innovation and social enterprise.

Bloomberg Philanthropies also advocates for collaboration across disciplines and sectors. Its "Champion Cities" convene groups of local universities, NGOs, private industry, and other partners to pull together diverse expertise to solve urban problems.[45] The city of Vallejo, California, took on the major challenge of repairing its infrastructure, especially broken water pipes, by forging a coalition whose diverse partners include the Water Department, residents, water customers, a research team from the University of Vermont, and the Silicon Valley technology firm Civic Foundry. The goal was to test the hypothesis that water resources will be conserved by combining crowdsourced data with radar/acoustic-based GIS mapping, allowing the city to identify leaks before they happen and thereby increase sustainability and reduce costs.

Working with partners allows for ways of working that may be routine for a university or a company but can be risky or novel for public-sector agencies. For example, government does not have institutional review boards, yet conducting experiments can be risky without ethics oversight. Partnering with universities like MIT and its Abdul Latif Jameel Poverty Action Lab, which conducts randomized controlled trials on behalf of states, enables government institutions to get external institutional review board approval; this ensures that the design of experiments protects the rights of the people involved in the research study.

Similarly, the New Jersey Office of Innovation partners with Rutgers University to design and build tools for the long-term unemployed. The partnership gives the office access to the university's subject-matter expertise and assurance that its project is ethically designed. Rutgers, in turn, advances its research while doing real-world social good.

The New Jersey Office of Innovation was established as a nonprofit specifically to fulfill the role of partner for other state agencies. The office was able to accept a generous grant from Schmidt Futures, the family foundation of the former Google CEO Eric Schmidt, for a project to make the offerings and outcomes of job-training programs more transparent to residents. The state's Department of Labor might have struggled to accommodate the grant, given its lack of experience in accepting philanthropic donations. Similarly, the office can hire technologists quickly, when most government agencies lack established processes to do so.

Government, nonprofit, and philanthropic partners all have their own separate practices for procurement, contracting, hiring, firing, and accepting and giving away money, among other tasks. Sharing and exchanging these different ways of working can multiply the benefits for all.

More Hands on Deck

As government as well as nonprofits are often short on time and people, working with others can bring in more help.[46] The veteran White House policy maker Tom Kalil served in four presidential administrations; his signature science accomplishments include a policy to make solar energy competitive with other fuel sources by 2020. Just as significantly, the BRAIN (Brain Research through Advancing Innovative Neuro-technologies) Initiative that he conceived invests in neuro-technologies to treat, prevent, and cure brain disorders such as Alzheimer's, Parkinson's, schizophrenia, autism, epilepsy, and traumatic brain injury.[47] To advance the BRAIN Initiative, Kalil worked with the Kavli Foundation to convene potential partners. Kavli aims to benefit humanity through advanced science and runs an international program of research institutes, symposia, and professorships in astrophysics, nanoscience, neuroscience, and theoretical physics. Late in 2011, the foundation organized a workshop for researchers who came from different fields but were all looking for a transformative project to advance neuroscience in the same way that the Human Genome Project had advanced genetics. In 2012, Kavli and Kalil built a coalition of researchers, foundations, and federal agencies to advance the idea. The following year, President Obama unveiled the BRAIN Initiative, a multiagency "grand challenge" to accelerate understanding of the human brain.

BRAIN increased annual federal investment from $100 million in the 2014 financial year to more than $430 million three years later. Philanthropic organizations came on board. Congress provided an extra $1.5 billion to support the National Institutes of Health to participate in the BRAIN Initiative. This brought the total for public and private investment to $3 billion.[48] Kalil explains how this was possible:

> In order to be effective, not only would I have to come up with an idea, but I would need to figure out how to build a coalition around that idea, even though the people who I ultimately had to convince to say "Yes" in no way reported to me. The ability to do that, to build coalitions around ideas that you're excited about, is very important in a policy role when it's not like you have dedicated funding that you have direct responsibility for and a large staff that is reporting to you, that you have this command-and-control relationship with.[49]

During my time working for the Obama White House as the deputy chief technology officer and the head of open government in the Office of Science and Technology Policy (OSTP), we frequently turned to partners to achieve greater scale and impact in our work. In OSTP, we supported the White House goal to advance STEM education. Between 2003 and 2011, the number of accredited math and science teachers had inched up by six and nine percentage points, respectively.[50] But it was not enough, especially in schools with high numbers of minorities. To quickly close the gap, we forged a coalition of over 190 public and private organizations, including the American Chemical Society, NASA, and the National Science Foundation. These groups, representing more than six and a half million STEM professionals and educators, committed to National Lab Day, which involved sending their members as volunteers into classrooms to teach hands-on lessons and forging individual connections between K–12 educators and STEM professionals. We aimed to build ten thousand "communities of support" with the potential to reach more than one million students. But, as I shall discuss, we did not succeed.[51]

As with sourcing solutions to problems, partnership in the form of crowdsourcing also helps to attract more hands on deck and to aid implementation and execution. The crowdsourcing effort run by the Arolson Archives, the world's largest devoted to the victims of Nazi persecution, took advantage of the COVID-19 quarantine to enlist more people to work as amateur archivists to digitize approximately twenty million records on its Every Name Counts Project.[52] The Federation of American Scientists (FAS) crowdsources the development of questions for congressional witnesses in hearings involving science and technology. Typically, members of Congress and their staff have to research and write questions for hearing witnesses. To run this Congressional Science Policy Initiative, FAS crowdsources expertise from its network of over six hundred volunteer scientists, consolidating information, including draft questions, for staff in one place. Most often, members of Congress simply use the questions that they like verbatim.[53]

Sharing Data

Sharing data and data-science expertise is a unique and important reason to partner. The amount of data we can access has grown exponentially in recent years, and data's role in helping to solve some of our most difficult public problems is increasingly clear.

Yet a lot of useful data are in private hands, not available for public purposes. For example, private companies hold data about our transactions, credit-card purchasing records, mobile-phone calling records, search-engine logs, and location. Some companies, however, are beginning to take part in data collaboratives, which share data and data-science talent for public good. These collaboratives, which can be studied further at http://www.datacollaboratives.org, involve private companies, universities, and/or public-sector organizations exchanging their data to create public value.

For example, when the category 5 Hurricane Irma hit the state of Florida, in 2017 thousands of people were forced to evacuate their homes at short notice, and information about fuel became critical. Without up-to-date information, people seeking to relocate to a safe place could have found themselves looking for fuel in the wrong place, diminishing their chance of successful evacuation and risking their lives.

The tech company GasBuddy was in a unique position to supply information about fuel during this crisis. Through its mobile and web application, GasBuddy shares data on fuel prices, fuel types, and other information about gas stations in an area, much of it crowdsourced from GasBuddy's user base. That enables it to provide real-time fuel prices from 140,000 gas stations in the United States, Canada, and Australia.

In response to Hurricane Irma, GasBuddy and the Florida Division of Emergency Management (DEM) launched a data collaborative to ensure that government agencies and the public had free access to accurate and up-to-date information about the fuel they needed to evacuate safely.

GasBuddy analysts traveled to Tallahassee and shared real-time data with response agencies in the state government. Analysts also studied the information as it arrived, informing government decision-making and public communications. Florida's then-governor, Rick Scott, went on television and social media to encourage people to use GasBuddy to check fuel availability and share information through the app.

Huge numbers of Florida evacuees both accessed and contributed up-to-date fuel information. In the space of twenty-four hours GasBuddy jumped from being the fifty-seventh to the second most downloaded iPhone app in the United States. It was downloaded 350,000 times on September 7, 2017—when the storm was quickly moving through the Caribbean and toward Florida—compared with 30,000 downloads on a typical day. The GasBuddy and Florida DEM data-sharing partnership is a powerful example of how collaboration combining public and private data streams can contribute to evidence-based disaster and emergency response.[54]

Another data collaborative is the Genomic Data Commons, a research program of the National Cancer Institute that enables cancer researchers to share clinical trial and research data. By giving more physicians and researchers access to a larger pool of standardized data, the collaborative creates a repository of shared knowledge that will help them to diagnose, treat, and ultimately cure cancer patients.[55]

While data collaboratives can be effective in solving public problems, how do the companies that provide the data benefit? Research by The GovLab suggests that private-sector partners join data-sharing coalitions for a number of reasons.[56] Corporations might share data with others for mutual benefit, especially when access to other data sources can inform their own business decisions. Opening up corporate data may also generate new insights and ideas for new lines of business.

Data collaboratives can also help corporations tap into new data-analytical skills, such as those of university researchers. They can then identify new sources of talent to hire. Data collaboratives are also a way to retain talent. Employees who get opportunities to work on projects that can improve people's lives, rather than selling more toothpaste or life insurance, are more likely to stay with the firm. And while sharing data is often done for free—sometimes known as "corporate data philanthropy"—companies can sometimes sell their data for social good, earning money in the process. Sharing data is a novel form of corporate social responsibility that companies engage in to enhance their reputation and gain media attention.

Access to Tech

In addition to providing data to accelerate identification of a problem or design and implementation of a solution, partners also provide technology and technology skills. I have already discussed how governments partnered with volunteer technologists and data scientists to create a data-driven response to COVID-19 in 2020. Partnerships are helping even the most local organizations gain access to cutting-edge technology.

The United Nations Development Programme (UNDP) partnered with the government of Singapore to establish the Global Centre for Technology, Innovation and Sustainable Development. The effort is designed specifically to curate partnerships between Asian technology companies, social innovators, and government partners to marry cutting-edge technology to challenges of development. The intent is to give people working in the field with vulnerable communities on development challenges access to the latest technology in areas such as sustainable agriculture, digital cities, and financial inclusion. Through partnerships, the aim of the center is to identify technology or support cocreation of technological solutions to accelerate solutions to sustainability. Similarly, USAID's Global Development Lab also develops and scales technologies to address development challenges.

Technology firms are frequently interested in partnering with public problem solvers and public entrepreneurs in order to apply their innovations for social good either pro bono or at reduced cost. Partnerships can also be used to spur the development of new technology. The Movement Cooperative Lab, for example, organizes partnerships among progressive, political nonprofits in order to lower the costs to each of building or acquiring cutting-edge technology. Workers Lab organizes "Design Sprints" among partners to develop and pilot technology solutions for challenges impacting workers and workplaces.

THE PROCESS OF PARTNERING

Creating partners for delivery and implementation is not a simple process. While private-sector collaboration is typically governed by standard contracting vehicles, such as joint venture agreements, partnerships that cross sectors can take many forms. They can be more or less formal. They can involve the sharing of a wide range of resource types. They can implicate actors from entirely different settings, who often lack common interests or even a shared vision of success.

Skills in establishing a public partnership are not formally taught, which explains why there are so many toolkits on the topic. Partnerships may involve some loss of control and power, could compromise accountability, and could even create added legal or reputational risk. All this means that it is essential to take time to consider and design the partnership. Harvard Kennedy School's scholars of collaborative governance John Donohue and Richard Zeckhauser explain the challenge this way: "Orchestrating collaborative arrangements calls upon skills that are frequently found among corporate executives, venture capitalists, or senior consultants, but less so among front-line public managers. We are not currently accustomed to selecting, compensating, or evaluating government workers on the basis of such competencies."[57] Not all collaborations succeed, nor is there yet much empirical evidence about the benefits of governing through partnerships compared with other forms of governance.

I have reviewed a wide range of resources and distilled them into the following six-step process to guide the formation of partnerships. The process includes key tasks through which partners can clarify and articulate their shared goals and mutual contributions. As Buffett and Eimicke sum up, "Thoroughly planning on, agreeing to, and coordinating shared investment throughout the collaboration helps reduce potential conflict."[58]

Step 1: Identifying Clear Value from Partnership

First consider whether partners are even needed. What is the rationale for the partnership? Will it speed the path to problem solving? Given that partners will add complexity to your project, it is important to be clear about why you need them and why you believe you can accomplish more together than alone. To know what others can contribute and to create the shared imperative for partnership, you should understand your limits: of capital, legitimacy, expertise, risk, need for more hands on deck, or other reasons.

The partnership must add intrinsic value to your goal and be a better alternative than if the parties were to work independently.

The Partnering Initiative, a UK nonprofit focused on supporting business partnerships with nonprofits and governments to tackle sustainable development, advises that the partnership has to add clear value for each partner, in addition to advancing implementation. It provides useful checklists to help individual partners and the collaborative to identify the value of working together. All partners need to understand how they will benefit. Is it to satisfy a sense of altruism or public purpose, or something more self-serving, or both? Whichever it is, partnerships "should only happen whenever there is an overlap of interest between organisations and sufficient compatibility between them." The Partnering Initiative also advises that "each partner should achieve a net benefit from the partnership, with the value generated after accounting for all input and transactional costs."[59]

The power of aligning incentives and interests can be seen in the case of Sense about Science, a UK-based nonprofit that challenges misrepresentations of science in politics and the media. In 2015, the organization launched the AllTrials campaign to promote research transparency in the United States. The campaign sought to ensure the registering and reporting of all clinical trials, after concerns that the results of up to half of all clinical trials are never reported, leaving doctors and patients in the dark about treatments they prescribe and take.

The National Institutes of Health had already built a superb resource to house these kinds of data at http://clinicaltrials.gov, an open-access library at which scientists can register and report the results of clinical trials. Yet although US law requires the pharmaceutical industry and academia to report trials, both have been slow to comply, perhaps because enforcement by the Food and Drug Administration has been weak.

To accelerate compliance, AllTrials created a petition calling for the transparency of clinical trials. Nearly 750 organizations and tens of thousands of individuals, including dozens of patient groups and leading medical societies, endorsed it.[60] Most importantly, AllTrials engaged some important global investors, who together represented more than €3.5 trillion in investment, as partners. Their involvement put significant pressure on the pharmaceutical industry. Partnering to support AllTrials was in the investors' interest because misleading claims about drug safety can lead to expensive lawsuits, product recalls, and declining market share.[61] The result has been intensified action by the US Food and Drug Administration, as well as by the UK Parliament and funders, to demand the publication of research data. Much more progress was made through this partnership than legal mandate alone would have achieved.

Step 2: Identifying and Recruiting Prospective Partners
After determining the need to partner, you should ascertain who those partners are. You need to create a clear plan, from which you can generate the to-do list that will propel the project forward, by showing who needs to do what and when.[62]

Such checklists have been popularized by the *New Yorker* writer and surgeon Atul Gawande in his book *The Checklist Manifesto*. Implementation checklists avoid what Gawande describes as errors of ineptitude—mistakes we make when we fail to use properly what we already know.[63] Such lists not only help you remember certain details but are a check and balance on the arrogance and hubris that can arise when creative leaders are assumed to hold instinctual and infallible powers.

However, creating a to-do list by working backward from the end point is not an obvious or easy task when time is tight and we want to focus on the next step. Our sense of urgency tends to crowd out the important process of reflection needed to chart the course. A further hazard is that professionals tend to think they know exactly what to do next after undertaking what they believe to be an adequate level of investigation. Pausing to document the implementation pathway, and revising it based on new knowledge, can actually speed up implementation. It also helps you to confirm which partners you might need.

To choose your partners, you need to examine your options for addressing your problem. Often, they are diverse. For example, increasing the number of STEM-ready teachers in schools might involve creating tax credits for new teachers or launching a pilot project to increase pay for STEM teachers in key jurisdictions. It might involve asking CEOs of companies to commit publicly to allow their employees to volunteer to teach, or it might mean developing an advanced market mechanism to guarantee a teaching position to those who invest the time to prepare. Playing through all the scenarios can inform a plan of action.

Identifying potential partners is not the same as identifying stakeholders —groups affected by a decision, whose interests need to be considered when designing a solution. As the nonprofit consulting firm FSG explains, partners need not be stakeholders; they might be entities such as foundations, businesses, and other influencers that have complementary assets and desire to accomplish the goal, without having a direct stake in the project at the outset, such as we have seen with data collaboratives.

In any case, it will sometimes be obvious which partners are essential to the project's success and which are optional. In your scan of the horizon for potential partners, you will also want to identify stakeholders affected by the outcomes. You will want to identify those with money, membership, skills and talent, or the capacity to publicize the project or with a different risk profile—in other words, anyone who can bring assets of value to the project. Finally, you should identify any linchpins, the connectors to support implementation, or, conversely, those with the potential to be roadblocks—people you will need to engage.

A range of helpful guides exists to support individuals and organizations to identify and map stakeholders and partners. For example, an exercise in chapter 5 lays out a nonexclusive list of potential stakeholders and partners. Another useful resource is the "Intersector Toolkit," designed to support collaborative problem solving, created by the Intersector Project, a Brooklyn-based nonprofit organization. It begins with steps to engage potential partners and usefully points to a variety of additional checklists.[64] Some of those checklists are reproduced among the exercises at the end of this chapter.

Once you have identified partners, you need to woo them. You need to set out a clear and compelling account of the problem and how solving it aligns with their interests. Even more importantly, you need to identify a person or organization that will have the greatest capacity to interest and perhaps impress your prospective partner. Getting an idea implemented usually depends on getting someone to say yes. Often this is a busy executive, philanthropist, legislator, or developer—someone who may be hard to reach, let alone persuade.

Once you have identified that middle person, you will usually need to write the letter you want him or her to send on your behalf.[65] When getting to yes means convincing a president, mayor, or manager, it is useful to craft the draft you want that person's adviser or chief of staff to send. To accelerate progress, make it simple for the budget officer to agree to your proposal by writing a draft budget for him or her. Industry lobbyists regularly employ this technique and write the legislation they want politicians to pass. The American Legislative Exchange Council (ALEC) drafts and shares model state-level legislation to accelerate the adoption of conservative policies.[66] Such networks and professional groups play a crucial role in policy diffusion simply by making it easy for a public official to choose among policies.[67]

Junior associates in professional firms are familiar with this trick of writing letters their boss will sign. But public problem solvers, with responsibilities and leadership authority, often lose sight of how valuable this shortcut can be for getting things done. (While we all write email, for most of us far more than we would like, writing a persuasive letter that prompts a busy person to say yes is an art, and I offer some suggestions on "writing the killer letter" at http://solvingpublicproblems.org.)

Step 3: Articulating the Mission and Defining Roles

Creating a shared picture of what success looks like and why we must change helps to sustain the momentum of engaged partnerships. We have seen firsthand the power of movements and coalitions to change the world. But not all collaboration succeeds. Even high-profile networks such as the Arab Spring or Occupy Wall Street fizzled out, even if some of their achievements were notable. Exciting collaborative projects such as Retos Jalisco, Mexico, which invited entrepreneurs and innovators to propose and develop digital solutions to social problems, can fail to survive a transition of political leadership. In 2019, the budget for Australia's foreign-affairs InnovationXchange was cut from AUD$50 million to AUD$10 million, despite the program's successful outcomes. The InnovationXchange foundered because broader department staff did not understand the role of the exchange or what its employees did. While its partnerships with outside organizations thrived, the program did not work well within its more traditional home department. An implementation partnership must be well designed, or it will fail.

Defining a common set of goals, vision of success, and objectives (and making those clear to your own and your partner organizations) is a key part of partnership development. Partners might have very different reasons to partner and different measures of success. Government goals are not the same as those of business or philanthropy. Success should be defined in a collaborative way, to arrive at a common mission. For public problem solvers, that should be for a public purpose. The shared goals of a partnership should be clarified and reconfirmed over time, or there is a risk they will diverge for different partners. So long as partners continue to articulate and acknowledge their differences, they can be overcome and even be welcomed.

Collaborations are stronger when each partner acknowledges its individual goals. David Smith of the Presidio Institute calls this "community-centered selfishness," emphasizing the need to ensure that the partnership creates value both for individual members and for the collective.[68] Even so, as the Intersector Project advises in its toolkit, "if partners cannot balance the collaboration's vision of success with their own organizational mission and goals, or if they perceive that the collaboration's goals begin to deviate significantly from their own, partners' commitment to the collaboration is likely to weaken."[69]

I had firsthand experience of the challenge of aligning partner goals while working on the White House National Lab Day initiative to send tens of thousands of STEM professionals into schools to teach hands-on lessons. The initiative ultimately failed, arguably because the goals of one partner, namely, national publicity, diverged from the substantive education goals of the others. National Lab Day garnered the president of the family foundation that volunteered to coordinate the effort a great deal of media attention. But when that president lost a subsequent election for political office and no longer needed the publicity, he lost interest, and his foundation stopped investing in the project. What started with a bang ended with a whimper. The governance was not in place to ensure competent leadership and a smooth and lasting transition. The episode provides further evidence of the need to think through a partnership strategy from end to beginning, anticipating such changes of heart.

These conflicts arise among other types of partners as well. I was involved in a research project to use data science to improve legal services for low-income people. The partners were my university and a major nonprofit. While the nonprofit was focused on the needs of people they serve, my academic collaborators were exclusively interested in more publications in academic journals. These interests were not inherently at odds until data analysis for the project revealed a surprising pattern of behavior with regard to police violence that was in conflict with the advocacy goals of the nonprofit. In another project I undertook with partners in several universities, we accepted a grant from a private company, only to find the company wanting to play an outsize role in shaping the writing and research. Not only were the academics in conflict with the funders' reluctance to show negative results, but the academics were also not aligned on how to respond. Fortunately, there was an agreement in place that anticipated such challenges.

To avoid those kinds of breakdowns, it is important to arrive at a shared vision for the partnership, its mission, objectives, and activities and how information will be shared with other partners and with the public, to ensure alignment. Knowing the difficulties of reaching agreement, the Intersector Project suggests that partners may find it easier first to agree on criteria for evaluating and selecting indicators, which are necessary in order to make shared claims about outcomes. Here are some questions they propose for consideration:

- How relevant are the indicators to the collaboration's vision of success?
- How relevant are the indicators to the facts that have been agreed are applicable to the issue at hand?
- Are the indicators accessible during the time span of the collaboration?
- Do the indicators provide insight into the "living experiences" of those affected by the issue the collaboration aims to influence?[70]

As well as articulating the vision and mission, the group has to assign roles to each partner, identifying what each needs to do and contribute in order to achieve the goals just outlined. As the P-TECH program for STEM careers illustrates, it is important to define each party's responsibilities within the group.[71] They may be funders or may be focused on advocacy. Perhaps their role is communication or community outreach. Increasingly, partners are needed that know how to use data or how to engage with citizens. These are special skills that often define the need for partners.

Taking the steps to talk through the process of implementation and each party's role, you will gradually identify the value of each partner. You will also clarify whether partners have the authority and acceptance in their own organization to be able to deliver on the commitments they make.[72]

Step 4: Designing the Type of Partnership
Organizations working together must have a clear vision of how they will collaborate. My colleagues at The GovLab Stefaan Verhulst and Andrew

Young define six types of arrangement for data collaboratives. This typology describes the most common forms by which public, private, and university or philanthropic sectors exchange data or data-science talent.

In the first type, a "data cooperative" or "data pool," organizations agree to combine data in a shared resource. The National Institutes of Health's Genomic Data Commons, for example, pools data from a variety of research organizations. In the second type, "prize-backed challenge collaboratives," corporations make data available to qualified applicants who compete to develop new apps or discover innovative uses for the data. In "research partnership data collaboratives," corporations share data with universities and other academic organizations. For example, the Harvard School of Public Health partnered with the mobile provider Safaricom to analyze aggregated cell-phone data from fifteen million people in Kenya along with the country's Malaria Atlas to better understand the spread of the disease and support eradication efforts.

An "intelligence product data collaborative" uses corporate data to build a dashboard or other tool to support a public or humanitarian objective. Application programming interfaces (APIs) allow software developers to access data across organizations for testing, product development, and data analytics. For example, the Ashoka Trust for Research in Ecology and the Environment uses the Google Earth API to provide forest information to policy makers to support ways they can protect tigers and elephants in Indian forest reserves.

The final type of collaborative is the "trusted intermediary data collaborative," in which corporations share data with a limited number of known partners for data analysis.[73]

Another way to characterize different types of partnership is provided by Arizona State University's Lodestar Center for Philanthropy and Nonprofit Innovation, which focuses on partnership among nonprofits. The center identifies eight different types of partnership based on different governance models, ranging from fully integrated merger to confederation among partnering organizations.[74]

It is not important to settle on a hard and fast typology for collaborative cross-sectoral partnerships. What matters is having a process through which partners can come to a shared understanding of the mission and goals of the collaboration and the roles and responsibilities of each partner.[75] These ideal types of partnerships offer models to help partners design their own, a process that should also include a risk assessment and a plan to mitigate risks and divergence of interests.

Again, there is a plethora of tools, checklists, and rubrics for this purpose. Intersector suggests six steps for designing any partnership, supported by a total of seventeen tools in its partnership-planning toolkit! The six steps are building a common fact base, agreeing on metrics of success, committing to information sharing, sharing power and decision-making, establishing a governance structure, and identifying a manager. The Harvard Graduate School of Education publishes another a partnership-design toolkit focused on the education domain. Drawing on research into hundreds of cases, the school offers an eight-point checklist of values, summarized in the acronym ELEMENTS:

- Excellently Executed (not haphazard or amateurish in process)
- Leadership Driven (not without a vision but not leader dominated or unnecessarily hierarchical)
- Engaging for Participants (not without meaning, not narrowly focused)
- Mission Focused (not all over the map, not with contradictory goals)
- Ethically Oriented (not self-serving, based on power, or exhibiting "compromised work")
- Nurtured Continuously (not neglected or left to whim)
- Time Well Spent (not time wasted, not reliant on impulse or rigid routine)
- Solution Inspired (not aimless or without a specific goal or product)[76]

Step 5: Articulating the Theory of Change

To cross the chasm from idea to implementation and to persuade others to embark on a partnership, you must be able to lay out the logic of the steps needed to achieve your goal. One way to ensure that partners are aligned in their vision is to collaborate on completing a logic model, sometimes called a "theory of change," which connects your planned activities to your intended impact. A logic model is "a picture of how your program works— the theory and assumptions underlying the program. . . . This model provides a road map of your program, highlighting how it is expected to work, what activities need to come before others, and how desired outcomes are achieved."[77]

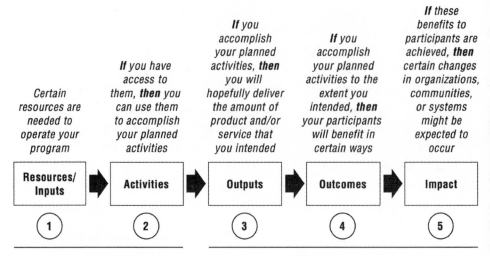

How to read a logic model (Courtesy of the W. K. Kellogg Foundation)

A logic model is a diagram that can focus attention on the anticipated goals of the project and why it is likely to work. Constructing it collaboratively, using participatory methods, will tap into the group's broader expertise and help to strengthen the partnership. More importantly, a logic model used in this way can reveal disagreements and divergences of opinion.

The most basic form of logic model is a roadmap for implementation that systematically connects initial resources with desired outcomes. It starts by documenting the inputs and activities of the intervention. The diagram then captures the outputs and finally the outcomes and ultimate impact. Each step depends on the previous one. The resources at step 1 define the human, financial, and organizational assets that go into making a program work. The activities—what the initiative does—at step 2 would not be possible without those resources. Developing this map of inputs and resources together creates the opportunity for partners to explain what each brings to the project. There are variations on the logic model to emphasize the theory of change, outcomes, and activities.

The activities will describe what you will do to produce the project's outputs and direct products, such as the service delivered or the website created as a result of the activities. As the W. K. Kellogg Foundation puts it in its guide for grantees, "Outcomes are the specific changes in program participants' behavior, knowledge, skills, status and level of functioning. Short-term outcomes should be attainable within 1 to 3 years, while longer-term outcomes should be achievable within a 4- to 6-year timeframe. The logical progression from short-term to long-term outcomes should be reflected in impact occurring within about 7 to 10 years."[78] Whereas outcomes might measure specific changes in attitudes or skills or status for individuals, impact measures the longer-term changes, whether intended or not, that emerge across a system or community as a result of the outcomes.

Step 6: Creating a Governance Structure
Unlike traditional corporate or public-sector organizations, with their hierarchical management structures and titles, no one actor in a collaboration should have legitimate authority "over" the others. The risk is that a lack of clarity about governance can scuttle even the most well-intentioned efforts. Management and governance must therefore be designed and agreed on if the partnership is to succeed.

Governance challenges are more serious than just poor communication and bad project planning. Multisectoral partnerships, especially with private-sector involvement, can pose ethical challenges and highlight tensions about priorities for achieving impact. Agribusiness and food conglomerates, for example, might sell products harmful to health even while they genuinely want to help fight hunger. Fast fashion, fossil fuel, and chemical companies want to be part of climate-focused public-private partnerships. Social media, finance, and credit-card companies may want to share data for public good, but only when it suits their purposes or for a limited time frame.

Care must be taken to avoid complicity in greenwashing and laundering of corporate malfeasance through the good publicity of public-interest partnerships. At the same time, the private sector can play a pivotal role to advance progress on public issues and bring attention to causes. The Obama administration, for example, formed partnerships with Walmart, Subway, and Pepsi to reformulate products and reduce their calorie count. Some people saw this as a sellout. Others argue that, without those partnerships, legislative progress on public-school lunches would not have been possible.[79] Also, arguably, if you want to change the American diet, making a small change at Walmart, Subway, and Pepsi may be more impactful for more people's lives than a new green market is. Companies are not always the most problematic partner. Politicians, too, can be difficult collaborators, especially when reelection season approaches. Even nonprofit and university partners that are keen not to offend their funders or that need to chase limited sources of funding can be more competitive than collaborative. No sector is exempt from its challenges. No matter what the organization, there will always be difficult personalities intent on self-aggrandizement at the expense of the partnership. Without a doubt, cross-sectoral partnerships can be fraught for the public problem solver, while also having significant potential impact.

There are significant risks when a partner loses commitment to the public-interest goals of the partnership. A transparent and accountable governance structure and related policies protect the ethical foundations of the collaboration and make it possible to exclude partners that try to manipulate the project for their own ends. Part of the work at this stage is to assess and anticipate these kinds of ethical risks.[80]

A democratic governance structure among partners provides insurance against the risk of being captured by any one partner. Citizens and stakeholders affected by the project should be included. The more inclusive the partnership, the more legitimacy and credibility it will have.[81] If the project relates to young people, then they should be included in governing structures.[82]

All of Us, a national public-health research program sponsored by the NIH and launched in 2018, attempts to integrate inclusivity and power sharing into its governance. All of Us is striving to collect big health data, including whole genome sequencing, from a million or more diverse American residents in order to accelerate health research and the development of individualized treatments. Collecting so much data means working with dozens of hospitals and health-care systems to enroll people via an app and to collect blood and urine samples and other information. Dozens of associations and interest groups, such as the American Medical Association, the National Black Nurses Association, and the National Pan-Hellenic Council, have committed to encourage people to sign up to this massive, nationwide public-health initiative.

Given the project's ambitious scope, and to ensure that partners agree on its goals, All of Us published a shared set of values. One of those principles is, "Participants are partners. Participants shape the program with their input and contribute to a project that may improve the health of future generations. They may also learn about their own health."[83] The governance structures support this principle: governance is participant centered. Since April 2018, thirty-two participant representatives—ordinary people representing participants—serve on All of Us Research Program committees. The project makes citizens part of the mix. Eight of them serve on the program's advisory and governing bodies—the Advisory Panel, Steering Committee, and Executive Committee. The other twenty-two individuals provide input on specific aspects of the program, such as research priorities, participant retention, privacy and security, and the meaningful return of information to participants.

There is no single model for governance. Partners may be accustomed to different models of management and authority in their own organizations. Discussion among partners will determine the governance structure that best fits the collaboration, the level of formality needed, and what is feasible and comfortable.

The StriveTogether partnership, a national, nonprofit network working to provide cradle-to-career educational opportunities for young people, recommends depicting in a diagram the governance structure and the roles of participants to create clarity and public accountability within the partnership.[84] RaiseDC, one of seventy national StriveTogether partnerships, shows the governance structure as a series of concentric circles to reinforce inclusivity. RaiseDC has organized the partnership's different groups, which include leaders in government, philanthropy, and business, into what it calls a "lasting civic infrastructure." The executive team is a core group of cross-sector leaders who provide strategic direction and oversight. A leadership council, a larger group of executive-level leaders across the member organizations, drives collaborative action for agreed outcomes. A third series of governing groups are called "change networks": practitioners and experts working in different areas, such as early-childhood development or disconnected youth, who identify promising strategies, design indicators for them, and develop data to inform the work of the leadership council. The networks are also responsible for implementing strategies in their respective programs.[85] RaiseDC's professional staff supports the partnership. Boundaries between the three groups are not neatly delineated; membership of the accountability structures can overlap, and members of one group in the structure might also participate in another.

One must stay attuned to the risk of inequality and real or perceived power imbalances among partners. To avoid this problem, the Rockefeller Foundation took an innovative approach to its 100 Resilient Cities partnership. To avoid political leaders from big cities dominating the project, the foundation created a new role of Chief Resiliency Officer in every city government it funded. These officials, helped by foundation staff, run the network, sharing ideas with each other and benefiting from the experience of building resilience in their highly diverse hometowns.[86]

TO DO

Exercise 1: Design a Partnership
Complete this exercise to design your partnership.

Identify Clear Value from the Partnership

- What is the reason for the partnership? Does collaboration speed up the progress of problem solving?

Identify and Recruit Prospective Partners

- Determine the supply of potential partners. Prioritize the individuals and organizations that can help you.

Work Backward from Goals

- Work backward from what you want to accomplish, identifying tangible goals. Then generate a to-do list that propels the project forward.

Articulate the Mission

- Define with partners a common set of goals, vision of success, and objectives. Given people's potentially diverse reasons to participate, recognize that partners can measure success differently, depending on who they are.

Here is a related set of questions (adapted from the Partnering Initiative) to help with articulating the mission:

- Vision: How will the world be different if we succeed?
- Mission: What is the purpose of the partnership?

- Objectives: What are the specific goals, deliverables, and time frames of the partnership?
- Activities: What specific actions will it undertake? Who will do what?
- Measurement: How will success for the partnership's activities be defined and measured?
- Transparency: How will information be shared with partners and the public?

Define Roles

In addition to articulating the vision and mission, the group has to assign roles to each partner, identifying what each needs to do and contribute in order to achieve the goals that have been outlined.

By talking through the process of implementation and each person's role in it, you will gradually identify the value of the partners and whether they have the authority in their own organization to play their part and make good on their commitments.

Exercise 2: Partnership Checklist (Intersector Project)

- Build a common fact base
- Agree on measures of success
- Commit to information sharing
- Share power and decision-making
- Establish a governance structure
- Identify a manager

Exercise 3: Construct a Logic Model

There are many examples of logic models and theory of change worksheets and courses online. The most basic form of logic model is a roadmap for implementation that systematically connects initial resources with desired outcomes.

- *Activities.* In order to address our problem or create this asset, we will conduct the following activities.
- *Resources.* In order to accomplish our planned activities, we will need the following resources.
- *Outputs.* Once completed or under way, the activities will produce the following evidence of service delivery.

- *Short- and long-term outcomes.* We expect that, if completed or ongoing, these activities will lead to the following changes in one to three, then four to six, years.
- *Impact.* We expect that, if completed, these activities will lead to the following changes in seven to ten years.

Exercise 4: Articulate Your Theory of Change
In the body of the chapter, we have included the Theory of Change diagram from the W. K. Kellogg Foundation, which has many good theory of change resources online, as does the Annie E. Casey Foundation. New Philanthropy Capital in the United Kingdom provides a ten-step workbook on theory of change (https://www.thinknpc.org/resource-hub/ten-steps/). A Googling may leave you overwhelmed by the choices. Thus, I have selected one other example here, from Nesta's DIY Toolkit (https://diytoolkit.org/tools/theory-of-change/).

Start at the left and note the problem you want to solve and, then jump all the way to the right and note your long-term goals. Take care to set goals that are specific, achievable, and measurable.

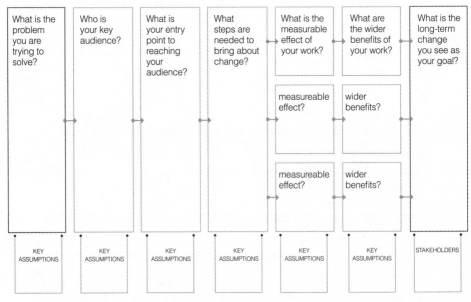

Theory of change worksheet from the DIY Toolkit, Nesta, 2014 (Worksheet licensed under Creative Commons 4.0)

In between, write down the activities, filling in the steps you plan to take to get from the left column to the right.

Underneath each activity, note your assumptions, or what must be true for it to succeed.

Keep in mind that this theory of change worksheet is most effective for facilitating planning discussions with others. It is not intended to help you formulate the definition of your problem, your goals, or the methods you use to solve it.

Exercise 5: Create a Governance Structure

- Create a transparent and accountable governance structure.
- Look at similar initiatives and learn from their structures.
- Create a visual diagram showing the governance structure and the roles of participants.
- Write a partnership agreement in the form of a memorandum of understanding, partnership bylaws, group constitution, or another document.
- Make citizens part of the mix.

CHAPTER TEN

Testing What Works

EVALUATION AND EVOLUTION

The country needs, and unless I mistake its temper, the country demands bold persistent experimentation. It is common sense to take a method and try it. If it fails, admit it frankly and try another.

Franklin Delano Roosevelt, Oglethorpe University address (1932)

EVALUATING WHAT WORKS

Chapter 8 discussed the need to conduct a rapid field scan using data and people to find solutions and evaluate their relevance to the problem in view quickly. Chapter 9 addressed the need to take advantage of the collective intelligence of organizations and individuals in order to plan and implement a solution. Now we need a way to gather information about whether our efforts are working.

By this point, we should be reasonably confident that we understand the solution being implemented, what will support it, and how it will work, including how to replicate what has worked elsewhere. But we still need to find out whether our theory of change is correct and our activities will work in the ways intended. Sometimes, we are not necessarily confident about the solution we are trying.[1] We need to work out how to evaluate our own project.

The evaluation field is vast, with countless and diverse methods and tools. We will focus here on some methods and tools to run our own experiments, set up our own pilots, and use social auditing to engage others to measure what works. As this book proposes for all initiatives, we will include as participants in evaluation activities the people who are intended to benefit from our activities.

Designing an Experiment

Randomized controlled trials (RCTs) can help to test whether small changes designed to influence human behavior can make a costly intervention more effective. We can try to implement our own RCTs as a way to generate evidence in real time about whether the intervention we plan to pursue works in practice.[2] This often involves breaking a project into its key components, testing what can make the difference, and attributing progress—or lack of it—to the relevant factors.

For example, the Supplemental Nutritional Assistance Program (SNAP) helps to feed families and improve their health. But whether it works might first depend on whether people can get through the application process to obtain the benefit. Transposing a food-benefit program from one jurisdiction to another might fail, not because food assistance is not effective but because the form families must fill out is too complicated. It might be faster and far cheaper, for example, to simplify the form and test what difference that made to the delivery of the benefit.

The UK Behavioural Insights Team has conducted more than four hundred RCTs. To test a solution in the field, it recommends a nine-step process divided into three parts: test, learn, adapt.[3] This framework provides a useful summary of how an RCT works.

Ideally, a properly conducted trial needs an ethics review from a relevant independent review board. The design of the experiment must be submitted for review, to ensure compliance with rules for human research on human subjects.

As we have previously discussed, during the testing phase, we identify two or more policy or service interventions to compare. We determine the outcome that the policy is intended to influence and how the trial will measure it. Then we decide on the randomization unit. For example, we might be dividing individuals into two groups, or we might be randomizing at the level of the institution and dividing a cohort of schools into groups. We need to judge how big our groups of institutions or people need to be to get meaningful results. Next we need to randomly assign our test participants into the experimental or control group and give the experimental group the intervention. Then we can observe and determine whether the trial has yielded any insight about the success of the intervention,

Good RCTs demand a large-enough sample size and the ability to randomly select subjects from the sample. Both are needed to ensure that the populations in each group are relatively similar and that it is reasonable to infer causality from the intervention. When those conditions can be satisfied, some people assert that RCTs can be run quickly and relatively inexpensively. Ideas42 estimates the cost of RCTs at a few hundred dollars.[4]

Others are more critical, pointing out that embracing experimental methods like RCTs demands significant investment of researchers' time, talent, and attention.[5] A study must be conceptualized and designed, groups sorted, data gathered, and permission obtained from relevant agencies and organizations. In field experiments, it can be challenging to be sure the right intervention is delivered to the right people and the outcomes are measured correctly. Fortunately, digital technology can help make it easier to more efficiently check on this kind of progress.

Designing Quasi-Experimental Tests

While RCTs have surged in popularity only in recent decades, there is a long-standing tradition of empirical study of natural data obtained from observations. We can return to this approach to measure impact when RCTs do not work. Difference-in-difference studies measure the difference between two naturally occurring groups. For example, the city of Chicago imposed a plastic-bag tax in order to deter single-use plastic. Because everyone in the city was subject to the tax, an RCT was not possible. Instead, the team conducted a natural experiment, comparing bag use before and after the tax went into effect in Chicago, as well as in suburbs that were not subject to a bag tax. The team was able to report that the intervention reduced disposable-bag use by 42 percent.[6]

The nineteenth-century English physician John Snow's famous study revealing that cholera is transmitted through the water supply rather than through the air is an example of difference-in-difference, quasi-experimental evaluation design. At the time, households in London were provided with water from one of two companies. One year, before the cholera outbreak of 1853, one of those companies changed the source of its water to a cleaner supply from outside the city.[7] People drinking the cleaner water died at a rate of only 37 per 10,000, whereas people drinking from the polluted Thames died at 315 per 10,000.[8] This natural experiment, involving diverse people divided into two large-enough groups, made it possible for Snow to draw a statistically significant comparison.

As this book has emphasized, RCTs are powerful tools, but they have limits and biases. When the intervention being tested is a simple behavioral prompt, for example, RCTs can identify whether that intervention works. But knowing what worked in a specific instance does not allow us to generalize or to answer important questions about the relevance of the solution. Designing other kinds of empirical experiments without a control group can be just as meaningful and efficient, if not more so.[9]

At the height of the California energy crisis at the turn of the millennium, the Cal State University psychologist P. Wesley Schultz and colleagues wanted to measure the impact on energy consumption of sending people messages that signaled to them where they stood relative to their neighbors. In the experiment, households were given weekly feedback about the amount of electricity they used compared with similar households in their neighborhood.

The researchers reasoned correctly that the messages would have different effects for those who were above-average energy users and those who were light users. While the heavy users would use less, the light users who were told how well they were doing would use more (a boomerang effect), with no net benefits in energy saved. The researchers added one additional condition. Light users who received an approving smiley-face emoticon did not suffer the boomerang effect, illuminating a novel strategy for reducing energy consumption, which has since become mainstream practice by utilities across the country. Trials of the strategy in more than a hundred subsequent deployments over ten years led to more than $1 billion saved in household energy costs and a reduction of nearly thirteen billion pounds of CO_2 emissions.[10]

Instead of a simple experiment with one intervention and a control group, this design used two interventions and no control group, simply studying the behavior of participants before and after the intervention. With big data becoming much more prevalent, and with easier ways to gather and analyze large quantities of data with machine learning, we are able to conduct statistically relevant empirical experiments without the cost or complexity of a traditional RCT.[11]

Using a Survey to Test a Solution

The RCT and other quantitative experiments discussed in the preceding section are relatively rapid and real time, allowing meaningful data to be

generated to assess an intervention quickly. But sometimes it can be difficult to get permission or find the time for these. When neither an RCT nor
a natural experiment are possible or practical, you may want to use a survey
to assess the effectiveness of an intervention. Surveys can be very effective
for revealing people's attitudes and state of mind in ways that observational
studies are not and can also be used to complement other experiments.

There are more ways to collect survey responses than through face-to-
face or phone surveys. For example, microsurveys via text message or chatbot can elicit answers to questions quickly and potentially at lower cost. As
my team at the Innovation Office of the state of New Jersey rolls out a new
platform (New Jersey Career Network) to help the long-term unemployed
get back to work, we regularly do a "pulse check" with our participants,
surveying them electronically about their satisfaction with the tools and
asking them for more detailed feedback on the experience. The pulse check
uses a series of emoticons that depict a range of moods from sad to happy
and invites users to choose one. This form of Likert scale is especially useful
with low-literacy individuals, who are among our customers, as well as children.[12]

Surveys are not perfect. Response rates can be low at a time when many
surveys compete for attention. The wording and sequencing of questions
affect the quality and reliability of responses, and even minor changes can
have an impact.[13] Professional survey designers often randomize responses
to avoid primacy effects—that is, people selecting whatever options are presented first because they have had more time to process and absorb those
responses.[14] It is important to avoid offering too many answer choices because people find it hard to keep too many options in mind.

Risks of bias and variance arise from the failure to frame and select
appropriately whom we ask to respond to the survey. It is vital that survey
respondents reflect the target population for a planned intervention.[15] Finally, it is not easy to be sure whether responses or nonresponses to a survey can be attributed to the intervention itself or to the survey. We can try to
address this issue by improving how we sample and by comparing re-
sponders and nonresponders using the data we do have.

More appealing survey content and design will increase the likelihood
that people will respond. Pew Research comments, "Researchers will sometimes conduct a pilot study using open-ended questions to discover which
answers are most common. They will then develop closed-ended questions

that include the most common responses as answer choices. In this way, the questions may better reflect what the public is thinking or how they view a particular issue."[16] Once Pew Research has created its surveys, it tests them to see how they can be improved.

Instead of replicating a long, paper-based questionnaire on the screen, we can take advantage of the Internet and mobile phones to change the way we ask questions. Collaborating with professional social scientists and survey-methods experts can help with formulating questionnaires for these kinds of survey options.

Most survey questions are closed, with participants choosing from among a list of preset responses. By contrast, wiki surveys, described in chapter 5, can obtain rapid and collaborative assessment of solutions. The All Our Ideas tool presents respondents with a question and the choice between two responses. Respondents can also submit their own text response or select "I cannot decide."

A wiki survey takes advantage of digital technology to solicit reactions from a larger number of people about why a solution works, allowing you to leverage the wisdom of the crowd to evaluate your solution.

PILOTING YOUR PROJECT

"What a man hears he may doubt, what he sees he may possibly doubt, but what he does himself he cannot doubt." Seamen Knapp, father of the Extension Service of the US Department of Agriculture (USDA) in 1903, used these words to describe the importance of farmers trying out innovations for themselves rather than have the government mandate what they should do. In order to speed up innovation in agriculture, the USDA formalized the agricultural clubs of the 1800s by establishing a network of learning organizations to distribute research and learning about farming in America. Writing about Knapp's innovation in the *New Yorker*, Atul Gawande noted that in 1900, more than 40 percent of a family's income went to paying for food. It became essential "to reduce food costs, so that families could spend money on other goods, and resources could flow to other economic sectors." Gawande explains how Knapp persuaded one farmer to agree to try some simple farming innovations like deeper plowing. Despite the boll weevil infestation that year, the farmer dramatically increased his output. Knapp expanded the program, hiring thirty-three more agents. "What seemed like a hodgepodge eventually cohered into a whole." Once the government shaped a feedback loop of experiment and learning and encouragement for farmers across the country, the results were beyond anyone's imagining. The productivity of US farmers began to outpace that of farmers in other Western countries. Prices fell by half. By 1930, food absorbed just 24 percent of family spending and 20 percent of the workforce. "Today, food accounts for just eight per cent of household income and two per cent of the labor force. It is produced on no more land than was devoted to it a century ago, and with far greater variety and abundance than ever before in history," marvels Gawande.[17]

Small-scale piloting and testing what works—instead of full implementation—represents both a new mind-set and a new skill set for the public entrepreneur.[18] Although pilots are commonplace in medical care, policy piloting has not been used widely, perhaps because of a perception that such experiments, which treat people differently, may be unfair or even illegal or because of concerns that randomization violates due process and equal protection under the Constitution.[19]

Nevertheless, for public problem solving, in which neither problem nor solution is well understood and there is no sure pathway to implementation, smaller-scale pilots, trials, and demonstration projects can help those problem solvers inside and outside government to determine what works before scaling up a project across a city, state, or nation. Pilots are invaluable for testing a policy, service, or product at the stage of implementation before a broader rollout. Far too often a new program has to be a big success, and big political egos get in the way of learning and adjusting as we go.

Bas Leurs and Kelly Duggan of Nesta in the United Kingdom advocate the use of pilots "when you believe you have an effective solution and are looking to iron out the creases and understand how it works in reality."[20] Exposing these "creases," which might include unintended consequences, unrealistic resource assumptions, or problems with reaching intended project beneficiaries, creates an opportunity to adjust a project's design and promote its chances of success. So much of the success of behavioral insights as an approach has been the practice of implementing small-scale pilots based on research to determine what works in practice, with the awareness that while many of those experiments might fail, the pilots create an evidence base for learning and eventual scale.

In this way, pilot programs can be used to help begin major initiatives without the risk that bigger programs create. Care must always be taken to roll out pilots so that they reach and reflect the populations that will use the program.[21] You can use the techniques of experimental design and evaluation discussed earlier to measure the effectiveness of your pilot.

AVOIDING PILOTITIS

One caveat to the prescription to start small is to avoid the problem of *pilotitis*. Pilotitis is the tendency to try many small proof-of-concept experiments without ever crossing the threshold to achieve real scale with an intervention. This leads to wasted effort and short-lived benefits that do not justify the work you have put into designing and planning your intervention and fail to achieve sustained impact. Worse yet, stopping with the pilot creates the opportunity cost of failing to act. "It is a tragedy and incomprehensible that it should cost life to give life," exclaimed Princess Mary of Denmark at the Danish Scaling Innovations to Save the Lives of Mothers and Babies Conference. "And it is unacceptable, because we know what to do and there exist effective solutions that can prevent the majority of these deaths."[22]

While there are significant benefits to trying something to see what works—and funders like to support pilots especially of "new" apps, interventions, and ideas—you need to prepare for success and scale before you even begin the pilot; otherwise you will also end with the pilot. Doing so requires significant attention to and support for the implementation that happens after the pilot, not simply the process of coming up with the idea. Scaling up needs to begin with defining what scaled-up success looks like and having that conversation with all partners.

It is not uncommon to start out excited to try something new, but then the innovation fails to achieve general acceptance or widespread adoption. But, if the desire is to achieve scale, then the pilot needs to be a stepping-stone in a project that is designed for and anticipates what is needed to expand the effort. It is exciting that more innovative projects are being undertaken and great ideas are getting traction, but too often they fail to have large-scale impact. Pilots proliferate; impact does not.

Given the costs of going from pilot to scale, it is necessary to explain the benefits and how costs are offset as a result of the project in order to justify the necessary outlay. For example, it has been shown that when police officers and social workers respond to emergency calls together, this "co-response" approach leads to fewer arrests and hospitalizations, thereby decreasing both violence and costs. While several cities have piloted the approach, it is not yet widespread in part because of a lack of rigorous research and the challenge of measuring money not spent.[23] There also needs to be agreement as to what constitutes success. As discussed in chapter 8 and in more depth in the next section on social auditing, an RCT is not the only option to measure results, and participatory approaches can help to accelerate more consensual assessment.

The process of planning for scale starts at the outset. The desire to get to scale and real impact is why we place so much emphasis, first, on defining the problem with the affected community to ensure that the intervention addresses a genuinely felt need. Going beyond borrowing a solution that worked elsewhere to ensure that a solution works "here" by developing the project in conjunction with the community is another important component. Incorporating participation—and taking account of needs, attitudes, and desires of the community—throughout will help to ensure that the intervention is legitimate as much as it is effective.

Then there is the need for the hard work of deciding how to get from pilot to scale. Pilots can be scaled in different ways. The project can grow to serve a bigger population and more "users" (scaling up). As the term "scaling up" implies, the pilot is iteratively expanded in new geographies and communities, reaching more and more people until it becomes sustainable. By contrast, sustainability and innovation can also be the result of "franchising" the innovation. Instead of growing the original project, new changemakers may copy and replicate the model in different geographies (scaling out). Scaling can involve simply providing the tools or standards as a basis for others to innovate and develop new but related projects. Take the example of an innovative training program. Imagine the difference between (1) developing a training program and teaching it to more and more people oneself, (2) creating "chapters" of a common training movement, and (3) setting standards but letting others develop their own training programs. All three are options for scaling. Wanting to reform public-administration education, a group of ten professors decided in 2020 that their best bet to achieve reform at scale was to publish a digital government curriculum online and let others copy it, rather than trying to create a new graduate degree.[24]

Deciding which path to follow requires careful consideration of how to traverse what the literature sometimes refers to as the "messy middle" between pilot and scale. Multiple solutions might be tested and considered for scaling. "Scaling pathways are usually not clear-cut in advance, nor can it be predicted how long the replication process might take. The right model needs to be discovered through an iterative process over time, often involving larger-scale 'failure' and iteration, which requires patient support from investors and partners."[25] Whether the goal is scaling up or scaling out, such expansion can be accomplished in different ways; growing the existing organization is only one. Safecast, the massively distributed air-quality and radiation-monitoring project that started in post-Fukushima Japan, has grown so much because it relies on a network of volunteers who want to participate, less out of altruism than because they are curious about the environmental conditions in their own neighborhoods. That is what drives the data collection, and the recognition that comparing their own communities to others is what drives the data sharing. While most of the work is done by volunteers, Safecast also has a handful of dedicated, professional staff like Sean Bonner, global director, and Angela Eaton, North America director, who are able, for example, to create strategic partnerships and to support growth while maintaining the organization's robust data-reporting standards. More important, they help to tell the story to their own community of what people are doing so that otherwise-isolated volunteers feel connected to something bigger. Having a generous and consistent set of funders has allowed the Safecast team to focus on its work, rather than fundraising. Key supporters like Joi Ito, the former head of the MIT Media Lab, and Reid Hoffman, the founder of LinkedIn, along with the Knight and Shuttleworth foundations, have allowed the effort to remain independent of government, free for its participants, and sustainable.

But there are other ways to grow beyond expanding the organization's network. As explored in this chapter, partnership is another way to scale. In Lakewood, Colorado, Jonathan Wachtel initially shared the learnings of and his colleagues in four cities replicated the Sustainable Neighborhoods Model that he began in 2012. Then, in 2020, they decided to institutionalize their efforts by spinning out a new nonprofit, responsible for scaling. The organizers attribute the growth of the Sustainable Neighborhoods Program to a variety of design features that empower residents to shape their own projects. By setting standards for projects, awarding points for successful projects, and certifying those neighborhoods that grow the program, Sustainable Neighborhoods creates incentives for partners to take the initiative to scale.

Deciding on a strategy for scaling requires considering often competing factors. There may be potent drivers and incentives, including the success of the intervention and its response to a long-felt need. But there are
also potential blockers, including resources (both human and financial capital) needed to expand the pilot, context (what is needed to adapt the intervention to the institutional and political reality), legal context (what regulatory
changes are needed to integrate the innovation more permanently), organization and incentives (what will motivate others to get involved and expand
the work of the original public problem solver), and owner (who is the right
entity to take the project to scale, which may not be the original creator). In
short, it is important to weigh the ease of implementation against the likely
impact. If an innovation conflicts with established norms, rules, or values,
more resources may be needed for scaling.

Finally, partnerships can be vital for going from pilot to evaluation to
scale and back to evaluation. Working with corporate or country funders
and community partners can provide the wherewithal—both funding and
talent—needed to expand and deepen the innovation. But, as discussed
throughout the chapter, partners need to share a common vision for growth,
scale, and success.

SOCIAL AUDITING

Evaluating implementation—measuring what works—creates a prime opportunity and need for public engagement and community accountability.
Affected community members can provide a vital assessment of on-the-
ground conditions and perceptions, both before and after an intervention. You
can ask the public how to define and measure the impact of your solution
and what data to use for that purpose. You can engage people in the process
of evidence gathering, crowdsourcing their efforts to help with progress
monitoring and reporting, to improve existing service delivery and to inform future policy formulation. Such participatory evaluation is sometimes
known as "social audits" or "civic auditing" and has immense potential to
enhance accountability and performance.

Many nonprofit organizations and governments are turning to online
technology, including web platforms and mobile phones, to enable this kind
of social auditing, collecting the data to support monitoring and evaluation.
People are simply asked to take pictures, gather data, and submit other

"evidence" of on-the-ground conditions. Partners and their members can also be enlisted to help with real-time monitoring and reporting, enabled by new technology. In addition to the surveys and wiki surveys already discussed, imagine asking people to report via text message, web platform, or social media. A watchful community can improve policy making by evaluating outcomes and impact.

An example of social and civic auditing was TransGov. Established in 2014 to help Ghanaian citizens monitor the progress of local development projects, TransGov curated a list of projects in communities and gave people the ability to comment on their progress. TransGov's six hundred thousand registered users provided feedback through the TransGov website, mobile app, SMS, or Interactive Voice Response. This feedback forum enabled greater reporting of project failures, such as an eighteen-unit classroom building of the Millennium City school project, funded by USAID, that was delayed by four years and a public toilet facility that is on indefinite hold.

A second example comes from Chile. The country's Senate uses a full-time facilitator who runs evaluative focus groups after a new law is implemented. The goal is to examine the implementation and its consequences. Focus groups evaluate three things: compliance with the metrics established when the law was enacted, public perceptions of the policy and its implementation, and corrective measures to bring the law into line with the metrics. The evaluation assesses whether the law or regulation was efficient and effective in its implementation.

In Brazil, public audits conducted in random municipalities by the national comptroller have exposed deficiencies in school infrastructure quality across the country. In 2016, the comptroller launched an experimental project, the Projeto Controladoria na Escola, to engage students in ten public schools to audit school infrastructure. Students were asked to collect data about their local school environments, report major problems they faced and their causes, and propose ideas to fix them. In one school alone, students identified 115 issues. Within three months, nearly half of them were fixed, either by the Department of Education or, where possible, by the students and school managers.[26]

The collective-intelligence techniques explored in chapter 7 are useful for evaluating project success and failure. You can engage people to contribute real-time data about project implementation. Crowdcrafting, built by the Spanish software firm Scifabric, is an additional example. Institutions such as the British Museum, CERN, and the United Nations Institute for Training and Research use Crowdcrafting for assorted crowdsourcing (not specifically social-auditing) projects. While the software is free and open source, a hosted Crowdcrafting platform costs a few hundred dollars a month for basic support. For an additional fee, Scifabric will customize a version for an organization's use. It is one of many examples of crowd-sourced data-collection platforms that make it possible to engage in social auditing. However, social auditing does not require any special software. Depending on the project design, you could and might even prefer to use a platform in common use, like Facebook, Twitter, Instagram, or other social media platforms, to invite people to gather and share pictures, data, and stories rather than asking people to download a new app or visit an unfamiliar website. PetaBencana, the project that crowdsources flooding data, intentionally uses the tools people already have in their pockets, including SMS and Twitter.[27]

This chapter has revisited using collective intelligence—including participatory data collection and social auditing, as well as experiments both controlled and quasi-experimental—to improve the implementation process and help with measuring what works. Through partnership and collaboration, we can accomplish projects faster and take them to scale. We can even collaborate to design the way partnerships and their governance will work, as well as evaluate projects as they are implemented.

Chapters 11 and 12 examine how institutions can create the environment in which individuals can use the methods and tools discussed in this book. We will also see how more educational institutions worldwide are beginning to train public problem solvers and public entrepreneurs to work differently and change the world.

TO DO

The best way to learn how to evaluate and scale your project is by learning from examples. On https://solvingpublicproblems.org/ we have posted interviews with leading public entrepreneurs from government, for- and not-for-profits, and other activists talking about how they have implemented and scaled their work to maximize impact.

Exercise 1: Design an RCT (adapted from UK Behavioural Insights)

Test

1. Identify two or more policy or program interventions to compare (e.g., old versus new policy or program; different variations of a policy or program).
2. Determine the change outcome sought and how it will be measured in the trial.
3. Decide on the randomization unit: whether to randomize to intervention and control groups at the level of individuals, institutions (e.g., schools), or geographical areas (e.g., local authorities).
4. Determine how many units (people, institutions, or areas) are required for robust results.
5. Assign each unit to one of the policy interventions, using a robust randomization method.
6. Introduce the policy interventions to the assigned groups.

Learn

1. Measure the results and determine the impact of the policy interventions.

Adapt

1. Adapt your policy intervention to reflect your findings.
2. Return to step 1 to continually improve your understanding of what works.

Exercise 2: The SUM Framework for Scaling Up (from Management Systems International)

Step 1: Develop a scaling-up plan
    Task 1: Create a vision
    Task 2: Assess scalability
    Task 3: Fill information gaps
    Task 4: Prepare a scaling-up plan
Step 2: Establish the preconditions for scaling up
    Task 5: Legitimize change

Task 6: Build a constituency

Task 7: Realign and mobilize the needed resources

Step 3: Implement the scaling-up process

Task 8: Modify organizational structures

Task 9: Coordinate action

Task 10: Track performance and maintain momentum[28]

CHAPTER ELEVEN

Doing Differently, Learning Differently

We've gotta get our civics, law school, nerd shit on right now.

Hasan Minhaj

DECLARE WAR ON 1,034: HOW INNOVATIVE INSTITUTIONS SAVE LIVES

Fifty years ago, roads in the Australian state of Victoria were dangerous places to be. In 1969, 1,034 people died on them, in a population of 3.44 million. Weak seatbelt, drunk-driving, and speeding laws and a state of inertia among policy makers and the public meant that across Australia, per capita road-fatality rates were among the highest among wealthy countries —higher than in the United States and twice as high as in Britain. To Harry Gordon, editor of the *Sun News Pictorial*, a newspaper in Victoria, these numbers were an outrage. In a blistering editorial in November 1970, Gordon said it was time to "declare war on 1034." To shock the public out of its complacency, his newspaper began publishing graphic accounts of car accidents and the deaths and horrific injuries they caused. Some of these accounts were even written by a columnist called "Death." The media campaign also worked with politicians to propose solutions, and legislation followed. In December 1970, the Victorian Parliament made wearing seatbelts compulsory, the first such law in the world. Breath tests on drivers were introduced in 1971, compulsory alcohol tests on all Victorian road casualties in 1974. In 1990, speed cameras were introduced across the state, along with an unsparing advertising campaign titled "Don't fool yourself— speed kills," reenacting the trauma of road accidents. Harsh penalties for speeding, including loss of license, were introduced. Road deaths had been going down since the seatbelt laws in 1970, but police, doctors, and legislators continued to push for change, not only to laws but to the medical treatment of victims. What they created came to be called the Victorian State Trauma System (VSTS).

A critical challenge for the state was how to pay for improved trauma care. In 1986, the Transport Accident Commission (TAC) was created to provide transport accident insurance to cover all Victorians and a stable source of funding for addressing the road toll. The legislation that created TAC dramatically curtailed lawsuits for accidents and replaced them with a no-fault system that provided enhanced care for victims. TAC's prudent financial management of car registration fees (which include the insurance premium) ensured the system's viability and capacity to invest in cost-saving improvements such as trauma-care research, more policing, and "booze buses" to administer breathalyzer tests.

The creation of a comprehensive data registry supported change. Recording and reporting of preventable death rates helped to dispel the sense that road deaths were somehow inevitable. Making the costs of injuries more transparent helped to define the problem of long-term care for the injured and the need to address rehabilitation and lost productivity.

These concerted efforts, along with an unusual degree of political bipartisanship and collaboration, created the demand to overhaul trauma care and improve procedures for treating victims. A large number of smaller but vital changes, including improvement in the training of paramedics and changes in manufacture to create safer cars, also played their part in reducing deaths and injuries.

Anyone who has worked in or with government knows how difficult change inside it can be. Even small, innovative projects can be a herculean task to drive through. Yet the creation of the VSTS was anything but small. It was expensive (at least initially—decrease in injuries has reduced costs over time). It challenged cultural norms. It required massive transformation of institutions and individual behavior. And, if you are seeking to bring about change from outside government, it can be extraordinarily challenging to get people and systems to change, whether the ask is to stop doing something they do now, to start doing something new, or to continue a practice.

Whereas public and political apathy initially impeded reform, once new initiatives were shown to succeed, they spurred more motivation to continually improve the system, write Peter Bragge and Russell Gruen in their book *From Roadside to Recovery: The Story of the Victorian State Trauma System*. "For the Victorian paramedics, nurses, doctors and others involved in the immediate care of severely injured patients, high-performance is self-motivating. They recognise the privilege of working in a system that consistently produces exceptional actions that make a real difference to patients' lives." The authors conclude, "Rarely in the history of medicine had there been an intervention so effective at saving lives. That it had done so in just ten years earned the Victorian State Trauma System (VSTS) the reputation of being 'penicillin-esque.'"[1]

As a result of fifty years of intelligent, courageous policy making, traffic deaths in Victoria *had fallen by 2018 to 213* in a state of 6.27 million people, their lowest levels ever. Few other states or countries have accomplished anything similar.[2]

The Victoria road-trauma story shows how effective and determined public entrepreneurs can radically transform whole systems with a combination of complementary initiatives, each designed to solve a piece of a complex puzzle, including the problem of comprehensive financing, leading to systems-level change. The vision of zero road fatalities now seems a goal within reach. Articulating this once seemingly unattainable target helped to galvanize energy and focus political will and private commitment.

Eliminating traffic deaths is what policy wonks sometimes call a "moon shot." The term comes from John F. Kennedy's famous speech at Rice University in 1962, when he declared, "We choose to go to the Moon in this decade and do the other things, not because they are easy, but because they are hard; because that goal will serve to organize and measure the best of our energies and skills, because that challenge is one that we are willing to accept, one we are unwilling to postpone, and one we intend to win, and the others, too."[3]

The idea of moon shots describes defining an audacious goal, generally articulated by the government and designed to inspire and attract partners to join the effort by contributing concrete, practical solutions to address the public problem. Moon shots help to elevate public problem solving from the small to the grand scale. They help to set a clear vision and direction for the problem to be solved. They are a form of "mission," another term used with increasing frequency in public policy. Often the terms "mission," "moonshot," and "challenge" are used interchangeably for the concept of articulating an ambitious goal to give an aim and purpose to innovation. Missions help to scale individual problem-solving efforts by encouraging many individuals and teams within and across organizations and across sectors to row in the same direction. Thus, the Kennedy moon shot created shared agency, impetus, and funding for scientific and technological innovation by government, universities, and the private sector.

The European Commission defines a mission as an approach to policy making that involves setting defined goals, with specific targets, and working to achieve them in a set time.[4] The economist Mariana Mazzucato, one of the better-known proponents of mission-driven innovation, proposes that many of our public problems can and should be reframed as missions. She argues that problems should be broad enough to attract cross-sectoral investment but focused enough to show measurable impact.[5] Unlike public challenges of old, mission-driven initiatives do not focus on a single policy or single innovation. They undertake both incremental and radical steps, crossing silos and sectors. They are not about picking winners but about picking willing partners to collaborate to solve problems in the ways discussed in chapter 9. Of course, there is no hard-and-fast rule about what constitutes a mission. Some challenges are very broad, like restoring the rule of law or curing cancer, while others are much more specific and designed to achieve a target, such as putting a man on the moon and bringing him safely back or reducing carbon emissions by a given percentage.

Road fatalities are just one of a huge number of missions: complex, interconnected, system-level problems that, in the case of Victoria, helped to scale innovation from the individual to the systems level. Obesity in the United States is another example, albeit a less successful one. A third of Americans are overweight, and more than a third are obese, leading to increased risk of comorbidities like diabetes, heart disease, stroke, and COVID-19. Since the 1970s, obesity has tripled around the world. We now know that this is due to American food companies manipulating the composition of processed food to feed our addiction. They have also funded research to spread the falsehood that a lack of exercise—and not diet—is responsible for obesity. Compounding the problem is the cheap cost of junk food: American subsidies of corn farming induce more food producers to add corn syrup to their products to bring down production costs. Free-trade agreements, intended to promote peace and economic growth by opening up national markets to one another, allow junk-food producers to export their products, ruining once healthy and sustainable food-production systems in other countries and creating the same addictive cycle of obesity.

Michelle Obama's Let's Move! was "a comprehensive initiative, launched by the First Lady, dedicated to solving the problem of obesity within a generation, so that children born today will grow up healthier and able to pursue their dreams." Let's Move! was intended to galvanize government, industry, the health-care profession, and individual action through a series of initiatives. "Sure, this is an ambitious goal. But with your help, we can do it," exhorts the website.[6] Like many missions, it adopted a specific and measurable target: reducing obesity in the United States to 5 percent by 2030. Obama used all the institutional levers at her and her husband's disposal, including enacting an executive order, pushing for legislation regarding healthier school lunches, and also using her convening power to get a dozen federal agencies working on changes in policy and practice and, despite hefty criticism, to engage the processed-food industry to make changes. Further, she used her star power to produce videos and hold events to inspire individuals to make changes to their own lifestyles. While there was significant anecdotal evidence of success, with rollbacks of the policies under Trump and increasing childhood obesity, the effort has arguably foundered. *But*

But having a well-articulated challenge helps to galvanize concerted action. Such ambition is vital for individuals to tackle difficult challenges, from racial discrimination to gun violence to mental health to climate change and many other moon shots, using new skills. Thinking and talking "big" even while acting "small" connects well-defined problems to more ambitious societal goals and attracts more people to get engaged in problem solving. Mission-driven thinking gives coherence and structure to bottom-up problem solving by connecting the efforts of individuals to a broader and bolder story of societal progress and innovation.

To round out the individual-skills discussion, I focus on the mind-set of innovative institutions and how to create institutional environments to support innovators, laying out a series of policy prescriptions for developing more agile, experimental, and open institutions that foster innovation. It is important to go beyond the micro or individual approach and adopt such a meso-level focus on institutions as well. To explain by analogy, food producers have blamed obesity on lack of exercise, rather than diet, to lay the responsibility at the feet of individuals to change their habits. Similarly, manufacturing companies invented the term "litterbug" and launched the "Keep America Beautiful" campaign to shift attention away from regulating them to blaming individuals for throwing away the packaging the companies never should have created in the first place. Instead of requiring packaging producers to change their containers, the campaign encouraged fines and jail time for litterbugs.

I do not want the focus on individual skill building and the practices of public problem solving to inadvertently divert attention away from the need for political and institutional reform. Changing how each of us works is no substitute for institutional transformation. We will not solve the creeping crisis of trust in our institutions or tackle our hardest problems without a commitment to and investment in public-sector talent after decades of eviscerating problem-solving capacity in our public-sector institutions. Increased outsourcing to the market and to consultants, derision of civil and public servants in government, and excessive investment in business-entrepreneurship education have led to a hollowing out that needs to be reversed. Routing corruption and restoring the rule of law are essential first steps that must also be followed by restoring capacity and major investment, especially by governments and universities, in training public problem solvers at scale. Recommendations for how to do so and how to create institutions that foster more ambitious problem solving are the focus of the remainder of this chapter and of chapter 12.

FROM INDIVIDUAL SKILL SET TO INSTITUTIONAL MIND-SET
Systems like the Victorian State Trauma System encourage, support, and celebrate visionaries and innovators who not only make incremental changes but build support for more radical reforms. They actively engage big data and collective intelligence to make problems visible, and they forge alliances and partnerships to make change feasible.

In order for more of us to be able to function as public entrepreneurs, we need institutions that unlock the capacity of individuals to adopt more innovative ways of thinking and working. It is not enough for individuals to possess the right skill set; we also need institutions with the right mind-set. Innovative institutions make it easier—the best ones make it imperative—to work differently.

For MindLab in Denmark (now disbanded), GovTech in Singapore, and other organizations discussed in this book, it has been normal to involve the public—academic and industry experts and citizens—in the design or planning of new or improved services, products, and policies.

Organizations (like Victoria's Transport Accident Commission) increasingly collect and use data for decision-making and track outcomes as a matter of course, not as an exception. Institutions like NASA in the United States or Australia's Innovation Exchange in its Department of Foreign Affairs encourage the use of open innovation to source new solutions. As mentioned in chapter 8, leaders of organizations such as the Health Ministry in Ontario demand the use of evidence synthesis to identify what has worked elsewhere.

However, beyond organizations like the Defense Advanced Research Projects Agency (DARPA) or the Advanced Research Projects Agency-Energy (ARPA-E) that support cutting-edge science and technology research or some of the urban labs funded by outside philanthropy, there are not enough institutions that bring together cross-disciplinary, high-performing teams or give high priority to developing new ideas, including providing funding to develop and test innovations. Too few, if any, public institutions combine the systematic use of data *and* collective intelligence across all problem-solving stages.

For public entrepreneurs to feel supported and encouraged in their work, their institutions need mind-sets that differ from those of traditional bureaucracy. Such organizations are characterized by three values. They are agile, experimental, and open.

Values

Agile Organizations

Agile involves developing problem-solving policies and practices that are more incremental and less prematurely conclusive but nonetheless designed to lead to action and implementation. This necessitates policy and rule changes to create the more flexible working conditions necessary for eliminating the clumsy and clunky way government, especially, too often operates.

We have seen during the COVID-19 pandemic how too many public organizations that were unused to rapid response struggled to keep up with the demands for more testing, personal protective equipment, contact tracing, food deliveries, digital services, and more. The absence of "delivery units" or people trained and ready to implement hobbled response efforts (and led to outsourcing to consultants). Arguably, people died in long-term-care facilities not because government was unaware of the problem but because it was not equipped to do more than set policy and demand that industry comply. It was not set up to take the on-the-ground actions needed to move patients, change living arrangements, and train workers. So much of the burden of readying hospitals, sanitizing workplaces, and procuring supplies fell to unprepared private-sector actors who could not depend on help from the government or, in other cases, who did not want to change.

When government does take on projects, too many of those are delivered late or are over budget and then do not work well. Government is notorious for its over-budget projects. The US Air Force spent 1.1 billion taxpayer dollars on a software project, the Expeditionary Combat Support System, that was ultimately scrapped.[7] Technology is creating the ability and incentive to work more effectively by working "smaller." Instead of large-scale "waterfall" projects that require extensive gathering of evidence to support them and then take years to implement without any evidence that they will work, better public institutions are moving toward agile or "lean" project management. This approach applies not only to technology projects but also to infrastructure.[8]

"Agile" is less a specific methodology than a new way of thinking about policy design and service delivery. Rather than creating a fully developed solution, agile organizations are willing to try, fail, improve, and try again. But they are hands-on. This approach is adapted to today's fast pace of technological development, in contrast to traditional cycles of legislation and policy making that typically unfold over many years. Software makes it much easier to try something, test it out, see what works, and iterate, emphasizing successful outcomes over following rules.

The agile approach is not always welcomed, because it threatens to upend long-standing programs with established stakeholders. Any model that embraces "failing fast" in a culture where change and failure are not tolerated will struggle to take root. I often meet public officials who, seeking to preserve their role as conflict broker, resist the agile model of frequent iteration and public user testing.

Nevertheless, this new approach, which emphasizes working in small teams, engagement with citizens, frequent iteration, and continuous improvement, learned from the tech industry, is beginning to reshape both law and policy making.[9] Public servants are beginning to break down larger projects into smaller components that can be developed and tested in shorter time frames, sometimes known as "sprints." As many US agencies adopted agile processes and new technology between 2004 and 2015, the length of major federal-government IT projects went from an average of nine years to less than two, with significant cost savings.[10] Agile ways of working—agile governance—combined with an ambitious mission help an institution to organize, direct, and scale up innovative problem solving. Thus, red tape, rule-based compliance mania, and excessive and accreted policies and customs that limit the creation of small-team efforts, inhibit the use of human-centered and data-driven practices, and impede problem-solving practices need to be eliminated. This is not a call for deregulation— for eliminating red tape—but for green tape, that is to say, freeing individuals to be agile and to do sensible work that leads to results. The US federal government's pay-scale system, known as the General Schedule (GS), established in 1959, is an outdated compensation structure. The GS pays civil servants on the basis of time in service. But more agile institutions that work differently and that will attract new kinds of talent need to compensate people on the basis of outcomes and performance.

Today's problems are complex and interdependent. Agile public servants need to be able to work across departments and agencies in multidisciplinary teams of people with complementary skill sets to tackle problems more effectively. Thus, embracing commonsense ways of working, reducing mindless compliance, eliminating requirements that impede agility, changing pay scales to reward performance, and restructuring budgets to enable collaboration will all be necessary to foster new ways of working.

#2 Experimental Organizations

Experimental describes another change of perspective that rejects rigid, rule-based compliance in favor of more evidence-based ways of working in institutions. Again, it is not yet typical in large organizations, including the public sector, where "citizens expect governments to pour concrete, not play with cardboard"—in other words, to create permanent and durable policies and services, not experimental prototypes or pilots.[11]

But it is not enough to train individuals in rapid evidence review, pilots, and experiments without having institutions that embrace trial and error. That is why, in 2009, I circulated a memo within the White House and to potential partners to create an "i-Lab."

President Obama has committed to create a 21st century open
government and connected democracy. . . . Innovative technology
is key to fulfilling this presidential mandate. . . . Currently, there
are limitations to designing and implementing such innovations
in government. There are almost no agile technology development resources. When the Office of Science and Technology
Policy wants to experiment with using citizen juries to assess
nanotech policy or the NIH wants to test a second generation of
Grants.Gov, there is no process or platform by which to undertake such pilot projects quickly and no place to experiment safely.
There is a shortage of technically proficient personnel in the
Executive Office of the White House or the agencies to build new
websites. When the Office of Management and Budget needs to
build Recovery.gov, organizational stovepipes make it hard to pull
together an interdisciplinary team of experts on technology,
contracting, grants, data quality, and state and local collaboration.
There is no mechanism to tap the myriad volunteers, who would
happily participate in creating software for open government just
as so many developers now undertake for Mozilla and other open
source projects. Despite the knowledge that those outside
government have tremendous expertise to contribute, complex
legal rules like the Federal Advisory Committee Act make it hard
to solicit their engagement. Procurement processes and budget
cycles retard the ability to acquire cutting-edge tools and, more
important, to experiment and try new tools before adopting a
single solution.[12]

The memo (the first of many) went on to describe an implementation plan
for a fellowship program (that later became the White House Presidential
Innovation Fellows) and the i-Labs Rapid Prototyping Team, which would
design and build prototypes of new tools and software for both citizen services and civic engagement. The MacArthur Foundation funded the first
version of such a government lab, housed originally at the American Association for the Advancement of Science because it was too hard to set up
quickly inside government. This original lab eventually grew into permanent labs inside government, including the United States Digital Service
and 18F.

Around the world, governments have established so-called design labs, policy labs, innovation labs, reality labs, public labs, or living labs. Like the agile i-Labs I proposed over a decade ago, these units hire people who not only have new skills like data science, design, engineering, and anthropology but are more likely to practice new methods than the rest of the bureaucracy is. My own exposure to efforts to forge a more experimental mind-set in an otherwise-hidebound bureaucracy came in 2005 when my students at New York Law School, where I worked prior to the Obama White House, convinced the US Patent and Trademark Office to experiment with allowing volunteer scientists and technologists to comment on draft patent applications. We did so by persuading companies filing the patents to consent and running the initiative as an experimental pilot.[13] We called ourselves the Democracy Design Workshop and conceived of ourselves as a lab, helping government to experiment by modeling the change from outside.

A decade later and governments are beginning to create labs internal to government. In the United Arab Emirates, the Mohammed bin Rashid Centre for Government Innovation has established a formal experimentation methodology to accelerate the development of innovative new policies and services. It created the Afkari investment fund to support experimentation in the delivery of citizen services on the part of federal government employees by investing in innovative ideas.[14] Similarly, the United Kingdom created a £10 million Regulatory Pioneers Fund, a competitive process for investing in fifteen public projects, rewarding regulators who want to undertake more experimental work in connection with new technologies, such as AI-lawyering or flying taxis.[15] While the outcomes of these efforts are still indeterminate, they reflect an effort to encourage experimentation in an otherwise-bureaucratic culture.

Some public-sector institutions are opening new spaces for testing real-world solutions. The UN Global Pulse, an experimental unit within the United Nations, seeks to provide data-science expertise for tackling the Sustainable Development Goals. One goal of these experiments in governance is to shift bureaucratic and slow-moving public agencies from a rules-based compliance culture led by lawyers toward staffing plans that include engineers, designers, technologists, and a culture that encourages experimentation.[16]

Although the methods of these experimental organizations differ, they all seek to accelerate the rate and effectiveness of problem solving. For example, the United Nations Development Programme (UNDP) is setting up 90 Innovation Accelerators to serve 114 countries, all designed to create spaces within large, conservative bureaucracies for creative and distributed experimentation. The idea behind the labs is to unlock the creativity of citizens in solving problems on the ground in developing countries but also to change the culture across the seventy-thousand-person UNDP organization by spurring innovation at the edges and forcing headquarters to relinquish control. "The labs will transform our collective approach by introducing new services, backed by evidence and practice, and by accelerating the testing and dissemination of solutions within and across countries."[17] Sense-making, collective intelligence, solutions mapping, and experimentation are touted as being part of the new offer from UNDP to governments.

Such experimentation units are often focused on a particular sector. For example, the Swedish government set up Experio Lab to get designers working specifically on health-care challenges. The United States Digital Service, a design and technology unit within the Executive Office of the President that helps to improve the delivery of citizen services, doubled-down in 2020 on collaboration with states to the end of improving antiquated unemployment systems.

Of course, some labs have failed. MindLab and the public labs in Bogotá and Mexico City all closed in 2018.[18] Some observers suggest that these innovation outposts were too small and understaffed or that their toolkit for change was too limited to yield the desired outcomes. Another theory is that such experimental units were shut down because their emphasis on doing things differently threatened traditional political officials.

One unique form of experimental organization that is, thus far, thriving, however, is the *regulatory sandbox*, because businesses like it. Regulatory sandboxes are a mechanism to enable businesses to test out new products and services free from government intervention. By relaxing or waiving normal regulations for a period of time, regulatory sandboxes allow businesses to reduce the time and cost needed to bring an idea to market while facilitating the testing necessary to protect consumers. Regulatory sandboxes are designed expressly to introduce legal and regulatory experiments into the regulatory process.[19]

In 2016, Britain launched a regulatory sandbox and since then has conducted 140 regulatory experiments, whereby the Financial Conduct Authority (FCA), the United Kingdom's financial-services regulator, has relaxed rules, provided legal expertise, or waived enforcement of rules to enable firms from the banking, pension, insurance, and other industries to test new products and services, such as blockchain and cryptocurrency offerings. These time-limited tests allow companies to focus on getting investors and getting to market instead of complying with rules, and the hope is that it allows them to succeed while still protecting consumers. Companies that can demonstrate that they are doing something innovative apply to be part of a six-month testing cohort. The vast majority of participants in these tests have been start-ups. "By supporting individual firms to get to market, we believe that this creates positive competitive pressures on existing firms to evolve and improve their offering, creating more positive outcomes for consumers, such as lower cost and higher quality products and services," reports the FCA.[20] In addition to the regulatory sandbox, where companies test on real consumers, the FCA digital sandbox gives firms a "digital testing environment" to support early-stage proof of concept development.

Other countries that have implemented regulatory sandboxes are Abu Dhabi, Australia, Canada, Denmark, Hong Kong, Malaysia, and Singapore, and they have been proposed in Indonesia, Japan, Russia, Switzerland, Taiwan, Thailand, and the United States.[21] Although financial technology has been the hotbed for regulatory experimentation, test beds are emerging in other fast-developing fields such as transportation, especially autonomous vehicles, where sandboxes enable inventors to test their hardware and software on real roads. The US Federal Transit Administration has also launched a regulatory sandbox to allow for testing of "mobility on demand" solutions that use predictive analytics and real-time data to give people personalized transportation choices. But sandboxes remain confined, at present, to these few areas of innovative economic development, and we need to avoid limiting a culture of innovation and experimentation to a few places. Thus, in order to foster more experimental organizations, in addition to training individuals to work differently, we need to invest in more lab-like units, not walled off from the rest of government or the company or nonprofit but within every part of the institution, in order to "infect" the broader culture with a problem-solving mind-set. In the United States, that means investing in and growing organizations like United States Digital Service and 18F.

Strengthening experimental culture demands more talent. The scholar of bureaucracy James Q. Wilson argued that talent is in shockingly short supply in government. "Some things literally cannot be done—or cannot be done well—because there is no one available to do them who knows how. The supply of able, experienced executives is not increasing nearly as fast as the number of problems being addressed by public policy."[22] Wilson felt that a key impediment to the smooth functioning of administration and the ability to implement equitable, efficient, and responsive policy was a lack of talent, rendering large, hierarchical institutions ill suited to carry out many desired solutions. Wilson was not sanguine about the prospects for increasing the supply of talent at any scale.

While Wilson's denigration of those who work in government might be too extreme, there is no doubt that achieving a more experimental mindset will necessitate proactively hiring people, not for generic roles like deputy-this or assistant-that but to tackle specific public problems. To get there, our governments have to start by knowing who works for them. We need a better and more detailed picture than we currently have of who works for government, what they do, and what they accomplish. The federal government's handbook of executive positions, known as the "Plum Book" (because it contains the best job listings in government) is a 236-page list of nothing more than titles, with nothing in it to attract innovative people to public service and nothing to hold those whom it does attract accountable for results.[23]

Achieving more experimentation calls for our leaders to put out a national call to service to attract more people to do a stint in government or to take on mission-driven roles in nonprofits, at universities, and in companies. These call-to-service jobs will be positions for passionate problem solvers aimed at improving people's lives. Instead of today's Plum Book listings, job descriptions will have in common that they articulate a compelling problem to solve and impose few limitations on the public entrepreneur for how to do so.

Open Organizations

Open describes the sea change from an organizational culture focused on walling off employees from the undue influence of politics and public opinion to thinking about how to share information and partner with others, especially in different sectors: transparent, participatory, collaborative.

Technology is making more diverse information and ideas accessible across more institutions. But the capacity to collaborate is not enough; there has to be the will. This is a matter both of individual skill set and also of institutional mind-set. For public entrepreneurs to be able to work across silos and boundaries, their organizations must embrace openness and public engagement.[24] Organizations must dramatically shift their mind-set, breaking with traditions that reach deep into the past.

The late nineteenth and early twentieth centuries saw the rise both of the professions—medicine, law, engineering, and social sciences—and of the civil service. To overcome the cronyism of the past, professional civil servants were meant to be chosen on talent and to do their work behind closed doors, at arm's length from the people.[25] Institutions and bureaucracies were designed to be hierarchical and rules based, in order to support the new vision of the public servant as a lone and impartial decision-maker.

This culture persists today. Resistance to collaboration stems from the insularity of the public service, exacerbated by the Mandarin stance designed to ward off undue influence and reject collaboration across sectors and across agencies. Mike Bracken, former head of the UK Government Digital Service, writes, "As public administrators, we need to work differently and more collaboratively in a system that is not set up to do that. Whitehall was described to me when I started as a warring band of tribal bureaucrats held together by a common pension scheme."[26]

Many public servants choose a lifelong career in government. In the United States, the average tenure for workers in the federal government is 9.5 years, compared with the private-sector median of 3.8 years.[27] Because it can take forever to get a job in the federal government, the incentive to keep it once accepted is higher. David T. Ellwood, former dean of Harvard University's Kennedy School of Government, describes it as a "19th-century hiring system" in which applications can disappear into a "black hole" for nine months or a year, "even at the best of times."[28]

Things are no better at the state level. In an open online forum for public servants, an employee of the state of New Jersey wrote that hiring for many state positions often takes six months or longer. "A lot can happen in six months. If you are looking to advance or change jobs, this can be really discouraging to the applicant. Plus, there is often little to no communication between the hiring agency and the applicant, so the applicant cannot even tell if they are being considered for a position."[29]

Mobility is much higher in the tech organizations of Silicon Valley. The average employee tenure at Uber is only 1.8 years; at Facebook, 2.5

years.[30] The Berkeley professor AnnaLee Saxenian has shown how high turnover rates and moves between Silicon Valley companies spur an exchange of knowledge and ideas, helping to explain the region's high rates of growth and innovation. She comments, "Job-hopping, rather than climbing the career ladder within a corporation, facilitates flows of information and know-how between individuals, firms, and industries. When combined with venture capital, it supports unanticipated re-combinations of technologies and skill."[31]

Whereas long tenures and a relative lack of mobility were once seen as great attractions of government work, some public institutions are changing their organizational dynamics and allowing exchanges, sabbaticals, and shorter-term stints. Instead of promoting lifelong careers walled off from industry and academia, some governments are exploring new forms of talent exchange designed to bring fresh ideas into the public sector. Governments in France and Korea, for example, are using sabbaticals, exchanges, and short-term stints in government to recruit outsiders with cutting-edge experience to work on public problems.

Other governments, conversely, are encouraging public servants to gain experience in the private sector or in academia. The United Kingdom, for example, is encouraging civil servants to leave government for a stint in the private sector, which Whitehall refers to as a "career break."[32] Scotland and Ireland also offer working sabbaticals for public servants.[33] The cities of London and New York have held "innovation exchanges," where public servants from one city go work in the other, to learn from one another about their methods of combating climate change and congestion.[34]

Although President Obama reversed piecemeal reforms of the GS pay scale in response to union pressure, at the start of his first term, he ordered agencies to accelerate their hiring in order to bring in more talent from outside government.[35] The goal was to eventually process applications and hire new employees in no more than eighty days (still a remarkably long period). Yet across government, rapid hiring remains a major challenge. And a collaboration mind-set across agencies and sectors, so vital for solving problems with a human-centered approach, is far from the norm. Thus, in addition to institutions adopting policies of transparency and open data as well as public engagement and open innovation, achieving a more open culture necessitates both more hiring and also more rapid hiring, such as bringing in people for a "tour of duty" and doing so quickly. We need to

shorten the time it takes to hire the brightest and
from a wide range of backgrounds and fields into g(
attention to ensuring the hiring and advancemen
We need to foster the addition and hiring of mul'
just individuals, and the flexible matching of talen'
Finally, changing our institutions will necessitate
for a handful of public entrepreneurs but widely aᴄᵣ...
and across disciplines in universities.

INNOVATION SKILLS TRAINING IN THE PUBLIC SECTOR:
A GLOBAL SCAN

Under President Trump, there has been a profound disregard of government experience, integrity, and competence. To solve tomorrow's challenges and reimagine how we govern, we need to invest in talent by preparing public servants at every level to solve public problems (and outside government, as will be discussed in chapter 12).

If we want to achieve more success stories like Victoria's State Trauma System, we need to provide individuals with the skill set, and organizations with the mind-set, to solve problems. That will require public-sector organizations (and the philanthropies and universities that serve them) to invest more in training prospective public entrepreneurs in and outside government in public problem solving.[36] It will require the public entrepreneurship curriculum to be spread across roles and levels of government and training to be connected to improved outcomes in real-world problems.

Survey data identify gaps in problem-solving skills at all levels of government. There is a significant disparity between awareness and practice of these skills, reflecting the lack of formal training and an environment that does not promote use of these skills. The demand for innovation skills training is largely not being met: while respondents in The GovLab's surveys in Australia and the United States expressed broad interest in learning these skills, very few said they had been formally trained in them. There is no widespread training in data science. There is no program to teach open innovation and collective intelligence practices. There is no science of problem solving taught at the federal level at all and no courses on taking projects from idea to implementation. Some states and cities do teach Lean Six Sigma project management. Bloomberg Philanthropies does train mayors and other key city leaders. There are also wonderful but selective pro-for political leaders, such as the Aspen Institute's Rodel Fellowship, which young (under fifty) elected leaders analyze and discuss historical texts and contemporary commentaries on topics such as democracy and leadership. Only twenty-four people get this honor each year. (I want to run for office just to participate!) But public-sector skills training needs to extend beyond political leaders to include people inside and outside government more broadly. We need to overhaul the curriculum of training in both civil service training colleges and universities to impart the skills of public problem solving, taking advantage of new technology to deliver training and coaching at scale. To guide recommendations for changing how training is done in government, let us look at what leading-edge public institutions are already doing.

RECOMMENDATIONS FOR IMPROVING PUBLIC-SECTOR TRAINING

Start with Training Needs Analysis

Very little is known about the existing skills and competencies of the public sector. Many governments are already investing in training that seeks to change the way their public servants work. Yet even as they work to teach skills such as data analysis and human-centered design, these same public organizations are not using those skills to assess their employees' training needs prior to developing their training programs.[37]

Public organizations wanting to boost their performance in solving public problems should first measure the state of innovative problem-solving skills and the extent of any skill gaps within their workforce. They need to understand what their people know, what they would like to know, and how they learn best.

When the Chilean government wanted to inform its training strategy, it commissioned the OECD in 2017 to conduct a world-first study of the depth of innovation skills in its public workforce.[38] While the OECD surveyed and interviewed only a small number of people, the study paved the way for more recent empirical research into public-sector innovation skills. In 2018, the Canada Digital Service put out a survey asking public servants, "What digital training do you need?" The survey asked a random sample of fifty-five hundred recipients about their knowledge of thirty digital trends, including cybersecurity, data visualization, and machine learning. The gov-

Canada

ernment used the results to shape its rollout of the Digital Academy in 2019. The Digital Academy teaches digital literacy through a series of courses that target public servants at all levels of government—from short course videos aimed at the nation's 250,000 public servants to intensive multiday workshops for executives and senior leaders. The academy's use of a skills survey prior to rolling out its training has led to a better-informed design and a more-cost-efficient rollout. This earlier work inspired the skills survey that my colleagues and I developed in collaboration with the International City and County Managers Association (ICMA), which I have cited throughout this book and details of which can be found on the website for this volume (https://solvingpublicproblems.org/.) Similarly, the investment of the Australia New Zealand School of Government (ANZSOG) in a skills survey in Oceania has inspired work to create a new skills curriculum in 2021. In Latin America, The GovLab collaborated with the government of Paraguay to administer this innovation skills survey to over four hundred public servants in 2020.

Hybrid Learning

In the surveys in the United States, Australia, and Paraguay, more than twelve hundred public servants told The GovLab they wanted to learn new innovation skills such as problem definition, human-centered design, and open innovation. But, when asked (before the pandemic) *how* they wanted to learn, they were equally divided in their desire for traditional face-to-face workshops or training via the Internet. Some of the most promising approaches to public-sector innovation training around the world blend both, combining the flexibility and scale of online education with the community building of standard classes.

The public sector around the world offers many strong examples of in-person learning programs. Many take the form of a workshop, in which people meet with an instructor to master a new skill in a short period of time—usually one or a handful of days. Prior to COVID-19, ANZSOG, for example, trained about fifteen hundred professionals through in-person workshops each year. With a limited class size, trainers can adapt the course to address unanticipated questions. Yet live workshops also have drawbacks, such as transport and scheduling issues that can prevent participants from attending and, since COVID-19, of course, the challenges of following social distancing.

The main challenge, however, is to prevent participants from leaving the workshop, returning to "business as usual," and struggling to apply their newly acquired skills on the job. Training classes often leave people feeling abandoned when they return to their desks to face the challenge of innovating within a bureaucracy that is resistant to change.

Online training has emerged as an exciting new alternative to traditional classes that has become the new norm since COVID-19. It offers flexibility of time and place, access at all hours, ease of distribution, enhanced student-to-student and faculty-to-student communication, and the potential for a wider variety of guest speakers and coaches from far-flung places. New technology can also help public-sector institutions lower the cost and expand the reach of new training programs to new markets.[39]

While initial production costs can be high, depending on the quality and depth of the program, online training can be reused to train new hires or to enable alumni to brush up on the material. It can be repeated at no marginal cost and without the expense of venues, teachers, and other costly logistical tasks that come with an in-person program. Online courses like The GovLab's "Solving Public Problems with Data" lectures—an online crash course on data analytics and responsible data use in the public sector—are openly available and free. The GovLab's course on "open justice"—a course for legal reformers on uses of data to promote more equitable, efficient, and effective administration of justice—combines online lectures with live instruction delivered by Mexico's Tribunal Electoral, the country's highest electoral court.[40]

Despite the advantages of online learning, especially in the era of COVID-19, there are challenges. Despite the potential ease of communication, students learning at a distance may struggle without the direct help or attention of an instructor. It is hard to find the time and motivation to finish online courses. Online courses come under fire for their minuscule completion rates. A study from the *Journal of Labor Economics*, in which a group of microeconomics students was divided between an in-person lecture course and an online lecture course, found that the latter exacerbated the struggles of lower-achieving students and students of color.[41] These students in the online course performed significantly worse compared with students of similar academic caliber in the in-person course.

Furthermore, online programs may be harder to update, compared to changing the delivery of a live lecture. To get the best of both approaches, some organizations are combining traditional and online training in a hybrid (or blended) learning program. The Online Learning Consortium defines hybrid courses as either one of the following:

1. A classroom course in which online activity is mixed with classroom meetings, replacing a significant portion of but not all face-to-face activity
2. An online course that is supplemented by required face-to-face instruction such as lectures, discussions, or labs[42]

A hybrid course can effectively combine the short-term activity of an in-person workshop with the longevity and scale of an online course. Hybrids are also a way to stagger attendance to reduce the number of in-person participants and, thereby, lower any attendant health risks.

For example, Israel's Digital Leaders program is a nine-month hybrid course designed to train two cohorts of forty leaders each in digital innovation. The program contains live workshops and a series of online courses, which learners from Israel and a similar program in the United Kingdom can both take.[43] This style of blended learning allows a wider range of participants to take advantage of the content and make more optimal use of participants' time.

Blended classrooms are believed to increase engagement and collaboration among participating students. One study found that blended learning improves student engagement and learning even if the participant only takes advantage of the traditional classroom resources.[44] While designing for traditional classroom and online environments adds complexity for the designers, the approach provides multiple ways for public servants to learn, a clear benefit.

Digital Government
In order to master the quantitative and qualitative skills needed at each stage of problem identification, solution identification, implementation, and evaluation, it is important to have a basic understanding of the underlying technologies enabling these new ways of working. As Canada's Treasury Board president and minister of digital government Scott Brison explains, "In the age of smartphones, social media and apps that do everything, Canadians expect their government to serve them as seamlessly and as well as they've come to expect from the best digital service providers. Government

exists to improve the lives of people, and a digitally enabled public service gives us an unprecedented opportunity to improve government services."[45]

Whether it is big data or machine learning or the technologies of collective intelligence, knowing what these technologies are, how they work, and the ethical risks of these tools is a form of twenty-first-century literacy and a prerequisite for public problem solving. That is why the government of Singapore's Civil Service Training College, to achieve its vision of creating a "smart nation," mandates technology and digital skills training for the 145,000 public servants it trains (which excludes the military and medical personnel). Although civil servants are free (in conversation with their supervisors) to choose among a wide array of offerings from public and private partners via the college's new Learn.sg.gov training platform, including courses offered by US online learning providers like Coursera and EdEx, the Civil Service College is making a concerted push to teach digital literacy as the core competence.[46] The country's national upskilling initiative, SkillsFuture, also encourages training in new technology, including learning how to code, for all citizens, not simply public servants. The government even has a program to teach digital literacy to one hundred thousand senior citizens. Civil servants are learning basic web development and hands-on coding skills. In addition to tech basics, the goal is to train twenty thousand people in data analytics by 2023.[47]

The German federal government hired a chief information officer, Markus Richter, to advance digital literacy across the civil service. Based in the Ministry of the Interior, he is responsible for establishing an online and offline digital training academy, the Digitalakademie, to provide government-wide training using new technology. Information technology is not simply the delivery mechanism; it is one of the key learning domains.[48] These digital competencies include ten areas of knowledge: UX design, automation, software development methods and management, IT security, artificial intelligence, data analytics, big data, blockchain, cloud computing, and networked systems. While data-driven and people-centered methods are not yet connected into a curriculum, under Richter's leadership, there are plans to change that. Finally, Barcelona wants to take digital training one step further and ensure that public servants are trained not simply in technology but in ethical and responsible uses of technology, making sure that officials understand the risks as much as the rewards. As a first step, the city created a "manifesto in favor of technological sovereignty and digital rights for cities" to declare its values with regard to technology. It is anticipated that the city will issue a request for proposals to develop training in ethical technology.[49]

Qualitative and Quantitative Skills

The public entrepreneur knows how to use data-analytical methods and evidence-based decision-making in order to complement qualitative approaches such as collaboration and active listening. The best programs teach both qualitative and quantitative skills. Most, however, teach only one, focusing either on the skill of interpreting individual-level design approaches (human-centered design) or on population-level analysis (big data). For example, WeGov in Brazil focuses on teaching human-centered design, while the Universidad Adolfo Ibáñez in Chile focuses on data analysis. At the start of a three-day workshop on data science for public managers, about eighty participants arrive with a problem from their government department or agency and apply the introductory data-science skills they learn to develop a potential solution.[50] Since COVID-19, the workshop is now available as an online course, and participants get the benefit of learning from an instructor and through conversation with their peers.

The Coleridge Initiative, created by faculty from the University of Chicago, the University of Maryland, and NYU, offers more advanced applied data analytics programs for computer-savvy agency staff working on real-world microdata.[51] The program teaches the use of administrative data, some of which is sensitive material, for policy analysis. It shows how to use microdata in the SQL and Python programming languages for tasks such as managing and visualizing data, linking records, and machine learning. Programs often have a thematic focus, such as social benefits, economic development, or employment outcomes. Such a course requires participants to commit a significant amount of time: several weeks of online coursework interspersed with two week-long seminars.

Singapore's Civil Service Training College focuses on delivering a basic digital-literacy curriculum to all public servants. Other innovation and leadership topics, however, are optional, and there is a great deal of diversity in what people learn. There is no formal problem-solving curriculum and no requirement to develop both quantitative and qualitative skills.

Similarly, Apolitical, a commercial online community for public servants, teaches courses like digital transformation, behavioral insights, and evidence-based policy making, but these microcourses, too, are not connected into a curriculum.[52]

Strive for Scale

Many of these innovation skills programs are small. Israel trains forty at a time. Bloomberg Philanthropies selects thirty-five "Champion Cities," where it trains a handful (but growing number) of people each year. However, to transform whole agencies and public-sector culture, it is not enough to train a lone innovator or a data scientist in a unit or even a few dozen innovators. By contrast, governments like Canada and Argentina are trying to train large numbers of innovators, scaling their programs across public administrations of a quarter million people each. It is still too early to tell if these programs are any good or if and how they are changing ways of working and, more important, what the outcomes are with regard to policies and services. But there are interesting examples of jurisdictions taking advantage of new technology to try to train more people at scale.

The Canada Digital Academy offers short online readings, videos, and podcasts called "Busrides" that have the potential to reach all 250,000 Canadian public servants.[53] The content, designed to expand public servants' digital awareness, includes modules on digital skills, data analysis, design, development and automation, evolutionary technologies, artificial intelligence, and machine learning.[54]

The city of Denver's Colorado Peak Academy aims to "turn 10,300 employees into innovators." The academy trains municipal employees in the Lean Six Sigma analytical methods to make their agencies more efficient. The city contends that its public-works department saved $1 million thanks to skills developed in the academy. For example, one employee saved $46,000 a year for the wastewater division by devising a way to scrap the use of certified mail to send eleven thousand lien letters each year.[55]

Since 2016, Argentina's LabGob says it has trained thirty-six thousand federal, provincial, and local officials in its Design Academy for Public Policy, and the goal is to scale to a quarter million.[56] The academy teaches iteration, design and digital thinking, data use as evidence, curiosity and flexibility, and new narratives and collaboration. Courses include "Big Data: Let Data Speak," "Learning Dialogues: Evaluation and Big Data," "Learning Dialogues: Education Innovation in the Public Sector," and "Introduction to Civil Innovations." Programs range from one day to four weeks.

Create Incentives for Learning

Instructional design experts report that only between 5 and 15 percent of students who start free, open, online courses end up finishing. By contrast, more expensive online courses, such as a Harvard Business School $1,500 online class, have completion rates of over 85 percent because students are more engaged and invested.[57] Creators explain that this engagement is the result in part of the cost but also of feeling like classes are selective to join. Deadlines and interactive exercises help to propel forward progress, and a basic level of participation and collaboration is demanded of learners.

Governments, too, are taking steps to add incentives for training. In Argentina, for every class taken, a public servant earns points, which are a prerequisite for promotions and pay raises in the Argentinian civil service. This points system uses the behavioral insight of gamification to create the motivation for people to take the training despite otherwise busy schedules and competing demands for their time and attention. Furthermore, striving for scale and training tens of thousands of people creates a buzz around the training that makes people want to sign up or risk being left out. In Singapore, there previously was a mandate for civil servants to take a hundred hours of training each year, or about one day each month. Instead, the government now creates incentives in other ways. In some cases, courses are compulsory. But the Civil Service College also makes some courses competitive so that when a civil servant's boss nominates an employee to participate, it is considered a reward and an honor. Song Hsi Ching, senior researcher at the Singapore Institute of Governance and Policy, explains that the "fear factor" motivates people to learn of their own accord. Civil servants are scared into believing they will fall behind the private sector if they do not do training. "Here the norms are quite strong," she explains.[58]

Sector-Specific Innovation

Instead of going broad, some training programs go deep by teaching sector-specific innovation skills. Britain's NHS (National Health Scheme) Digital Academy, run in collaboration with Imperial College, London, the University of Edinburgh, and Harvard Medical School, provides six online and four live sessions designed to "develop a new generation of excellent digital leaders who can drive the information and technology transformation of the NHS."[59] The curriculum includes essentials of health systems, implementing transformational change, user-centered design, citizen-driven informatics, decision support and actionable data analytics, leadership, and workplace project coaching.

The first two cohorts comprised a total of 220 health professionals. Students who complete the program can take another year of study at their own expense in order to complete an MSc in digital health leadership from Imperial College.

In Taiwan, the government is "going deep" on citizen engagement training, specifically, teaching public servants how to work with the public. The Office of the Digital Minister is educating public officials in how to engage residents in decision-making. Public servants across agencies are invited to join a Participation Officers Network, made up of public servants who learn how to consult with citizens when making policy.[60] Modeled on the concept of the open government officer appointed to each federal agency in the United States, the Taiwanese model goes one step further and trains these civil servants in citizen engagement. As Taiwan's digital minister, Audrey Tang, explains,

> I have established a network of Participation Officers in each ministry. They serve as the links between the general public and the public sectors, and as channels for inter-agency collaboration. Whenever a proposal is raised, a collaborative meeting can be held, with participants from government departments and the public invited to join the discussion and to jointly create new policies. So far we have held more than 40 collaborative meetings. We gathered stakeholders to find solutions, be it to improve the experience of filing income tax, the allocation of medical resources in remote towns, or balancing the fishery and marine biodiversity in national parks.[61]

Tang and her team have offered the same training program in English in the United States.[62]

Citizens as Trainers, Training Citizens

As governments invest in developing new training programs, especially scalable online programs, there is the opportunity to offer high-quality training to other levels of government and to the public in order to create more public problem solvers. The Office of Innovation in the state of New Jersey maintains a free, online training program in public entrepreneurship that my team and I launched in 2019. The Innovation Skills Accelerator is a twelve-part series with videos on public problem solving, available at https://skills.innovation.nj.gov. It is designed to introduce people to the basic skills for moving from idea to implementation. The state also strives for scale by offering the program at no cost to seventy thousand public servants via the state's training platform and, at the same time, to local officials, university students, and state residents (and the rest of the world) via a free and open website. More work needs to be done to advertise the programs and create demand so that more people take advantage of the training.

The city of Orlando's Digital Service Academy shares stories of residents' experiences with city services in order to build empathy among civil servants. The latter "secret shop" another agency's services in order to understand the hidden struggles that residents experience. The GovLab's MultiCity Challenge program trains public servants and residents together. Five cities in Mexico and five in Africa undertook such training in fall 2020 (https://multicitychallenge.org/). They learn to take ideas developed in these open innovation competitions to fruition. The public brings outside expertise, passion, and know-how to the team, while the public servants understand how to navigate the city's rules to get things done. Jurisdictions like São Paulo are taking the relationship with residents further: São Paulo's Abierta program uses citizens to train the city's public servants. More than twenty-three thousand have studied with these lay trainers, who possess innovation skills that are in short supply in government. Citizens apply to be teachers by submitting a course proposal. The selection committee approves about thirty courses per cycle, and the courses are free and accessible to all municipal public servants. Potential trainers must demonstrate at least a year of knowledge, expertise, or experience in the subject. Public employees or elected government officials cannot be instructors.[63]

Coaching and Mentoring

Coaching and mentoring are essential to ensuring that developing public entrepreneurs maintain the knowledge they acquire in training. Australia's BizLab Academy, a school for public servants in Canberra, the nation's capital, uses alumni of their human-centered-design training as mentors for new students.[64] The academy teaches human-centric design principles, tools, and techniques to classes of ten to fifteen participants. It also offers programs to train more experienced designers in how to effectively use human-centric design principles in order to teach others in their own agency. "Our challenge is to make the training 'stick,'" writes Leanna Douglas of BizLab. "We have all been on training courses where we have left all excited but failed to apply the learnings to our work once we leave the classroom. To try to address this, we have established an alumni program to stay in touch with our graduates and support them once they return to their jobs."[65]

Coaching was also a significant theme in responses to the Australian New Zealand School of Government 2019 survey of Australian public servants. While respondents' preferences for training content and methods varied widely, there was significant support for coaching and mentoring programs ahead of traditional training methods. Nearly a third of public servants surveyed expressed interest in help from subject-matter experts to advance their work.

This preference for coaching over training is widespread, and explains why The GovLab at New York University is using coaches to help public entrepreneurs take their public-interest projects from idea to implementation.[66] The highest quality training program can leave people feeling abandoned when they return to their desk to face the challenge of innovating within a bureaucracy. With hands-on mentoring from global leaders and peer-to-peer support, The GovLab coaching programs try to ensure that public servants are getting the help they need to advance innovative projects.

The curriculum comprises live but online sessions typically delivered over ten to twelve weeks. Session topics reflect the same skills and methods discussed here, including (1) defining the problem, (2) defining the problem with data, (3) rapid results research and field scanning, (4) open innovation, (5) convincing others, (6) prototyping, testing, and development, and (7) measuring impact. Over the years, our training has connected thousands of public employees, civil-society leaders, and students to mentors who can help them to advance their projects.

Learning by Doing: Teaching the Skills to Solve Real Problems
Most training programs take a conceptual approach to teaching digital skills, AI for government, or human-centered design, among other subjects.

Yet learning a skill is one thing; knowing how to use and apply it in everyday practice is another. More training needs to focus on applying these skills to the practical work of a public servant.

In 2019, Nesta's States of Change program began offering six to nine coaching programs for public servants in the United Kingdom and Australia. It took a page from The GovLab coaching model, which focuses on teaching public servants how to adopt new ways of working to solve problems for real citizens. An evaluation of Nesta's first such program in Victoria, Australia, showed that "working on real-world projects over an extended period enabled public servants to take action and develop an innovation mindset."[67]

In interviews, participants say that Nesta's approach to training builds their skills and changes their beliefs, behavior, and identity. As a result, they are both keen and able to use the human-centered design and other skills they have learned in the program in their everyday work. They feel empowered to set up their own innovation labs within their agencies.

In Latin America, Chile's Laboratorio del Gobierno has begun training civil servants in building innovation skills to address real-world problems. The program's success has been linked to its learning-by-doing approach. A report on the program for Nesta found that "working on real life issues makes learning relevant and enhances the participants' learning experience, while at the same time serving the strategic agenda of their institution."[68] While working on these projects, teams are trained and mentored. In the training sessions, teams learn how to use specific innovation methods and tools. In the mentoring sessions, teams discuss their challenges and reflect on their experiences. Both sessions are facilitated by experienced innovation practitioners.

The New Jersey Innovation Skills Accelerator also connects normally disconnected and disjointed skills into a learning pathway that contains quantitative and qualitative approaches. Covering a dozen skills, the program begins with an introduction to new technologies to ensure that participants share a common vocabulary. It then introduces problem identification, human-centered design, data-analytical thinking, and other problem-solving methods discussed in this book. A series of short lectures focused on how to apply the skill, combined with how-to exercises, are accompanied by practitioner interviews, readings, and self-assessments. Successful participants in the online course are eligible for intensive coaching focused on applying the skills they have learned to the problems they are working on in their jobs. Our first skills "bootcamp," conducted both online and face-to-face, was offered to winners of the governor's ENJINE competition, which rewards public servants who have proposed innovation to solve public problems and save taxpayers' money. The early 2020 bootcamp was interrupted by the pandemic but was intended to focus on helping participants to take the ideas developed in that competition and implement them using new methods learned in the online program.[69]

The MultiCity Challenge model also offers a curriculum, rather than disjointed methods courses, that combines problem-definition with data-analytics and citizen-engagement training to help public officials refine effective and legitimate definitions of problems before asking the public to help solve those problems in an open innovation competition. Finally, in 2020–2021, the Australia New Zealand School of Government is planning to launch a nationwide curriculum in Australia in public-problem-solving skills.

Key Lessons about Training

All over the world, forward-looking public-sector institutions are looking to change how they train public servants, using new technology to deliver training differently but also teaching people to use new technology to work differently and acquire design, data, and engagement skills. There is still a long way to go to scale systematic training in problem-solving competencies rather than simply to teach one-off courses on design thinking or data analysis. But there is much to be learned from these novel offerings. In sum, these global experiences with innovative skills training suggest ten recommendations for enhancing training in public problem solving going forward and pave the way for a reorganization and reinvestment in the management of public personnel:

1. *Diagnose skill gaps.* To increase efficiency and effectiveness of training and stimulate demand, organizations need to survey people about what and how they want to learn first.
2. *Go hybrid.* To make training more convenient and take advantage of the best of both modalities, the best programs offer both face-to-face and online training. The pandemic, especially, has shown the need to create purely digital training as an alternative.

3. *Teach digital government skills.* To learn problem solving requires having basic tech and digital literacy skills. While there is disagreement about how deep this digital competency needs to go, the Internet and new technologies of big data and collective intelligence must be familiar.

4. *Teach quantitative and qualitative skills.* To enable effective new ways of working, the best training programs teach "data" and "people" skills rather than exclusively one or the other.

5. *Strive for scale.* To change the culture of governing, training must not be limited to a handful of public entrepreneurs. Rather, there must be a strategy to train people in different roles at scale using new technology.

6. *Create incentives for training.* To transform how government works, programs need to offer inducements for training; otherwise, day-to-day demands will crowd out the time for training.

7. *Focus on sector-specific innovation.* To impart problem-solving skills, it might be appropriate to customize offerings for specific domains like health or education, as well as procurement, enabling people to understand how these skills apply to their own projects.

8. *Use the public as trainers, train the public.* To spread the learning of public problem solving, governments can use citizens, who have useful specialty knowledge, as teachers. At the same time, they should open up their training offerings to other levels of government and to citizens.

9. *Coach and mentor.* To enable people to take projects from idea to implementation and cultivate their problem-solving skills, combine coaching and mentoring with training in order to translate skills learned in theory into day-to-day practice. Working on real-world problems is an added incentive for learning.

10. *Connect the dots.* To create true public entrepreneurs, it is essential to teach the curriculum to solve problems, not disconnected skills. The learning pathway is essential.

All these different ways to build capacity reflect a common view that changing the ability of individuals to innovate will improve institutional effectiveness and legitimacy, restore trust in government, and lead to more public problem solving. As the British website Apolitical writes, "Government is the world's largest employer, and its success in solving the world's wicked problems depends on its public servants. For government to be all the things we want it to be—innovative, citizen-centred, transparent, experimental and data-driven—its employees need to be constantly learning future-ready skills on the job. Governments around the world are finally realising that."[70] These programs enable new sources of information to be applied to the development of more effective solutions to public problems. Collectively, the initiatives offer us a new way to think about and measure public service, not through an inchoate notion of public value but by implementing solutions with communities that work and stick.

Too many training programs still measure success by how many people take a course or listen to a podcast. We should be measuring whether learning these innovation skills enables public entrepreneurs to better solve public problems. Are public servants better able to progress from idea to implementation? Are they able to accomplish what they set out to do? Did the program achieve its stated aims? We are still a long way from investing in, conducting, and evaluating training using measures that matter in the real world.

CHAPTER TWELVE

Training the Next Generation of Leaders and Problem Solvers

> We have many modern tools at our disposal, but instead of assigning messy problems that would require the synthesis of concepts from multiple courses, the application of logical boundary conditions and a thoughtful examination of outcomes to make sure they are reasonable, we assign problems that could be solved with a slide rule. They are easier to grade and explain, but they are not all that realistic or inspiring.
>
> *Sheryl Sorby, speech at the annual conference of the American Society for Engineering Education (June 26, 2020)*

Just as the private sector needs workers to obtain new in-demand skills to keep up with changing technologies, the public sector needs to finance and support new forms of training for its employees if we are to make government more effective and a more enjoyable place to work. As discussed in chapter 11, our countries deserve governments that work, and the fall in trust in government, coupled with the rise of increasingly complex public problems, makes it essential to train public servants in using technology, data, and innovative ways of working.

However, to create better government and to solve the challenges of our time, we cannot limit that training to people in the public sector. First, we need to stimulate interest in public-interest (not only public-sector) work by introducing young people to the skills of public problem solving much earlier. Second, we need to train people to solve public problems no matter what sector they choose to work in. The World Economic Forum identifies problem solving as one of the most important skills a graduate must have in the twenty-first century. Yet as a tenured academic, previously in law and now in engineering, who also taught in a public policy school, I can report that our universities are failing to teach future professionals how to tackle complex problems in a rapidly changing world.[1]

The primacy of technology in our lives, combined with the urgent need to design and implement solutions to public problems, requires a new curriculum of public problem solving and public entrepreneurship in universities and professional schools as well as in governments. As we have seen, public problem solving teaches students to work together in teams and with real-world partners across disciplinary silos. It teaches participants to go beyond vague issues to define specific problems. It teaches how to use both data and collective intelligence to get smarter about problems and solutions. It teaches how to design solutions in equitable partnership with people affected by real problems and how to implement measurable solutions that improve lives.

WHAT IS WRONG WITH PROFESSIONAL EDUCATION NOW?

Engineering and computer science courses teach technological craft, but all too often they do not teach how to implement solutions in the real world of institutions. Engineering, in particular, is often taught without regard for cultural, social, and political context. Internships and capstones, while they can be useful, can also vary widely in quality and are no substitute for acquiring the formal skills and methods of problem solving.

The toolkit given to law students is also far too limited. Of course, public-interest litigation, strategic use of contracts, and knowledge of how to craft legislation and regulation are vital mechanisms for advancing social justice and the public interest. Yet the agile and flexible tools of technology, data, and innovation have been woefully absent from the curriculum.

Business schools (with notable exceptions) have largely focused on private markets as the preferred solution to every public problem. As a result, they have unquestioningly accepted the central tenets of capitalism. Public-administration schools still teach policy analysis but rarely digital or data skills, let alone policy implementation and getting things done. You may recall Francis Fukuyama's complaint from chapter 3 that these schools train students to become policy analysts but with no understanding of how to implement policies in the real world.

Our universities should be dedicated to teaching students to advance the common good by learning how to wrestle with solving public problems. Problem-based learning is a more inclusive student-centered pedagogy in which all students learn by engaging with the complex situation either that is presented to them or that they choose themselves. By working on a messy, real-world problem, students become active and engaged learners who are accountable for outcomes, rather than just for content.

Sadly, this is too rarely the case. A statement published by a group of deans and educators convened by Stanford University to address reforming public-administration education said, "In the United States, and other consolidated democracies, the system of educating and training people to solve public problems is radically insufficient. Often such education and training, especially for professionals, simply does not exist."[2] (I am a member of the group and signatory to the statement.)

THE KNOWLEDGE-PRACTICE GAP

The absence of widespread public problem-solving education in US universities is no surprise, given that only small numbers of faculty are engaging with policy makers and NGOs themselves. The COVID-19 epidemic led many university professionals to emerge from the ivory tower and offer to help. Their data scientists cranked out predictive analytics. They turned on their 3-D printers and maker labs to manufacture masks and face shields. Their public-health experts lent expertise and trained contact tracers. Of course, scientific and medical researchers develop the much-needed vaccines. But such a high level of engagement, especially outside of professions like medicine that have a significant clinical component, is unusual.

Academic achievement is generally measured by citations in peer-reviewed journals, not societal impact. Michael Lindsey, executive director of the McSilver Institute for Poverty Policy and Research and Constance and Martin Silver Professor of Poverty Studies at New York University, comments about the knowledge-practice gap between academia and the world of public policy: "We're all busy. We have demands that relate to our success as academics. Many folks are still trying to get tenure or be promoted, and so how does that [public interest] work align with their interest in getting promoted or tenure?"[3]

Arguably, most faculty are not engaged in public problem solving because it conflicts with the demands of a job that emphasizes scholarship over service. According to an original survey of NYU faculty conducted by Caitlin Gebhard and Nelson James, students in my public-problem-solving class in 2020, who set out to develop solutions to the knowledge-practice gap at universities, faculty are eager to do socially impactful work. When asked to identify high-impact endeavors from a list of nineteen common faculty activities, 53 percent of NYU faculty surveyed believe proposing or drafting new policies or legislation is a highly effective way to impact change, yet only 22 percent of surveyed faculty have done so.

Of those surveyed, 47 percent think op-ed writing is socially impactful, but only 31 percent of that group have actually done so.[4] Other activities that faculty identified as being socially impactful included providing expert opinions (64 percent), research (51 percent), training (42 percent), and data collection/analysis for government, NGO, and/or industry (40 percent). Interestingly, 45 percent said they had supervised a student working for an outside organization, but only 23.3 percent found that to be impactful.[5] Traditional faculty activities like attending conferences and writing academic journal articles, while done most frequently, were rated least impactful.

In addition to direct engagement with policy makers and practitioners, surveyed faculty also identified contributing to nonacademic media, such as appearing on TV and other popular broadcast media (47 percent), and contributing to more mainstream newspapers and magazines (43 percent) as activities that have a greater impact on policy and social change than producing academic publications such as journal articles (30 percent), books (29 percent), and conference presentations (26 percent). However, faculty are more likely to engage in academic communication.

A vital part of bridging scholarship and social impact is communicating academic work outside academia. Publications such as *The Conversation*, the *Stanford Social Innovation Review*, and the *Harvard Business Review* are all well-known examples of media that "translate" between the academy and leaders in government, civil society, and business. The concept of translational research is well understood in medical schools, which assist faculty to connect research to better clinical outcomes. It is expected that a medical researcher does work that has real-world application.

Similarly, at Harvard Business School, the administration provides assistance with drafting case studies designed to translate research into practical lessons for CEOs and managers. Helping the business world innovate and become more productive and more ethical is part and parcel of the work of business-school faculty, who regularly conduct executive education.

In social sciences, however, faculty are not measured by their real-world impact. Universities do not typically provide resources to translate research into public policy outcomes like decreasing poverty and homelessness, reducing police brutality, or improving educational outcomes. Obviously, there are many notable exceptions among media-savvy faculty, who regularly advise government, philanthropy, and business and appear on the news to explain how research connects to practice, but hands-on problem solving or even advisory work are not the norm.

Interestingly, when NYU faculty were asked why they had not participated in activities that they considered to be socially impactful, the most common response among those surveyed was that they "don't know how." They overwhelmingly expressed a great deal of interest in receiving training in areas they felt to be ways to impact social change, especially learning how to advise government, how to draft policy, and how to package research for policy makers.

Ali Nouri of the Federation of American Scientists and creator of the Congressional Science Policy Initiative, which crowdsources scientific expertise for Congress, explains that such expertise, were it available, is desperately needed. Out of the 535 lawmakers, he points out, only 17 have a background in a field related to science and technology policy. "There is a simple solution to the science deficit in Congress. If you lack in-house expertise, get expert advice from outside. . . . There are more than 10,000 research institutions across the country, filled with experts on everything from infectious disease to cancer research to artificial intelligence."[6] However, there is an absence of training, education, and brokering to help academics "translate" their expertise into a format that is useful for policy makers, leaders of NGOs, and even businesses. Given the knowledge-practice gap among faculty, it is no wonder that students do not have enough opportunities to solve public problems.

PUBLIC-PROBLEM-SOLVING EDUCATION
Over fifty years ago, the Ford Foundation made a decision to start funding the creation of clinical programs at law schools around the country and consciously shift legal education from more theoretical to more practical pedagogy. Since the late nineteenth century, in an effort to professionalize legal education and render it more scholarly (and its graduates more elite), the academy (with the exception of the University of Denver) had previously exclusively taught legal doctrine and theory, meaning students had no con-

tact with real people or real problems. But over the ensuing generation, thanks to Ford's investment in defining the field, every law school now offers clinical education.

If we want to raise a next generation of civic-minded leaders willing to advance social justice, then, just as Ford supported the creation of a clinical law-school curriculum fifty years ago, so too must philanthropy, investors, universities, and government work together to invest in public-problem-solving teaching for all undergraduates and professional students, regardless of discipline.

Most law schools have a public-interest law program and provide career counseling for those who wish to do public-interest law. But unlike clinical or public-interest legal education, there is no common vocabulary across schools and disciplines to capture the idea of public problem solving. The awkward terms "mission driven," "service learning," "social impact," "social innovation," and "public interest" are not universally understood. It does not connote a common and coherent field with defined skills and measures the way that public-interest law does.

Today, students lack adequate access to training in public-problem-solving methods to complement the domain content and expertise they are developing. There is an overall dearth of adequate opportunities for problem-based (as distinct from project-based) learning and unmet demand for social-change courses, especially in the wake of the Black Lives Matter protests. Of the 100 students in my Solving Public Problems class at NYU during fall semester 2020, the overwhelming plurality indicated a passion for tackling climate change, racial injustice, inequality, poverty alleviation, or education reform.

Where private entrepreneurship has clear return-on-investment metrics, there are no clearly defined or easy-to-measure performance indicators for public entrepreneurship education.[7] Whereas nonacademic measures of social and emotional learning cover such positive psychological traits as grit or resilience or problem solving (understood as interpersonal information processing),[8] there are no assessments of student interest in or commitment to helping others, despite empirical evidence that service to others correlates with personal well-being.[9]

Especially in light of the global and shared sense of public challenge created by the COVID-19 pandemic, there is momentum to address the opportunity for expanding public-problem-solving opportunities and inspire more students to go into public service either inside or outside government. In the NYU 2020 course, over 76 percent of those who responded to the initial intake survey said they were interested in pursuing mission-driven work as a lifelong career or as part of a career that might involve other kinds of work. As Sheryl Sorby, the incoming head of the American Society for Engineering Education (ASEE), writes, "Personally, I think it is time that we take a long, critical look at our curricula to ensure that we are preparing our students for their unknown and perhaps unseeable future careers in the current century. To ensure that we are attracting and retaining a diverse pool of learners to our programs, we need to examine what we are teaching and how we are teaching it. We need to examine the type of problems we expect our students to solve so they are inspired to continue in engineering and to solve problems that change the world for the better."[10]

In 2015, 120 deans at US engineering and computer science schools announced plans to educate a new generation of engineers to expressly tackle some of the most pressing issues of the twenty-first century. The deans argued that computer science and engineering students, as much as their law and policy counterparts, are keen, as they put it, to "do stuff that matters."[11] But, if we look at our curricula in subjects from engineering to law to public administration that have hardly changed in a generation and sometimes longer, it is urgent to solve the problem of how we train people to make these disciplines more service oriented by imparting the entrepreneurial know-how of learning how to implement a project in a real world beset by political conflict.

To move in this direction, schools must create opportunities for teams of students, not only in policy courses but in engineering, computer science, law, and business, who will work on public-interest problems in collaboration with outside institutions. There is no shortage of important problems to solve. The National Academy of Engineering's Fourteen Grand Challenges and the United Nations' seventeen Sustainable Development Goals name just a few. At New York University's Tandon's Ability Lab, computer science, engineering, design, and occupational therapy students are designing tools to improve the lives of people with disabilities. The student-run computer science programs at the Rensselaer Center for Open Source endeavor to empower students to develop open-source solutions to real-world problems.[12]

Although collaborative programs exist across different branches of engineering, for example, such as computer and biological engineering, a century-long effort to create distinct professions by narrowly defining academic fields has led most professional schools not to teach any kind of problem solving or, if they do, only with the toolkit of their own discipline. They do project- or team-based learning within their school but all too rarely across schools, despite the real-world need to develop shared agency and to function in global cross-disciplinary and diverse teams.[13] By contrast, the newly founded London Interdisciplinary School (LIS), led by the polymath Carl Gombrich, aspires to prepare "students to tackle some of the most complex problems that we face in the world. The LIS curriculum cuts across the disciplines, equipping students with knowledge and methods from the arts, sciences, and humanities." LIS aims to teach undergraduates a combination of quantitative and qualitative research methods—survey design, ethnography, coding, and a range of methods that can be applied to different problems.[14] Real-world problems—and methods for tackling them—drive the intended learning and design of LIS's novel (and as-yet-untested) programs.

Over years of teaching public problem solving in law, policy, and engineering schools, I have found that teams get more done when students are exposed to each other's substantive knowledge and diverse problem-solving heuristics and vocabularies. Sharing such experience also helps students to develop a multidisciplinary competency and to learn the skills of collaboration. This is why Arizona State's Humanities Lab offers courses where students and faculty work as interdisciplinary and intergenerational teams. According to its website, "The Humanities Lab at ASU is designed as an experimental space in which interdisciplinary faculty teams work with students from a variety of academic and cultural backgrounds to investigate grand social challenges, to construct researchable questions that delve deeply into those challenges, and to generate possible approaches to complex, 'wicked' issues like immigration, health, and climate change, for which there are no easy answers."[15]

Even more important than teamwork and shared agency, professional schools must teach problem solving by beginning with problem definition, not by handing students a problem. Too often students are taught to solve well-structured problems working from preexisting cases. Even so-called capstone or research assistantships assign prescribed tasks to students or predefine the problem. By contrast, the Berlin-based University of Applied

Sciences CODE program teaches students a variety of hard and soft skills building toward creating "your own project from scratch" and putting together a team of fellow students to solve it.[16] At the University of Toronto, the Reach Alliance is an honors capstone where students from medical engineering, public policy, management, and biology form teams to address complex development challenges. Their work centers around conducting the research needed to define real-world problems. To date, ninety-three students have conducted eighteen case studies in fifteen countries.[17]

Problems of the kind tackled in Toronto's Reach program, such as eliminating malaria in Sri Lanka or addressing food insecurity in Ethiopia, are rarely well structured. Empirical research shows that learning only to solve well-structured problems leaves graduates poorly equipped to tackle open-ended, complex, real-world problems. Instead, as they do in Reach or in Fukuyama and Weinstein's Policy Engineering at Stanford, real innovators must discover the problem, not work on one already presented. They must learn the epistemic craft of how to define a problem, its historical and social context, and its root causes.[18]

Problem-based learning had its origins in medical-school education. In the 1950s, the curriculum of Case Western Reserve University Medical School began to incorporate new instructional methods and strategies, including teaching students through real-world problems. Medical faculty at McMaster University in Ontario, Canada, further developed the practice, pioneering the use of problem scenarios for students to work through instead of the Socratic method. Professor Donald Woods of McMaster has been credited with coining the term "problem-based learning" and starting the practice.[19] McMaster's first class of problem-based learning began in 1969 with nineteen medical students. They worked in small teams and did not receive traditional lectures; instead they received a "problem pack" in a card-deck format. In a randomized and controlled study, students who learned using the problem-based learning approach were seen to have increased motivation and problem-solving and self-study skills. Students' knowledge and, more importantly, their ability to apply it in clinical care demonstrably improved. Other medical schools, including Harvard, followed suit, integrating problem-based learning with traditional lecture courses and combining training in basic science with clinical approaches throughout the four years of medical school, not merely at the end.[20] The embrace of problem-based learning challenged the primacy of the biomedical model that had become the gold standard of twentieth-century medical training.[21]

It is a commonplace that defining a problem depends on understanding root causes. But to define a problem well, as I have argued throughout, teams must use both quantitative and qualitative methods—getting smarter from data and from human insight to frame the problem to solve. Acquiring these skills is even more important for younger professionals and university students, for whom a knowledge of both human-centered design and data-analytical methods will prepare them early to thrive in their careers. To do so, they must abandon a dogmatic adherence to either human-centered design or data analysis as the exclusive means of problem discovery. Good programs across a range of disciplines teach both methods. In the Open Seventeen program, a partnership among Tsinghua University in China and the Universities of Zurich and Geneva in Switzerland, students from computer science and informatics, design, history, policy, and other fields received online project coaching from The GovLab in how to apply both human-centered design *and* data-analytical methods to advance projects that address one of the seventeen United Nations Sustainable Development Goals.[22]

But we also need to teach students, as much as adults, the undervalued and challenging task of implementing solutions, not just designing them. Accordingly, at Purdue University in Indiana, the Engineering Projects in Community Service program offers students the opportunity to learn about the social context of the projects they undertake.[23] Arizona State has emulated the program and even created EPICS High, a similar program for local high and middle schools. In 2013, five high school students designed a mobile dental clinic. They went on to study at Arizona State University and in 2017 got the project off the ground with $80,000 in funding.[24]

Design for America (DFA), founded by the Northwestern professor Elizabeth Gerber, is a national social innovation organization with university-based chapters running extracurricular design-based problem-solving training and projects. For the past decade, DFA has trained students in participatory design practices to develop and implement solutions to problems in their own communities. Anyone can join, but "the only requirement is that participants must develop, test, and implement the ideas, not just discuss the enormity of the problems."[25]

As chapter 1 discussed, most universities offer programs in private entrepreneurship, and the language of entrepreneurship is well-known and

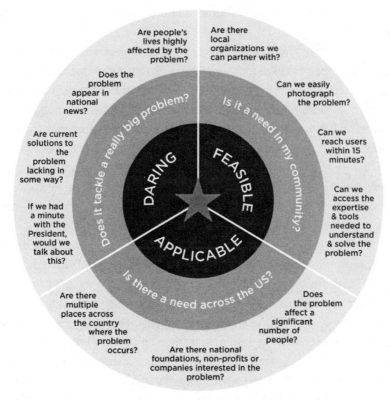

Design for America scoping wheel (D. G. Rees Lewis, M. W. Easterday, and E. M. Gerber, "Supporting Project Scoping: The Scoping Wheel," poster presented at Harvey Mudd Design Workshop IX, 2015). Courtesy of Elizabeth Gerber

understood. Yet the pedagogy of problem solving taught in those clubs and classes has critical limitations. Private entrepreneurship focuses on a person's ability to devise his or her own original solution, launch an app, or start a company. But public problem solving demands solutions that are legitimate and equitable as well as effective. That is why students must go beyond learning prepackaged and mechanical problems to which they develop solutions on their own and, instead, learn participatory and democratic methods for defining and solving problems in partnership with communities. Public problem solving and public entrepreneurship shift the focus from oneself to a sense of responsibility to the group and to the problem. They cultivate a sense of public purpose, not private ambition. While they teach the same creative leadership that students learn in an entrepreneurship class, these multidisciplinary methods for getting things done are applied to doing good in the world.

This involves, however, going beyond human-centered practices of talking with individuals to include methods that incorporate the use of data and the use of collective intelligence to identify and implement solutions against the backdrop of existing legal and governmental institutions. As emphasized through this volume, government has an important role to play in bringing about change and stewarding those conversations. Rather than ignore public institutions in favor of focusing on the innovator, as so many entrepreneurship programs do, public problem solving needs to incorporate a relevant understanding of law, policy, and governance—and how to partner with public institutions—to make change happen.

Xavier Briggs, former vice president of the Ford Foundation and currently a distinguished visiting professor at NYU, teaches Leadership and Social Transformation. In his course, students learn the interplay between institutions and social innovation. They "focus on the role of change makers, strategy, and context in shifting big systems. His course explores how social actors in a range of positions, using a range of platforms and tools, work to conceptualize, animate and scale change, often through (a) cultural beliefs and norms, (b) markets and (c) public policy reform."[26] But importantly, they learn all three stratagems rather than only one and develop a bigger toolkit for changing the world than just market-based mechanisms.

At the turn of the century, the Carnegie Foundation made improving the health-care system its major goal. To achieve its aim, Carnegie focused on improving the state of medical education and training, sponsoring a review of medical-school training by the education reformer Abraham Flexner. Flexner's 1910 report, which extolled the German scientific model, argued that medical education should be taken out of the hands of clinicians and brought in line with university education and that the way to fix health care is to fix how we train doctors by changing the curriculum in universities.

If we believe that poverty, racial injustice, and climate change are not going to solve themselves and we believe that improving the quality of our government—those who are on the front line of tackling public problems—matters and that political will is needed for change, then we have to ask, How are we training those who govern? How are we teaching the leaders of tomorrow to be problem solvers instead of mere bureaucrats? How are we engaging more young people in doing stuff that matters? How are we creating equitable educational opportunities by imbuing every student with the ability to improve one's own community and imparting domain expertise and problem-solving methods to help them become truly powerful?

We do not need another Flexner Report. Flexner was myopic, racist, and excessively focused on research to the detriment of clinical care. But if we want more effective institutions, then we do need to change how we educate. We do need to rethink how we train young people across disciplines to solve problems. This cannot be a problem only for public policy or public administration or law schools. Rather, we have to look at infusing an ethos of ethical public problem solving across engineering, law, business, computer science, and other disciplines, in order to ensure that more young people have the opportunity to work on real-world challenges. Ideally, we have to start far before professional school. United4SocialChange (U4SC), for example, started in 2017, trains college, high school, and middle school students to become civic leaders, teaching advocacy, writing, and speaking skills as a means to bring about social change.[27]

As the management and public policy professor Anita McGahan writes, "I truly hope that we can transform the culture of business schools, and in doing so, transform the culture of business. Our students have the potential, power, capability and insight to change the way we work in companies, government, NGOs, philanthropic organizations—in all aspects of life."[28] In the era of Greta Thunberg, the teenage climate activist; the Parkland survivors, youthful crusaders for gun control; Teens Take Charge, high schoolers fighting school segregation in New York City; and a growing cadre of YouTube influencers and start-up kids speaking out for social justice, the time is ripe to ensure that more young people, especially, have access to the tools to take a project from idea to implementation. We cannot continue to teach as we have before simply because it is how we have always done things. Our curricula are outdated, unattractive, too exclusionary, and too silent on issues of social and racial justice. The way we teach fails to take seriously the power and passion of young people to bring about change. Rigid rules and the failure to work on stuff that matters alienate too many diverse students from pursuing higher education. If we were genuinely concerned about academia's effect on the world, we should be doing things very differently, recognizing students not simply as tomorrow's leaders but as today's problem solvers who, with the right training, could make a significant dent in the universe.

Professor McGahan's words could apply to virtually any school in any university. Complementing traditional education—subject-matter expertise —with learning the methods of public problem solving would allow us to cultivate many more and more diverse public problem solvers, who know how to work with rather than for communities, transforming education while producing the leaders and problem solvers we so desperately need to improve people's lives, transform how we govern, and rescue humanity.

ACKNOWLEDGMENTS

After twenty years of coaching and learning from public entrepreneurs and public problem solvers, I have had the privilege of meeting countless change makers inside and outside government whose creative ideas and selfless actions have inspired this book. Happily for the world, they are too numerous to mention here, and the greatest joy of writing this book has been the opportunity to share their stories. While their accomplishments fill the pages of this book, I limit myself here to thanking some of those people who assisted in putting their exploits between two covers.

This is a better book because of original survey work about the skills of public problem solvers, and I must acknowledge the thousands of people who took the time to respond to our questions in five countries. Tad Mc-Gillard and Laura Godderis at the International City and County Managers Association and James Anderson at Bloomberg Philanthropies generously made possible that research in the United States, while Ken Smith and Janine O'Flynn of the Australia New Zealand School of Government supported comparable research in Australia and New Zealand. Thank you to Alejandra Mendoza at the Monash Sustainable Development Institute for her help administering and analyzing the survey down under. Thank you to Dan Zahs and Lisa Holland at the University of Michigan for their advice with survey design. I am indebted to Lee Rainie at Pew Research Center, who is an always ready, always generous, and always delightful interlocutor on all things technology, society, or research design. Victoria Alsina, Jason Williams-Bellamy, and Anirudh Dinesh at The GovLab provided invaluable assistance with administering and analyzing the survey in the United States and Paraguay as well as additional research throughout the project. Victoria's use, reuse, and significant improvement on the public-problem-solving teaching materials have made this a better book and her friendship and collaboration have made me a better teacher and coach.

Additional grant support from the MacArthur Foundation, which has supported my work on governance innovation since its inception, the Nesta Center for Collective Intelligence, and the Democracy Fund made possible the writing of many of the case studies you find throughout this book. Dane Gambrell and Matt Ryan and the entire team at The GovLab have been wonderful collaborators in investigating and writing earlier versions of those stories and helping me to translate them into training curricula. I have also benefited from the work and insights of Stefaan Verhulst, Andrew Young, and Henri Hammond Paul at The GovLab as well.

Thank you to my departmental colleagues, including Jonathan Soffer, Luke Dubois, Richard Wener, Krysta Batterby, Paulette Bancroft, and my NYU colleagues Jelena Kovacevic, Sayar Lonial, Charlton McIlwain, Cybele Raver, and Ellen Schall for their professional and personal support, in particular for their encouragement to develop public problem solving as a course at NYU, which I hope will mark a sea change in exposing more students to the joys of mission-driven work. Caitlin Gebhard and Nelson James gave of their tremendous talents to make that course a reality.

Jack Balkin, Peter Bragge, Bradley Busetto, Soon Ae Chun, Laurie Claus, Fred DeJohn, Seth Harris, Carl van Horn, Sarah Jackson, Eric Klinenberg, Carl Malamud, José L. Martí, Alfons Martinez, Jose Manuel Martinez Sierra, Lex Paulson, Agueda Quiroga, Lakshmi Subramanian and Eileen Twiggs in ways various and sundry deserve special thanks. I owe much to their intelligent conversations and to the much-needed intellectual, moral, and emotional support they provided.

I am not alone in my passion for public problem solving or commitment to rethinking how we use data and technology to train tomorrow's leaders. Elizabeth Gerber, Francois Grey, Joi Ito, Anita McGahan, Geoff Mulgan, Francois Taddei, Mitchell Weiss, and Connie Yowell have been pioneers in this field.

With support from the Knight Foundation for The GovLab's earliest work on coaching public entrepreneurs, Alan Kantrow and Dinorah Cantu were early collaborators in efforts to design public-problem-solving coaching for thousands of participant collaborators over the past decade.

More recently, Rod Glover at Monash Sustainable Development Institute has been my closest collaborator in developing new curricula for public entrepreneurs and rethinking the relationship between innovative individuals and public institutions. Himself a true public entrepreneur, Rod is one of those rare and wise renaissance thinkers of great insight who is also a tremendous doer, investing passion and energy to bring about change.

Thank you to Caroline Paulick-Thiel of Politics for Tomorrow and Sam DeJohn at The GovLab, who have shared the work with me of organizing a quarterly online gathering for the growing field of public-sector innovation skills training. Jeremy Bailenson and Francis Fukuyama organized an important conference on rethinking public-administration education at Stanford in early 2019 from which I benefited enormously. One of the participants at that event, Tom Kalil, formerly of the White House and now of Schmidt Futures, is the consummate public entrepreneur. I am always learning from him. He uses all the tools in an ever-expanding toolkit for change to inspire and enable new ways of working in government, especially.

Thank you to Governor Phil Murphy of New Jersey, who believed in the ideas in this book enough to support the creation of an experimental Innovation team for the state of New Jersey, especially the development of the Innovation Skills Accelerator, which has allowed me to test many of the ideas in this book with public servants in New Jersey and around the world. Thank you to the Innovation team in New Jersey, especially Kai Feder and Giuseppe Morgana, who daily demonstrate how to get into good trouble and do things differently for public good.

Thank you to the editorial team at Yale University Press, especially Joseph Calamia, Seth Ditchik, Elizabeth Sylvia, and Margaret Otzel for taking a chance on this project. David Dembo, Andy Oram, May Lam, and Andrew Katz provided indispensable and painstaking editorial assistance during the lifetime of this project.

If this book is at all readable or well written, it is thanks to the indefatigable efforts of James Button. To have had a writer of his caliber and credentials lend his sharp eye and loving hand to this manuscript was more than any author could hope. I am so thankful and truly in his editorial debt for the joyous experience of collaborating with him.

Finally, I would like to acknowledge with love and gratitude the support of my family. As with any book project, the greatest investment is made by those who pay the price in lost weekends, museums not visited, concerts missed, foregone outings, and rushed meals. I am grateful to my mother, Doris Noveck, and my son, Amedeo Bettauer, for their forbearance. Amedeo, aka Kid Pundit, also contributed substantively to the manuscript with myriad quotes, facts, and research assistance far beyond his eleven years. His "polito-graphic" memory, whereby he can remember any fact or figure so long as it pertains to history, politics, or government, saved me in more than one instance. He is already more knowledgeable about US government than anyone I know. His deep commitment to progressive ideals, public service, and the belief that government can be a force for good, despite what he knows about partisan politics, instills me with hope for the future. If anyone is going to grow up to be a public problem solver, it is he.

NOTES

INTRODUCTION

1. United States Digital Response, accessed October 12, 2020, https://www.us
digitalresponse.org/.

2. Mitchell Weiss, "'Government Entrepreneur' Is Not an Oxymoron," *Harvard
Business Review*, March 28, 2014.

3. Elinor Ostrom, "Public Entrepreneurship: A Case Study in Ground Water Basic
Management," PhD diss., University of California, September 29, 1964, http:
//dlc.dlib.indiana.edu/dlc/bitstream/handle/10535/3581/eostr001.pdf?sequence
$=$1. See also Rowan Conway, "How to Be a Public Entrepreneur," *The RSA*
(blog), July 25, 2018, https://www.thersa.org/discover/publications-and-articles
/rsa-blogs/2018/07/how-to-be-a-public-entrepreneur; Center for Public Impact,
"Enter the Public Entrepreneur," 2016, https://resources.centreforpublicimpact.
org/production/2016/12/5284-CPI-Public-Entrep-singles1.pdf; Mitchell Weiss,
*We the Possibility: Harnessing Public Entrepreneurship to Solve Our Most Urgent
Problems* (Cambridge, MA: Harvard Business School Press, 2021).

4. Bertrand Russell, *Power: A New Social Analysis* (1938; repr., London: Routledge,
2004), 23.

5. Moises Naïm, *The End of Power: From Boardrooms to Battlefields and Churches to
States, Why Being in Charge Isn't What It Used to Be* (New York: Basic Books, 2014).

6. Yuval Levin, "How Did Americans Lose Faith in Everything?," *New York Times*,
January 18, 2020, https://www.nytimes.com/2020/01/18/opinion/sunday
/institutions-trust.html?fbclid=IwAR2BiMBKMRahvW_rumZZ_Sd3kBMw
5vmbMiDVAH7xVFQYSIl1DtlM1bw_p-w.

7. "Rapper Killer Mike Speech Transcript during Atlanta Protests," *Rev*, May 30,

2020, https://www.rev.com/blog/transcripts/rapper-killer-mike-speech-transcript
-during-atlanta-protests.

1. PUBLIC PROBLEM SOLVING AND THE NEW PUBLIC ENTREPRENEUR

1. See Open Source Drug Discovery, "About Us," accessed June 18, 2019, http://www.
   osdd.net/about-us.
2. See Open Source Drug Discovery, home page, accessed May 10, 2019, http://
   www.osdd.net/home. See also Mark Stevenson, *We Do Things Differently: The
   Outsiders Rebooting Our World* (New York: Harry N. Abrams, 2018), 40–73;
   Christine Ardal and John-Arne Rottingen, "Open Source Drug Discovery in
   Practice: A Case Study National Center for Biotechnology Information," *PloS
   Neglected Tropical Diseases* 6, no. 9 (2012): e1827, https://www.ncbi.nlm.nih.gov
   /pmc/articles/PMC3447952/.
3. Nisha Chandran and Samir K. Brahmachari, "A Decade of OSDD for TB: Role
   and Outcomes," *Current Science*, February 5, 2019, doi: 10.18520/cs/v115/i10
   /1858-1864.
4. Municipio San Pedro Garza García, The GovLab, and Codeando México,
   "Desafío San Pedro Primera Edición (2016–18)," accessed October 11, 2020,
   http://desafios.sanpedro.gob.mx/.
5. Beth Simone Noveck and Dinorah Cantu Pedrazza, "City Challenges: Collaborative Governing for Public Problem Solving," *Forbes*, January 24, 2018, https://
   www.forbes.com/sites/bethsimonenoveck/2018/01/24/city-challenges-collabora
   tive-governing-for-public-problem-solving/#3948f666df34.
6. Beth Simone Noveck, Dane Gambrell, and Matt Ryan, "Collective Intelligence
   Case Studies," The GovLab, accessed October 11, 2020, https://www.thegovlab
   .org/collective-intelligence.html.
7. Jonathan Wachtell, interview with author, October 27, 2019.
8. Public Service Jobs Database, https://www.psjd.org/.
9. Art Barnard, Thomas Pittz, and Jeff Vanevenhove, "Entrepreneurship Education
   in U.S. Community Colleges: A Review and Analysis," *Journal of Small Business
   and Enterprise Development*, April 23, 2019, https://www.emerald.com/insight
   /content/doi/10.1108/JSBED-06-2018-0178/full/html.
10. Horst Rittel and Melvin Webber, "Dilemmas in a General Theory of Planning,"
    Policy Sciences 4, no. 2 (1973): 155–169, http://doi:10.1007/bf01405730.
11. Beth Simone Noveck, *Wiki Government: How Technology Can Make Government
    Better, Democracy Stronger, and Citizens More Powerful* (Washington, DC:
    Brookings Institution Press, 2010); Noveck, *Smart Citizens, Smarter State: The
    Technologies of Expertise and the Future of Government* (Cambridge, MA: Harvard
    University Press, 2015).
12. For more on the debate on innovators as rule breakers, see Sandford Borins, *The
    Persistence of Innovation in Government* (Washington, DC: Brookings Institution
    Press, 2014), 4.
13. Ian MacDougall, "How McKinsey Makes Its Own Rules," ProPublica, December
    14, 2019, https://www.propublica.org/articlehow-mckinsey-makes-its-own-rules.

14. World Economic Forum, *Towards a Reskilling Revolution Industry-Led Action for the Future of Work* (Geneva: World Economic Forum, 2019), http://www3.we forum.org/docs/WEF_Towards_a_Reskilling_Revolution.pdf.

15. Jeff Dyer, Hal Gregersen, and Clayton Christensen, *The Innovator's DNA: Mastering the Five Skills of Disruptive Innovators* (Boston: Harvard Business Review Press, 2011), 22.

16. Blue Wooldridge, "Increasing the Productivity of Public-Sector Training," *Public Productivity Review* 12, no. 2 (1988): 205–217.

17. Michael Gove, "The Privilege of Public Service," Ditchley Lecture, reprinted in *New Statesman*, June 28, 2020, https://www.newstatesman.com/politics /uk/2020/06/privilege-public-service-michael-gove-s-ditchley-lecture-full-text.

18. For details on the public entrepreneurship innovation skills surveys sponsored by the International City and County Managers Association (ICMA), see http:// www.publicentrepreneur.org/skills.

19. Beth Simone Noveck and Rod Glover, "The Public Problem Solving Imperative," ANZSOG, August 13, 2019, https://www.anzsog.edu.au/resource-library/news -media/todays-problems-yesterdays-toolkit-public-service.

20. Beth Simone Noveck, Victoria Alsina, and Alejandra Mendoza, "Encuesta de habilidades de innovación en el sector público de Paraguay" (The GovLab white paper, August 2020), https://www.thegovlab.org/publications.html.

21. Observatory for Public Sector Innovation, *Core Skills for Public Sector Innovation* (Paris: OECD, April 2017), https://www.oecd.org/media/oecdorg/satellitesites /opsi/contents/files/OECD_OPSI-core_skills_for_public_sector_innovation -201704.pdf. This OECD report builds on earlier work by the OECD, which did the first countrywide study of the pervasiveness of innovation skills in a survey of 150 Chilean public servants and subsequently elaborated on this work in a report on core governance innovation skills, both in 2017.

22. Noveck and Glover, "Public Problem Solving Imperative."

23. "4G Leaders Will Work with Singaporeans to Design, Implement Public Policies: DPM Heng," Channel News Asia, June 15, 2019, https://www.channelnewsasia .com/news/delmaneheng-swee-keat-4g-leaders-will-work-with-singaporeans -policies-11629932.

24. Author interview with twenty-five citizen-engagement officials in Singapore, hosted by the Ministry of Youth and Culture, Singapore, November 5, 2019.

25. The TrimTab Conspiracy was the name of the "salon" that David Johnson, Susan Crawford, and I ran between 2003 and 2008 in New York and then in Washington, DC. It was self-consciously styled as an opportunity to discuss strategies for public problem solving using new technologies. We met either every two weeks or once a month for these discussions for many years. See Buckminster Fuller, "A Candid Interview with R. Buckminster Fuller," *Playboy* 19, no. 2 (February 1972), available at http://www.bfi.org/sites/default/files/attachments/pages /CandidConversation-Playboy.pdf.

26. The Australian Public Service Commission identified lack of skills as a "major barrier to generate, select, implement, and sustain public sector innovation."

Australian Public Service Commission, "Barriers to Innovation in the APS," accessed October 10, 2020, https://www.apsc.gov.au/4-barriers-innovation-aps. See also OECD, *Innovation Skills in the Public Sector: Building Capabilities in Chile*, OECD Public Governance Reviews (Paris: OECD, 2017), 30, http://dx.doi.org/10.1787/9789264273283-en.

27. Barry Schwartz, "Rethinking Work," *New York Times*, August 28, 2015, https://www.nytimes.com/2015/08/30/opinion/Sunday/rethinking-work.html.

28. Adam Grant and James Berry, "The Necessity of Others Is the Mother of Invention: Intrinsic and Prosocial Motivations, Perspective-Taking, and Creativity," *Academy of Management Journal* 54 (2011): 73–96.

29. Teresa M. Amabile, K. G. Hill, B. A. Hennessey, and E. M. Tighe, "The Work Preference Inventory: Assessing Intrinsic and Extrinsic Motivational Orientations," *Journal of Personality and Social Psychology* 66, no. 5 (1994): 950–967, http://dx.doi.org/10.1037/0022-3514.66.5.950.

30. Robert Lavigna, "Employee Engagement Low, Especially in Government," Association for Talent Development, October 19, 2017, https://www.td.org/insights/employee-engagement-low-especially-in-government. See also Lavigna, *Engaging Government Employees: Motivate and Inspire Your People to Achieve Superior Performance* (New York: HarperCollins Leadership, 2013).

31. For more on the literature of public entrepreneurship, see Sandford Borins, *The Persistence of Innovation in Government* (Washington, DC: Brookings Institution Press, 2014), 20–25.

32. Samir Brahmachari, interview, "Expert Conversation: Using Open Source Drug Discovery to Help Treat Neglected Diseases," *The Conversation*, January 14, 2017, https://theconversation.com/expert-conversation-using-open-source-drug-discovery-to-help-treat-neglected-diseases-79318.

33. Rohit Vashisht and Samir K. Brahmachari, "Metformin as a Potential Combination Therapy with Existing Front-Line Antibiotics for Tuberculosis," *Journal of Translational Medicine* 13 (2015): art. 83, https://doi.org/10.1186/s12967-015-0443-y.

34. Joseph A. DiMasia, Henry G. Grabowski, and Ronald W. Hansen, "Innovation in the Pharmaceutical Industry: New Estimates of R&D Costs," *Journal of Health Economics* 47 (May 2016): 20–33.

35. Capítulo Tercero del Programa Desafíos, Artículo 509 Bis 7, et seq., September 13, 2017, https://www.sanpedro.gob.mx/gobierno/Reglamentos/PDFs/ReglamentoParticipaci%C3%B3nCiudadanaparapublicaci%C3%B3np%C3%A1ginainterntetGobMunicipalrevisado_XBDXNGDiIK.pdf.

2. THE GOVERNMENT THAT GOVERNS LEAST GOVERNS BEST

1. Laura Bliss, "How Louisville Is Using GPS to Control Asthma," City Lab, August 9, 2017, https://www.citylab.com/environment/2017/08/how-high-tech-inhalers-are-helping-louisville-clear-the-air/535749/.

2. Service to America Medals (The "Sammies"), "2020 Samuel J. Heyman Service to America Medals," accessed October 9, 2020, https://servicetoamericamedals.org/.

3. Mariana Mazzucato, *The Entrepreneurial State: Debunking Public vs. Private Sector Myths* (London: Anthem, 2013).

4. Edelman, "Edelman Trust Barometer Spring Update: Trust and the Covid-19 Pandemic," May 5, 2020, https://www.edelman.com/research/trust-2020-spring -update. See also Sabrina Tavernise, "Will the Coronavirus Kill What's Left of Americans' Faith in Washington?," *New York Times*, May 24, 2020, A4.

5. Paul C. Light, "Six Ways the Demand for Government Reform Will Shape the 2020 Election," *FixGov* (blog), Brookings Institution, February 26, 2020, https:// www.brookings.edu/blog/fixgov/2020/02/26/six-ways-the-demand-for-govern ment-reform-will-shape-the-2020-election/.

6. "Regulation is currently under attack from all quarters as inefficient, ineffective, and undemocratic." Jody Freeman, "Collaborative Government in the Administrative State," *UCLA Law Review* 45, no. 1 (1997): 3. "More than 6 out of 10 Americans in Gallup polls conducted this year have consistently said 'most members of Congress' do not deserve re-election. . . . The most frequently given response . . . is fairly straightforward and direct, if not a bit tautological: Members of Congress are doing a bad job or just are not doing their job, period." Frank Newport, "Americans See Congress as Ineffective, Self-Serving, Entrenched," Gallup, June 23, 2010, https://news.gallup.com/poll/141008/americans-congress -ineffective-self-serving-entrenched.aspx. "Today we notice when the president doesn't show up. . . . No one man—or woman—can possibly represent the varied, competing interests of 327 million citizens. And it may be that no man— or woman—can perform the ever-expanding duties of office while managing an executive branch of 2 million employees (not including the armed forces) charged with everything from regulating air pollution to x-raying passengers before they board an airplane." John Dickerson, "The Hardest Job in the World," *Atlantic*, May 2018, https://www.theatlantic.com/magazine/ archive/2018/05/a-broken-office/556883/.

7. Ian MacDougall, "How McKinsey Is Making $100 Million (and Counting) Advising on the Government's Bumbling Coronavirus Response," ProPublica, July 15, 2020, https://www.propublica.org/article/how-mckinsey-is-making-100-mil lion-and-counting-advising-on-the-governments-bumbling-coronavirus-response.

8. Megan Brenan, "Americans' Trust in Government to Handle Problems at New Low," Gallup, January 31, 2019, https://news.gallup.com/poll/246371/americans -trust-government-handle-problems-new-low.aspx.

9. Peter Schuck, *Why Government Fails So Often: And How It Can Do Better* (Princeton, NJ: Princeton University Press, 2014), 3. See also Joseph S. Nye Jr. and Philip D. Zelikow, "Conclusion: Reflections, Conjectures, and Puzzles," in *Why People Don't Trust Government*, ed. Joseph S. Nye Jr., Philip D. Zelikow, and David C. King (Cambridge, MA: Harvard University Press, 1997), 253–281.

10. Washington Post, *The Great Society: 50 Years Later* (New York: Diversion Books, 2014), 4.

11. "Democracy Index 2019," *Economist*, accessed October 10, 2020, http://www.eiu .com/topic/democracy-index.

12. Schuck, *Why Government Fails So Often*, 23.

13. John Bridgeland and Peter Orszag, "Can Government Play Moneyball? How a New Era of Fiscal Scarcity Could Make Washington Work Better," *Atlantic*, July–August 2013, https://www.theatlantic.com/magazine/archive/2013/07/can-government-play-moneyball/309389/.

14. Paul C. Light, "A Cascade of Failures: Why Government Fails, and How to Stop It," Brookings Institution, July 14, 2014, https://www.brookings.edu/research/a-cascade-of-failures-why-government-fails-and-how-to-stop-it/.

15. Seth J. Hill and Chris Tausanovitch, "A Disconnect in Representation? Comparison of Trends in Congressional and Public Polarization," *Journal of Politics* 77, no. 4 (2015): 1058–1075.

16. Bryan Caplan, *The Myth of the Rational Voter: Why Democracies Choose Bad Policies* (Princeton, NJ: Princeton University Press, 2007); Ilya Somin, *Democracy and Political Ignorance: Why Smaller Government Is Smarter* (Stanford, CA: Stanford University Press, 2013); Rick Shenkman, *Just How Stupid Are We: Facing the Truth about the American Voter* (New York: Basic Books, 2008).

17. Anthony Downs, *An Economic Theory of Democracy* (New York: Harper, 1957); see also Guido Pincione and Fernando Tesón, *Rational Choice and Democratic Deliberation: A Theory of Discourse Failure* (Cambridge: Cambridge University Press, 2006). For a scathing critique of this "anti-democratic" viewpoint, see Roslyn Fuller, *In Defence of Democracy* (London: Policy, 2019).

18. Christopher H. Achen and Larry M. Bartels, *Democracy for Realists: Why Elections Do Not Produce Responsive Government* (Princeton, NJ: Princeton University Press, 2017).

19. See Lawrence Lessig, *Republic Lost: Version 2.0* (New York: Twelve, 2015); and Paul Pierson and Jacob Hacker, *Winner-Take-All Politics: How Washington Made the Rich Richer—and Turned Its Back on the Middle Class* (New York: Simon and Schuster, 2011).

20. Stephen M. Teles, "Kludgeocracy in America," *National Affairs* 25 (Fall 2013): 97.

21. See Center for Responsive Politics, Open Secrets, "Lobbying Data Summary," accessed October 10, 2020, https://www.opensecrets.org/federal-lobbying/summary. See also John B. Judis, *The Paradox of American Democracy: Elites, Special Interests, and the Betrayal of Public Trust* (New York: Knopf, 2013).

22. Steven H. Woolf and Heidi Schoomaker, "Life Expectancy and Mortality Rates in the United States, 1959–2017," *JAMA* 322, no. 20 (2019): 1996–2016, https://doi.org/10.1001/jama.2019.16932.

23. National Academies of Science, Engineering, and Medicine, *The Growing Gap in Life Expectancy by Income: Implications for Federal Programs and Policy Responses* (Washington, DC: National Academies Press, 2015), https://doi.org/10.17226/19015.

24. S. Jay Olshanky et al., "Differences in Life Expectancy Due to Race and Educational Differences Are Widening, and Many May Not Catch Up," *Health Affairs*, August 2012, available at https://www.healthaffairs.org/doi/full/10.1377/hlthaff.2011.0746.

25. Jacob Bor, Gregory H. Cohen, and Sandro Galea, "Population Health in an Era of Rising Income Inequality: USA, 1980–2015," *Lancet* 389, no. 10077 (April 8, 2017), https://doi.org/10.1016/S0140-6736(17)30571-8; Samuel L. Dickman, David U. Himmelstein, and Steffie Woolhandler, "Inequality and the Health-Care System in the USA," *Lancet* 389, no. 10077 (April 8, 2017), https://doi.org/10.1016/S0140-6736(17)30398-7.

26. Shervin Assari, "George Floyd and Ahmaud Arbery Deaths: Racism Causes Life-Threatening Conditions for Black Men Every Day," *The Conversation*, June 1, 2020, https://theconversation.com/george-floyd-and-ahmaud-arbery-deaths-racism-causes-life-threatening-conditions-for-black-men-every-day-120541?.

27. United Nations Human Rights Office of the High Commissioner, "Statement on Visit to the USA, by Professor Philip Alston, United Nations Special Rapporteur on Extreme Poverty and Human Rights," December 15, 2017, https://www.ohchr.org/EN/NewsEvents/Pages/DisplayNews.aspx?NewsID=22533. See also Kathryn Edin and H. Luke Shaefer, *$2.00 a Day: Living on Almost Nothing in America* (New York: Mariner Books, 2016).

28. Ashish P. Thakrar, "Child Mortality in the US and 19 OECD Comparator Nations: A 50-Year Time-Trend Analysis," *Health Affairs* 37, no. 1 (2018): 140–149, https://doi.org/10.1377/hlthaff.2017.0767.

29. Centers for Disease Control and Prevention, "Pregnancy Mortality Surveillance System," accessed October 20, 2020, https://www.cdc.gov/reproductivehealth/maternalinfanthealth/pregnancy-mortality-surveillance-system.htm?CDC_AA_refVal=https%3A%2F%2Fwww.cdc.gov%2Freproductivehealth%2Fmaternalinfanthealth%2Fpmss.html; United Health Foundation, "Health of Women and Children," America's Health Rankings 2019, accessed October 10, 2020, https://www.americashealthrankings.org/explore/health-of-women-and-children/measure/maternal_mortality/state/NJ.

30. Centers for Disease Control and Prevention, "Health Equity Considerations and Racial and Ethnic Minority Groups," accessed October 10, 2020, https://www.cdc.gov/coronavirus/2019-ncov/need-extra-precautions/racial-ethnic-minorities.html.

31. Andrea Polonijo, "How California's COVID-19 Surge Widens Health Inequalities for Black, Latino and Low-Income Residents," *The Conversation*, July 30, 2020, https://theconversation.com/how-californias-covid-19-surge-widens-health-inequalities-for-black-latino-and-low-income-residents-143243.

32. Fernando G. De Maio, "Income Inequality Measures," *Journal of Epidemiology & Community Health* 61, no. 10 (2007): 849–852, doi: 10.1136/jech.2006.052969; Lawrence Mishel, Elise Gould, and Josh Bivens, "Wage Stagnation in Nine Charts," Economic Policy Institute, January 6, 2015, https://www.epi.org/publication/charting-wage-stagnation/.

33. Heather Long and Andrew van Dam, "U.S. Unemployment Rate Soars to 14.7 Percent, the Worst since the Depression Era," *Washington Post*, May 8, 2020, https://www.washingtonpost.com/business/2020/05/08/april-2020-jobs-report/.

34. James Bessen, "Scarce Skills, Not Scarce Jobs: The 'Real' Challenge Technology Presents Isn't That It Replaces Workers, but Rather Displaces Them," *Atlantic*, April 27, 2015. See also Bessen, *Learning by Doing* (New Haven, CT: Yale University Press, 2015), 106–109.

35. World Economic Forum, "Future of Work 2018," accessed May 25, 2020, http://reports.weforum.org/future-of-jobs-2018/preface/.

36. Mark Knickrehm, "How Will AI Change Work? Here Are 5 Schools of Thought," *Harvard Business Review*, January 25, 2018, https://hbr.org/2018/01/how-will-ai-change-work-here-are-5-schools-of-thought.

37. "America's Gun Culture in 10 Charts," BBC, October 27, 2018, https://www.bbc.com/news/world-us-canada-41488081.

38. Centers for Disease Control and Prevention, "Underlying Cause of Death 1999–2017," CDC WONDER, 2017, https://wonder.cdc.gov/wonder/help/ucd.html. See also Erin Grinshteyn and David Hemenway, "Violent Death Rates: The U.S. Compared with Other High-Income OECD Countries, 2010," *American Journal of Medicine* 129, no. 3 (2016): 266–273, https://doi.org/10.1016/j.amjmed.2015.10.025.

39. "1011 People Have Been Shot and Killed by Police in the Past Year," Fatal Force, *Washington Post*, May 29, 2020.

40. APM Research Lab, "COVID-19 Deaths by Race and Ethnicity in the U.S.," May 27, 2020, https://www.apmresearchlab.org/covid/deaths-by-race.

41. Michael Sandel, *The Tyranny of Merit* (New York: Farrar, Straus and Giroux, 2020), 18–27.

42. Charles Larson and Alec Mercer, "Global Health Indicators: An Overview," *Canadian Medical Association Journal* 171, no. 10 (2004): 1199–1200, doi: 10.1503/cmaj.1021409.

43. Moises Naím, "Why the People in Power Are Increasingly Powerless," *Washington Post*, March 1, 2013, https://www.washingtonpost.com/opinions/why-the-people-in-power-are-increasingly-powerless/2013/03/01/6dc7905c-7f70-11e2-8074-b26a871b165a_story.html.

44. OECD, "Inequality," accessed September 20, 2020, http://www.oecd.org/social/inequality.htm.

45. Oxfam International, "Reward Work, Not Wealth," January 22, 2018, https://www.oxfam.org/en/research/reward-work-not-wealth.

46. United Nations Environment Programme, "Bridging the Emissions Gap: The Role of Non-State and Subnational Actors," UN Environment Emissions Gap Report 2018, accessed September 20, 2020, http://hdl.handle.net/20.500.11822/26093.

47. Hiroyuki Murakami et al., "Dominant Effect of Relative Tropical Atlantic Warming on Major Hurricane Occurrence," *Science* 362, no. 6416 (2018): 794–799, https://science.sciencemag.org/content/362/6416/794; Union of Concerned Scientists, "Is Global Warming Fueling Increased Wildfire Risks?," July 24, 2018, https://www.ucsusa.org/global-warming/science-and-impacts/impacts/global-warming-and-wildfire.html#.XC_6GM9Ki1s; National Aeronau-

tics and Space Administration, "The Effects of Climate Change," accessed September 20, 2020, https://climate.nasa.gov/effects/.

48. Jeff Tollefson, "Humans Are Driving One Million Species to Extinction," *Nature*, May 6, 2019, https://www.nature.com/articles/d41586-019-01448-4.

49. "The 10 Hottest Global Years on Record," *Climate Central* (blog), February 6, 2019, https://www.climatecentral.org/gallery/graphics/the-10-hottest-global -years-on-record.

50. Institute for Economics and Peace, "Global Terrorism Index 2017: Measuring and Understanding the Impact of Terrorism," 2018, http://visionofhumanity .org/app/uploads/2017/11/Global-Terrorism-Index-2017.pdf.

51. United Nations Refugee Agency, "Figures at a Glance," June 18, 2020, https:// www.unhcr.org/ph/figures-at-a-glance.

52. Internal Displacement Monitoring Centre, "Global Report on Internal Displace- ment 2019," accessed October 10, 2020, http://www.internal-displacement.org /global-report/grid2019/.

53. Phillip Connor and Jens Manuel Krogstad, "Many Worldwide Oppose More Migration—Both into and out of Their Countries," Pew Research Center, December 10, 2018, https://www.pewresearch.org/fact-tank/2018/12/10 /many-worldwide-oppose-more-migration-both-into-and-out-of-their-countries/.

54. Connor and Krogstad.

55. Richard Wike, Laura Silver, and Alexandra Castillo, "Many across the Globe Are Dissatisfied with How Democracy Is Working," Pew Research Center, April 29, 2019, https://www.pewglobal.org/2019/04/29/many-across-the-globe-are -dissatisfied-with-how-democracy-is-working/.

56. Steven Levitsky and Daniel Ziblatt, *How Democracies Die* (New York: Crown, 2018).

57. Ryan Struyk, "By the Numbers: 7 Charts That Explain Hate Groups in the United States," CNN, August 15, 2017, https://www.cnn.com/2017/08/14 /politics/charts-explain-us-hate-groups/index.html.

58. "Full Text: 2017 Donald Trump Inauguration Speech Transcript," *Politico*, January 20, 2017, https://www.politico.com/story/2017/01/full-text-donald -trump-inauguration-speech-transcript-233907.

59. Walter Williams, *Honest Numbers and Democracy: Social Policy Analysis in the White House, Congress, and the Federal Agencies* (Washington, DC: Georgetown University Press, 1998), 2, 61.

60. Paul Light, "The True Size of Government: Tracking Washington's Blended Workforce, 1984–2015," Volcker Alliance, October 2017, https://www.volckeralli ance.org/sites/default/files/attachments/Issue%20Paper_True%20Size%20 of%20Government.pdf.

61. Daniel Schuman, "Keeping Congress Competent: The Senate's Brain Drain," Sunlight Foundation, November 30, 2012, https://sunlightfoundation.com /taxonomy/term/Congressional-salaries/.

62. Demand Progress and Lincoln Network to Rep. Nita Lowey et al., "Strengthen- ing the Legislative Branch by Increasing Its 302(b) Allocation," June 22, 2020,

https://docs.google.com/document/d/1DUMYLysANqdhngwUjYIDhP bFFr5CjLY1Kvz0KvOYxt8/edit?ts=5ee6d91c.

63. Bill Pascrell, "Pascrell Testifies before Select Modernization Committee on Congress," press release, March 12, 2019, https://pascrell.house.gov/news /documentsingle.aspx?DocumentID=3869.

64. OpenSecrets.org, "Lobbying Database," accessed May 4, 2019, https://www .opensecrets.org/lobby/.

65. Bill Pascrell, "Why Is Congress So Dumb?," *Washington Post*, January 11, 2019, https://www.washingtonpost.com/news/posteverything/wp/2019/01/11 /feature/why-is-congress-so-dumb/?utm_term=.127a60220713.

66. Daniel Schuman and Zach Graves, "The Decline of Congressional Expertise Explained in 10 Charts," *Techdirt*, October 18, 2018, https://www.techdirt .com/articles/20181018/10204640869/decline-congressional-expertise -explained-10-charts.shtml ("committee funding is down by $88 million, from $327 million in the 111th Congress to $239 million").

67. Kevin Kosar, "Why I Quit the Congressional Research Service," *Washington Monthly*, January–February 2015, https://washingtonmonthly.com/magazine /janfeb-2015/why-i-quit-the-congressional-research-service/.

68. Kathy Goldschmidt, *State of the Congress: Staff Perspectives on Institutional Capacity in the House and Senate* (Washington, DC: Congressional Management Foundation, 2017).

69. Drew Desilver, "Congress' Productivity Improves Somewhat in 2015," Pew Research Center, December 29, 2015, http://www.pewresearch.org/fact-tank /2015/12/29/congress-productivity-improves-somewhat-in-2015/. Following two remarkably unproductive years, Congress picked up the pace in 2015. In 1947, the so-called Do Nothing Congress passed 906 bills, compared to 74 in the 1995–1996 session or 55 in the 2013–2014 session.

70. GovTrack, "Bills and Resolutions," accessed May 25, 2020, https://www.gov track.us/congress/bills/#bystatus.

71. Frank Baumgartner and Bryan Jones, *The Politics of Information: Problem Definition and the Course of Public Policy in America* (Chicago: University of Chicago Press, 2015), 64.

72. White House, "President Trump Holds a Listening Session with High School Students and Teachers," YouTube, February 21, 2018, https://www.youtube.com /watch?v=vKblXAikzEc.

73. John Cassidy, "Trump's Idea of Arming Teachers Is Crazy but Clarifying," *New Yorker*, February 27, 2018, https://www.newyorker.com/news/our-columnists/ trumps-idea-of-arming-teachers-is-crazy-but-clarifying.

74. Rick Noack, "Trump Supports Arming Some Teachers in the U.S.: Other Countries Have Different Ideas," *Washington Post*, February 22, 2018, https:// www.washingtonpost.com/news/worldviews/wp/2018/02/22/trump-wants -teachers-in-the-u-s-to-be-armed-other-countries-have-different-ideas/.

75. Aimee Huff and Michelle Barnhart, "Why Trump's Idea to Arm Teachers May Miss the Mark," *The Conversation*, February 26, 2018, https://theconversation

.com/why-trumps-idea-to-arm-teachers-may-miss-the-mark-92335. See also Elizabeth Chuck and Corky Siemaszko, "Trump's Proposal to Arm Teachers Panned by Experts as a 'Colossally Stupid Idea,'" NBC News, February 22, 2018, https://www.nbcnews.com/news/us-news/trump-s-proposal-arm-teachers -panned-experts-colossally-stupid-idea-n850286.

76. Terry Spencer, "Education Unions Oppose Calls to Arm Teachers," Associated Press, February 11, 2019, https://www.apnews.com/a6239079b84a459291b 69d3c17c0e455.

77. Elaine Kamarck, John Hudak, and Christine Stenglein, "Immigration by the Numbers," Brookings Institution, August 15, 2017, https://www.brookings.edu /interactives/immigration-by-the-numbers/.

78. Michael Nelson, "Presidential Competence," in *The Presidency and the Political System* (Washington, DC: CQ Press, 2018), 155.

79. Michael Lewis, *The Fifth Risk* (New York: Norton, 2019).

80. Coral Davenport, "In the Trump Administration Science Is Unwelcome, So Is Advice," *New York Times*, June 9, 2018, https://www.nytimes.com/2018/06/09 /climate/trump-administration-science.html.

81. Evan Osnos, "Only the Best People: Trump vs. the 'Deep State,'" *New Yorker*, May 21, 2018, https://www.newyorker.com/magazine/2018/05/21/trump -vs-the-deep-state.

82. Merrit Kennedy, "Scientists Desert USDA as Agency Relocates to Kansas City Area," NPR, July 17, 2019, https://www.npr.org/sections/thesalt/2019/07/17 /742519999/future-of-key-farming-research-uncertain-as-2-3-of-usda-staff -say-they-wont-move.

83. Brad Plumer and Coral Davenport, "Science under Attack: How Trump Is Sidelining Researchers and Their Work," *New York Times*, December 29, 2019, A1. See Silencing Science Tracker, Columbia Law School, accessed September 20, 2020, https://climate.law.columbia.edu/Silencing-Science-Tracker.

84. "Read the Scrapped USPS Announcement to Send 5 Masks to Every American Household," *Washington Post*, September 17, 2020, https://www.washington post.com/context/read-the-scrapped-usps-announcement-to-send-5-masks-to -every-american-household/39cd11c9-3e38-4d8a-9d70-7c3215ab9cf8/?tid=ss_tw.

85. Arthur Schlesinger Jr., *The Cycles of American History* (Wawa, PA: Franklin Library, 1986); Samuel P. Huntington, *American Politics: The Promise of Disharmony* (Cambridge, MA: Harvard University Press, 1981); Frank Baumgart-ner and Bryan Jones, *The Politics of Information: Problem Definition and the Course of Public Policy in America* (Chicago: University of Chicago Press, 2015).

86. Niall Ferguson, "The Regulated States of America," *Wall Street Journal*, June 18, 2013, https://www.wsj.com/articles/SB100014241278873240211045785512911 60259734.

87. Baumgartner and Jones, *Politics of Information*, 72.

88. Michael Tanner, "Budget Deficits Are Only Getting Bigger under Trump," CATO Institute, July 25, 2018, https://www.cato.org/publications/commentary /budget-deficits-are-only-getting-bigger-under-trump.

89. Schuck, *Why Government Fails So Often*, 9.

90. James Q. Wilson, *American Politics, Then and Now, and Other Essays* (Washington, DC: AEI Press, 2010), 8.

91. John DiIulio Jr., "Facing Up to Big Government," *National Affairs* 11 (Spring 2012): 22–41; Meena Bose, James Wilson, and John DiIulio Jr., *American Government: The Essentials: Institutions and Policies*, 12th ed. (Boston: Cengage Learning, 2011).

92. Baumgartner and Jones, *Politics of Information*, 3.

93. Ben Wright, "There's a Sinister Strain of Anti-Intellectualism to Gove's Dismissal of 'Experts,'" *The Telegraph*, June 21, 2016, https://www.telegraph.co.uk/business/2016/06/21/in-defence-of-experts-whether-they-support-leave-or-remain/.

94. Mariana Mazzucato, *The Entrepreneurial State: Debunking Public vs. Private Sector Myths* (London: Anthem, 2013).

95. Anand Giridharadas, *Winners Take All: The Elite Charade of Changing the World* (New York: Knopf, 2018), 253.

96. Edelman, "Edelman Trust Barometer 2019," accessed January 1, 2020, https://www.edelman.com/trust-barometer ("Despite a high lack of faith in the system, there is one relationship that remains strong: 'my employer.' Fifty-eight percent of general population employees say they look to their employer to be a trustworthy source of information about contentious societal issues.").

97. Giridharadas, *Winners Take All*, 54–55.

98. Paul C. Light, *The Search for Social Entrepreneurship* (Washington, DC: Brookings Institution Press, 2008).

99. Giridharadas, *Winners Take All*, 17.

100. Gregory Dees, *The Meaning of Social Entrepreneurship* (Kansas City, MO: Kauffman Foundation, 1998), 1.

101. Alex Nicholls, introduction to *Social Entrepreneurship: New Models of Sustainable Social Change*, ed. Alex Nicholls (Oxford: Oxford University Press, 2008), 10.

102. Mike Monterio, *Ruined by Design: How Designers Destroyed the World, and What We Can Do to Fix It* (San Francisco: Mule Books, 2019).

103. Jigsaw, home page, accessed October 10, 2020, https://jigsaw.google.com/.

104. Facebook Social Good, home page, accessed September 20, 2020, https://socialgood.facebook.com/.

105. Robert Hackett, "How This Startup Plans to Use Blockchain to Revolutionize the Coffee Supply Chain," *Fortune*, October 24, 2017, https://fortune.com/2017/10/24/blockchain-coffee-bext360/.

106. Sanford Borins, *The Persistence of Innovations in Government* (Washington, DC: Brookings Institution Press, 2016), 11.

107. See, e.g., Christopher Pollitt, *Managerialism and the Public Services: The Anglo-American Experience* (London: Basil Blackwell, 1990); Michael Barzelay, *The New Public Management* (Berkeley: University of California Press, 2001); David Osborne and Ted Gaebler, *Reinventing Government: How the Entrepreneurial Spirit Is Transforming the Public Sector* (New York: Plume, 1993).

108. Owen E. Hughes, *Public Administration or Public Management*, 3rd ed. (London: Palgrave Macmillan, 2003), 6.

109. Osborne and Gaebler, *Reinventing Government*. See also Jim Nussle and Peter Orszag, eds., *Moneyball for Government* (Austin, TX: Disruption Books, 2014).

110. Patrick Dunleavy, Helen Margetts, Simon Bastow, and Jane Tinkler, "New Public Management Is Dead—Long Live Digital-Era Governance," *Journal of Public Administration Research and Theory* 16, no. 3 (July 2006): 467–494, https://doi.org/10.1093/jopart/mui057.

111. Mark Moore, *Recognizing Public Value* (Cambridge, MA: Harvard University Press, 2013); Moore, *Creating Public Value: Public Management in Government* (Cambridge, MA: Harvard University Press, 1995).

112. Rowan Conway et al., "Move Fast and Fix Things: How to Be a Public Entrepreneur," RSA Lab and Innovate UK, July 2018, 15, https://www.thersa.org/global assets/pdfs/reports/1331_move-fast-and-fix-things_final.pdf.

113. James Scott, *Seeing Like a State: How Certain Schemes to Improve the Human Condition Have Failed* (New Haven, CT: Yale University Press, 1999).

3. FROM IDEA TO IMPLEMENTATION

1. Beth Simone Noveck, *Wiki Government: How Technology Can Make Government Better, Democracy Stronger, and Citizens More Powerful* (Washington, DC: Brookings Institution Press, 2009).

2. Michael Barber, Paul Kihn, and Andy Moffit, "Deliverology: From Idea to Implementation," McKinsey and Company, February 2011, https://www.mc kinsey.com/industries/public-sector/our-insights/deliverology-from-idea-to -implementation; Mike Bracken, "On Strategy: The Strategy Is Delivery. Again," *Digital Transformation* (blog), January 6, 2013, https://mikebracken .com/blog/the-strategy-is-delivery-again/.

3. Jaykumar Menon, interview with author, February 15, 2020.

4. Genrich Altshuller, *And Suddenly the Inventor Appeared: TRIZ, the Theory of Inventive Problem Solving* (Worcester, MA: Technical Innovation Center, 1996). TRIZ, like other frameworks such as Lean Six Sigma for manufacturing or SCRUM for software development, is very complex and often difficult to adhere to in politically contested and resource-constrained public environments.

5. Alan Newell and Herbert A. Simon, *Human Problem Solving* (New York: Prentice Hall, 1972).

6. Jake Chapman, *System Failure: Why Governments Must Learn to Think Differently*, 2nd ed. (London: Demos, 2004), 19, https://www.demos.co.uk/files /systemfailure2.pdf.

7. Center for International Development at Harvard University, "PDIA Toolkit," Building State Capability, accessed September 23, 2020, https://bsc.cid .harvard.edu/PDIAtoolkit.

8. David Jonassen, *Learning to Solve Problems: A Handbook for Designing Problem-Solving Learning Environments* (Oxfordshire, UK: Taylor and Francis, 2010), 16.

9. Vinod Goel and Peter Pirolli, "The Structure of Design Problem Spaces,"

Cognitive Sciences 16, no. 3 (July 1992): 395–429, https://doi.org/10.1207/s1551
6709cog1603_3.

10. Jonassen, *Learning to Solve Problems*, 19.

11. In fairness, Nesta does some of the most pathbreaking work on collective
    intelligence and has developed the "Collective Intelligence Design Playbook"
    (2019) with strategies for engagement. But this is separate from the innovation
    spiral.

12. Thomas W. Malone and Michael S. Bernstein, eds., *Handbook of Collective
    Intelligence* (Cambridge, MA: MIT Press, 2015).

13. "Building State Capability," https://bsc.cid.harvard.edu.

14. Jeff Ubois, "Seeking Both Problems and Solutions: The MacArthur Foundation's
    100&Change Team Learned a Lot from the First Round of Grants That Will
    Boost Collaboration and Knowledge-Sharing in the Next Round," *Stanford Social
    Innovation Review*, Winter 2019, https://ssir.org/articles/entry/seeking_both
    _problems_and_solutions.

15. Safecast, home page, accessed October 3, 2020, http://www.safecast.org.

16. For an extended case study on Better Reykjavik, see The GovLab, "CrowdLaw
    Case Studies," accessed May 11, 2019, http://congress.crowd.law.

17. Ezra Klein, "The Vox Conversation: Hillary Clinton," *Vox*, June 22, 2016, https://
    www.vox.com/a/hillary-clinton-interview.

18. Simon Willis, "Managing Innovation Teams in Complex Environments,"
    Medium, January 8, 2019, https://medium.com/@simon_30495/manag
    ing-innovation-teams-in-complex-environments-b3b32049c58b.

19. Michael D. Shear, "Obama Lesson: 'Shovel Ready' Not So Ready," *New York
    Times*, October 15, 2010.

20. Peter Baker, "Education of a President," *New York Times*, October 12, 2010.

21. Francis Fukuyama, "What's Wrong with Public Policy Education," *American
    Interest*, August 1, 2018, https://www.the-american-interest.com/2018/08/01
    /whats-wrong-with-public-policy-education/.

22. Jeffrey Drushal and Alex Brubaker, "It's Time to Rebuild Our Culture of
    Deployment Readiness," *Army Sustainment*, February 20, 2018, https://www
    .army.mil/article/200643/its_time_to_rebuild_our_culture_of_deployment
    _readiness.

23. ICMA, "Innovations and Emerging Practices in Local Government 2016 Survey
    Summary Report of Results," 2, accessed September 27, 2020, https://icma.org
    /sites/default/files/309068_ICMA%20Innovation%20Survey%20Summary
    %20Report.pdf.

24. Nobel Prize, "The Sveriges Riksbank Prize in Economic Sciences in Memory of
    Alfred Nobel," accessed October 12, 2020, https://www.nobelprize.org/prizes
    /economic-sciences/.

25. Abhijit Banerjee et al., "Improving Immunization Coverage in Rural India: A
    Clustered Randomized Controlled Evaluation of Immunization Campaigns with
    and without Incentives," *British Medical Journal*, May 2010, https://economics
    .mit.edu/files/5579.

26. Defense Advanced Research Projects Agency, "Heilmeier Catechism," accessed October 11, 2020, https://www.darpa.mil/work-with-us/heilmeier-catechism.

27. George H. Heilmeier, "Some Reflections on Innovation and Invention," *The Bridge*, Winter 1992, 12–16, https://isi.edu/~johnh/TEACHING/CS651/AR CHIVE/Heilmeier92a.pdf.

4. DEFINING A PUBLIC PROBLEM

1. Skip Descant, "Nashville Experiments with Court Date Text Alerts," *Government Technology*, June 13, 2018, https://www.govtech.com/applications/Nashville -Experiments-with-Court-Date-Text-Alerts.html.

2. Citymart, "How Philadelphia Developed a Comprehensive Smart City Strategy," accessed March 19, 2019, http://info.citymart.com/success-stories.

3. Center for Education Policy Research, "Basic Literacy: Building Children's Potential as Learners," policy brief, November 2019, 3, https://www.inovasi .or.id/wp-content/uploads/2019/10/Policy-Brief-7-Literacy-2011-2019.pdf.

4. George Adam Sukoco Sikatan et al., "Local Problems, Local Solutions to the Indonesian Education Sector," *Building State Capability Blog*, December 6, 2019, https://buildingstatecapability.com/2019/12/06/pdia-course-journey -local-problems-local-solutions-to-the-indonesian-education-sector/.

5. Harry Farra, "The Reflective Thought Process: John Dewey Revisited," *Journal of Creative Behavior* 22, no. 1 (March 1988): 3, Creative Education Foundation, https://doi-org.proxy.library.nyu.edu/10.1002/j.2162-6057.1988.tb01338.x.

6. John Dewey, *The Later Works of John Dewey*, vol. 8, *1925–1953: 1933, Essays and How We Think*, rev. ed., ed. Jo Ann Boydston (Carbondale: Southern Illinois University Press, 1986), 118–124. See also Farra, "Reflective Thought Process."

7. Jacob Getzels and Mihaly Csikszentmihalyi, *The Creative Vision: A Longitudinal Study of Problem Finding in Art* (Hoboken, NJ: Wiley, 1976).

8. Albert Einstein and Leopold Infeld, *The Evolution of Physics: The Growth of Ideas from Early Concepts to Relativity and Quanta* (Cambridge: Cambridge University Press, 1938).

9. Robert Merton and Robert Nisbet, *Contemporary Social Problems: An Introduction to the Sociology of Deviant Behavior and Social Disorganization* (New York: Harcourt, Brace and World, 1961).

10. Getzels and Csikszentmihalyi, *Creative Vision*, 250.

11. Getzels and Csikszentmihalyi, 250.

12. For a brief history of Toyoda's "5 Whys," see "5 Whys," Wikipedia, accessed May 13, 2019, https://en.wikipedia.org/wiki/5_Whys#History.

13. Harold Lasswell, *The Policy Sciences: Recent Developments in Scope and Method* (Stanford, CA: Stanford University Press, 1951); Charles Lindblom, "The Science of 'Muddling Through,'" *Public Administration Review* 19, no. 2 (Spring 1959): 79–88.

14. Seyyed Khandani, "Engineering Design Process," Saylor Academy, August 2005, http://www.saylor.org/site/wp-content/uploads/2012/09/ME101-4.1-Engineering -Design-Process.pdf.

15. Einstein and Infeld, *Evolution of Physics*, 77–78.

16. Brenda Bushouse et al., "Crossing the Divide: Building Bridges between Public Administration Practitioners and Scholars," *Journal of Public Administration Research and Theory: J-PART* 21, supp. 1 (January 2011): i99–i112 ("We specifically propose that the field more fully embrace the notion of engaged scholarship, use innovative teaching techniques that connect theory and practice, and promote opportunities for academic-practitioner exchange.").

17. Travis Wagner, "Using Root Cause Analysis in Public Policy Pedagogy," *Journal of Public Affairs Education* 20, no. 3 (2014): 429–440, http://www.jstor.org /stable/24369813, citing Arnost Vesely, "Problem Delimitation in Public Policy Analysis," *Central European Journal of Public Policy* 1, no. 1 (October 2007): 80–100.

18. The Hallway, University of Washington, https://www.hallway.org/; Harvard Kennedy School Case Program, Harvard University, https://case.hks.harvard.edu/.

19. David Dery, *Problem Definition in Policy Analysis* (Lawrence: University Press of Kansas, 1984), 3.

20. "To date, our students' educational experience was largely within a 'teaching paradigm,' taking lectures and classes traditional formats." Chris McInerney and Maura Adshead, "Problem-Based Learning and Civic Engagement—Shifting the Focus of Learning in Public Policy Education," *PS: Political Science and Politics* 46, no. 3 (July 2013): 634.

21. Malcolm Sparrow, *The Character of Harms: Operational Challenges in Risk Control* (Cambridge: Cambridge University Press, 2008), 51–52.

22. Daniel Katz and Robert Kahn, *The Social Psychology of Organizations* (New York: Wiley, 1966), 277; Dery, *Problem Definition in Policy Analysis*, 94–95.

23. Mark Moore, *Creating Public Value: Strategic Management in Government* (Cambridge, MA: Harvard University Press, 1997), 17.

24. Sanderijn Cels, Jorrit de Jong, and Frans Nauta, *Agents of Change: Strategy and Tactics for Social Innovation* (Washington, DC: Brookings Institution Press, 2012), 53.

25. Thomas Wedell-Wedellsborg, "Are You Solving the Right Problems?," *Harvard Business Review*, January–February 2017, https://hbr.org/2017/01/are-you-solving -the-right-problems.

26. Peter Koen, "Lean Startup in Large Enterprises Using Human-Centered Design Thinking: A New Approach for Developing Transformational and Disruptive Innovations," Howe School of Business at Stevens Institute of Technology, Hoboken, NJ, January 27, 2015, http://dx.doi.org/10.2139/ssrn.2556187. (Large companies, on the basis of implementation experiences from over thirty large companies, typically make the following mistakes: (1) define the problem incorrectly; (2) confuse solution attributes and the solution.)

27. James Anderson (Government Innovation, Bloomberg Philanthropies), interview with author, April 23, 2019.

28. TEDx Talks, "Everyone Has a Problem: Grant Fry—TEDxAlmaCollege," YouTube, February 27, 2015, https://www.youtube.com/watch?v=3lR9TbMY2Cs.

29. The GovLab, "Alan Kantrow: Academy Intro—Defining a Problem," YouTube, July 27, 2016, https://www.youtube.com/watch?v=8Xq2goRGTLo.

30. James Lewis, *Fundamentals of Project Management*, 3rd ed. (New York: AMACOM, 2006), 12.

31. Big Think, "Think Small to Solve Big Problems, with Stephen Dubner," YouTube, July 23, 2014, https://www.youtube.com/watch?v=fypkPgeQxBQ.

32. Paul Glewwe, Albert Park, and Meng Zhao, "A Better Vision for Development: Eyeglasses and Academic Performance in Rural Primary Schools in China" (HKUST IEMS Working Paper No. 2015-37, June 2016), https://www.poverty actionlab.org/sites/default/files/publications/424_542_A%20better%20vision %20for%20development_PaulGlewwe_May2016.pdf.

33. Smarter Crowdsourcing for Zika, The GovLab, "Garbage and Standing Water," June 2017, https://zika.smartercrowdsourcing.org/la-basura-y-el-agua-estancada .html.

34. Russell L. Ackoff, *The Art of Problem Solving* (New York: Wiley, 1978), 52–53.

35. Ackoff, 53–54.

36. Citymart, "How Philadelphia Developed a Comprehensive Smart City Strategy."

37. "Bogotá: Creating a Safer, Shorter and More Engaging School Commute for Bogotá's Youth," Bloomberg Mayors' Challenge, accessed September 27, 2020, https://mayorschallenge.bloomberg.org/ideas/bogota/.

38. "How Complexity Thinking Cut Malnutrition in Vietnam by Two-Thirds," *From Poverty to Power* (blog), November 8, 2013, http://oxfamblogs.org/fp2p/how -complexity-thinking-cut-malnutrition-in-vietnam-by-two-thirds/.

39. DIY Toolkit, "DIY Toolkit: Problem Definition," YouTube, April 15, 2014, http:// www.youtube.com/watch?v=o4dddmOpQ5s.

40. Ken Watanabe, *Problem Solving 101: A Simple Book for Smart People* (Rutherford, NJ: Penguin, 2009).

41. Mark Warren, "The Cure for Cancer Is Data—Mountains of Data," *Wired*, October 19, 2016, https://www.wired.com/2016/10/eric-schadt-biodata-genomics-medi cal-research/.

42. Center for Innovation in Legal Education, "Episode 5.1 Identifying and Defining Problems," YouTube, September 27, 2013, https://www.youtube.com/watch?v =2m-xgti19-U.

43. Watanabe, *Problem Solving 101*.

44. Beth Simone Noveck, "Public Entrepreneurship and Policy Engineering," *Communications of the ACM*, December 2019, 29–31.

45. Eugene Bardach, *A Practical Guide for Policy Analysis: The Eightfold Path to More Effective Problem Solving* (Washington, DC: Congressional Quarterly, 2000), 1–14. See also Dery, *Problem Definition in Policy Analysis*, 14.

46. Michael Cooper, "Defining the Problem: The Most Important Business Skill You've Never Been Taught," *Entrepreneur*, September 26, 2014, http://www .entrepreneur.com/article/237668.

47. Getzels and Csikszentmihalyi, *Creative Vision*, 90.

48. Pagan Kennedy, *Inventology* (New York: Houghton Mifflin Harcourt, 2016), 4.

49. For a paradigmatic example, see Tom Kalil's description of getting excited about other people's ideas. Robert Wiblin and Keiran Harris, "How to Have a Big Impact in Government and Huge Organisations, Based on 16 Years' Experience in the White House," *80,000* podcast, April 23, 2019, https://80000hours.org/podcast/episodes/tom-kalil-government-careers/. ("There are definitely ideas that I have come up with personally, but I think I have a higher than average ability to get excited about other people's ideas. What that means is that the range of things that I can work on goes up considerably. I was not sitting at my desk and saying, 'Gee, I think we should launch a bit neuroscience initiative,' but the fact that a group of scientists and engineers contacted me and told me about this idea and I said, 'Wow, this seems like a big idea' and was able to get excited about pushing it. For me, I didn't need to be the person to originate the idea, I just had to be someone who was in a position to help it in order for me to get intrinsically motivated to work on it.")
50. Tina Seelig, "Shift Your Lens: The Power of Re-Framing Problems," *Stanford eCorner*, January 14, 2013, https://ecorner.stanford.edu/article/shift-your-lens-the-power-of-re-framing-problems/.
51. The GovLab, "Alan Kantrow."
52. Thomas Wedell-Wedellsborg, "Are You Solving the Right Problems?," *Harvard Business Review*, January–February 2017, https://hbr.org/2017/01/are-you-solving-the-right-problems.
53. Harvard Business School, "Karim R. Lakhani," Faculty and Research, accessed October 12, 2020, https://www.hbs.edu/faculty/Pages/profile.aspx?facId=240491&click=bestbet.
54. Hot Mess (PBS), "How to Survive a Climate Disaster," YouTube, June 7, 2018, https://www.youtube.com/watch?v=-C6UQiUt-eg.
55. Citymart, "How Philadelphia Developed a Comprehensive Smart City Strategy."
56. Molly Jackman, "ALEC's Influence over Lawmaking in State Legislatures," Brookings Institution, December 6, 2013, http://www.brookings.edu/articles/alecs-influence-over-lawmaking-in-state-legislatures/.
57. Public Entrepreneurship: Class Project with New York City Council, https://www.publicentrepreneur.org/copy-of-tcs-governing-the-city.
58. Citymart, "How Philadelphia Developed a Comprehensive Smart City Strategy."
59. The GovLab, "City Challenge Project," accessed October 10, 2020, https://www.thegovlab.org/project-city-challenges.html.
60. The GovLab, "Multi-City Challenge Mexico 2020," accessed September 27, 2020, http://multicitychallenge.org/.
61. Matthew Scheider, "Problem, Definition of," in *Encyclopedia of Community Policing and Problem Solving*, ed. Kenneth Peak (Los Angeles: Sage, 2013).
62. TEDx Talks, "Everyone Has a Problem."
63. Karen Schrier, *Knowledge Games: How Playing Games Can Solve Problems, Create Insight, and Make Change* (Baltimore: Johns Hopkins University Press, 2016), 66.
64. Dery, *Problem Definition in Policy Analysis*, 29.

65. The GovLab, "Problem Definition by Alph Bingham," YouTube, June 27, 2016, http://www.youtube.com/watch?v=3tYj_6Pbf04.

66. Dalgobind Mahto and Anjani Kumar, "Application of Root Cause Analysis in Improvement of Product Quality and Productivity," *Journal of Industrial Engineering and Management* 1, no. 2 (2008): 16–53, http://dx.doi.org/10.3926/jiem .v1n2.p16–53.

67. Travis Wagner, "Using Root Cause Analysis in Public Policy Pedagogy," *Journal of Public Affairs Education* 20, no. 3 (2014): 429–440, http://www.jstor.org /stable/24369813. See also Mahto and Kumar, "Application of Root Cause Analysis."

68. Bjorn Andersen and Tom Fagerhaug, *Root Cause Analysis: Simplified Tools and Techniques* (Milwaukee: ASQ Quality Press, 2000).

69. The GovLab, "Problem Definition by Alph Bingham."

70. Wagner, "Using Root Cause Analysis." See also Shri Ashok Sarkar, Arup Ranjan Mukhopadhyay, and Sadhan Kumar Ghosh, "Root Cause Analysis, Lean Six Sigma and Test of Hypothesis," *TQM Journal* 25, no. 2 (2013): 170–185, https:// doi.org/10.1108/17542731311299609.

71. Center for International Development at Harvard University, "PDIA Toolkit," Building State Capability, accessed October 10, 2020, https://bsc.cid.harvard .edu/PDIAtoolkit.

72. Seelig, "Shift Your Lens."

73. Dery, *Problem Definition in Policy Analysis*, xi.

74. Seelig, "Shift Your Lens."

5. HUMAN-CENTERED DESIGN, OR UNDERSTANDING PROBLEMS WITH HELP FROM PEOPLE

1. Lee Mindel, "Inside Vienna's Church of St. Leopold and Sanatorium Purkersdorf," *Architectural Digest*, March 31, 2015, https://www.architecturaldigest.com /story/otto-wagner-josef-hoffmann-vienna-article.

2. Mark Lamster, "The Virtues, and Perils, of Design Thinking," *Architect*, July 8, 2010, https://www.architectmagazine.com/design/the-virtues-and-perils-of -design-thinking_o.

3. Adam M. Grant and James Berry, "The Necessity of Others Is the Mother of Invention: Intrinsic and Prosocial Motivations, Perspective Taking, and Creativity," *Academy of Management Journal* 54, no. 1 (2011): 73–96.

4. "User-Centered Design," in *Berkshire Encyclopedia of Human-Computer Interaction*, ed. William Sims Bainbridge, vol. 2 (Great Barrington, MA: Berkshire, 2004), 763–768.

5. Herbert Simon, *The Sciences of the Artificial* (Cambridge, MA: MIT Press, 1969). Simon identifies design as the knowledge that is in the domain of professions such as engineering, management, or medicine. He believed that these fields all concern "what ought to be" and contrast with the sciences, which are concerned with "what is."

6. See, generally, Peter Rowe, *Design Thinking* (Cambridge, MA: MIT Press, 1987).

7. Russell L. Ackoff, *The Art of Problem Solving* (New York: Wiley, 1978), 38.

8. Jo Szczepanska, "Design Thinking Origin Story Plus Some of the People Who Made It All Happen," *Medium*, January 13, 2017, https://medium.com/@szcz panks/design-thinking-where-it-came-from-and-the-type-of-people-who-made -it-all-happen-dc3a05411e53.

9. John Zeisel, *Inquiry by Design* (New York: Norton, 2006) (a classic text on environmental behavior research methods, explaining the similarities and differences between research and design methods).

10. Ganesh Nathan, "Design Thinking Approach to Ethical (Responsible) Techno- logical Innovation," in *Responsible Research and Innovation: From Concepts to Practices*, ed. Robert Gianni, John Pearson, and Bernard Reber (Abingdon, UK: Routledge, 2017).

11. International Standardization Organization, "Ergonomics of Human-System Interaction—Part 210: Human-Centered Design for Interactive Systems," 2010.

12. Donald A. Norman and Pieter Jan Stappers, "DesignX: Complex Sociotechnical Systems," *She Ji: The Journal of Design, Economics, and Innovation* 1, no. 2 (2015): 83–106, https://doi.org/10.1016/j.sheji.2016.01.002.

13. Elizabeth Sanders, Erika Braun, and Sapna Singh, "Co-Designing with Commu- nities," Community Engagement Conference, The Ohio State University, January 24, 2018, https://kb.osu.edu/bitstream/handle/1811/84231/1/ES_V6 _2018_Sanders.pdf, 5.

14. Smart Start, https://smartstart.services.govt.nz/#47.

15. J. B. Wogan, "How Bloomberg's Still Changing the Way Cities Operate," *Governing*, April 2015, https://www.governing.com/topics/urban/gov-bloom berg-philanthrophies-urban-innovation.html.

16. Beth Simone Noveck, *Smart Citizens, Smarter State: The Technologies of Expertise and the Future of Governing* (Cambridge, MA: Harvard University Press, 2015), chap. 2.

17. Noveck, 47–48.

18. Neal K. Katyal, "Why Barr Can't Whitewash the Mueller Report: We Have a System in Place for Our Government to Uncover Evidence against a Sitting President. And It's Working," *New York Times*, May 1, 2019, https://www .nytimes.com/2019/05/01/opinion/barr-mueller-report.html.

19. Paul Jaeger and John Bertot, "Designing, Implementing, and Evaluating User-Centered and Citizen-Centered E-Government," *International Journal of Electronic Government Research* 6, no. 2 (April 2010): 1–7, https://doi. org/10.4018/jegr.2010040101; Noveck, *Smart Citizens*.

20. Pete Buttigieg, *Shortest Way Home: One Mayor's Challenge and a Model for America's Future* (New York: Liveright, 2019), 88.

21. James Scott, *Seeing Like a State: How Certain Schemes to Improve the Human Condition Have Failed* (New Haven, CT: Yale University Press, 1999), 2.

22. Max Weber, *From Max Weber: Essays in Sociology*, ed. H. H. Gerth and C. Wright Mills (1948; repr., Abingdon, UK: Routledge, 1991), 216.

23. Noveck, *Smart Citizens*.

24. Scott, *Seeing Like a State*, 103–147; Jane Jacobs, *The Death and Life of Great American Cities* (New York: Vintage, 1992).

25. Bruce Nussbaum, "Design Thinking Is a Failed Experiment. So What's Next?," *Fast Company*, April 5, 2011, http://www.fastcodesign.com/1663558/beyond -design-thinking.

26. Bo Burlingame, "The Entrepreneur of the Decade: An interview with Steven Jobs, Inc.'s Entrepreneur of the Decade," *Inc.*, April 1, 1989.

27. Alev Scott and Andronike Makres, *Power and the People: Five Lessons from the Birthplace of Democracy* (London: Riverrun, 2019), 42 (citing Thucydides 2.37).

28. Brook Manville and Josiah Ober, *A Company of Citizens: What the World's First Democracy Teaches Leaders about Creating Great Organizations* (Brighton, MA: Harvard Business Review Press, 2003).

29. Code for America, "Get CalFresh: Improving How Government Delivers Food Assistance to Californians in Need," accessed October 20, 2020, https://www .codeforamerica.org/programs/getcalfresh.

30. Lucy Kimbell, *Applying Design Approaches to Policy Making: Discovering Policy Lab* (Brighton, UK: University of Brighton Press, 2015), 60, https://researchingde signforpolicy.files.wordpress.com/2015/10/kimbell_policylab_report.pdf.

31. Beth Noveck and Rod Glover, "Today's Problems, Yesterday's Toolkit," ANZSOG, August 13, 2019, 31.

32. Elizabeth M. Gerber, Jeanne Marie Olson, and Rebecca L. D. Komarek, "Extracur ricular Design-Based Learning: Preparing Students for Careers in Innovation," *International Journal of Engineering Education* 28, no. 2 (2011): 317–324.

33. Australian Government, Department of Industry, "Australian Biz Lab Academy," accessed December 30, 2019, https://www.industry.gov.au/government-to-gov ernment/bizlab-academy/. See also Australia's "BizLab Human-Centered Design Curriculum," OECD, accessed October 10, 2020, https://oecd-opsi.org /toolkits/australias-bizlab-human-centered-design-curriculum/.

34. Kristofer Kelly-Frere and Jonathan Veale, "Essay: Advanced Design for the Public Sector," *Jonathan Veale Blog, Medium*, January 7, 2018, https://medium.com /@jonathanveale/essay-advanced-design-for-the-public-sector-223dedo8f7d9.

35. Fredrik Olausson, "Policy Labs for Quick Tests Done Right," *Swedish Design Research Journal* 1 (2017), http://www.svid.se/en/Research/Design-Research -Journal/Read-and-download-Design-Research-Journal/Swedish-Design-Research -Journal-no-1-2017/Policy-Labs-for-quick-tests-done-right-/.

36. Maria Hermosilla, "MindLab: The Evolution of a Public Innovation Lab," *The GovLab Blog*, March 7, 2016, http://thegovlab.org/mindlab-the-evolution-of-a -public-innovation-lab/.

37. Henry Chesbrough and Jim Spohrer, "A Research Manifesto for Services Science," *Communications of the ACM* 49, no. 7 (July 2006): 35–40.

38. Lucy Kimbell, "Rethinking Design Thinking: Part 1," *Design and Culture* 3, no. 3 (April 2015), https://www.tandfonline.com/doi/pdf/10.2752/175470811X 13071166525216?needAccess=true; Daniela Sangiorgi, "Design Strategies for

Paradigm Shifts," *Foresight* 17, no. 4 (August 2015): 332–348, doi: 10.1108/FS-08-2013-0041.

39. Emma Diamond, "The Systemic Challenge of Childhood Obesity," *FutureGov Blog*, November 12, 2019, https://blog.wearefuturegov.com/the-systemic-challenge-of-childhood-obesity-60b89355bd0b.

40. Theo Keane, "Human-Centred Design," *Nesta Blog*, July 4, 2013, http://www.nesta.org.uk/blog/human-centred-design/.

41. Bella Martin and Bruce Hanington, *Universal Methods of Design* (Beverly, MA: Rockport, 2019).

42. Rikke Dam and Teo Siang, "Personas—A Simple Introduction," Interaction Design Foundation, May 6, 2019, https://www.interaction-design.org/literature/article/personas-why-and-how-you-should-use-them.

43. Matthew Salganik, *Bit by Bit: Social Research in the Digital Age* (Princeton, NJ: Princeton University Press, 2017), 87–88.

44. Sam Ladner, *Practical Ethnography: A Guide to Doing Ethnography in the Private Sector* (Oxfordshire, UK: Taylor and Francis, 2014), 12.

45. OECD, *Innovation Skills in the Public Sector: Building Capabilities in Chile*, OECD Public Governance Reviews (Paris: OECD, 2017), 33, http://dx.doi.org/10.1787/9789264273283-en.

46. Nesta, IDEO, and Design for Europe, *Designing for Public Services* (London: Nesta, 2017), 30, https://media.nesta.org.uk/documents/nesta_ideo_guide_jan2017.pdf.

47. Ladner, *Practical Ethnography*, 106.

48. Mary Jo Bitner, Amy Ostrom, and Felicia Morgan, "Service Blueprinting: A Practical Technique for Service Innovation," *California Management Review* 50, no. 3 (Spring 2008): 66–94; see also J. Will Roberts, "The Use of Service Blue-Printing as a Method of Improving Non-Academic College Student Experiences" (EdD diss., Creighton University, 2017), ProQuest, http://search.proquest.com/docview/1896975489/fulltextPDF/4A30D36C6B6A40B8PQ/2?accountid=12768.

49. Lynn G. Shostack, "Designing Services That Deliver," *Harvard Business Review*, January 1984, http://hbr.org/1984/01/designing-services-that-deliver.

50. Beth Simone Noveck and Daniel Goroff, *Information for Impact: Liberating Nonprofit Sector Data* (New York: Aspen Institute, 2013).

51. Peter Olsen-Phillips, "IRS Releases Flood of Searchable Charity Data," *Chronicle of Philanthropy*, June 16, 2016.

52. Matthew Salganik and Karen Levy, "Wiki Surveys: Open and Quantifiable Social Data Collection," *PLoS ONE* 10, no. 5 (2015), https://journals.plos.org/plosone/article?id=10.1371/journal.pone.0123483.

53. Matthew Salganik, "3.5.2 Wiki Surveys," in *Bit by Bit: Social Research in the Digital Age* (Princeton, NJ: Princeton University Press, 2017), https://www.bitbybitbook.com/en/asking-questions/how/wiki/.

54. CrowdLaw for Congress, The GovLab, "Governador Pergunta Municipal Open Innovation," accessed October 12, 2020, https://congress.crowd.law/case-aarp

-and-all-our-ideas.html. See also All Our Ideas, "About This Project," accessed October 12, 2020, https://www.allourideas.org/about.

55. "Four Tips for Making a Successful Wiki Survey," *All Our Ideas Blog*, August 11, 2010, https://blog.allourideas.org/post/937848848four-tips-for-making-a-suc cessful-wiki-survey.

56. The GovLab and AARP, "Identifying the Opportunities and Challenges of Using Big Health Data," accessed October 12, 2020, http://aarp.crowd.law.

57. Tom Atlee, "vTaiwan (Part 2)—Notes on Aspects of the vTaiwan Phenome-non," *Tom Atlee Blog*, April 23, 2018, http://www.tomatleeblog.com/archives /175327882.

58. Pol.is, "Report: Overview," accessed May 7, 2019, https://pol.is/report/r6xd52 6vyjyjrj9navxrj.

59. Emi Kolawole, "Empathy," IDEO Design Kit, accessed October 20, 2020, http:// www.designkit.org/mindsets/4.

60. Adam Gopnik, "Younger Longer," *New Yorker*, May 20, 2019.

61. Erika Weisz and Jamil Zaki, "Empathy-Building Interventions: A Review of Existing Work and Suggestions for Future Directions," in *The Oxford Handbook of Compassion Science*, ed. Emma M. Seppälä et al. (Oxford: Oxford University Press, 2017), chap. 16, doi: 10.1093/oxfordhb/9780190464684.013.1.

62. Paul Bloom, *Against Empathy: The Case for Rational Compassion* (New York: Ecco, 2016).

63. Sabine Junginger, "Design Research and Practice for the Public Good: A Reflection," *She Ji: The Journal of Design, Economics, and Innovation* 3, no. 4 (Winter 2017): 290–302, https://doi.org/10.1016/j.sheji.2018.02.005.

64. Karl Pillemer, Lakshminarayanan Subramanian, and Nathaniel Hupert, "The Importance of Long-Term Care Populations in Models of COVID-19," *Journal of the American Medical Association (JAMA)* 324, no. 1 (2020): 25–26, https:// jamanetwork.com/journals/jama/fullarticle/2767062?resultClick=1.

65. Priyanka Dutt, "Design Thinking and Health Communication: Learning from Failure," *Media Action Insight* (blog), BBC, April 20, 2017, https://www.bbc .co.uk/blogs/mediaactioninsight/entries/bbf66eff-b109-4f14-8cd9-8473442a7da9.

66. IDEO, "Redefining Parent-Child Engagement," accessed May 7, 2019, https:// www.ideo.org/project/vroom.

67. Eric Nee, "Don't Forget the Public Sector," *Stanford Social Innovation Review*, Spring 2020, https://ssir.org/articles/entry/dont_forget_the_public_sector.

68. Anna Rylander, "Design Thinking as Knowledge Work: Epistemological Foundations and Practical Implications," *Design Management Journal*, December 29, 2009, https://doi.org/10.1111/j.1942-5074.2009.00003.x. See also Lucy Kimbell, "Rethinking Design Thinking: Part 1," *Design and Culture* 3, no. 3 (April 2015): 289, https://www.tandfonline.com/doi/pdf/10.2752/1754708 11X13071166525216?needAccess=true.

69. Antonella Guiddoccio (former designer with LabGob Argentina), interview with author, May 4, 2019.

70. Tara McGuinness and Anne-Marie Slaughter, "The New Practice of Public Problem Solving," *Stanford Social Innovation* Review, Spring 2019, https://ssir .org/articles/entry/the_new_practice_of_public_problem_solving#.

71. Tim Brown, *Change by Design: How Design Thinking Transforms Organizations and Inspires Innovation* (New York: HarperCollins, 2009); Christian Bason, *Design for Policy* (Brighton, UK: Routledge, 2014).

72. Chelsea Mauldin et al., "High-Need Student Services," Policy Lab, accessed May 13, 2019, http://publicpolicylab.org/projects/high-need-student-services/.

73. Liana Dragoman, "By the People: A New Series on Participatory Service Design," *Blog of the City of Philadelphia*, January 29, 2019, https://www.phila.gov/2019 -01-29-by-the-people-a-new-series-on-participatory-service-design/.

74. Andrew Young et al., *People-Led Innovation: Toward a Methodology for Solving Urban Problems in the 21st Century* (The GovLab, January 2018), 16–17, http:// www.thegovlab.org/static/files/publications/people-led.pdf.

75. Roger Martin, *The Design of Business: Why Design Thinking Is the Next Competitive Advantage* (Brighton, MA: Harvard Business Review Press, 2009).

76. Barney Glaser and Anselm Strauss, *Discovery of Grounded Theory: Strategies for Qualitative Research* (Chicago: Aldine, 1967).

77. Mary Jo Bitner, Amy Ostrom, and Felicia Morgan, "Service Blueprinting: A Practical Technique for Service Innovation." *California Management Review* 50, no. 3 (Spring 2008): 66–94.

78. G. Lynn Shostack, "Designing Services That Deliver," *Harvard Business Review*, January–February 1984, http://hbr.org/1984/01/designing-services-that-deliver.

79. "Four Tips for Making a Successful Wiki Survey," *All Our Ideas Blog*, August 11, 2010, https://blog.allourideas.org/post/937848848/four-tips-for-making-a-suc cessful-wiki-survey.

6. UNDERSTANDING PROBLEMS USING DATA

1. Office of the Governor of New Jersey, "Transcript: April 6th, 2020 Coronavirus Briefing Media," April 7, 2020, https://www.nj.gov/governor/news/news /562020/20200407b.shtml.

2. Teo Armus, "Social Distancing a Week Earlier Could Have Saved 36,000 American Lives, Study Says," *Washington Post*, May 21, 2020.

3. Jordan Weissman, "It Sure Looks like the Trump Administration Used Some Bad, High School–Level Math to Justify 'Reopening' the Economy," *Slate*, May 6, 2020, https://slate.com/business/2020/05/trump-models-coronavirus-dumb .html.

4. Mitch Landrieu, "New Orleans' Top Priority: Cut Its Murder Rate," CNN, December 16, 2014, https://money.cnn.com/2014/12/09/news/economy /new-orleans-landrieu/index.html.

5. "30-2-2 Programs Encourage Companies to Hire Ex-Offenders," Jails to Jobs, February 1, 2018, https://www.jailstojobs.org/30-2-2-programs-encourage -companies-hire-ex-offenders/.

6. "New Orleans: Lowest Number of Killings in 47 Years," *US News*, January 1,

2019, https://www.usnews.com/news/best-states/louisiana/articles/2019-01-01/new-orleans-lowest-number-of-killings-in-47-years.

7. City of Boston Mayor's Office, "New Investments to Aid Emergency Medical Services Response Times," March 30, 2018, https://www.boston.gov/news/new-investments-aid-emergency-medical-services-response-times.

8. City of Boston Mayor's Office.

9. Alexi Cohan, "EMS Facts and Figures," *Boston Herald*, April 29, 2019, https://www.bostonherald.com/2019/04/29/boston-ems-facts-and-figures/.

10. Shelley H. Metzenbaum, "The Future of Data and Analytics," in *Government for the Future: Reflection and Vision for Tomorrow's Leaders*, ed. Mark A. Abramson, Daniel J. Chenok, and John M. Kamensky (Lanham, MD: Rowman and Littlefield, 2018), 243.

11. Stephen Goldsmith and Susan Crawford, *The Responsive City: Engaging Communities through Data-Smart Governance* (New York: Wiley, 2014), 3.

12. Justin Longo and Alan Rodney Dobell, "The Limits of Policy Analytics: Early Examples and the Emerging Boundary of Possibilities" (University of Victoria White Paper, 2018), 5, https://dspace.library.uvic.ca/bitstream/handle/1828/10364/Longo_Justin_PolitGovern_2018.pdf.

13. Elizabeth Day, Maria Fitzpatrick, and Thomas O'Toole, "NASPAA Data Science Curriculum for Public Service Summary of Proposed Approach at Cornell University's Institute for Public Affairs," Network of Schools of Public Policy, Affairs, and Administration (NASPAA), September 2019, https://www.naspaa.org/sites/default/files/docs/2019-09/Cornell%20CIPA%20NASPAA%20Data%20Science.pdf.

14. Day, Fitzpatrick, and O'Toole, 2.

15. Patrick Fiorenza, "Government Workforce in Focus: Closing the Data and Analytics Skills Gap," GovLoop, November 21, 2014, https://www.govloop.com/resources/government-workforce-focus-closing-data-skills-gap/.

16. Beth Simone Noveck and Rod Glover, "The Public Problem Solving Imperative," ANZSOG, August 13, 2019, https://www.anzsog.edu.au/resource-library/news-media/todays-problems-yesterdays-toolkit-public-service.

17. "LinkedIn Workforce Report: United States, August 2018," *Economic Graph* (blog), LinkedIn, August 10, 2018, https://economicgraph.linkedin.com/resources/linkedin-workforce-report-august-2018?trk=lilblog_08-20-18_data-scientists-America-great_tl&cid=70132000001AyziAAC.

18. Jascha Franklin-Hodge, foreword to *The Smart Enough City: Putting Technology in Its Place to Reclaim*, by Ben Green (Cambridge, MA: MIT Press, 2019), xi.

19. Metzenbaum, "Future of Data and Analytics," 244–245.

20. "Flint, Michigan: Winner," *Engaged Cities Award Blog*, Cities of Service, accessed October 12, 2020, https://engagedcities.jhu.edu/flint-michigan-2019-winner/; Christina Kelly, Director of Planning and Neighborhood Revitalization, Genesee County Land Bank Authority, interview with author, November 14, 2019.

21. Quoted in Svetlana Sicular, "Gartner's Big Data Definition Consists of Three Parts, Not to Be Confused with Three 'V's," *Forbes*, May 27, 2013.

22. Mansoor Iqbal, "Tinder Revenue and Usage Statistics (2018)," *Business of Apps*, February 27, 2019, https://www.businessofapps.com/data/tinder-statistics/#1; and see Zephoria, "Strategic Insights: The Top 20 Valuable Facebook Statistics —Updated July 2019," July 2019, https://zephoria.com/top-15-valuable-facebook -statistics/.

23. Matthew J. Salganik, *Bit by Bit* (Princeton, NJ: Princeton University Press, 2019), 16, 82–83.

24. Diana Farrell et al., "The Online Platform Economy in 27 Metro Areas: The Experience of Drivers and Lessons," JPMorgan Chase & Co. Institute, April 2019, https://institute.jpmorganchase.com/content/dam/jpmc/jpmorgan -chase-and-co/institute/pdf/institute-ope-cities-exec-summary.pdf. ("The JPMorgan Chase Institute is harnessing the scale and scope of one of the world's leading firms to explain the global economy as it truly exists. Its mission is to help decision-makers—policymakers, businesses, and nonprofit leaders— appreciate the scale, granularity, diversity, and interconnectedness of the global economic system and use better facts, timely data, and thoughtful analysis to make smarter decisions to advance global prosperity. Drawing on JPMorgan Chase's unique proprietary data, expertise, and market access, the Institute develops analyses and insights on the inner workings of the global economy, frames critical problems, and convenes stakeholders and leading thinkers.")

25. mongoDB, "Unstructured Data in Big Data," accessed July 29, 2019, https:// www.mongodb.com/scale/unstructured-data-in-big-data.

26. Seth Stephens-Davidowitz, "The Cost of Racial Animus on a Black Candidate: Evidence Using Google Search Data," *Journal of Public Economics* 118 (2014): 26–40, https://people.cs.umass.edu/~brenocon/smacss2015/papers/Stephens Dawidowitz2014.pdf.

27. Jens Ludwig, Jeffrey B. Liebman, Jeffrey R. Kling, Greg J. Duncan, Lawrence F. Katz, Ronald C. Kessler, and Lisa Sanbonmatsu, "What Can We Learn about Neighborhood Effects from the Moving to Opportunity Experiment?," *American Journal of Sociology* 114, no. 1 (July 2008): 144–145, https://doi.org/10.1086 /588741.

28. Louisiana Department of Health, "Louisiana Receives Approval for Unique Strategy to Enroll SNAP Beneficiaries in Expanded Medicaid Coverage," press release, June 1, 2016, http://ldh.la.gov/index.cfm/newsroom/detail/3838.

29. Brian Heaton, "New York City Fights Fires with Data," *Emergency Management*, GovTech, May 18, 2015, https://www.govtech.com/em/safety/New-York-City -Fights-Fire-Data.html.

30. Jenni Bergal, "To Combat Potholes, Cities Turn to Technology," *FutureStructure*, GovTech, June 18, 2018, https://www.govtech.com/fs/infrastructure/To-Com bat-Potholes-Cities-Turn-to-Technology.html.

31. Beth Simone Noveck, "Five Hacks for Digital Democracy," *Nature* 544, no. 7650 (April 19, 2017): 287–288.

32. Daniel T. O'Brien, *The Urban Commons: How Data and Technology Can Rebuild Our Communities* (Cambridge, MA: Harvard University Press, 2018).

33. O'Brien, 3.

34. City of Chicago Mayor's Press Office, "Chicago Department of Streets and Sanitation Crews Increase Preventive Rodent Baiting by 30 Percent over 2012: Resident Requests for Rodent Control Services Down 15 Percent," press release, July 2, 2013, https://www.chicago.gov/city/en/depts/mayor/press_room/press _releases/2013/july_2013/chicago_departmentofstreetsandsanitationcrews increasepreventiver.html.

35. Julia Lane, "Data Analytical Thinking and Methods I: How to Define a Research Question and Introduction to Statistical Approaches to Draw Inference," recorded lecture for "Solving Public Problems with Data," The GovLab, 2017, http://sppd.thegovlab.org/lectures/data-analytical-thinking-and-methods-i -how-to-define-a-research-question-and-introduction-to-statistical-approaches -to-draw-inference.html.

36. John Byrne, "The Plural of Anecdote Is Not Data," *Skeptical Medicine Blog*, accessed October 12, 2020, https://sites.google.com/site/skepticalmedicine /the-plural-of-anecdote-is-not-data.

37. Beth Simone Noveck, *Smart Citizens, Smarter State: The Technologies of Expertise and the Future of Governing* (Cambridge, MA: Harvard University Press, 2015).

38. Rashida Richardson, "Can Technology Help Undo the Wrongs of the Past?," *Medium* (August 10, 2018).

39. Christina Rogawski, Stefaan Verhulst, and Andrew Young, "Kennedy vs. The City of Zanesville, United States: Open Data as Evidence," The GovLab, accessed October 3, 2020, https://odimpact.org/case-kennedy-vs-the-city-of-zanesville- united-states.html.

40. ProPublica, "Documenting Hate," accessed October 3, 2020, https://projects. propublica.org/graphics/hatecrimes; "Fatal Force," *Washington Post*, September 28, 2020, https://www.washingtonpost.com/graphics/investigations/police -shootings-database/; Jackson Heart Study, accessed October 3, 2020, https:// www.jacksonheartstudy.org.

41. Centers for Disease Control, "COVID-19 Hospitalization and Death by Race/ Ethnicity," accessed October 10, 2020, https://www.cdc.gov/coronavirus/2019 -ncov/covid-data/investigations-discovery/hospitalization-death-by-race-ethnicity .html.

42. William Josiah Goode and Paul Hatt, *Methods in Social Research* (New York: McGraw-Hill, 1952), 56. See also Ethel Shanas, "Review of William Josiah Goode and Paul Hatt, *Methods in Social Research*," *American Journal of Psychology* 59, no. 6 (1954): 595, https://www.jstor.org/stable/2772617.

43. Jessica Gover, "How to Do Data Analytics in Government," GovTech, July 16, 2018, https://www.govtech.com/data/How-to-Do-Data-Analytics-in-Government .html.

44. NYC Analytics, "Mayor's Office of Data Analytics (MODA)," accessed July 29, 2019, https://www1.nyc.gov/assets/analytics/downloads/pdf/MODA-project -process.pdf.

45. See "CDC Diabetes Cost-Effectiveness Group: Cost-Effectiveness of Intensive

Glycemic Control, Intensified Hypertension Control, and Serum Cholesterol Level Reduction for Type 2 Diabetes," *Journal of the American Medical Association* 287, no. 19 (2002): 2542–2551, cited in Rebecca Myerson et al., "Medicaid Eligibility Expansions May Address Gaps in Access to Diabetes Medications," *Health Affairs (Project Hope)* 37, no. 8 (2018): 1200–1207, doi: 10.1377/hlthaff .2018.0154.

46. Mejora Tu Escuela, http://mejoratuescuela.org.

47. Stefaan Verhulst and Andrew Young, "The Global Impact of Open Data: Key Findings from Detailed Case Studies around the World" (The GovLab white paper, 2016), 207.

48. Carter Hewgley, "Discovering and Collecting Data: Practical Advice for Government Managers," recorded lecture for "Solving Public Problems with Data," The GovLab, 2017, http://sppd.thegovlab.org/lectures/discovering-and-collecting -data-practical-advice-for-government-managers.html.

49. See Data Coalition, "The DATA Act," accessed July 30, 2019, https://www .datacoalition.org/issues/data-act/; US Census Bureau, "Explore Data," accessed July 30, 2019, https://www.census.gov/data.html; FBI, "Uniform Crime Reporting," accessed September 22, 2020, https://www.fbi.gov/services/cjis /ucr.

50. See Open Data Census, https://census.okfn.org/en/latest/.

51. US Census Bureau, "Data," accessed July 29, 2019, https://www.census.gov /data.html.

52. Humanitarian Data Exchange, https://data.humdata.org/.

53. National Neighborhood Indicators Partnership, "Data Sources," accessed July 29, 2019, https://www.neighborhoodindicators.org/data-tech/sources; Urban Institute, "Data/Viz," accessed July 29, 2019, https://www.urban.org/data-viz.

54. Alexander V. Laskin, *Social, Mobile, and Emerging Media around the World* (Lanham, MD: Rowman and Littlefield, 2018); Stefaan Verhulst and Andrew Young, "The Potential of Social Media Intelligence to Improve People's Lives," The GovLab, accessed October 12, 2020, http://datacollaboratives.org/social -media.html.

55. Stefaan Verhulst, "Building the Smarter State: The Role of Data Labs," Living Library, December 13, 2017, https://thelivinglib.org/ building-the-smarter-state-the-role-of-data-labs/.

56. New Jersey's Education to Earnings Data System is available at http://njed2 earndata.org/.

57. Office of Management and Budget, Executive Office of the President, "Analytical Perspectives, Budget of the United States Government, Fiscal Year 2016," August 9, 2017, https://obamawhitehouse.archives.gov/sites/default/files /omb/budget/fy2016/assets/spec .pdf.

58. Anirudh Dinesh, "Building the Smarter State: The Role of Data Labs," *Medium*, December 13, 2017, https://medium.com/data-labs/building-the-smarter-state -the-role-of-data-labs-5b5428920f0f.

59. Fred Wulczyn, Senior Research Fellow, Chapin Hall at the University of

Chicago, interview with author, July 5, 2017. See also The GovLab, "Data Labs: The Center for State Child Welfare Data," December 12, 2017, https://medium .com/data-labs/the-center-for-state-child-welfare-data-fbe64f1b743.

60. See Actionable Intelligence for Social Policy, home page, accessed October 3, 2020, https://www.aisp.upenn.edu.

61. Executive Office of the President, National Science and Technology Council, "Smart Disclosure and Consumer Decision Making: Report of the Task Force on Smart Disclosure," May 2013, https://obamawhitehouse.archives.gov/sites /default/files/microsites/ostp/report_of_the_task_force_on_smart_disclosure.pdf.

62. UK government, "Accessing the Justice Data Lab Service," last updated May 25, 2018, https://www.gov.uk/government/publications/justice-data-lab?source =post_page.

63. Benedict Rickey, "Unlocking Offending Data: How Access to Offending Data Could Help Charities Improve Outcomes for Offenders," New Philanthropy Capital (NPC), December 11, 2012, https://www.thinknpc.org/resource-hub /unlocking-offending-data/?source=post_page.

64. UK Ministry of Justice, "Justice Data Lab: General Annex to Accompany Re- Offending Reports," 2017, https://assets.publishing.service.gov.uk/government /uploads/system/uploads/attachment_data/file/650894/jdl-general-annex -oct-17.pdf.

65. UK Ministry of Justice, "Justice Data Lab Statistics," last updated July 13, 2017, https://www.gov.uk/government/collections/justice-data-lab-pilot-statistics.

66. Recidiviz, https://www.recidiviz.org/.

67. Safecast, "About," accessed October 12, 2020, https://safecast.org/about/. See also Azby Brown et al., "Safecast: Successful Citizen-Science for Radiation Measurement and Communication after Fukushima," *Journal of Radiological Protection* 36 (2016): S85.

68. Suzanne Perry, "IRS Plans to Begin Releasing Electronic Nonprofit Tax Forms Next Year," *Chronicle of Philanthropy*, June 30, 2015, https://www.philanthropy .com/article/IRS-Plansto-Begin-Releasing/231265.

69. Beth Simone Noveck and Daniel Goroff, *Information for Impact: Liberating Non-Profit Data* (New York: Aspen Institute, 2013), https://assets.aspeninstitute .org/content/uploads/files/content/docs/pubs/Informationfo rImpactReport FINALREPORT_9-26-13.pdf.

70. IRS, "IRS Makes Electronically Filed Form 990 Data Available in New Format," IR-2016-87, June 16, 2016, https://www.irs.gov/uac/newsroom/irs-makeselec tronically-filed-form-990-data-available-in-new-format.

71. Hewgley, "Discovering and Collecting Data."

72. Jessica Gover, "How to Do Data Analytics in Government," GovTech, July 16, 2018, https://www.govtech.com/data/How-to-Do-Data-Analytics-in-Govern ment.html.

73. Mayor of London, "Piloting the London Office of Data Analytics," Nesta, February 2018, https://londondatastore-upload.s3.amazonaws.com/LODA%20 pilot%20report.pdf.

74. Beth Blauer, "Barriers to Building a Data Practice in Government," recorded lecture for "Solving Public Problems with Data," The GovLab, 2017, http://sppd .thegovlab.org/lectures/barriers-to-building-a-data-practice-in-government.html.
75. Salganik, *Bit by Bit*, 41.
76. Henry S. Farber, "Why You Can't Find a Taxi in the Rain and Other Labor Supply Lessons from Cab Drivers," *Quarterly Journal of Economics* 130, no. 4 (2015): 1975–2026, https://www.nber.org/papers/w20604.
77. Scott T. Leatherdale, "Natural Experiment Methodology for Research: A Review of How Different Methods Can Support Real-World Research," *International Journal of Social Research Methodology*, July 2, 2018, https://www.tandfonline .com/doi/full/10.1080/13645579.2018.1488449.
78. World Bank, "Mexico's Opportunidades Program," accessed July 29, 2019, http://web.worldbank.org/archive/website00819C/WEB/PDF/CASE_-62.PDF.
79. Ricardo Perez-Truglia, "The Effects of Income Transparency on Well-Being: Evidence from a Natural Experiment" (National Bureau of Economic Research Working Paper, February 23, 2019), https://www.nber.org/papers/w25622.
80. Noveck, "Five Hacks for Digital Democracy," 287–288.
81. Gideon Mann, "Machine Learning Applications for the Public Sector," recorded lecture for "Solving Public Problems with Data," The GovLab, 2017, http://sppd .thegovlab.org/lectures/machine-learning-applications-for-the-public-sector.html.
82. Scott E. Page, *The Model Thinker* (New York: Basic Books, 2018), 15, 4.
83. Beth Simone Noveck, "In the Fight against Hunger, Technology Brings Power to the People," *Medium*, September 19, 2016, https://medium.com/@bethnoveck /in-the-fight-against-hunger-technology-brings-power-to-the-people-4cb2c5888146.
84. Rockefeller Foundation, "News & Media: New Partnership to Boost Food Security in Africa by Use of Artificial Intelligence," April 2, 2019, https://www.rockefel lerfoundation.org/about-us/news-media/new-partnership-boost-food-security -africa-use-artificial-intelligence/.
85. Rockefeller Foundation, "YieldWise Food Loss," accessed July 29, 2019, https://www.rockefellerfoundation.org/our-work/initiatives/yieldwise/.
86. Betsy Anne Williams et al., "How Algorithms Discriminate Based on Data They Lack: Challenges, Solutions, and Policy Implications," *Journal of Information Policy* 8 (2018): 78–115, http://www.jstor.org/stable/10.5325/jinfopoli.8.2018 .0078.
87. Tonya Riley, "Artificial Intelligence Was Supposed to Reduce Hiring Discrimination. It's Already Backfiring," *Mother Jones*, January 3, 2019, https://www.mother jones.com/politics/2019/01/artificial-intelligence-was-supposed-to-reduce-hiring -discrimination-its-already-backfiring.
88. Solon Barocas and Andrew Selbst, "Losing Out on Employment Because of Big Data Mining," *New York Times*, August 6, 2014, https://www.nytimes.com/room fordebate/2014/08/06/is-big-data-spreading-inequality/losing-out-on-employment -because-of-big-data-mining.
89. Elena Cresci, "Russian Photographer Identifies Strangers with Facial Recognition App," *The Guardian*, April 14, 2016, https://www.theguardian.com/world

/2016/apr/14/russian-photographer-yegor-tsvetkov-identifies-strangers-facial
-recognition-app; Jordan G. Teicher, "What Do Facial Recognition Technologies
Mean for Our Privacy?," *New York Times*, July 18, 2018, https://www.nytimes
.com/2018/07/18/lens/what-do-facial-recognition-technologies-mean-for-our
-privacy.html; Ben Guarino, "Russia's New FindFace App Identifies Strangers
in a Crowd with 70 Percent Accuracy," *Washington Post*, May 18, 2016, https://
www.washingtonpost.com/news/morning-mix/wp/2016/05/18/russias-new
-findface-app-identifies-strangers-in-a-crowd-with-70-percent-accuracy/.

90. Lane, "Data Analytical Thinking and Methods I."

91. Page, *Model Thinker*, 6.

92. Solon Barocas, Andrew Selbst, and Arvind Narayanan, "Fairness in Machine
Learning Limitations and Opportunities" (unpublished ms., February 21, 2020),
22, https://fairmlbook.org/pdf/fairmlbook.pdf.

93. Kelly Dwyer, "Data Breaches Up Nearly 45 Percent According to Annual Review
by Identity Theft Resource Center and Cyberscout," Identity Theft Resource
Center, January 25, 2018, https://www.idtheftcenter.org/data-breaches-up-nearly
-45-percent-according-to-annual-review-by-identity-theft-resource-center-and
-cyberscout/; Cathy O'Neil, *On Being a Data Skeptic* (Beijing: O'Reilly Media, 2013).

94. Latanya Sweeney, "Simple Demographics Often Identify People Uniquely"
(Data Privacy Working Paper 3, Carnegie Mellon University, Pittsburgh,
2000), https://dataprivacylab.org/projects/identifiability/paper1.pdf.

95. Bruce Schneier, "Why 'Anonymous' Data Sometimes Isn't," *Medium*, December
12, 2017, https://www.wired.com/2007/12/why-anonymous-data-sometimes
-isnt/.

96. Adam Entous and Ronan Farrow, "Private Mossad for Hire," *New Yorker*,
February 18, 2019, https://www.newyorker.com/magazine/2019/02/18
/private-mossad-for-hire. See also Christopher Wylie, *Mindf*ck: Cambridge
Analytica and the Plot to Break America* (New York: Random House, 2019).

97. Justin Longo et al., "Technology Use, Exposure to Natural Hazards, and Being
Digitally Invisible: Implications for Policy Analytics," *Policy & Internet* 9, no. 1
(2017): 76–108, https://jlphd.files.wordpress.com/2017/02/longo_et_al-2017
-policy__internet.pdf.

98. As it currently stands, ISPs are required to deliver Form 477 data to the FCC
indicating broadband availability and speed twice a year. But the FCC does not
audit the accuracy of this data, despite the fact that ISPs are heavily incentivized
to overstate speed and availability to downplay industry failures. The FCC also
refuses to make the pricing data provided by ISPs available to the public. Carl
Bode, "How Bad Maps Are Ruining American Broadband," *The Verge*, September
24, 2018, https://www.theverge.com/2018/9/24/17882842/us-internet
-broadband-map-isp-fcc-wireless-competition.

99. Ziad Obermeyer et al., "Dissecting Racial Bias in an Algorithm Used to Manage
the Health of Populations," *Science* 366, no. 6464 (October 25, 2019): 447–453,
doi: 10.1126/science.aax2342. See also Sendhil Mullainathan, "Biased Algorithms Are Easier to Fix Than Biased People: Racial Discrimination by Algo-

rithms or By People Is Harmful—but That's Where the Similarities End," *New York Times*, December 8, 2019, BU5.

100. Breach Level Index, accessed July 29, 2019, https://breachlevelindex.com/.

101. Gartner, "Dirty Data Is a Business Problem, Not an IT Problem," May 13, 2004, https://www.gartner.com/newsroom/id/501733.

102. Mapping Police Violence, https://mappingpoliceviolence.org/; and "Fatal Force," *Washington Post*, accessed June 4, 2020, https://www.washingtonpost.com /graphics/2019/national/police-shootings-2019/.

103. Federal Bureau of Investigation, "UCR Offense Definitions," US Department of Justice, August 9, 2017, https://www.ucrdatatool.gov/offenses.cfm.

104. Janet L. Lauritsen and Daniel L. Cork, *Modernizing Crime Statistics: Report 1: Defining and Classifying Crime* (Washington, DC: National Academies Press, 2016), 10.

105. Eugene Volokh, "Chief Justice Robots," *Reason*, January 14, 2019, https:// reason.com/2019/01/14/chief-justice-robots/; Chris Johnston, "Artificial Intelligence 'Judge' Developed by UCL Computer Scientists," *The Guardian*, October 23, 2016, https://www.theguardian.com/technology/2016/oct/24 /artificial-intelligence-judge-university-college-london-computer-scientists#_=_.

106. Carl Benedikt Frey and Michael A. Osborne, "The Future of Employment: How Susceptible Are Jobs to Computerisation?" (working paper, Oxford Martin School of Business, September 17, 2013), 16.

107. Mireille Hildebrandt et al., "Preregistration of Machine Learning Research Design. Against P-Hacking," in *Being Profiled: Cogitas Ergo Sum*, ed. Emre Bayamlioglu, Irina Baraliuc, Liisa Janssens, and Mireille Hildebrandt (Amsterdam: Amsterdam University Press, 2019), 103–105, https://library.oapen.org /bitstream/handle/20.500.12657/25118/9789048550180.pdf?sequence=1& isAllowed=y; also available at https://papers.ssrn.com/sol3/papers.cfm?abstract _id=3256146.

108. See, e.g., Miranda Bogen and Aaron Rieke, "Help Wanted: An Examination of Hiring Algorithms, Equity, and Bias," *Upturn*, December 2018, https://apo.org .au/sites/default/files/resource-files/2018/12/apo-nid210071-1229641.pdf.

109. Mann, "Machine Learning Applications for the Public Sector."

110. Page, *Model Thinker*, 58.

111. Jeff Larson et al., "How We Analyzed the COMPAS Recidivism Algorithm," ProPublica, May 23, 2016, https://www.propublica.org/article/how-we-ana lyzed-the-compas-recidivism-algorithm. See also Frank Pasquale, *Black Box Society* (Cambridge, MA: Harvard University Press, 2015); and Pedro Domingos, *Master Algorithm* (New York: Basic Books, 2015).

112. Cecilia Muñoz, Megan Smith, and D. J. Patil, *Big Data: A Report on Algorithmic Systems, Opportunity, and Civil Rights* (Washington, DC: Executive Office of the President, White House, May 2016), https://obamawhitehouse.archives.gov /sites/default/files/microsites/ostp/2016_0504_data_discrimination.

113. Megan L. Head et al., "The Extent and Consequences of P-Hacking in Science,"

PLoS Biology, March 13, 2015, https://journals.plos.org/plosbiology/article?id
=10.1371/journal.pbio.1002106.

114. Brett Dahlberg, "Cornell Food Researcher's Downfall Raises Larger Questions
for Science," National Public Radio, September 26, 2018, https://www.npr.org
/sections/thesalt/2018/09/26/651849441/cornell-food-researchers-downfall
-raises-larger-questions-for-science.

115. Tarun Wadhwa, "Lessons from Crowdsourcing: The Boston Bombing
Investigation," *Forbes*, April 25, 2013, https://www.forbes.com/sites/tarun
wadhwa/2013/04/22/lessons-from-crowdsourcing-the-boston-marathon
-bombings-investigation/#20d870cd4424.

116. Jay Caspian Kang, "Should Reddit Be Blamed for the Spreading of a Smear?,"
New York Times, July 25, 2013, https://www.nytimes.com/2013/07/28/maga
zine/should-reddit-be-blamed-for-the-spreading-of-a-smear.html?pagewanted
=all&_r=1&.

117. Nicolas Henke, Ari Libarikian, and Bill Wiseman, "Straight Talk about Big
Data," *McKinsey Quarterly*, October 2016, https://www.mckinsey.com/busi
ness-functions/digital-mckinsey/our-insights/straight-talk-about-big-data.

118. Blauer, "Barriers to Building a Data Practice in Government."

7. USING COLLECTIVE INTELLIGENCE TO SOLVE A PROBLEM

1. The GovLab, "Multi-City Challenge Africa," accessed October 7, 2020, http://
africa.multicitychallenge.org.

2. WeFarm, home page, accessed October 7, 2020, https://wefarm.co/.

3. SynAthina, "Statistics," accessed October 3, 2020, https://www.synathina.gr
/en/synathina/statistics.html.

4. Aaron Smith, "Part 1: Online and Offline Civic Engagement in America,"
Pew Research Center, April 25, 2013, https://www.pewresearch.org/internet
/2013/04/25/part-1-online-and-offline-civic-engagement-in-america/.

5. "Strengthening Democracy: What Do Americans Think?," Public Agenda and
the Kettering Foundation, 2019, https://www.publicagenda.org/wp-content
/uploads/2019/08/Strengthening_Democracy_WhatDoAmericansThink
FINAL.pdf.

6. J. Richard Hackman and Nancy Katz, "Group Behavior and Performance," in
Handbook of Social Psychology, 5th ed., ed. Susan T. Fiske, Daniel T. Gilbert, and
Gardner Lindzey (Hoboken, NJ: Wiley, 2010), 1208–1252.

7. Philip Pettit and Christian List, *Group Agency: The Possibility, Design, and Status
of Corporate Agents* (Oxford: Oxford University Press, 2011).

8. Jeff Howe, *Crowdsourcing: Why the Power of the Crowd Is Driving the Future of
Business* (New York: Random House, 2008). See also Howe, "The Rise of
Crowdsourcing," *Wired*, January 6, 2006.

9. Economic Opportunity Challenge, "Announcing the Economic Opportunity
Challenge," October 15, 2019, https://www.economicopportunitychallenge.org
/news/announcing-the-economic-opportunity-challenge-26; Racial Equity

2020, "Awarding $90 Million," accessed October 17, 2020, https://www.racial
equity2030.org/.

10. The White House, "Transparency and Open Government," January 21, 2009,
https://obamawhitehouse.archives.gov/the-press-office/transparency-and-open
-government.

11. America Creating Opportunities to Meaningfully Promote Excellence in
Technology, Education, and Science Reauthorization Act of 2010 ("America
Competes"), P.L. 111-358 (January 4, 2011).

12. Challenge.gov, "Bridging the Word Gap Challenge," accessed October 12, 2020,
https://www.challenge.gov/toolkit/case-studies/bridging-the-word-gap-challenge/.

13. Solving Public Problems, home page, accessed October 7, 2020, https://solving
publicproblems.org/.

14. Open Innovation, NASA, "About Us," accessed October 12, 2020, https://www
.nasa.gov/offices/oct/openinnovation/aboutus.

15. Beth Simone Noveck, *Wiki Government: How Technology Can Make Government
Better, Democracy Stronger, and Citizens More Powerful* (Washington, DC:
Brookings Institution Press, 2010), 18.

16. Simon Winchester, *The Meaning of Everything: The Story of the Oxford English
Dictionary* (Oxford: Oxford University Press, 2004).

17. Beth Simone Noveck, "How to Mobilize Group Intelligence," *Nature*, November
28, 2017.

18. Anirudh Dinesh et al., "Briefing Notes: Social Audits," *CrowdLaw for Congress
Playbook*, May 2019, 137, http://congress.crowd.law.

19. Local Motors, "Meet Olli," accessed January 1, 2020, https://localmotors.com
/meet-olli/.

20. Royal Society for the Arts, "Future of Work Award Winners," accessed January 1,
2020, https://www.thersa.org/action-and-research/rsa-projects/economy-enter
prise-manufacturing-folder/future-work-awards/winners.

21. Mark Elliott, *Collaboration Design: Step-by-Step* (Melbourne: Collaborge, 2019).

22. Eric von Hippel, "The Dominant Role of Users in the Scientific Instrument
Innovation Process," *Research Policy* 5, no. 3 (July 1976): 212–239.

23. Henry Chesbrough, *Open Innovation: The New Imperative for Creating and
Profiting from Technology* (Cambridge, MA: Harvard Business Review Press,
2003).

24. Kevin Boudreau and Karim Lakhani, "Using the Crowd as an Innovation
Partner," *Harvard Business Review* 91, no. 4 (March 31, 2013): 60–69, 140.

25. Thomas Kalil, "Incentive Prizes Deliver Important Results for the Nation,
Offer More 'Bang for the Buck,'" *White House Blog*, January 9, 2017, https://
obamawhitehouse.archives.gov/blog/2017/01/09/incentive-prizes-deliver
-important-results-nation-offer-more-bang-buck.

26. Vicky Hallett, "Whatever Happened to . . . the Car Mechanic Who Invented a
Device to Pop Out a Baby?," National Public Radio, August 26, 2018, https://
www.npr.org/sections/goatsandsoda/2018/08/26/637472896/whatever
-happened-to-the-car-mechanic-who-invented-a-device-to-pop-out-a-baby.

27. Carlos Bernal, "CrowdLaw in the Judiciary: Designing a Public Participation Initiative for a Judicial Public Hearing" (unpublished ms. on file with author, January 20, 2020).

28. Office of Innovation, State of New Jersey, "The Future of Work Policy and Practice Catalog," accessed October 12, 2020, https://fow.innovation.nj.gov/.

29. The GovLab, "Smarter Crowdsourcing," accessed October 7, 2020, http://www.smartercrowdsourcing.org.

30. The organizational theorist Jay Galbraith offers a useful map of the planning choices you have in establishing an organization. He identifies five significant design decisions that together constitute what he calls an organization's "star model." The first, strategy, determines direction. The second, structure, determines the location of decision-making power. Processes to manage the flows of information, including information technologies, is the third. The fourth is rewards and reward systems, to influence the motivation of people to perform and address organizational goals. The fifth design decision is to adopt policies relating to people: human resource policies, which influence and frequently define the employees' mind-sets and skills. Galbraith, "Star Model," accessed October 12, 2020, https://www.jaygalbraith.com/images/pdfs/StarModel.pdf.

31. Aaron Wildavsky, *Speaking Truth to Power: The Art and Craft of Policy Analysis* (Boston: Little, Brown, 1979).

32. John Gastil and Erik Olin Wright, eds., *Legislature by Lot: Transformative Designs for Deliberative Governance* (London: Verso Books, 2019).

33. Administration for Community Living, "ACL Launches Health IT Prize Competition," accessed October 7, 2020, https://acl.gov/news-and-events/announcements/acl-launches-health-it-prize-competition (the competition was halted for COVID and restarted in October 2020).

34. Edward Paulino, "How New Jersey Asked Workers about the Future of Work: The Importance of Partnership," New Jersey Office of Innovation, *Medium*, September 25, 2020, https://medium.com/njinnovation/how-new-jersey-asked-workers-about-the-future-of-work-the-importance-of-partnership-dc9c71ce34c1.

35. Daren C. Brabham, "Using Crowdsourcing in Government," Collaborating Across Boundaries Series, IBM Center for the Business of Government, 2013, 8, http://bit.ly/17gzBTA.

36. C. P. Cerasoli, Jessica M. Nicklin, and Michael T. Ford, "Intrinsic Motivation and Extrinsic Incentives Jointly Predict Performance: A 40-Year Meta-Analysis," *Psychological Bulletin* 140 (2014): 980–1008, doi: 10.1037/a0035661.

37. Edward L. Deci, Richard Koestner, and Richard M. Ryan. "A Meta-Analytic Review of Experiments Examining the Effects of Extrinsic Rewards on Intrinsic Motivation," *Psychological Bulletin* 125, no. 6 (1999): 627–668, https://doi.org/10.1037/0033-2909.125.6.627.

38. All of Us, https://participant.joinallofus.org/.

39. Nashin Mahtani, "Chat Bots and Social Media Strategies for Crisis," Covid Course, The GovLab, accessed June 2, 2020, http://covidcourse.thegovlab.org/modules/chatbots-social-media.html.

40. The GovLab, "PetaBencana Case Study," October 20, 2020, https://www.thegov
lab.org/collective-intelligence.html.

41. The White House, "We the People," accessed October 6, 2020, https://petitions
.obamawhitehouse.archives.gov/.

42. Stefaan Verhulst et al., "Identifying Citizens' Needs by Combining Artificial
Intelligence (AI) and Collective Intelligence (CI)," The GovLab, September 2019,
9, http://www.thegovlab.org/static/files/publications/CI-AI_oct2019.pdf.

43. James E. Katz, Michael Barris, and Anshul Jain, *The Social Media President:
Barack Obama and the Politics of Digital Engagement* (Berlin: Springer, 2013); Beth
Simone Noveck, *Smart Citizens, Smarter State: The Technologies of Expertise and
the Future of Government* (Cambridge, MA: Harvard University Press, 2015).

8. FAST FIELD SCANNING

1. "California Gives Teenagers a Lie-In," *Economist*, October 19, 2019, https://www
.economist.com/united-states/2019/10/19/california-gives-teenagers-a-lie-in.

2. Lisa Lewis, "Why School Should Start Later in the Day," *Los Angeles Times*, September 18, 2016, https://www.latimes.com/opinion/op-ed/la-oe-lewis-school
-too-early-20160918-snap-story.html.

3. Adolescent Sleep Working Group, Committee on Adolescence, Council on
School Health, "School Start Times for Adolescents," *Pediatrics* 134, no. 3
(September 2014): 642–649, doi: 10.1542/peds.2014-1697.

4. Gideon Dunster, "Sleepmore in Seattle: Later School Start Times Are Associated
with More Sleep and Better Performance in High School Students," *Science
Advances* 4, no. 12 (December 12, 2018), https://advances.sciencemag.org/con
tent/4/12/eaau6200.

5. Stefaan G. Verhulst, "Re-Imagining Action Research as a Tool for Social
Innovation and Public Entrepreneurship," The GovLab, February 2020, http://
thegovlab.org/wordpress/wp-content/uploads/2020/02/Re-imagining-Action
-Research-as-a-Tool-for-Social-Innovation-and-Public-Entrepreneurship-1.pdf.

6. The reality of much contemporary evidence-based policy and practice as it is, or
is meant to be, carried out today is that good evidence for a policy has come to
mean a good RCT, an RCT that shows that the policy has worked. See Nancy
Cartwright and Jeremy Hardie, *Evidence-Based Policy: A Practical Guide to Doing
It Better* (New York: Oxford University Press, 2012), http://ebookcentral.proquest
.com/lib/nyulibrary-ebooks/detail.action?docID=3054984.

7. John Lavis et al., "Towards Systematic Reviews That Inform Health Care
Management and Policy-Making," *Journal of Health Service Research Policy* 10,
supp. 1 (July 2005): 35–48.

8. David L. Sackett et al., "Evidence-Based Medicine: What It Is and What It Isn't:
It's about Integrating Individual Clinical Expertise and the Best External
Evidence," *British Medical Journal* 312, no. 7023 (January 13, 1996): 71–72.

9. Lynn Olson, "Growing Pains," *Education Week*, November 2, 1994, 29.

10. Cartwright and Hardie, *Evidence-Based Policy*, 5.

11. Eugene S. Bardach, *A Practical Guide for Policy Analysis: The Eightfold Path to*

More Effective Problem Solving, 6th ed. (Washington, DC: Congressional Quarterly, 2020), 105.

12. Esmée Fairbairn Foundation, *Street (UK): Learning from Community Finance*, (London: Esmée Fairbairn Foundation, 2005), https://esmeefairbairn.org.uk /Street-Learning-from-Community-Finance.

13. Peter Bragge, "Three Day Evidence Review," video, Crisis Collective Intelligence Course, The GovLab, accessed June 3, 2020, http://covidcourse.thegovlab.org /modules/evidence-review.html.

14. Eileen Munro, "Evidence-Based Policy," in *Philosophy of Social Science: A New Introduction*, ed. Nancy Cartwright and Eleonora Montuschi (Oxford: Oxford University Press, 2014), 49.

15. D. L. Sackett et al., "Evidence Based Medicine: What It Is and What It Isn't," *British Medical Journal* 312 (1996): 71–72.

16. Beth Simone Noveck, *Smart Citizens, Smarter State: The Technologies of Expertise and the Future of Governing* (Cambridge, MA: Harvard University Press, 2015), chap. 2.

17. Munro, "Evidence-Based Policy," 49.

18. Ron Haskins and Greg Margolis, *Show Me the Evidence: Obama's Fight for Rigor and Results in Social Policy* (Washington, DC: Brookings Institution Press, 2014).

19. Deborah Stone, *The Policy Paradox: The Art of Political Decision Making*, rev. ed. (New York: Norton, 2001), 376.

20. Union of Concerned Scientists, "Attacks on Science," January 20, 2017, https:// www.ucsusa.org/resources/attacks-on-science.

21. National Research Council, *Using Science as Evidence in Public Policy* (Washington, DC: National Academies Press, 2012), chapter 4, https://doi.org/10.17226 /13460.

22. Justin Longo and Rob Dobell, "The Limits of Policy Analytics: Early Examples and the Emerging Boundary of Possibilities," *Politics and Governance* 6, no. 4 (2018): 5–17.

23. John A. List, "An Introduction to Field Experiments in Economics," *Journal of Economic Behavior and Organization* 70, no. 3 (2009): 439–442.

24. Commission on Evidence-Based Policymaking, *The Promise of Evidence-Based Policymaking* (Washington, DC: Commission on Evidence-Based Policymaking, 2017), https://www.cep.gov/report/cep-final-report.pdf.

25. Commission on Evidence-Based Policymaking.

26. David Halpern, "What Works? The Rise of 'Experimental' Government," *Civil Service Quarterly Blog*, UK government, January 27, 2015, https://quarterly.blog .gov.uk/2015/01/27/what-works-the-rise-of-experimental-government/.

27. Sara B. Heller et al., "Thinking, Fast and Slow? Some Field Experiments to Reduce Crime and Dropout in Chicago" (National Bureau of Economic Research Working Paper No. 21178, issued May 2015, revised August 2016), https://www .nber.org/papers/w21178.

28. Richard H. Thaler and Cass Sunstein, *Nudge: Improving Decisions about Health, Wealth and Happiness* (New York: Penguin, 2009); and Cass Sunstein, *How*

Change Happens (Cambridge, MA: MIT Press, 2019) and *Cost-Benefit Revolution* (Cambridge, MA: MIT Press, 2018).

29. Doris Weichselbaumer, "Discrimination against Female Migrants Wearing Headscarves," *EconPapers*, Institute of Labor Economics, 2016, https://Econ Papers.repec.org/RePEc:iza:izadps:dp10217.

30. Marianne Bertrand and Sendhil Mullainathan, "Are Emily and Greg More Employable than Lakisha and Jamal? A Field Experiment on Labor Market Discrimination," *American Economic Review* 94, no. 4 (2004): 991–1013, doi: 10.1257/0002828042002561.

31. Applied Ltd., https://www.beapplied.com/.

32. OECD, "Behavioural Insights," 2019, http://www.oecd.org/gov/regulatory-policy /behavioural-insights.htm.

33. US Government, Office of Evaluation Sciences, "Evaluation Methods," accessed October 12, 2020, https://oes.gsa.gov/methods/; Sarah Stillman, "Can Behavioral Science Help in Flint?," *New Yorker*, January 23, 2017; US Government, Social and Behavioral Sciences Team, accessed October 12, 2020, https://web .archive.org/web/20160213143327/https://sbst.gov/.

34. The Lab@DC, http://thelabprojects.dc.gov/.

35. Behavioural Economics Team of the Australian Government, https://behavioural economics.pmc.gov.au/.

36. Beth Simone Noveck and Rod Glover, "Today's Problems, Yesterday's Toolkit," ANZSOG, August 2019, https://www.anzsog.edu.au/preview-documents /publications-and-brochures/5425-today-s-problems-yesterday-s-toolkit/file.

37. Noveck, *Smart Citizens*.

38. John Stuart Mill, *A System of Logic*, book 3, chapter 8 (London, 1843).

39. Laura Haynes et al., "Test, Learn, Adapt: Developing Public Policy with Randomised Controlled Trials" (policy paper, UK Cabinet Office: Behavioural Insights Team, 2012), 9, https://assets.publishing.service.gov.uk/government /uploads/system/uploads/attachment_data/file/62529/TLA-1906126.pdf; Cartwright and Hardie, *Evidence-Based Policy*, 33.

40. Munro, "Evidence-Based Policy," 56–57, citing Alan B. Krueger, "Experimental Estimates of Education Production Functions," *Quarterly Journal of Economics*, 114, no. 2 (1999): 497–532.

41. Urban Institute, "Data and Methods: Experiments," accessed October 12, 2020, https://www.urban.org/research/data-methods/data-analysis/quantitative-data -analysis/impact-analysis/experiments.

42. Royal Swedish Academy of Sciences, "The Prize in Economic Sciences 2019," accessed October 12, 2020, https://www.nobelprize.org/uploads/2019/10 /popular-economicsciencesprize2019-2.pdf.

43. Royal Swedish Academy of Sciences, "Press Release: The Prize in Economic Sciences 2019," Nobel Prize, October 14, 2019, https://www.nobelprize.org /prizes/economic-sciences/2019/press-release/. See also Michael Kremer, "The Origin and Evolution of Randomized Evaluations in Development," YouTube, January 27, 2014, https://www.youtube.com/watch?v=YGL6hPgpmDE.

44. Peter Bragge et al., "Towards Systematic Reviews That Inform Health Care Management and Policy-Making," *Journal of Neurotrauma* 33, no. 16 (August 15, 2016): 1461–1478, http://doi.org/10.1089/neu.2015.4233.

45. Peter Bragge, "Ten Ways to Optimize Evidence-Based Policy," *Journal of Comparative Effectiveness Research* 8, no. 15 (November 7, 2019), https://www.future medicine.com/doi/10.2217/cer-2019-0132.

46. National Health and Medical Research Council, "NHMRC Additional Levels of Evidence and Grades for Recommendations for Developers of Guidelines: Stage 2 Consultation Early 2008–End June 2009," 6, accessed January 10, 2019, https://www.mja.com.au/sites/default/files/NHMRC.levels.of.evidence.2008 -09.pdf.

47. Sally Green et al., introduction to *Cochrane Handbook for Systematic Reviews of Interventions*, ed. Julian P. T. Higgins et al. (West Sussex, UK: Cochrane Collaboration and Wiley, 2008).

48. Peter Bragge, "Opinion: Google Searches Are No Substitute for Systematic Reviews When It Comes to Policymaking," *The Mandarin*, May 26, 2020, https://www.themandarin.com.au/134365-opinion-google-searches-are-no -substitute-for-systematic-reviews-when-it-comes-to-policymaking/.

49. Jeremy M. Grimshaw, Martin P. Eccles, John N. Lavis, Sophie J. Hill, and Janet E. Squires, "Knowledge Translation of Research Findings," *Implementation Science* 7 (2012): art. 50, https://doi.org/10.1186/1748-5908-7-50.

50. Institute of Education Sciences, "What Works Clearinghouse," accessed October 12, 2020, https://ies.ed.gov/ncee/wwc/ReviewedStudies#/OnlyStudiesWith PositiveEffects:false,SetNumber:1ht.

51. Education Endowment Foundation, "Evidence Summaries," accessed October 12, 2020, https://educationendowmentfoundation.org.uk/evidence-summaries/.

52. Evidence for Learning, https://www.evidenceforlearning.org.au/.

53. US Department of Labor, Clearinghouse for Labor Evaluation and Research (CLEAR), https://clear.dol.gov/.

54. The foundation has funded trials in over 150 programs, creating more RCTs in education than any other organization across the globe.

55. UK government, "Guidance: What Works Network," accessed October 12, 2020, https://www.gov.uk/guidance/what-works-network#the-what-works-network. The What Works network includes the following organizations: the Education Endowment Foundation, College of Policing What Works Centre for Crime Reduction, Early Intervention Foundation, What Works Centre for Local Economic Growth, Centre for Ageing Better, What Works Centre for Wellbeing, and What Works for Children's Social Care, as well as three affiliates and one associate.

56. College of Policing, "Crime Reduction Toolkit," accessed October 12, 2020, https://whatworks.college.police.uk/toolkit/Pages/Toolkit.aspx.

57. Campbell Collaboration, home page, accessed October 12, 2020, https://www .campbellcollaboration.org.

58. Julia Littell and Howard White, "The Campbell Collaboration: Providing Better

Evidence for a Better World," *Research on Social Work Practice*, May 4, 2017, https://journals.sagepub.com/doi/10.1177/1049731517703748.

59. Campbell Collaboration, "Training for Authors," accessed October 12, 2020, https://www.campbellcollaboration.org/research-resources/training-courses .html; and Campbell Collaboration, "Resources for Policymakers," accessed October 12, 2020, https://www.campbellcollaboration.org/evidence-portals.html.

60. Cochrane, "Our Evidence," accessed October 12, 2020, https://www.cochrane .org/evidence.

61. Cochrane Methodology Reviews, "Reviews of Methodology," accessed October 6, 2020, https://training.cochrane.org/handbook/current/chapter-i#section-i-2-2-5.

62. Cochrane Methodology Reviews, "Reviews of the Effects of Interventions," accessed October 6, 2020, https://training.cochrane.org/handbook/current /chapter-i#section-i-2-2-1; "Definitions That Apply to All Department Pro- grams," 34 CFR 77.1.

63. Ideas42, https://www.ideas42.org/.

64. Bloomberg Philanthropies, "About What Works Cities," accessed October 12, 2020, https://whatworkscities.bloomberg.org/about/.

65. BehaviourWorks Australia, https://www.behaviourworksaustralia.org/.

66. BehaviourWorks Australia, "About Us," accessed October 12, 2020, https:// www.behaviourworksaustralia.org/about/.

67. BehaviourWorks Australia.

68. Breanna Wright, Nicholas Faulkner, Peter Bragge, and Mark Graber, "What Interventions Could Reduce Diagnostic Error in Emergency Departments? A Review of Evidence, Practice and Consumer Perspectives," *Official Journal of the Society to Improve Diagnosis in Medicine (SIDM)* 6, no. 4 (2019), https://doi.org /10.1515/dx-2018-0104.

69. Peter Bragge et al., "Container Deposit Schemes Work: So Why Is Industry Still Opposed?," *The Conversation*, June 5, 2016, https://theconversation.com/con tainer-deposit-schemes-work-so-why-is-industry-still-opposed-59599.

70. BehaviourWorks Australia, "The Method," accessed October 12, 2020, https:// www.behaviourworksaustralia.org/the-method/.

71. Poverty Action Lab, https://www.povertyactionlab.org/.

72. Cochrane Canada Collaboration, "About Us," accessed October 12, 2020, https://canada.cochrane.org/about-us.

73. Health Systems Evidence, "About," accessed October 7, 2020, https://www .healthsystemsevidence.org/about?lang=en.

74. Social Systems Evidence, https://socialsystemsevidence.org/.

75. J. N. Lavis, F.-P. Gauvin, C. A. Mattison, K. A. Moat, K. Waddell, M. G. Wilson, and R. J. Reid, "Rapid Synthesis: Creating Rapid Learning Health Systems in Canada," McMaster Health Forum, December 10, 2018, https://www.mcmaster forum.org/docs/default-source/product-documents/rapid-responses/creating -rapid-learning-health-systems-in-canada.pdf?sfvrsn=4.

76. Jonathan Breckon and Michael Sanders, "The Evidence Quarter: An Idea to Join Up the UK's What Works Centres," Alliance for Useful Evidence, May 23, 2019,

https://www.alliance4usefulevidence.org/the-evidence-quarter-an-idea-to-join
-up-the-uks-what-works-centres/.

77. "Table 1: General Comparison of Rapid Review versus Systematic Review
Approaches," in Sara Khangura, Kristin Konnyu, Rob Cushman, Jeremy
Grimshaw, and David Moher, "Evidence Summaries: The Evolution of a Rapid
Review Approach," *Systematic Reviews* 1 (2012): art. 10, https://systematicreviews
journal.biomedcentral.com/articles/10.1186/2046-4053-1-10/tables/1.

78. MIT Solve, "Solver Spotlight," accessed October 12, 2020, https://solve.mit.edu
/solver_spotlight.

79. Hunter Goldman and Kimberly Junmookda, "Exploring Innovative Solutions
to Resilience Building," Rockefeller Foundation, March 4, 2015, https://www
.rockefellerfoundation.org/blog/exploring-innovative-solutions-to-resilience
-building/.

80. Angus Deaton, "Randomization in the Tropics Revisited: A Theme and Eleven
Variations" (National Bureau of Economic Research Working Paper No. 27600,
July 2020), 20–21.

81. Angus Deaton and Nancy Cartwright, "Understanding and Misunderstanding
Randomized Controlled Trials" (National Bureau of Economic Research
Working Paper No. 22595, October 2017).

82. Mark Petticrew and Helen Roberts, *Systematic Reviews in the Social Sciences*
(Oxford, UK: Blackwell, 2006).

83. Jonathan Rothwell, "Sociology's Revenge: Moving to Opportunity (MTO)," *Social
Mobility Memos* (blog), Brookings, May 6, 2015, https://www.brookings
.edu/blog/social-mobility-memos/2015/05/06/sociologys-revenge-moving
-to-opportunity-mto-revisited/.

84. Jens Ludwig et al., "What Can We Learn about Neighborhood Effects from the
Moving to Opportunity Experiment?," *American Journal of Sociology* 114, no. 1
(July 2008): 182.

85. Raj Chetty, Nathaniel Hendren, and Lawrence F. Katz, "The Effects of Exposure
to Better Neighborhoods on Children: New Evidence from the Moving to
Opportunity Experiment," Harvard University and the National Bureau for
Economic Research, August 2015, http://www.equality-of-opportunity.org
/images/mto_paper.pdf; Opportunity Insights, "Policy," accessed October 12,
2020, https://opportunityinsights.org/policy/.

86. Michael Luca and Max H. Bazerman, *The Power of Experiments: Decision-Making
in a Data-Driven World* (Cambridge, MA: MIT Press, 2020); Jim Manzi, *Uncon-
trolled: The Surprising Payoff of Trial-and-Error for Business, Politics, and Society* (New
York: Basic Books, 2012), 128, 142. See also Laura M. Holson, "Putting a Bolder
Face on Google," *New York Times*, February 28, 2009, https://www.nytimes.
com/2009/03/01/business/01marissa.html?pagewanted=3&_r=0.

87. Kevin J. Boudreau and Karim R. Lakhani, "Innovation Experiments: Researching Technical Advance, Knowledge Production, and the Design of Supporting
Institutions," *Innovation Policy and the Economy* 16 (2016): 135–167.

88. York CVS, "People Helping People: Volunteering in York: Our Strategy,"

November 2017, https://www.yorkcvs.org.uk/wp-content/uploads/2017/10
/CVS_People_Helping_People_A4_V1.pdf.

89. Arjan Haring, "In the Age of Machine Learning, Randomized Controlled Trials
Are Unethical," *Towards Data Science, Medium*, January 14, 2019, https://towards
datascience.com/in-the-age-of-machine-learning-randomized-controlled-trials
-are-unethical-74acc05724af.

90. The Unorthodox Prize, home page, accessed October 12, 2020, https://www
.unorthodoxprize.org/.

91. Eugene Bardach, *A Practical Guide for Policy Analysis: The Eightfold Path to More
Effective Problem Solving*, 6th ed. (Washington, DC: Congressional Quarterly,
2020), appendix B.

92. Lester M. Salamon, *The Tools of Government: A Guide to the New Governance*
(Oxford: Oxford University Press, 2002).

93. Dane Gambrell, *Your Future of Work: What the New Jersey Future of Work Task
Force Learned from 4,000 Workers in the Garden State* (New Jersey State Office of
Innovation, September 2020), https://medium.com/njinnovation/what-we
-learned-about-the-future-of-work-from-4-000-workers-in-new-jersey-7c18ae
8dd4bb.

94. National Priorities Project, "Total Federal Spending," accessed October 12,
2020, https://www.nationalpriorities.org/.

95. White House, "Information Technology," in *FY 2018 President's Budget*, 2018,
https://www.whitehouse.gov/sites/whitehouse.gov/files/omb/budget/fy2018
/ap_16_it.pdf.

96. Pearl Eliadis, Margaret M. Hill, and Michael Howlett, *Designing Government:
From Instruments to Governance* (Montreal: McGill-Queen's University Press,
2005), 12. See also Marie-Louise Bemelmans-Videc, Ray C. Rist, and Evert
Vedung, *Carrots, Sticks, and Sermons: Policy Instruments and Their Evaluation*
(London: Routledge, 2011), chapter 2.

97. Linda A. Hill and Allison J. Wigen, "Tom Kalil: Leading Technology &
Innovation at the White House," Harvard Business School Case 417-021,
August 2016 (revised March 2019), 6.

98. For one list of innovative ways of solving problems, see Nesta's Innovation
Methods catalog, accessed October 12, 2020, https://www.nesta.org.uk/report
/compendium-innovation-methods/.

99. The original website has been modified to reflect the current administration's
priorities: https://www.healthcare.gov/.

100. United States Digital Service, "Helping Students Make More Informed College
Choices at Department of Education: 2016 Report to Congress," 2016, https://
www.usds.gov/report-to-congress/2016/college-scorecard/.

101. Beth Simone Noveck and Rod Glover, "Today's Problems, Yesterday's Toolkit,"
ANZSOG, August 2019, 48, https://www.anzsog.edu.au/preview-documents
/publications-and-brochures/5425-today-s-problems-yesterday-s-toolkit/file.

102. Diego Piacentini, "From Seattle to Rome: Digital Innovation for Citizens and
for the Development of the Country," *Medium*, September 29, 2016, https://

medium.com/team-per-la-trasformazione-digitale/from-seattle-to-roma-innova
tion-citizens-talents-6b8c6c06002b; Italian government, "Digital Transformation Team: About Us," 2019, https://teamdigitale.governo.it/en/49-content.htm.

103. Public and Commercial Services Union, "Career Breaks," April 22, 2016,
https://www.pcs.org.uk/pcs-in-hm-revenue-and-customs-group/latest-news
/career-breaks.

104. Scottish government, "Scottish Government Staff Handbook," 2007, https://
www.gov.scot/resource/doc/76007/0060961.pdf.

105. William Eggers and Shalabh Kumar Singh, *The Public Innovator's Playbook:
Nurturing Bold Ideas in Government* (New York: Deloitte Research, 2009), 20.

106. GovTech Singapore, "Our Role," accessed October 12, 2020, https://www.tech
.gov.sg/who-we-are/our-role/.

107. Jeff Ubois and Thomas Kalil, "The Promise of Incentive Prizes," *Stanford Social
Innovation Review*, Winter 2019, https://ssir.org/articles/entry/the_promise_of
_incentive_prizes.

108. Michael Kremer and Rachel Glennerster, *Strong Medicine: Creating Incentives for
Pharmaceutical Research on Neglected Diseases* (Princeton, NJ: Princeton University Press, 2004), 56.

109. Tracy Tullis, "How Game Theory Helped Improve New York City's High
School Application Process," *New York Times*, December 7, 2014, MB1.

110. Nancy Shute, "Matching Kidney Donors with Those Who Need Them—and
Other Explorations in Economics," *From Research to Reward*, National Academy
of Sciences, 2016, https://www.nap.edu/read/23508/.

111. Stefaan Verhulst et al., "Open Data's Impact" (The GovLab white paper),
accessed October 12, 2020, https://odimpact.org.

112. Owain Service, "Automatic Enrolment and Pensions: A Behavioural Success
Story," Behavioural Insights Team, November 10, 2015, https://www.bi.team
/blogs/automatic-enrolment-and-pensions-a-behavioural-success-story/.

113. Claudia Juech, "Influencing Human Behavior to Help Build Resilience and
More Inclusive Economies," *Ideas42 Blog*, July 7, 2016, https://www.ideas42
.org/blog/influencing-human-behavior-help-build-resilience-inclusive-eco
nomies/.

114. National Research Council, *Using Science as Evidence in Public Policy* (Washington, DC: National Academies Press, 2012), https://doi.org/10.17226/13460.

115. Behavioural Insights Team, "EAST," July 2015, https://www.behavioural
insights.co.uk/wp-content/uploads/2015/07/BIT-Publication-EAST_FA
_WEB.pdf.

116. Brooke Auxier and Lee Rainie, "Key Takeaways on Americans' Views about
Privacy, Surveillance and Data Sharing," *Fact Tank*, Pew Research Center,
November 15, 2019, https://www.pewresearch.org/fact-tank/2019/11/15
/key-takeaways-on-americans-views-about-privacy-surveillance-and-data
-sharing/.

117. YouTube: Vox, https://www.youtube.com/vox; Vox News, "About Us," accessed
October 7, 2020, https://www.vox.com/pages/about-us.

118. Results for America, "Our Work: State Policy," accessed October 12, 2020, https://results4america.org/our-work/state-policy/.

119. Results for America, "Videos," accessed October 7, 2020, https://results4amer ica.org/videos/.

120. "Harper's Index," *Harper's Magazine*, October 2019, https://harpers.org/archive /2019/10/harpers-index-october-2019/.

121. SciLine, "Covering and Communicating the Evidence: Adolescent Health," accessed October 7 ,2020, https://www.sciline.org/umbc?utm_campaign =umbc&utm_medium=direct&utm_source=homepage.

122. SciLine, "Fact Sheets: What the Science Says," accessed October 7, 2020, https://www.sciline.org/evidence.

123. The Conversation United States, "Expert Knowledge for the Public Good," annual report, 2019, https://cdn.theconversation.com/static_files/files/761 /TCUS_FY2019_Annual_Report_.pdf.

124. Marion Nestle, "Industry-Funded Scientific Argument of the Week: Do Blue-berries Prevent Dementia?," *Food Politics*, December 2, 2019, https://www .foodpolitics.com/2019/12/industry-funded-scientific-argument-of-the-week -do-blueberries-prevent-dementia/; Wolfgang Marx et al., "In Response to 'There Is No Meta-analytic Evidence of Blueberries Improving Cognitive Performance or Mood,'" *Brain, Behaviour and Immunity*, October 4, 2019, https://www.sciencedirect.com/science/article/pii/S0889159119312607.

125. Joachim Schöpfel, "Towards a Prague Definition of Grey Literature," Twelfth International Conference on Grey Literature: Transparency in Grey Literature; Grey Tech Approaches to High Tech Issues, Prague, December 6–7, 2010, Czech Republic, 11–26.

126. Lauder Institute Think Tanks and Civil Societies Program, University of Pennsylvania (Philadelphia), https://www.gotothinktank.com/.

127. Congressional Research Service, home page, accessed October 12, 2020, https://www.loc.gov/crsinfo/.

128. Congressional Research Service, "Child Welfare: An Overview of Federal Programs and Their Current Funding," January 2, 2018, https://crsreports .congress.gov/product/pdf/R/R43458.

129. Congressional Research Service, "Trade Dispute with China and Rare Earth Elements," June 28, 2019, https://crsreports.congress.gov/product/pdf/IF /IF11259.

130. "The Rapid Research Method," *Microsoft Blog*, May 12, 2012, https://blogs .msdn.microsoft.com/jmeier/2012/05/13/the-rapid-research-method/.

131. Bardach, *Practical Guide for Policy Analysis*, 25.

132. Eric von Hippel, Nikolaus Franke, and Reinhard Prügl, "'Pyramiding': Efficient Identification of Rare Subjects" (MIT Sloan School of Management Working Paper 4719-08, October 2008); Marion Poetz and Reinhard Prügl, "Find the Right Expert for Any Problem," *Harvard Business Review*, December 16, 2014, https://hbr.org/2014/12/find-the-right-expert-for-any-problem.

133. Noveck, *Smart Citizens*, 126.

134. Elisa Shearer and Katerina Eva Matsa, "News Use across Social Media Platforms: 2018," Pew Research Center, September 10, 2018, https://www .journalism.org/2018/09/10/news-use-across-social-media-platforms-2018/.

135. Stefaan Verhulst and Andrew Young, "R-Search: Rapid Re-Search Enabling the Design of Agile and Creative Responses to Problems," The GovLab, accessed January 12, 2020, https://www.thegovlab.org/static/files/publications/R-Search .pdf.

136. Noveck, *Smart Citizens*, 126.

137. Bardach, *Practical Guide for Policy Analysis*, 119.

138. Linda Hill and Allison Wigen, "Tom Kalil: Leading Technology and Innovation at the White House," Harvard Business School Case Collection, August 2016 (rev. March 2019), https://www.hbs.edu/faculty/pages/item.aspx?num=51561.

139. David Evans, "Hierarchy of Evidence: A Framework for Ranking Evidence Evaluating Healthcare Interventions," *Journal of Clinical Nursing* 12, no. 1 (2003): 77–84, https://doi.org/10.1046/j.1365-2702.2003.00662.x; Richard Grol and Jeremy Grimshaw, "From Best Evidence to Best Practice: Effective Implementation of Change in Patients' Care," *Lancet* 362 (2003): 1225–1230, http://dx.doi.org/10.1016/S0140=6736(03)14546-1.

140. Munro, "Evidence-Based Policy," 54–55.

141. Michael Schrage, "Q and A: The Experimenter," *MIT Technology Review*, 2011, http://www.technologyreview.com/news/422784/qa-the-experimenter/.

142. J. Chandler et al., introduction to *Cochrane Handbook for Systematic Reviews of Interventions, Version 6.0*, ed. J. P. T. Higgins et al. (Chicester, UK: Cochrane, 2019), http://www.training.cochrane.org/handbook.

143. Trisha Greenhalgh, "How to Read a Paper: Papers That Summarise Other Papers (Systematic Reviews and Meta-Analyses)," *BMJ Clinical Research* 315 (1997): 672–675, doi: 10.1136/bmj.315.7109.672.

144. "How to Read a Paper," *BMJ*, accessed October 12, 2020, https://www.bmj .com/about-bmj/resources-readers/publications/how-read-paper.

145. Pew, "Evidence-Based Policymaking Made Easy by 'Results First' Tool," You Tube, December 9, 2016, https://www.youtube.com/watch?v=MXUEBl0G-tU.

146. Pew, "Results First Clearinghouse Database," https://www.pewtrusts.org/en /research-and-analysis/data-visualizations/2015/results-first-clearinghouse -database.

147. "Definitions That Apply to All Department Programs," 34 CFR 77.1.

148. Jonathan Jacobson, "Understanding the Evidence Definitions Used for U.S. Department of Education Programs," slideshow, Institute of Education Sciences, accessed October 12, 2020, https://ies.ed.gov/ncee/wwc/Docs /Multimedia/wwc_definitions_transcript.pdf.

149. Lever for Change, "Economic Opportunity Challenge," accessed October 12, 2020, https://www.economicopportunitychallenge.org/.

150. John Mayne, "Addressing Attribution through Contribution Analysis: Using Performance Measures Sensibly," *Canadian Journal of Program Evaluation* 16, no. 1 (2001): 1–24.

151. Vidya Krishnamurthy, "Video: FSG Explains Collective Impact," Hewlett, July 29, 2016, https://hewlett.org/video-collective-impact-explained/.

152. Betty Hart and Todd Risley, *Meaningful Differences in the Everyday Experience of Young American Children* (Baltimore: Paul H. Brookes, 1995); Hart and Risley, "American Parenting of Language-Learning Children: Persisting Differences in Family-Child Interactions Observed in Natural Home Environments," *Developmental Psychology* 28, no. 6 (November 1992): 1096–1105.

153. Kenneth Wong, "Disrupting the Early Learning Status Quo: Providence Talks as an Innovative Policy in Diverse Urban Communities," Providence Talks, February 14, 2018, http://www.providencetalks.org/wp-content/uploads/2018/07/updated-brown-eval.pdf.

154. Jill Gilkerson et al., "Language Experience in the Second Year of Life and Language Outcomes in Late Childhood," *Pediatrics* 142, no. 4 (October 2018), https://doi.org/10.1542/peds.2017-4276.

155. Bloomberg Philanthropies, "Bloomberg Philanthropies Announces Replication of Mayors Challenge-Winning Early Childhood Learning Innovation in Five U.S. Cities," press release, September 24, 2019, https://www.bloomberg.org/press/releases/bloomberg-philanthropies-announces-replication-mayors-challenge-winning-early-childhood-learning-innovation-five-u-s-cities/.

156. Rafaela Lindeberg, "Man behind Sweden's Controversial Virus Strategy Admits Mistakes," Bloomberg News, June 3, 2020, https://www.bloomberg.com/news/articles/2020-06-03/man-behind-sweden-s-virus-strategy-says-he-got-some-things-wrong.

157. I am grateful to Jens Ludwig, University of Chicago, for the concept here of informational comparative advantage.

158. Amanda Ripley and Timothy Williams, "Body Cameras Have Little Effect on Police Behavior, Study Says," *New York Times*, October 20, 2017, A1.

159. Cartwright and Hardie, *Evidence-Based Policy*.

160. Cartwright and Hardie, 68.

161. Cartwright and Hardie, 113.

162. Bragge, "Ten Ways to Optimize Evidence-Based Policy."

163. Kaelan Moat et al., "Evidence Briefs and Deliberative Dialogues: Perceptions and Intentions to Act on What Was Learnt," *Bulletin of the World Health Organization* 92 (2013): 20–28, https://doi.org/10.2471/BLT.12.116806.

164. Moat et al., 25.

165. Beth Simone Noveck, "A Democracy of Groups," *First Monday* 10, no. 11 (2005), http://firstmonday.org/article/view/1289/1209.

166. Beth Simone Noveck, "The Electronic Revolution in Rulemaking," *Emory Law Review* 53 (2004): 504.

167. The GovLab, "Evidence Checks UK: Evidence-Based Policy Making in the UK," accessed October 12, 2020, https://congress.crowd.law/case-evidence-checks-uk.html.

168. Cartwright and Hardie, *Evidence-Based Policy*, 113.

9. IMPLEMENTING SOLUTIONS WITH PARTNERS

1. Olivia Elson, Thomas Feeny, and Luke Heinkel, "Experimentation, Partnership and Learning: Insights from a Review of the First Three Years of DFAT's InnovationXchange," Results for Development, 2019, https://bit.ly/2Sv9F4A.

2. Sarah Pearson, interview with author, December 17, 2019 (on file with author).

3. United Nations, "SDG 17," accessed October 17, 2020, https://sdgs.un.org /goals/goal17.

4. Pearson interview.

5. Tina Rosenberg, "Ideas Help No One on a Shelf. Take Them to the World," *Opinionator* (blog), *New York Times*, February 26, 2016, https://opinionator. blogs.nytimes.com/2016/02/29/dont-just-solve-a-problem-go-tell-the-world/.

6. R. Kent Weaver, "But Will It Work? Implementation Analysis to Improve Government Performance" (Issues in Governance Studies No. 32, Brookings, February 2010), 4.

7. Hilary Cottam, *Radical Help: How We Can Remake the Relationships between Us and Revolutionise the Welfare State* (London: Virago, 2018), 207.

8. Kofi Annan, "The Power of Partnerships in Africa," Kofi Annan Foundation, May 10, 2011, https://www.kofiannanfoundation.org/in-the-news/the-power-of -partnerships-in-africa/.

9. United Nations Global Compact, home page, accessed December 27, 2019, https://www.unglobalcompact.org/.

10. Felix Dodds, "Multi-Stakeholder Partnerships: Making Them Work for the Post-2015 Development Agenda," Global Research Institute, 2015, https://bit. ly/34YsHTD. See also Marianne Beisheim and Andrea Liese, eds., *Transnational Partnerships Effectively Providing for Sustainable Development?* (London: Palgrave Macmillan, 2014).

11. Ronald A. Heifetz, John V. Kania, and Mark R. Kramer, "Leading Boldly Foundations Can Move Past Traditional Approaches to Create Social Change through Imaginative—and Even Controversial—Leadership," *Stanford Social Innovation Review*, Winter 2004, https://ssir.org/articles/entry/leading_boldly.

12. Howard W. Buffett and William B. Eimicke, *Social Value Investing: A Management Framework for Effective Partnerships* (New York: Columbia University Press, 2018), 4.

13. Lindsay Holst, "P-TECH Is Proof of What Can Be Accomplished, but We've Got to Have the Courage to Do It," *White House Blog*, October 25, 2013, https:// obamawhitehouse.archives.gov/blog/2013/10/25/p-tech-proof-what-can-be -accomplished-we-ve-got-have-courage-do-it.

14. Anya Kamenetz, "Turmoil behind the Scenes at a Nationally Lauded High School," NPR, March 14, 2016, https://www.npr.org/sections/ed/2016/03/14 /469207779/turmoil-behind-the-scenes-at-a-nationally-lauded-high-school; Mengli Song and Christina Zeiser, "Early College, Continued Success," American Institutes for Research, 2016, ix–x, https://www.air.org/sites/default /files/downloads/report/Early-College-Continued-Success-Longer-Term-Impact -of-ECHS-September-2019-rev.pdf.

15. P-TECH, home page, accessed June 4, 2020, http://www.ptech.org/.
16. P-TECH, "Getting Started: The Roadmap," accessed December 27, 2019, http://www.ptech.org/getting-started/roadmap/.
17. Buffett and Eimicke, *Social Value Investing*, 71–72.
18. Paul R. Verkuil, *Outsourcing Sovereignty* (Cambridge: Cambridge University Press, 2007), 1–22, https://doi.org/10.1017/CBO9780511509926.
19. OECD, "Health Expenditure," accessed October 12, 2020, https://www.oecd.org/els/health-systems/health-expenditure.htm.
20. Katherine Barrett and Richard Greene, "What Happens When Privatization Doesn't Work Out," *Governing*, October 2016, https://www.governing.com/columns/smart-mgmt/gov-privatization-pensions-prisons.html.
21. Anita Mukherjee, "Impacts of Private Prison Contracting on Inmate Time Served and Recidivism," *American Economic Journal: Economic Policy*, June 6, 2019, http://dx.doi.org/10.2139/ssrn.2523238.
22. Tara Joy, "The Problem with Private Prisons," Justice Policy Institute, February 2, 2018, http://www.justicepolicy.org/news/12006. See also Amedeo Bettauer, "How Private Prisons Fail Inmates | Kid Pundit," YouTube, September 26, 2020, https://www.youtube.com/watch?v=S_PeYbJbUes&list=PLeMKJ1LDPNYeFZEthfoHSnQU7Uo1sJKhW&index=7.
23. Katherine Kim, "Private Prisons Face an Uncertain Future as States Turn Their Backs on the Industry," *Vox*, December 1, 2019, https://www.vox.com/policy-and-politics/2019/12/1/20989336/private-prisons-states-bans-califonia-nevada-colorado.
24. Oren Frank, Twitter post, June 1, 2020, https://twitter.com/orenfrank/status/1267504648275005440.
25. Victòria Alsina Burgués and Carles Ramió Matas, "Proactive and Reactive Reasons for Initiating Public-Private Collaboration and Its Consequences in Terms of Success" (XXII CLAD Conference Working Paper, last modified November 17, 2017), https://www.iappuebla.edu.mx/CLAD/pdfs/alsinvic.pdf.
26. Don Kettl, "The Transformation of Governance: Globalization, Devolution, and the Role of Government," *Public Administration Review* 60 (December 17, 2002): 488–497, doi: 10.1111/0033-3352.00112.
27. Hewlett, "FSG Explains Collective Impact," video, July 29, 2016, https://hewlett.org/video-collective-impact-explained/.
28. John Kania and Mark Kramer, "Collective Impact," *Stanford Social Innovation Review*, Winter 2011, https://ssir.org/articles/entry/collective_impact#.
29. StriveTogether, "Who We Are," accessed October 12, 2020, https://www.strivetogether.org/who-we-are/.
30. Connect4Climate, "About," accessed October 8, 2020, https://www.connect4climate.org/about.
31. Prevention Institute, "Our Approach," accessed October 12, 2020, https://www.preventioninstitute.org/about-us/our-approach.
32. Rutgers School of Public Health, "New Jersey COVID-19 Community Contact

Tracing Corps Program: Information about Student Contact Tracers," May 14, 2020, https://sph.rutgers.edu/covid19/index.html.

33. For an overview of the literature on partnerships, see Amelia Clarke and Andrew Crane, "Cross-Sector Partnerships for Systemic Change: Systematized Literature Review and Agenda for Further Research," *Journal of Business Ethics* 150, no. 2 (June 2018): 303–313, https://doi.org/10.1007/s10551-018-3922-2; and John D. Donahue and Richard A. Zeckhauser, *Collaborative Governance: Private Roles for Public Goals in Turbulent Times* (Princeton, NJ: Princeton University Press, 2012).

34. See, e.g., Intersector Project, "The Intersector Toolkit," accessed October 12, 2020, http://intersector.com/toolkit/; Partnering Initiative, "TPI Tools," accessed December 27, 2019, https://thepartneringinitiative.org/tpi-tools/; European Commission, "The European Commission Public-Private Partnership Toolkit," accessed December 27, 2019, https://ec.europa.eu/regional_policy /sources/docgener/guides/ppp_en.pdf; and David B. Smith and Jeanine Becker, "The Essential Skills of Cross-Sector Leadership," *Stanford Social Innovation Review*, Winter 2018, https://ssir.org/articles/entry/the_essential_skills_of_cross _sector_leadership#. The Collaboration Prize has a checklist for managing nonprofit partnerships. AIM Alliance, "Board Members' Guide to Partnership Planning," accessed October 12, 2020, https://lodestar.asu.edu/sites/default /files/aimboardmembersguide.pdf.

35. Donahue and Zeckhauser, *Collaborative Governance*, 35–36.

36. Central Park Conservancy, "About Us," accessed October 12, 2020, https://www .centralparknyc.org/abou.

37. "Public-Private Partnerships for Green Space" (SIPA Working Paper 14-0005.0, School of International and Public Affairs, May 2014), http://ccnmtl.columbia .edu/projects/caseconsortium/casestudies/128/casestudy/files/global/128/PPP %20Parks%20Final%20072214.pdf.

38. Intersector Project, "The Connecting Veterans to Resources in the Central Savannah River Area," accessed October 12, 2020, http://intersector.com/case /awpveterans_georgia/; ForcesUnited, "990 Form," accessed October 12, 2020, https://forcesunited.org/wp-content/uploads/2019/10/2018-Form-990-Public -Inspection-Copy.pdf.

39. ForcesUnited, home page, accessed October 9, 2020, https://forcesunited.org/.

40. Office of the Inspector General, "Review of Alleged Mismanagement at the Health Eligibility Center," September 2, 2015, https://www.va.gov/oig/pubs /VAOIG-14-01792-510.pdf.

41. Daariimaa Khurelbat et al., "Prevalence Estimates of Substandard Drugs in Mongolia Using a Random Sample Survey," *SpringerPlus* 3 (December 2, 2014): art. 709, doi: 10.1186/2193-1801-3-709.

42. Farmatrust, "Government and Regulators," accessed December 28, 2019, https://www.farmatrust.com/governments-regulators.

43. Rockefeller Foundation, "Resilient Cities, Resilient Lives: Learning from the 100 RC Network," July 2019, 99, http://www.100resilientcities.org/wp-content /uploads/2019/07/100RC-Report-Capstone-PDF.pdf.

44. Krista Cannelakis, interview with author, Washington, DC, October 27, 2019 (notes on file with author).

45. Bloomberg Philanthropies, "Chapter 3: New Ways of Working for Government," in "2018 Mayor's Challenge," accessed May 6, 2019, https://mayorschallenge .bloomberg.org/the-creative-city-report/Chapter3/.

46. Elizabeth Reynoso, "The Power of Ecosystems for Problem-Solving," Living Cities, March 28, 2018, https://www.livingcities.org/blog/1248-the-power-of -ecosystems-for-problem-solving.

47. White House Office of the Press Secretary, "Impact Report: 100 Examples of President Obama's Leadership in Science, Technology, and Innovation," press release, June 21, 2016, https://obamawhitehouse.archives.gov/the-press-office /2016/06/21/impact-report-100-examples-president-obamas-leadership-science.

48. Thomas Kalil, "Policy Entrepreneurship at the White House: Getting Things Done in Large Organizations," *Innovations: Technology, Governance, Globalization* 11, nos. 3–4 (Summer–Fall 2017): 4–21, https://doi.org/10.1162/inov_a_00253.

49. Robert Wiblin and Keiran Harris, "How to Have a Big Impact in Government and Huge Organisations, Based on 16 Years' Experience in the White House," 80,000 Podcast, April 23, 2019, https://80000hours.org/podcast/episodes /tom-kalil-government-careers/.

50. National Science Board, "Teachers of Mathematics and Science," *Science & Engineering Indicators 2018*, 2018, https://www.nsf.gov/statistics/2018/nsb20181/.

51. Beth Simone Noveck, "New York City Students Get Down and Dirty for National Lab Day," *White House Blog*, May 6, 2010, https://obamawhitehouse.archives .gov/blog/2010/05/06/new-york-city-students-get-down-and-dirty-national -lab-day.

52. Andrew Curry, "How Crowdsourcing Aided a Push to Preserve the Histories of Nazi Victims," *New York Times*, June 3, 2020, https://www.nytimes.com/2020 /06/03/world/europe/nazis-arolsen-archive.html?smid=tw-share.

53. "Congressional Science Policy Initiative: More than 600 Volunteer Scientists across the USA Informing the Work of Congress," The GovLab, accessed June 5, 2020, https://congress.crowd.law/case-congressional-science-policy-initiative .html.

54. Kelsey Sutton, "How Big Tech Is Working with Nonprofits and Governments to Turn Data into Solutions during Disasters," *AdWeek*, October 15, 2018, https:// www.adweek.com/digital/how-tech-companies-are-working-with-nonprofits -and-governments-to-turn-data-into-solutions/.

55. "California Data Collaborative ('CaDC') Coalition of Water Utilities," Data Collaboratives, The GovLab, accessed May 6, 2019, http://datacollaboratives.org /cases/california-data-collaborative-cadc-coalition-of-water-utilities.html; "Genomic Data Commons," Data Collaboratives, The GovLab, accessed May 6, 2019, http://datacollaboratives.org/cases/genomic-data-commons.html.

56. Stefaan Verhulst and Andrew Young, "Data Collaboratives Explorer," accessed December 27, 2019, https://datacollaboratives.org/canvas.html.

57. John D. Donahue and Richard A. Zeckhauser, "Public Private Collaboration," in

The Oxford Handbook of Public Policy, ed. Michael Moran, Martin Rein, and Robert E. Goodin (Oxford: Oxford University Press, 2006), 522.

58. Buffett and Eimicke, *Social Value Investing*, 73.

59. Darian Stibbe, Stuart Reid, and Julia Gilbert, "Maximising the Impact of Partnerships for the SDGs," Partnering Initiative and UN DESA, 2019, 11, https://www.thepartneringinitiative.org/wp-content/uploads/2018/07/Maximising-partnership-value-for-the-SDGs.pdf.

60. AllTrials, "All Trials Registered | All Results Reported," accessed October 12, 2020, https://www.alltrials.net/find-out-more/.

61. Beth Simone Noveck, "Data Collaboratives: Sharing Public Data in Private Hands for Social Good," *Forbes*, September 24, 2015, https://www.forbes.com/sites/bethsimonenoveck/2015/09/24/private-data-sharing-for-public-good/#a59321851cda.

62. Linda Hill and Allison Wigen, "Tom Kalil: Leading Technology and Innovation at the White House," Harvard Business School Case Collection, August 2016 (rev. March 2019), https://www.hbs.edu/faculty/pages/item.aspx?num=51561.

63. Atul Gawande, *The Checklist Manifesto* (New York: Metropolitan Books, 2009), 11.

64. Intersector Project, "The Intersector Toolkit," accessed December 27, 2019, http://intersector.com/toolkit/.

65. Hill and Wigen, "Tom Kalil."

66. Molly Jackman, "ALEC's Influence over Lawmaking in State Legislatures," Brookings, December 6, 2013, https://www.brookings.edu/articles/alecs-influence-over-lawmaking-in-state-legislatures/. ("First, ALEC model bills are, word-for-word, introduced in our state legislatures at a non-trivial rate. Second, they have a good chance—better than most legislation—of being enacted into law. Finally, the bills that pass are most often linked to controversial social and economic issues.")

67. David Lazer, "Regulatory Capitalism as a Networked Order: The International System as an Informational Network," *Annals of the American Academy of Political and Social Science* 598, no. 1 (2005): 52–66, http://doi.org/10.1177/0002716204272590.

68. David Smith, "Community Centered Selfishness," Independent Sector, February 7, 2017, https://independentsector.org/news-post/community-centered-selfishness/.

69. "Share a Vision of Success," The Intersector Toolkit, accessed December 27, 2019, http://intersector.com/toolkit/share-a-vision-of-success/#tab-9c202eec-ee35-6.

70. Intersector Project, "Agree on Measures of Success," accessed December 27, 2019, http://intersector.com/toolkit/agree-on-measures-of-success/.

71. StriveTogether, "Building an Accountability Structure," accessed December 27, 2019, https://www.strivetogether.org/wp-content/uploads/2017/03/AccountabilityStructureToolkit_Final_2015_1.pdf.

72. Prescott and Stibbe, "Better Together."

73. The GovLab, "There Are Six Main Types of Data Collaborative," Data Collaboratives, accessed October 12, 2020, http://www.datacollaboratives.org.

74. Collaboration Prize, "Models of Collaboration: Nonprofits Working Together,"

accessed October 12, 2020, https://lodestar.asu.edu/sites/default/files/coll_models
_report-2009.pdf.

75. Collective Impact Forum, "What Is Collective Impact?," accessed October 12, 2020, https://www.collectiveimpactforum.org/what-collective-impact.

76. The Good Project, "The Good Collaboration Toolkit: Getting Started," accessed October 12, 2020, http://thegoodproject.org/collaborationtoolkit/.

77. W. K. Kellogg Foundation, "Logic Model Development Guide," January 2004, 1, https://www.bttop.org/sites/default/files/public/W.K.%20Kellogg%20Logic Model.pdf. See also C. C. Schmitz and B. A. Parsons, "Everything You Wanted to Know about Logic Models but Were Afraid to Ask," W. K. Kellogg Foundation, October 20, 1999.

78. W. K. Kellogg Foundation, "Logic Model Development Guide," 2.

79. Julia Belluz, "How Michelle Obama Quietly Changed What Americans Eat," *Vox*, October 3, 2016, https://www.vox.com/2016/10/3/12866484/michelle -obama-childhood-obesity-lets-move.

80. World Bank, "A Framework for Disclosure in Public-Private Partnerships," August 2015, http://pubdocs.worldbank.org/en/773541448296707678/Dis closure-in-PPPs-Framework.pdf.

81. Dodds, "Multi-Stakeholder Partnerships," 12.

82. Community Tool Box, "Section 8. Including Youth on Your Board, Commission, or Committee," accessed December 28, 2019, https://ctb.ku.edu/en/table-of -contents/structure/organizational-structure/include-youth/main.

83. All of Us, "Core Values," accessed October 12, 2020, https://allofus.nih.gov /about/core-values.

84. StriveTogether, "Building an Accountability Structure," March 2017, https:// www.strivetogether.org/wp-content/uploads/2017/03/AccountabilityStructure Toolkit_Final_2015_1.pdf, 17.

85. StriveTogether, 21.

86. Rockefeller Foundation, "Resilient Cities, Resilient Lives," 101.

10. TESTING WHAT WORKS

1. "How Do We Choose the Most Promising Theory of Change? Building on the Context-Intervention 2×2," *From Poverty to Power* (blog), Oxfam, December 9, 2016, https://oxfamblogs.org/fp2p/how-do-we-chose-the-most-promising-theory -of-change-building-on-the-context-intervention-2x2/.

2. Ideas42, "A/B Testing Tool," accessed October 9, 2020, http://abtesting.ideas42 .org/.

3. Laura Haynes et al., "Test, Learn, Adapt: Developing Public Policy with Ran-domised Controlled Trials" (policy paper, UK Cabinet Office: Behavioural Insights Team, 2012), https://assets.publishing.service.gov.uk/government /uploads/system/uploads/attachment_data/file/62529/TLA-1906126.pdf.

4. Anthony Barrows et al., "Behavioral Design Teams: A Model for Integrating Behavioral Design in City Government," Ideas42, April 2018, 12, https://www .ideas42.org/wp-content/uploads/2018/04/BDT_Playbook_FINAL-digital.pdf.

5. Kevin J. Boudreau and Karim R. Lakhani, "Innovation Experiments: Researching Technical Advance, Knowledge Production, and the Design of Supporting Institutions," *Innovation Policy and the Economy* 16, no. 1 (2016): 137.

6. Barrows et al., "Behavioral Design Teams," 32–33.

7. Steven Johnson, *The Ghost Map: The Story of London's Most Terrifying Epidemic— and How It Changed Science, Cities, and the Modern World* (New York: Riverhead Books, 2007), 73.

8. Duke University, "ModU: Powerful Concepts in Social Science," accessed October 12, 2020, https://modu.ssri.duke.edu/module/examples-experiments/london -cholera-outbreak-was-it-natural-experiment.

9. Matt Salganik, "Who to Ask," in *Bit by Bit: Social Research in the Digital* Age (Princeton, NJ: Princeton University Press, 2017), open review edition, section 3.4, https://www.bitbybitbook.com/en/1st-ed/asking-questions/who/.

10. Wesley P. Schultz et al., "The Constructive, Destructive, and Reconstructive Power of Social Norms," *Psychological Science* 18, no. 5 (2007): 429–434, https:// doi.org/10.1111/j.1467-9280.2007.01917.x.

11. Tom Frieden, "Why the 'Gold Standard' of Medical Research Is No Longer Enough," *STAT*, August 2, 2017, https://www.statnews.com/2017/08/02 /randomized-controlled-trials-medical-research/.

12. Linda Kaye, Stephanie Malone, and Helen Wall, "Emojis: Insights, Affordances and Possibilities for Psychological Science," *Trends in Cognitive Sciences* 21 (2017): 66–68, doi: 10.1016/j.tics.2016.10.007.

13. Amos Tversky and Daniel Kahneman, "The Framing of Decisions and the Psychology of Choice," *Science* 211, no. 4481 (January 30, 1981): 453–458, doi: 10.1126/science.7455683.

14. Jon A. Krosnick and Duane F. Alwin, "An Evaluation of Cognitive Theory of Response Order Effects in Survey Measurement," *Public Opinion Quarterly* 51, no. 2 (Summer 1987): 201–229.

15. Salganik, "Who to Ask."

16. "Questionnaire Design," *Methods* (blog), Pew Research Center, accessed October 12, 2020, https://www.pewresearch.org/methods/u-s-survey-research/question naire-design/.

17. Atul Gawande, "Testing, Testing," *New Yorker*, December 7, 2009, https://www .newyorker.com/magazine/2009/12/14/testing-testing-2.

18. Jesper Christiansen, "Skills, Attitudes and Behaviours That Fuel Public Innovation: A Guide to Getting the Most from Nesta's Competency Framework for Experimenting and Public Problem Solving," Nesta, accessed December 28, 2019, https://www.nesta.org.uk/toolkit/skills-attitudes-and-behaviours-fuel -public-innovation/.

19. Colleen V. Chien, "Rigorous Policy Pilots: Experimentation in the Administration of the Law," *Iowa Law Review* 104 (2019): 2319–2350, http://dx.doi.org /10.2139/ssrn.3312696.

20. Bas Leurs and Kelly Duggan, "Proof of Concept, Prototype, Pilot, MVP—What's in a Name? Four Methods for Testing and Developing Solutions," *Nesta Blog*,

December 20, 2018, https://www.nesta.org.uk/blog/proof-of-concept-prototype
-pilot-mvp-whats-in-a-name/.

21. Katherine Barrett and Richard Greene, "Six Tips for Piloting New Programs,"
Governing, August 28, 2019, https://www.governing.com/columns/smart-mgmt
/gov-six-tips-piloting-new-programs.html.

22. "Moving Beyond 'Pilot-itis' and Getting to Scale," Concern Worldwide, accessed
June 5, 2020, https://www.concernusa.org/scaling-innovations-to-save-the-lives
-of-mothers-and-babies/.

23. "Why American Departments Are Sending Social Workers to Answer 911 Calls,"
Economist, May 11, 2019, https://www.economist.com/united-states/2019/05/11
/why-american-departments-are-sending-social-workers-to-answer-911-calls.

24. Bennett Institute for Public Policy, "Teaching Public Service in a Digital Age,"
July 31, 2020, https://www.bennettinstitute.cam.ac.uk/news/teaching-public
-service-digital-age/.

25. Isabel Vogel, "Challenge Brief: How Do We Advance the Pace and Success of
Innovation for Development in Tackling Poverty and Other Global Challenges?"
Ideas to Impact, March 2017, http://www.ideastoimpact.net/sites/default/files
/doc_research/challenge_brief_v8a.pdf.

26. Claudio Ferraz, Frederico Finan, and Diana B. Moreira, "Corrupting Learning:
Evidence from Missing Federal Education Funds in Brazil," *Journal of Public
Economics* 96, nos. 9–10 (2012): 712–726. See also Gabriela Moll, "Horta
comunitária será usada na merenda do CEF 404, em Samambaia," Agência
Brasília, November 7, 2016, http://www.agenciabrasilia.df.gov.br/2016/11/07
/horta-comunitaria-sera-usada-na-merenda-do-cef-404-em-samambaia/.

27. Scifabric, "Crowdcrafting," accessed October 12, 2020, https://scifabric.com
/crowdcrafting/.

28. Larry Cooley, *Scaling Up—From Vision to Large-Scale Change: A Management
Framework for Practitioners*, 3rd ed. (Arlington, VA: Management Systems
International, 2016), 1, https://www.msiworldwide.com/sites/default/files
/additional-resources/2018-11/ScalingUp_3rdEdition.pdf.

11. DOING DIFFERENTLY, LEARNING DIFFERENTLY

1. Peter Bragge and Russell Gruen, *From Roadside to Recovery: The Story of the Victorian State Trauma System* (Melbourne: Monash University Publishing, 2018), 318.

2. Australian Bureau of Statistics, "Population Size and Growth," *Yearbook Australia*,
last modified May 24, 2012, https://www.abs.gov.au/ausstats/abs@.nsf/Lookup
/by%20Subject/1301.0~2012~Main%20Features~Population%20size%20
and%20growth~47. See also Bragge and Gruen, *From Roadside to Recovery*, 33.

3. John F. Kennedy, "Moonshot Speech," delivered September 12, 1962, available at
https://er.jsc.nasa.gov/seh/ricetalk.htm.

4. European Commission, "Mission-Oriented Policy for Horizon Europe," accessed
December 28, 2019, https://ec.europa.eu/info/horizon-europe-next-research-and
-innovation-framework-programme/mission-oriented-policy-horizon-europe_en.

5. Rainer Kattel et al., "The Economics of Change: Policy Appraisal for Missions,

Market Shaping and Public Purpose" (working paper, UCL Institute for Innovation and Public Purpose, 2018), https://www.ucl.ac.uk/bartlett/public-purpose/wp2018-06.

6. Let's Move!, "About," accessed October 9, 2020, https://letsmove.obamawhitehouse.archives.gov/about.

7. Kevin Desouza and Kendra Smith, "Mega-Scale IT Projects in the Public Sector," *TechTank* (blog), Brookings Institution, May 28, 2015, https://www.brookings.edu/blog/techtank/2015/05/28/mega-scale-it-projects-in-the-public-sector/.

8. Obama White House, "Contracting Guidance to Support Modular Development," June 14, 2012, https://obamawhitehouse.archives.gov/sites/default/files/omb/procurement/guidance/modular-approaches-for-information-technology.pdf.

9. World Economic Forum, "Agile Governance: Reimagining Policy-Making in the Fourth Industrial Revolution," January 2018, http://www3.weforum.org/docs/WEF_Agile_Governance_Reimagining_Policy-making_4IR_report.pdf.

10. Peter Viechnicki and Mahesh Kelkar, "Agile by the Numbers: A Data Analysis of Agile Development in the US Federal Government," *Deloitte Insights*, May 5, 2017, https://www2.deloitte.com/insights/us/en/industry/public-sector/agile-in-government-by-the-numbers.html.

11. Kristofer Kelly-Frere and Jonathan Veale, "Essay: Advanced Design for the Public Sector," *Jonathan Veale Blog, Medium*, January 7, 2018, https://medium.com/@jonathanveale/essay-advanced-design-for-the-public-sector-223ded08f7d9.

12. Beth Simone Noveck, "Open Government iLabs" (memo), January 31, 2009 (on file with author).

13. Beth Simone Noveck, *Wiki Government: How Technology Can Make Government Better, Democracy Stronger, and Citizens More Powerful* (Washington, DC: Brookings Institution Press, 2010).

14. Mohammed bin Rashid Centre for Government Innovation, "Government Innovation Labs," accessed May 10, 2019, https://www.mbrcgi.gov.ae/en/experiment/government-innovation-labs.

15. UK government, "Projects Lay the Groundwork for a Future of Robolawyers and Flying Cars," press release, October 5, 2018, https://www.gov.uk/government/news/projects-lay-the-groundwork-for-a-future-of-robolawyers-and-flying-cars.

16. Geoff Mulgan, "The Radical's Dilemma: An Overview of the Practice and Prospects of Social Public Labs—Version 1," Nesta, February 2014, https://media.nesta.org.uk/documents/social_and_public_s_-_and_the_radicals_dilemma.pdf. See also Zaid Hassan, *The Social Labs Revolution: A New Approach to Solving Our Most Complex Challenges* (San Francisco: Berrett-Koehler, 2014).

17. United Nations Development Programme, "Accelerator Labs," accessed January 6, 2020, https://acceleratorlabs.undp.org/.

18. Apolitical, "Public Innovation Labs around the World Are Closing—Here's Why," February 27, 2019, https://apolitical.co/solution_article/public-innovation-labs-around-the-world-are-closing-heres-why/.

19. Administrative Conference of the United States, "Administrative Conference Recommendation 2017–6: Learning from Regulatory Experience," adopted

December 15, 2017, https://www.acus.gov/sites/default/files/documents/Recommendation%202017–6%20%28Learning%20from%20Regulatory%20Experience%29_0.pdf.

20. UK Financial Conduct Authority, "The Impact and Effectiveness of Innovate," April 2019, https://www.fca.org.uk/publication/research/the-impact-and-effectiveness-of-innovate.pdf. See also FCA, "Regulatory Sandbox," May 10, 2020, https://www.fca.org.uk/firms/innovation/regulatory-sandbox.

21. James Q. Wilson, "The Bureaucracy Problem," *National Affairs*, Winter 1967, 7.

22. United States Government, "Policy and Supporting Positions," December 1, 2016, https://www.govinfo.gov/content/pkg/GPO-PLUMBOOK-2016/pdf/GPO-PLUMBOOK-2016.pdf.

23. Khushboo Agarwal, "Playing in the Regulatory Sandbox," *NYU Journal of Law and Business*, January 8, 2018, https://www.nyujlb.org/single-post/2018/01/08/Playing-in-the-Regulatory-Sandbox.

24. Beth Simone Noveck, "Rights-Based and Tech Driven: Open Data, Freedom of Information, and the Future of Government Transparency," *Yale Human Rights and Development Journal* 19, no. 1 (2017), https://digitalcommons.law.yale.edu/cgi/viewcontent.cgi?article=1140&context=yhrdlj.

25. "The role of the professional civil servant is enshrined by the law itself, which reinforces the profession's control over the flow of information into and out of institutions—what Pierre Bourdieu calls the 'officializing strategy' of bureaucracy—in ways designed to dissuade citizens from engagement. There is a wealth of administrative law that limits control over speech in the public sector to public management professionals and treats their decisionmaking with legal deference. For example, key information law statutes intentionally limit information sharing and collaboration and preserve the domain of the public servant distinct from and closed to others. The public earned a right to access information held by government relatively late in the twentieth century, and even then, only upon request and with significant limitations. For those of us outside the curtain, the effect is impressive." Beth Simone Noveck, *Smart Citizens, Smarter State: The Technologies of Expertise and the Future of Governing* (Cambridge, MA: Harvard University Press, 2015), 49.

26. Brian Glick, "Interview: Government Digital Chief Mike Bracken—Why I Quit," *Computer Weekly*, August 13, 2015, https://www.computerweekly.com/news/4500251662/Interview-Government-digital-chief-Mike-Bracken-why-I-quit.

27. US Office of Personnel Management, "Profile of Federal Civilian Non-Postal Employees," September 30, 2017, https://www.opm.gov/policy-data-oversight/data-analysis-documentation/federal-employment-reports/reports-publications/profile-of-federal-civilian-non-postal-employees/.

28. Joe Davidson and Ed O'Keefe, "Obama Wants Federal Agencies to Hit the Gas on Hiring," *Washington Post*, May 11, 2010, http://www.washingtonpost.com/wp-dyn/content/article/2010/05/10/AR2010051004898.html.

29. Lynn Certo, "Streamline Hiring Process," Innovation ENJINE Challenge, accessed May 10, 2019, https://enjine.smarter.nj.gov/post/170.

30. US Department of Labor, Bureau of Labor Statistics, "Employee Tenure in 2018," press release, September 20, 2018, https://www.bls.gov/news.release/pdf/tenure.pdf.

31. "Laid Off? It's Good for You and Good for the Tech Industry," *Wired*, July 20, 2009, https://www.wired.com/2009/07/st-essay-10/. See also AnnaLee Saxenian, *Regional Advantage: Culture and Competition in Silicon Valley and Route 128* (Cambridge, MA: Harvard University Press, 1996).

32. Public and Commercial Services Union, "Career Breaks," April 22, 2016, https://www.pcs.org.uk/pcs-in-hm-revenue-and-customs-group/latest-news/career-breaks.

33. Scottish government, "Scottish Government Staff Handbook," 2007, https://www.gov.scot/resource/doc/76007/0060961.pdf.

34. William Eggers and Shalabh Kumar Singh, *The Public Innovator's Playbook: Nurturing Bold Ideas in Government* (New York: Deloitte Research, 2009), 20.

35. John Buckner, "OPM Gives Agencies New Way to Measure Time-to-Hire," *Federal News Network*, April 21, 2011, https://federalnewsnetwork.com/management/2011/04/opm-gives-agencies-new-way-to-measure-time-to-hire/. See also Obama White House, Office of the Press Secretary, "Presidential Memorandum —Improving the Federal Recruitment and Hiring Process," May 11, 2010, https://obamawhitehouse.archives.gov/the-press-office/presidential-memorandum-improving-federal-recruitment-and-hiring-process.

36. Beth Simone Noveck, "Public Entrepreneurship: How to Train 21st-Century Leaders Opinion: Public Sector Innovation Learning Goes to the Next Level," Apolitical, June 19, 2019, https://apolitical.co/solution_article/public-entrepreneurship-how-to-train-21st-century-leaders/.

37. Beth Simone Noveck and Jason Williams-Bellamy, "Before Training Public Servants, You Must Educate Yourself," Apolitical, July 22, 2019, https://apolitical.co/solution_article/dont-teach-public-servants-before-educating-yourself/.

38. Kevin Richman, OECD, interview with author, February 15, 2019 (notes on file with author).

39. OECD, Observatory for Public Sector Innovation, *Core Skills for Public Sector Innovation* (Paris: OECD Publishing, April 2017), https://www.oecd.org/media/oecdorg/satellitesites/opsi/contents/files/OECD_OPSI-core_skills_for_public_sector_innovation-201704.pdf.

40. The GovLab, "Solving Public Problems with Data," accessed December 30, 2019, https://sppd.thegovlab.org/.

41. David Figlio, Mark Rush, and Lu Yin, "Is It Live or Is It Internet? Experimental Estimates of the Effects of Online Instruction on Student Learning," *Journal of Labor Economics* 31, no. 4 (2013): 763–784.

42. Frank Mayadas, Gary Miller, and John Sener, "Definitions of E-Learning Courses and Programs," accessed April 4, 2015, https://onlinelearningconsortium.org/updated-e-learning-definitions-2/.

43. Digital Leaders, "DL Israel Aims to Bring Together Leaders to Bridge the Digital

Divide," accessed December 29, 2019, https://digileaders.com/dl-israel-aims
-bring-together-leaders-bridge-digital-divide/.

44. Linda De George Walker and Mary Keeffe, "Self-Determined Blended Learning:
A Case Study of Blended Learning Design," *Higher Education Research and
Development* 29, no. 1 (January 4, 2010): 1–13, doi: 10.1080/072943609032
77380.

45. Treasury Board, "Government of Canada Launches Digital Academy," news
release, October 16, 2018, https://www.canada.ca/en/treasury-board-secretariat
/news/2018/10/government-of-canada-launches-digital-academy.html.

46. Ms. Ong Toon Hui, Dean & CEO, Civil Service College, Singapore, interview
with author, November 4, 2019 (notes on file with author).

47. Mr. Yeo Whee Jim, Director, Institute of Governance and Policy, Civil Service
Training College, Singapore, interview with author, November 4, 2019 (notes
on file with author).

48. Interior Ministry, "Digitalakademie" (presentation at the Digitalakademie
Planning Workshop, September 23, 2020) (slides on file with author).

49. Barcelona, "Ethical Digital Standards," accessed October 12, 2020, https://www
.barcelona.cat/digitalstandards/manifesto/0.2/.

50. Escuela de Gobierno, "Proyecto Curso Ciencia de Datos para Directivos Públicos,"
accessed December 30, 2019, https://gobierno.uai.cl/centros/goblab/proyecto
-ciencia-de-datos-para-directivos-publicos/.

51. Coleridge Initiative, https://coleridgeinitiative.org/.

52. Apolitical, "Microcourses," accessed October 17, 2020, https://apolitical.co/micro
courses.

53. Busrides, https://en.busrides-trajetsenbus.ca/.

54. Kent Aitken, Canada School of Public Service, interview with author, December
7, 2018 (notes on file with author).

55. David Edinger and Scotty Martin, "Investing in Future Innovators: Denver's
Peak Academy," *Living Cities Blog*, March 8, 2013, https://www.livingcities.org
/blog/224-investing-in-future-innovators-denver-s-peak-academy. See also
Project on Municipal Innovation Team, "Improving Performance by Investing
in People," *Living Cities Blog*, December 10, 2014, https://www.livingcities.org
/blog/738-improving-performance-by-investing-in-people.

56. Jonatan Beun, "Moving 'the Elephant': Scaling Innovation Capabilities to Foster
Government's Transformation" (presentation to the States of Change Festival,
June 18, 2020).

57. Bharat Anand, Jan Hammond, and V. G. Narayanan, "What Harvard Business
School Has Learned about Online Collaboration from HBX," *Harvard Business
Review*, April 14, 2015, https://hbr.org/2015/04/what-harvard-business-school
-has-learned-about-online-collaboration-from-hbx#:~:text=The%20completion
%20rate%20%E2%80%94%20typically%20in,on%20a%205%2Dpoint%20
scale.

58. Song Hsi Ching, Singapore Civil Service Training College, interview with author,
November 4, 2019 (notes on file with author).

59. Imperial College, Centre for Health Policy, "NHS Digital Academy," accessed December 30, 2019, http://www.imperial.ac.uk/centre-for-health-policy/edu cation/nhs-digital-academy/.

60. Participation Officers, PDIS, "The Ultimate Guide of Participation Officers Network," accessed May 10, 2019, https://po.pdis.tw/en/.

61. Audrey Tang, "Inside Taiwan's New Digital Democracy," *Economist*, March 12, 2019, https://www.economist.com/open-future/2019/03/12/inside-taiwans -new-digital-democracy.

62. "vTaiwan Open Consultation & Participation Officers Training June 11–12, 2018," accessed October 10, 2020, http://training.gov.network/.

63. City of São Pablo Government, "Open Government Agents Program," accessed June 18, 2019, https://www.prefeitura.sp.gov.br/cidade/secretarias/governo /governo_aberto_na_cidade_de_sao_paulo/index.php?p=253369.

64. Australian Government, Department of Industry, "Australian Biz Lab Academy," accessed December 30, 2019, https://www.industry.gov.au/government-to-gov ernment/bizlab-academy/. See also Australia's "BizLab Human-Centered Design Curriculum," OECD, accessed October 12, 2020, https://oecd-opsi .org/toolkits/australias-bizlab-human-centered-design-curriculum/.

65. Leanne Douglas, "Sharing Our Lessons from Teaching Design," OECD Office of Public Sector Innovation, March 6, 2019, https://oecd-opsi.org/sharing-our -lessons-from-teaching-design/.

66. GovLab Academy, The GovLab, http://govlabacademy.org/.

67. Nesta, "States of Change," accessed December 30, 2019, https://states-of -change.org.

68. Bas Leurs, Paulina González-Ortega, and Diana Hidalgo, "Experimenta: Build- ing the Next Generation of Chile's Public Innovators," Nesta, March 2018, 8, https://states-of-change.org/assets/downloads/nesta_experimenta_report _english.pdf.

69. NJ Innovation Skills Accelerator, https://innovation.nj.gov/skills/index.html.

70. Apolitical, "Mapped: 100+ Teams Teaching Government the Skills of the Future," accessed October 11, 2020, https://apolitical.co/government-learn ing-directory/.

12. TRAINING THE NEXT GENERATION OF LEADERS AND PROBLEM SOLVERS

1. This section is adapted from Beth Simone Noveck, "Public Entrepreneurship and Policy Engineering," *Communications of the ACM* 62, no. 12 (December 2019), https://doi.org/10.1145/3325811. See also Beth Simone Noveck and Dinorah Cantu, "Training the Next Generation of Public Leaders and Problem Solvers," *Medium*, March 30, 2016, https://medium.com/@bethnoveck /training-the-next-generation-of-public-leaders-and-problem-solvers-7d41523ddo9.

2. "Statement on Education for Public Problem Solving," Freeman Spogli Institute for International Studies, Stanford University, accessed October 12, 2020, https://fsi.stanford.edu/publicproblemsolving/docs/statement-education-public -problem-solving.

3. Michael Lindsey, interview with Technology and Social Change Clinic, New York University, Spring 2020 (notes on file with author).

4. The list of activities included the following: published research in an academic journal; published a book; presented at an academic conference; presented at a nonacademic conference; written an op-ed; contributed to a blog; written for popular media (newspaper, magazine); been interviewed for popular media (newspaper, magazine); appeared on popular broadcast media (TV, radio, YouTube); maintained a Twitter account; supervised students working with outside groups/organizations; provided expert opinion to government, NGO, and/or industry; proposed/drafted new policies/legislation; collected or analyzed data for government or NGO; provided research for government or NGO; provided design or technology advising for government or NGO; designed or conducted an experiment for government or NGO; conducted training for government or NGOs.

5. Caitlin Gebhard and Nelson James, "Survey on Faculty Engagement with Policymakers and NGOs," conducted March 16, 2020, results analyzed May 3, 2020, https://www.publicentrepreneur.org/nyu-tandon.

6. Ali Nouri, "Congress Needs More Scientific Expertise to Fight COVID-19," *Scientific American*, April 6, 2020, https://blogs.scientificamerican.com /observations/congress-needs-more-scientific-expertise-to-fight-covid-19/.

7. Jiaqi Dong and Christine Vandevoorde, "NYU Prepares the Next Generation of Public Problem Solvers," May 18, 2020, final paper prepared for Technology and Social Change, Spring 2020 (on file with author).

8. P. Paul Heppner and Dong-gwi Lee, "Problem-Solving Appraisal and Psychological Adjustment," *Handbook of Positive Psychology*, ed. C. R. Snyder and Shane J. Lopez (Oxford: Oxford University Press, 2002), 288–298.

9. Oliver Scott Curry, Lee A. Rowland, Caspar J. Van Lissa, Sally Zlotowitz, John McAlaney, and Harvey Whitehouse, "Happy to Help? A Systematic Review and Meta-Analysis of the Effects of Performing Acts of Kindness on the Well-Being of the Actor," *Journal of Experimental Social Psychology* 76 (May 2018): 320–329.

10. Sheryl Sorby, speech at the annual conference of the American Society for Engineering Education, June 26, 2020.

11. National Academy of Engineering, "Grand Challenge Scholars Program," accessed December 30, 2019, https://www.nae.edu/169108/Grand-Challenges -Scholars-Program.

12. NYU Ability Lab, http://ability.nyu.edu; Rensselaer Center for Open Source, http://rcos.rpi.edu.

13. Valeri A. Werpetinski, "Engaging Engineering Students with Non-Engineering Majors in Interdisciplinary Service-Learning Projects: A Model for Engineering Everywhere for Everyone" (paper presented at the 2017 ASEE Zone II Conference, American Society for Engineering Education), accessed January 6, 2020, http://people.cst.cmich.edu/yelam1k/asee/proceedings/2017/3/130.pdf.

14. Carl Gombrich, interview with author, June 30, 2020. See also London Interdisciplinary School, https://www.londoninterdisciplinaryschool.org/.

15. Humanities Lab, Arizona State University, "About," accessed June 6, 2020, https://humanities.lab.asu.edu/about/.

16. CODE, University of Applied Sciences, "Curiosity-Driven Education," accessed June 6, 2020, https://code.berlin/en/concept/.

17. Dong and Vandevoorde, "NYU Prepares the Next Generation of Public Problem Solvers." See also the Reach Alliance, http://reachprojectuoft.com/.

18. Maggi Savin-Baden, "The Problem-Based Learning Landscape," *Planet* 4, no. 1 (2001): 4–6, doi: 10.11120/plan.2001.00040004.

19. Maggi Savin-Baden and Claire Howell, *Foundations of Problem-Based Learning* (London: Society for Research into Higher Education and Open University Press, 2014), 17.

20. H. S. Barrows and R. M. Tamblyn, *Problem-Based Learning: An Approach to Medical Education* (New York: Springer, 1980).

21. Thomas P. Duffy, "The Flexner Report—100 Years Later," *Yale Journal of Biology and Medicine* 84 (2011): 269–276.

22. Open Seventeen, http://bopenseventeen.org.

23. EPICS, Purdue University, https://engineering.purdue.edu/EPICS.

24. Kaila White, "ASU Students Finish $80,000 Mobile Dental Clinic for Charity," *Arizona Republic*, May 9, 2017, https://www.azcentral.com/story/news/local/tempe/2017/05/09/tempe-asu-students-mobile-dental-clinic-charity/314594001/.

25. Elizabeth Gerber et al., "Extracurricular Design-Based Learning: Preparing Students for Careers in Innovation," *International Journal of Engineering Education* 28, no. 2 (2012): 317–324; Elizabeth Gerber, "Design for America: Organizing for Civic Innovation," *Interactions*, March–April 2014, https://interactions.acm.org/archive/view/march-april-2014/design-for-america.

26. Leadership and Social Change: Sparking Social Change, syllabus, accessed June 6, 2020, https://wagner.nyu.edu/files/syllabi/202001/HPAM-GP.2186.001.pdf.

27. United for Social Change, "Mission," accessed July 5, 2020, https://united4sc.org/misson/.

28. Anita McGahan, "The New Agenda for Business Schools: Creating Problem Solvers for the World," *Rotman Magazine*, Spring 2012, 27.

INDEX

Figures and notes are indicated by f and n following the page number.

knowledge-practice gap, 337–39
Kramer, Mark, 256–57
Kremer, Michael, 209, 223
Kukharenko, Artem, 162

LabGob design academy (Argentina), 52, 121, 326
Laboratorio del Gobierno (Chile), 331
Lakewood, Colorado: open innovation in, 189; scaling solutions in, 297; Sustainable Neighborhoods Program in, 10–11, 181
Lakhani, Karim, 217
Landrieu, Mitch, 135
Laney, Doug, 140
LASSO (limited, (capable of being) acted (on), specific, supported, owned), 91–92
Latin America: COVID-19 response, 81, 112; public entrepreneurship in, 10; public-sector training in, 321, 331; Zika virus crisis (2016), 77, 112. *See also specific countries*
Lauritsen, Janet, 165
Lavis, John, 242
Lawrence Livermore National Laboratories, 205
law school curriculums, 339–40
Lean Six Sigma, 319, 326, 365n4
Le Corbusier, 101
Legend, John, 42
Lego Group, 182
Let's Move! campaign, 307
Leurs, Bas, 294
Levin, Yuval, 7
Lewis, Dana, 180
Lewis, John, 8
Library of Congress, 140
life expectancy, 28
Light, Paul, 25
Lindsey, Michael, 337
lobbyists, 26–27, 35–36
Local Motors, 181
Lodestar Center for Philanthropy and Nonprofit Innovation, 278
logic model, 279–80, 280f, 285–86

London: data-driven policy making in, 156; innovation exchanges with New York, 222, 318
London Interdisciplinary School (LIS), 342
Longo, Justin, 164
long-term care facilities, 117, 134–35, 310
Los Angeles: Business One Stop website in, 117; dog adoption programs in, 86
Louisiana, data-driven policy making in, 142
Louisville: air quality in, 23–24; collective intelligence used to solve problems in, 174
Lyft, 141

Ma, Yo-Yo, 198
MacArthur Foundation, 178, 236, 237
Machiavelli, Niccolò, *The Prince*, 23
machine learning, 159–62, 218
Maduro, Nicolas, 33
Majora Tu Escuela (Improve Your School) platform, 149
Malamud, Carl, 155
Malaria Atlas (Kenya), 278
Malaysia, regulatory sandbox in, 315
Malinowski, Branislaw, 120
Mann, Gideon, 165
Mapaton CDMX, 139
Martin, Bella, 106
Maryland StateStat program, 168–69
Massachusetts Institute of Technology (MIT), 116, 212, 214–15, 265
Matheny, Jason, 183
Mazdoor Kisan Shakti Sangathan (MKSS), 145
Mazzucato, Mariana, 24, 306
McGahan, Anita, 347–48
McKinsey (consulting firm), 16, 25, 118, 119, 199
McMaster University, 212, 242, 343
Mead, Margaret, 2, 120
Medicare and Medicaid, 34, 142, 152
MemFix project, 99
Memphis, Tennessee, human-centered design in, 98–99
MemShop project, 99

rapid field scanning. *See* fast field scanning
Rasmussen Reports, 226–27
Reach Alliance, 343
REACH program, 43
Reagan, Ronald, 2, 34–35, 258
Recidiviz (organization), 154
Re:Coded program, 5
Reddit, 168, 233
Red Innovadores Publicos (Chile), 234
reframing: exercise, 92–93; in problem
    definition stage, 79, 87; of public
    servants as public entrepreneurs, 20
Regulatory Pioneers Fund (UK), 313
regulatory sandboxes, 314–15
Remesh tool, 115
Render, Michael Santiago (Killer Mike), 7–8
Rensselaer Center for Open Source, 341
Research Gate, 226
Resilience Project, 80
Results First, 236
Results for America, 227
Retos Jalisco project (Mexico), 275
Reyes, Graciela, 10, 21
Richardson, Rashida, 145–46
Richter, Markus, 324
Rikers Island Prison, 119
RiskMap, 175, 189, 300
Rittel, Horst, 14
road safety initiatives, 303–4
Rockefeller Foundation, 161, 263, 284
Rodel Fellowship, 320
Roosevelt, Franklin, 260; Oglethorpe
    University address, 288
root cause analysis, 43, 59, 71–74, 82–87,
    90–91
Roper Center for Public Opinion Research,
    227
Rosenberg, Tina, 252–53
Rosenfeld, Michael J., 227
Roth, Alvin E., 223–24
Rotich, Juliana, 5
Rowan University, 3
Royal Society for the Arts (RSA), 181
Rush, Benjamin, *Observations upon
    the Present Government of Penn-
    sylvania,* 94

Russell, Bertrand, 7
Russia: public entrepreneurship in, 5;
    regulatory sandbox in, 315
Rutgers University, 3, 151, 266

Sackett, David, 201
Safaricom, 278
Safecast, 5–6, 60, 154, 175, 297
Salamon, Lester, 219, 245
Salganik, Matt, 112–13, 131, 157–58
Sandel, Michael, 30–31
Sanders, Bernie, 15
Sanders, Liz, 98, 104
San Francisco: Business One Stop website
    in, 117; partnerships for solution
    implementation in, 263–65
São Paulo, public-sector training in, 329
Save the Children, 79–80
Saxenian, AnnaLee, 318
scaling up: pilot projects and, 296–97;
    Providence Talks program, 237–38;
    SUM framework for, 301–2; training
    issues, 326–27
Scandinavian cooperative design, 96–97
Scared Straight programs, 211
Schadt, Eric, 80
Schmidt, Eric, 266
Schmidt Futures, 266
Schneier, Bruce, 163
Scholars Strategy Network, 234
Schrier, Karen, 90
Schuck, Peter, 25, 40
Schultz, P. Wesley, 291
Schuman, Daniel, 35
Schwartz, Barry, 19
Schwarzenegger, Arnold, 42
Scifabric, 300
SciLine, 228
Scopus, 226
Scott, James, 48, 100–101
Scott, Rick, 269
Sense about Science, 272
service blueprinting, 109–10, 130–31, 155
service delivery improvements, 262–63
Shapley, Lloyd, 224
Shute, Nancy, 224